FROM BETTY CROCKER TO FEMINIST FOOD STUDIES

cash   8 - bolocco

cash   10 - T

cash   2.90 - chocolate

credit card   36.66 - sandwiches
         - get reimbursed
          for 30.00

cash   17.50 - kirkland formal
            ticket

cash   30 - Lovell formal
           tickets
          - Hunter owes 15

From Betty Crocker to Feminist Food Studies

CRITICAL PERSPECTIVES ON WOMEN AND FOOD

Arlene Voski Avakian
Barbara Haber

Editors

UNIVERSITY OF MASSACHUSETTS PRESS

Amherst & Boston

LC 2005010628

ISBN 1-55849-512-6 (library cloth ed.); 511-8 (paper)

Designed by Lisa K. Clark
Set in Janson by Binghamton Valley Composition, Inc.
Printed and bound by The Maple-Vail Book Manufacturing Group

Library of Congress Cataloging-in-Publication Data

From Betty Crocker to feminist food studies : critical perspectives on
women and food / edited by
Arlene Voski Avakian and Barbara Haber.
p. cm
Includes bibliographical references and index.
ISBN 1-55849-512-6 (library cloth : alk. paper)—
ISBN 1-55849-511-8 (pbk. : alk. paper)
1. Women—Social conditions. 2. Food—Social aspects. 3. Cookery—Social
aspects. 4. Feminist theory. I. Avakian, Arlene Voski. II. Haber, Barbara.
HQ1111.F76   2005
394.1'2'082—dc22   2005010628

British Library Cataloguing in Publication data are available.

Contents

Preface

ARLENE VOSKI AVAKIAN

BARBARA HABER

When Barbara Haber developed the large cookbook collection at the Schlesinger Library at Harvard University's Radcliffe Institute for Advanced Studies, many feminists and women's studies scholars were not supportive of her interest in these works. Cookbooks, they argued, were a mark of women's oppression and should not be collected in a major American library committed to the history of American women. The idea that cookbooks are documents of women's history, a perspective that seems so obvious now, was not generally accepted when Haber made this argument in the 1970s. Decades later when Avakian told colleagues in women's studies she was working on an anthology of writing by feminists about their relationship to food and cooking, most smiled and changed the subject. Some would occasionally ask her how her cookbook was coming along despite her repeated attempts to explain she was using food, a constant and necessary presence in human life, to investigate the complexity of women's intersecting social identities. She was not, she reminded them, editing a cookbook. They were, however, puzzled. Had she not said she was including some recipes in the book? Yes, she had. Reading a recipe along with an essay, she was convinced, could provide another perspective on an issue, a relationship, or an individual. Much could be learned about contents by knowing both the specific ingredients and the techniques of cooking. To her dismay, when the book was published bookstores often shelved it with cookbooks rather than with women's studies volumes.

We now expect many bookstores to be creating sections for works such as Avakian's because of the publication of a plethora of volumes on what has come to be called food studies. We welcome the recognition of scholars and publishers that the study of food can be an important avenue to understanding both historical and contemporary society. These exciting new works, along with the many conferences on the subject, have resulted in significant insights about a variety of subjects in diverse fields. But while we have been gratified that the dailiness of the cooking and serving of food, these most mundane activities, is now being seen as its most valuable asset, we have at the same time been frustrated that so much of the work in food studies has neglected gender, despite women's centrality to food practices. And while a number of women's studies scholars are writing about food, many of these new works look at gender in isolation from other social formations, sometimes entirely omitting women who are defined as "other," or "including" them while keeping white, EuroAmerican women at the center.

We began to consider editing a volume by scholars and food writers whose work incorporated gender with the most exciting of women's studies approaches: interdisciplinary analyses that embed women's lives in race/ethnicity, class, colonialism, and capitalism. We wanted to know what women's studies scholars and food writers whose previous writings had addressed women's issues were thinking about women and food within these contexts. What fundamental questions would they raise? How would they push food studies and women's studies to an analysis beyond "inclusion"?

Rather than providing detailed studies in one discipline or limiting the range of essays to a time period or region of the world, we solicited contributions from the scholars we considered to be among the more exciting in the fields, asking them to write original essays for this collection. By allowing them to give us their latest thinking, we hoped these essays would bring new approaches to the study and conceptualization of women and food, provoking new questions as well as providing some answers. We were not disappointed by essays that asked: how the food industry constructs who does what in the kitchen, for whom, with what ingredients, and on what appliances; how in their food practices women resist oppression through racism, colonialism, and globalization; how women survive starvation conditions; how ethnicity intersects with gender, race, and class through cooking, serving, and eating food; how food practices are implicated in the construction of American whiteness; how we may be complicit in racialized gender constructions as consumers of both food and representations of gender and food.

These essays cross many borders. Their interdisciplinary analyses do not separate gender from other social formations, and many essays also consider power relations of nation and state, placing women into their globalized geopolitical contexts. Such essays are difficult to group into categories. After trying many combinations with various titles, we came to recognize that these pieces could not be satisfactorily kept within rigid boundaries. We intended to edit a volume of essays that addressed gender and food from an integrative women's studies perspective, giving authors latitude to define the issues, and many of the resulting essays defy boundaries, pushing against their placement, wandering into other categories. Finally, we saw that they are better put into loosely titled groupings that are more suggestive than definitive. The questions these essays raise and the arguments they present are beginning to map the terrain of what we may now call feminist food studies.

From Betty Crocker to Feminist Food Studies

Feminist Food Studies: A Brief History

Arlene Voski Avakian

Barbara Haber

The study of food, cooking, and eating, once a subject limited to nutritionists and a few anthropologists studying the symbolic importance of foodways among "natives,"[1] has expanded to include sociology, history, philosophy, economics, and the interdisciplinary fields of Women's Studies, American Studies and Cultural Studies.[2] Articles on food have recently appeared in a diverse list of scholarly periodicals and anthologies, while new books on the topic continue to be published in ever greater numbers by both university and trade presses. In the last decade an avalanche of books on food has appeared, and conferences on food are no longer the sole concern of food professionals. In addition to the annual conference of the Association for the Study of Food and Society (ASFS) other organizations have sponsored conferences addressing food such as The New School for Social Research's 1998 conference "Food: Nature and Culture," and its published proceedings,[3] and the 77th Annual Asians in America Conference 2001, "Palates of Pleasure: The Philosophy and Politics of Southeast Asian Food," complete with Southeast Asian meals catered by restaurants or prepared by guest chefs. ASFS also publishes a journal and has a listserve with lively discussions and debates on everything from the origins of barbecue to sources for research on a variety of topics.[4] In addition to the journal *Food and Foodways*, published since 1985, *Gastronomica*, a journal devoted to food and culture, published its first issue in 2000. Common among these works is the notion that studying the most banal of human activities can yield crucial information and insights about both daily life and world view, from what is in the pot to the significance of the fire that heats it. Particularly within the context of the postmodern questioning of reality[ies], looking closely at the material culture of the food of ordinary people has the appeal of the concrete within a world of uncertainty.

The excitement associated with this new scholarly interest in food, cooking, and eating is reminiscent of the early 1970s explosion of work in women's studies. Like women's studies, the emerging field of food studies is interdisciplinary and includes attention to the daily lives of ordinary people within its purview. Until recently, however, few scholars in food studies brought a gendered or feminist perspective to their work on food, and feminist scholars focused only on women's food pathologies. While work on anorexia, bulimia, and other eating disorders among women is vitally important, other aspects of women's relationship to food are at least equally significant. Feminists organized around housework and women's studies scholarship addressed domesticity, but cooking was ignored as if it were merely a marker of patriarchal oppression and, therefore, not worthy of attention. Similarly, food studies whether in anthropology, sociology, nutrition, or agricultural studies ignored or distorted what could be learned from and about women's relationship to food practices. Despite the fact of women's centrality to food practices, until the last decade, few in this plethora of new works on food focused on women, and only a minority of those had a feminist analysis.

Avakian's anthology, *Through the Kitchen Window: Women Writers Explore the Intimate Meanings of Food and Cooking* (1997, 1998), was among the first to address the varied and complex aspects of women and food, and many of the pieces consider the possibility that, like the gardens of poor southern African American women which served as an outlet for their creativity when no other existed, cooking may have provided a vehicle for women's creative expression. The essays in that volume provide glimpses into the lives of women in their various contexts and tell us about the meanings embedded in women's relationships to food. The recent scholarship on women and food conclusively demonstrates that studying the relationship between women and food can help us to understand how women reproduce, resist, and rebel against gender constructions as they are practiced and contested in various sites, as well as illuminate the contexts in which these struggles are located.

The first section of this introduction will discuss the work that established the study of food as a legitimate scholarly topic and the work that was done on women and food prior to 1990. The second section will address the scholarship on women and food studies that has emerged since the 1990s.

By the middle of the twentieth century, European historians were recognizing the importance of food in understanding the development of civilization. The influential Fernand Braudel saw history in sweeping

2

terms, believing, for instance, that how humans changed such natural conditions as the land, vegetations, and animals by introducing stock-breeding and agriculture was the stuff of history. His work as a social historian drew from such other disciplines as sociology, geography, psychology, and linguistics as well as anthropology. (See *The Mediterranean and the Mediterranean World in the Age of Philip II*, 1972, and *Capitalism and Material Life, 1400–1800*, 1974.) In America, most academic writing before the 1970s grew out of anthropology, where the study of what was described as "primitive" and often "exotic" cultures brought food into focus as an aid to interpreting cultural patterns. (For an overview of the development of culinary history, see "Culinary History" by Messer et al. in *The Cambridge World History of Food*, 2000, ed. K. F. Kiple and K. C. Ornelas.)

Two influential anthropologists, Claude Lévi-Strauss, who was French, and the British Mary Douglas, used food to illustrate their theories. Lévi-Strauss saw patterns as humans moved away from a natural into a cultural state—speaking languages, learning to cook—and believed that people did not invent them but instead obeyed laws that were a function of the human brain. In *The Raw and the Cooked*, he associates the "raw" with nature while the "cooked" is connected with culture. In her highly acclaimed *Purity and Danger* (1966), Douglas analyzes the food taboos laid out in Leviticus and Deuteronomy and interprets them as the ways in which tribal societies maintained their separateness and reinforced their sense of group identity, a pattern that still exists. Douglas also saw that an awareness of food-related convictions is crucial to policy makers who must avoid violating taboos.

Anthropologist Sidney Mintz is as concerned with history and political economy as his own discipline in his influential *Sweetness and Power: The Place of Sugar in Modern History* (1985). Here he brings together his field work with Caribbean sugar cane workers with a study of the social and political history of a major food. He points out that in England before 1800, sugar was a scarce food available only to the rich. How it later became a cheap commodity that supplied almost a fifth of the calories in the British diet is a complicated story that involves slavery, industrialization, changing consumer habits, and the power of trade. Mintz's focus is on the interconnections between the development of plantation slavery in Jamaica and industrial capitalism in England with sugar as the major commodity. Other major works on food by historians were soon to follow. Harvey Levenstein's *Revolution at the Table: The Transformation of the American Diet* (1988) gives academic weight to the study of food by relating changing eating habits in America to such major forces as immigration, urbanization, developing technologies, and the growth and power of the corporate food industry. And in *Paradox of Plenty: A Social History of Eating in Modern America* (1993), Levenstein looks at the ways in which the American diet has been shaped by cultural, political, and economic forces from the 1930s until today. British scholar Stephen Mennell's 1985 *All Manners of Food*, a sweeping social history of eating in England and France from the Middle Ages to the present, addresses domestic cooking and women's magazines. And Margaret Visser, a classicist, produced the wildly popular *Much Depends on Dinner: The Extraordinary History and Mythology, Allure and Obsession, Perils and Taboos of an Ordinary Meal* (1986), which illustrates the depth of information one can draw from such elemental foods as salt, butter, and rice. In *Appetite for Change* (1989) American Studies professor Warren Belasco analyzes how corporate America moved in on such counterculture foods as brown rice and whole wheat bread in order to profit from the very products that had symbolized radical opposition to capitalism. With such books as these, the serious study of food had taken on academic respectability, setting the scene for work to follow.

But academic work is not the only influence on scholars now writing about food. Good writing in this area requires something of a sensual response to food and the knowledge that comes from cooking and serving it. Two writers have made this point better than most—Elizabeth David, a British author of cookery books and numerous magazine and newspaper columns, and the American writer on gastronomy M. F. K. Fisher, who has become something of a cult figure. Before other writers were alert to the possibilities of food as a way to gauge human mood and behavior, these women intuitively understood that food allowed them the scope they needed to express their views. Their firm, sometimes quirky opinions about what constitutes a good meal breaks with conventional advice about diet. Fisher, for instance, took issue with the notion of "a well-balanced meal," believing that people were within their rights to eat just toast for breakfast if that was all they wanted, finding other occasions to take in required nutrients. Such strong views have had an impact on their readers, whose perceptions about food were probably changed forever. Elizabeth David's philosophy of food was formed when she lived in Provence as a young teenager, and later when she lived in the warm climates of Greece and Egypt during the Second World War. She later referred to the cooking of Provence as "the rational, right and proper food for human beings to eat" in contrast to the food she found in Britain after the war, which she described as "produced with a kind of bleak triumph which amounted almost to a hatred of humanity and humanity's needs" (vii, introduction to *South Wind through the Kitchen*). In *A Book of Mediterranean Food*, published in 1950,

4

four years before the end of food rationing in Britain, she communicated her belief that humans could find joy in simply prepared foods using correct ingredients. Even though such Mediterranean foods as olive oil, anchovies, and artichokes were not yet available to her English readers, her sun-drenched recipes served as an inspiration to a deprived and war-weary public. David continued her mission by writing for such publications as the *Sunday Times*, *Wine and Food*, and especially *The Spectator*, where she was allowed to write about the simple pleasures of real food without always having to produce recipes. Her reputation as an excellent researcher and fine writer was soon established, culminating in what many regard as her masterpiece, *English Bread and Yeast Cookery* (1980). At the time, David rightly believed that the British population was eating inferior manufactured loaves, putting up with caramel coloring added to white bread that was passed off as whole wheat, for instance. She set about to awaken her public to the pleasures of good, honest bread, first by telling the whole complicated story of the ingredients that go into it, and then following up with recipes for traditional British loaves. David received many honors from her country including the OBE (Order of the British Empire) awarded by the queen; the CBE (Commander of the British Empire), and honorary doctorates from the Universities of Essex and Bristol; and in 1982 was elected Fellow of the Royal Society of Literature, the recognition that meant the most to her. At the time of her death in 1992, Elizabeth David was widely regarded as a writer who advanced the cause of better food and how to investigate and write about it.

M. F. K. Fisher, who wished to be thought of as a writer and not more narrowly as a "food writer," nevertheless will best be remembered for what she wrote about food. Her gastronomical works—*Serve It Forth* (1937), *Consider the Oyster* (1941), *How to Cook a Wolf* (1942), *The Gastronomical Me* (1943), and *An Alphabet for Gourmets* (1943)—are still in print and inspire followers. Much of Fisher's appeal comes from her extraordinary ability to communicate her sensual response to food and the way she always found deep emotional meaning in what others might see as mere ordinary experience. In *How to Cook a Wolf*, her book about eating well during wartime, she makes clear that she intuitively knew that people under stress need more from food than just its nutritional content. For Fisher, the sense of well-being came from such simple dishes as polenta, spaghetti, baked apples, and rice pudding, favorite foods made from cheap and available ingredients. Now and then she includes recipes with scarce ingredients, advising, "if by chance you can indeed find some anchovies, or a thick slice of rare beef and some brandy, or a bowl of pink curled shrimps, you are double blessed, to

5

possess in this troubled life both the capacity and the wherewithal to forget it for a time." It is for good reason that this wartime book continues to be read with pleasure and has not been shelved as an artifact of a bygone era. At a time when most other food writers of the day were concerned with extending cheap cuts of meat into hashes or watering down butter, Fisher was advising her readers that "'since we must eat to live, we might as well do it with both grace and gusto."

The most important legacy left by Elizabeth David and M. F. K. Fisher is the convincing case they make for food as a worthy and dignified area of study. They followed their intuitions and wrote about the qualities of good food and what it means to people, establishing a literary genre that drew attention to the satisfaction and beauty of simple dishes made from fresh ingredients. This was a different line from earlier food writers, most often men, who identified as epicures and concerned themselves mainly with only the finest and most expensive of foods and the wines that went with them.[5]

In *Perfection Salad: Women and Cooking at the Turn of the Century* (1986) Laura Shapiro brings together the skills of a fine writer with the systematic approach of a historian to write about women and food. Her pioneering book proves that women's long association with food held untold stories that could illuminate both women's history and the history of food. While a great deal of scholarship on women had been flourishing since the early 1970s, almost none of it had concerned itself with the history of food, a subject that had not appealed to early generations of women's history scholars more interested in setting straight the public record on women's achievements. Shapiro establishes that the women at the center of the cooking school movement in America at the end of the nineteenth century were influenced by the scientific knowledge of the day applied to cooking. Fussy, over-sauced foods were the result of their deliberations, dishes unacceptable to modern tastes, but proudly offered by Fannie Farmer, her colleagues, and the students who learned from them. But Shapiro also explains that these teachers were serious and well intentioned, having found their way as professionals in a world where few such options were open to women. Shapiro had shown how the study of food shed new light on the study of women, and at the same time how women's history illuminated the history of food. Many more books and articles written by an array of scholars were to follow.

Over the last decade nearly twenty books on women and food and numerous scholarly articles have been published, authored by women's studies and food studies scholars. Recent feminist work, particularly in the last decade, has begun to move away from the invocation of a monolithic woman. Rather than merely adding on[6] women of color to theoretical frameworks constructed from the life experiences of white Western women, the most exciting new scholarship on women takes as its project the contextualization of gender within other significant social formations. Incorporating some of the critiques made by women of color and the theoretical positions of postcolonial and cultural studies, many women's studies scholars now focus on the specificities of women's lives in all of the complexity of their intersecting and embedded social formations. Some women's studies scholars have discovered that food practices and their representations, interwoven as they are into the dailiness of life, can reveal the particularities of time, place, and culture, providing an excellent vehicle to contextualize women's lives. Just as the kitchen is no longer off limits for women's studies, some of the latest work in food studies is beginning to recognize that food practices are gendered.

Like other interdisciplinary fields, food studies and women's studies cover a wide range of topics and use approaches and methodologies from more traditional disciplines or develop new interpretative modalities. This latest scholarship on women and food encompasses such diverse fields as philosophy, political economy, anthropology, sociology, history, and cultural studies, and the topics addressed range from minute studies of a single food item to close readings of food and its representation as the basis for broad cultural analyses. In order to describe the trends over the last decade, we have created a number of categories and will highlight selected works within them. These categories are neither intended as an analytic framework, nor are they definitive. Additionally, since scholarship on women and food brings new insights to both fields, and often cuts across disciplines, many of these categories overlap. We offer them only as one way to discuss the work of the last decade.

Sociocultural Analyses

Anthropology was among the first disciplines to recognize the importance of studying food practices, and much of contemporary scholarship that combines food studies and women's studies is also undertaken by anthropologists. Carole M. Counihan has been central to this effort, editing the journal *Food and Foodways*, co-editing a collection of articles from that journal (1998), co-editing another volume on food and culture that includes a number of articles on women (1997), and authoring a collection of her own articles on women and food (1999). Counihan's

7

perspective is that food practices are both constitutive and reflective of gender construction. Her essay "Bread as World: Food Habits and Social Relations" (in *The Anthropology of Food and Body: Gender, Meaning, and Power*) is a beautiful example of the value of focusing on food. Examining the changing place of a basic food as a way to look closely at the daily effects of modernization in Bosa, a town on the west coast of Sardinia, Counihan argues that Bosa experienced modernization without development. Using anthropologist's Marcel Mauss's framework of gift giving as a means of tying society together, and a political economy analysis of the demise of bread-baking, she posits that Bosan social relations became less communal and more individualistic because women neither baked bread together anymore, nor gifted family and friends with their homemade loaves. Store-bought bread was considered an unfit gift, and no longer allowed for the possibility of a means of artistic expression for the women baking it. Counihan also posits that the traditions of the region were maintained through the ritual baking of holiday breads, and have now been attenuated by their mass production. When women baked bread and the community had closer ties, males and females had interdependent relationships rather than men having power over women. What had once been a network of interconnections among people in Bosa was replaced by the impersonal monetary exchange of a commodity.

Also focusing on bread and the effects of industrialization, Aida Kanafani-Zahar (1997) examines the relationship between women's status and bread-making in Lebanon. In addition to being the basis of the diet, bread also has sacred significance in that region. Women's status is elevated, Kanafani-Zahar argues, because they have exclusive responsibility for baking bread. Bread-baking skills are valued, and are passed down from older women to their eldest daughters or daughters-in-law. With industrialization women do not need to bake, as bread is readily available for purchase, and like Counihan, Kanafani-Zahar posits that rather than being liberated from an arduous task, women actually lose the status they had as bakers.

Extending her analysis of bread-baking to cooking and cleaning among women in Florence in "Food, Power, and Female Identity in Contemporary Florence," Counihan contends that in a state society women gain influence (private power) through giving even as they may be locked out of coercive (public) power. In this analysis women feed others in return for "love, favors, good behavior and the power that comes from being needed" (48). In Florence before 1950, women were totally identified with their domestic role, providing nurturance for the families primarily by feeding them. Contemporary women are in conflict: not content with their influence in the private realm, they want and need to work, yet they are still wedded to the notion that "good" women are defined by a clean house and abundant home-cooked meals. While women may now have more economic power than their mothers did, Counihan argues that they have less security in their new identities as women, given the persistence of the demands of their former roles and their inability to satisfy these demands because of time constraints. They are also unhappy with their diminished ability to control what their children eat and the attendant feeling that they are not adequately passing on their cultural legacy. Both Counihan and Kanafani-Zahar agree that the interdependent relations between women and men which existed before industrialization have been supplanted; women now struggle for equal power (public) with men, while losing the influence (private) through giving which they enjoyed in the past.

Also exploring the construction of gender and family through food practices, the sociologist Marjorie DeVault (1991) argues that food preparation is work that defines family. Women's activities in the home, DeVault maintains, cannot be neatly divided into work versus leisure, the basis for much sociological theory on work and family. Based on the male experience of wage work in industrialized society, this framework conceptualizes work only as that done outside the home, while the family is assumed to be a respite from work. Despite the reality that for women the home is often the site of their work, labor in the family has been considered "only in terms of relationship and emotion," while "the necessary and arduous work of physical maintenance disappears" (10). Through the work of feeding, "women quite literally produce family life from day to day" (13). DeVault maintains that this work of feeding is invisible *as* work and, though it is central to the construction of family, women themselves often deny that it is work. Contrary to the contention of the women who perform it and the sociologists who ignore it, DeVault insists that this activity is work which is both physical and mental labor, and a social practice which constructs family. Citing the planning of meals as an example, she likens this activity to solving a puzzle. Decisions must be made in relationship to other people's desires, most importantly husbands and then children, and in accordance with what the culture considers a proper meal. "By solving this puzzle each day, the person who cooks for the family is continually creating one part of the reality of household life. At the same time, she . . . is constructing her own place within the family, as one who provides for the needs of others" (48). DeVault addresses issues of class by positing that the decision-making process to answer the question "what's for dinner" is dealt with by working-class women through the traditions in their families, and by middle-class women by reference to cookbooks and new trends in food preparation.

While DeVault does address class, she does not consider race and ethnicity, social formations central to work on women and food preparation among marginalized groups. Sociologist Josephine A. Beoku-Betts (1995) argues that because Gullah communities are under threat from economic development, the work of maintaining traditions through food is vital to the very survival of the group, and unlike the women in DeVault's study, the Gullah women are very conscious of their centrality to this effort. Jessica Harris's cookbooks (1989, 1995) make repeated connections, both in her introductions and in commentaries before each section, and often in recipes themselves, to African cuisine and what African Americans were able to preserve while in slavery. By recording and validating the African heritage of African American cuisine, Harris helps to repair cultural ties attenuated by slavery and white supremacy. Similarly, Barbara Kirshenblatt-Gimblett (1997) finds that the fairs and cookbooks produced by Jewish women in the nineteenth century sustained community institutions not only by raising funds for synagogues, but by bringing the community together. Unlike in African American communities, however, maintenance of this community did not necessarily rely on the adherence to traditional foods. Kirshenblatt-Gimblett's examination of the cookbooks and the food at these fairs reveals a diversified Jewish cuisine which often includes *tref*, food forbidden by Kosher rules.

Colonialism, Political Economy, Globalization

Some cultural analysts use food to examine colonialist constructions. Political scientist Uma Narayan (1995) examines contemporary Indian culture and identity through the lens of curry. Made from a mixture of many spices using different combinations for particular dishes, more turmeric in one *masala*, more cumin and chili in another, Indian curries have great variety. The "fabrication" of curry powder, a one-mixture-fits-all combination, was an English creation fixed onto Indian cuisine and accepted as quintessentially Indian by the colonizer, just as England "fabricated" an India from a variety of cultural and political entities (65). The precolonial history of India as a number of linguistic and religious entities rather than a unified nation can be readily seen in Indian cuisine, Narayan argues, which has enormous regional variations echoed in the contemporary cuisines of India, Pakistan, and Bangladesh. "'Pakistani food' has arguably more in common with certain North Indian cuisines than either has in common with a variety of South Indian cuisines, all of which have their regional variations" (71). In England however, non-Indians ignore these differences in the common practice of using the epithet "Pakis" for all South Asians and in the assumption that curry can describe all Indian food. Catering to this fabricated notion of Indian unity in order to make a living, many South Asian immigrants are engaged in feeding the English this version of "fabricated" Indian food.

Bringing a feminist analysis to the food practices of the Indian immigrant community in England, Narayan utilizes Partha Chatterjee's thesis that Indians have conflicting goals. They want "to cultivate the material techniques of modern western civilization" on the one hand, while "retaining and strengthening the distinctive spiritual essence of the national culture" on the other (74). The impulse to modernity, Chatterjee posits, is undertaken by males in the public sphere, while the work of resistance to assimilation is done by women in the private sphere. Narayan posits that the common practice of barring Indian women from waiting tables in the public space of Indian family-owned restaurants, though they are often permitted to work behind counters of family grocery stores, may be because the serving of food is associated with the maintenance of that distinctive spiritual "essence" since it takes place within the "intimacies of Indian family life" (75). The association of women with resistance to assimilation through their identification with tradition, Narayan worries, may have negative consequences for women by defining opposition to these traditions as abandoning Indian culture and assimilating to the West.

Narayan turns her attention to colonialist relations and the eating of curry by non-Indians by critiquing a 1993 paper by philosopher Lisa Heldke which argues that by "eating ethnic" without any concern for the people of the culture which produced the food, Westerners replicate colonialist relations of power. Westerners can become "anti-colonialist" eaters, Heldke posits, by educating themselves about the food, culture, and history of the people rather than merely unconsciously consuming their food. Narayan questions how much Westerners can learn about the cuisine of the "other," positing that few of us are aware of the historical and political realities of even the food of our own culture. While she agrees that gaining this knowledge and respect for "other" cultures is preferable to unconscious consumption, Narayan maintains that even if they attained this knowledge "mainstream eaters would remain privileged consumers, benefitting from the structural inequalities and unpleasant material realities that often form the contexts in which 'ethnic food' is produced and consumed" (78). Narayan also points out that from the perspective of Indian immigrants to England, many of whom survive economically through their restaurants, which cook food designed to appeal to English notions of Indian food, the food colonialism Heldke critiques is the basis of their livelihood.

Focusing directly on political economy manifestations of this historical colonial relationship, Deborah Barndt's edited collection, *Women Working the NAFTA Food Chain: Women, Food & Globalization* (1999), explores the exploitation and resistance of women food workers in the North and the South, as well as examining the relationships among them. The authors make the argument that this "food system . . . deepens inequalities between North and South as well as between men and women (with class and race complicating the picture); at the same time, it perpetuates human domination of the environment" (15). Historical and theoretical articles lay the groundwork for case studies of women food workers. Harriet Friedman's (1999) excellent historical and political economy analysis of globalization and food demonstrates how U.S. trade and agricultural policies after World War II, in particular the Marshall Plan and the Food for Peace program, transformed food production in the South from a peasant-based, integrated farm system of locally grown crops to mono-culture for export and international trade with the result that Third World countries once able to produce their own food became dependent on imports to feed their people. Relations between families and food were also transformed as many people, no longer growing their own food and unable to buy machines and chemicals necessary for raising export crops, were forced to leave for cities where they worked for low wages in order to buy food. Cheaper than men, women and children became the preferred work force. Rather than improving over the years since the end of the Second World War, this situation has been exacerbated by multinational agribusinesses, structural adjustment policies of the World Bank, and international trade agreements.

Following the tomato from fields in Mexico to fast food restaurants and supermarkets in Toronto, Deborah Barndt (1999) argues that the lives of Third World and First World women workers are both shaped by similar labor practices. Maquilization is defined as "1) the feminization of the work force, 2) extreme segmentation of skill categories, 3) the lowering of real wages and 4) a non-union orientation," while McDonaldization is "based on efficiency, predictability, calculability or quantifiability, substitution of non-human technology," and, most important, "'flexible' part-time labour" (63). The maquilization of the South, Barndt posits, is moving north while the McDonaldization of the North is moving south, with the result of further undermining women workers' earning capacity and worsening working conditions in both areas. These practices have decreased the proportion of skilled, permanent, usually male workers, and increased the proportion of de-skilled, part-time, temporary, usually female workers, with disastrous results for women workers. Using case studies of women food workers in Mexico, the southwest of the United States, and Toronto, the authors document both the exploitation and resistance of women workers and the connections among them.

Activist and scholar Vandana Shiva (1992) maintains that rather than being saved by development, Third World people need to be liberated from it. First colonialism and then development imposed Western patriarchy on indigenous cultures, both deepening women's impoverishment and degrading the environment. Women were displaced from productive activity by "removing land, water, and forests from their management and control, as well as through the ecological destruction of soil, water and vegetation systems so that nature's productivity and renewability were impaired" (337).

Examining the effect of colonialism on meal times in the parish of Zumbagua in the Andes, M. J. Weismantel (1996) also demonstrates how wage labor and the ideology of assimilation altered gender roles with negative results for women. Women resist, she argues, through their insistence on maintaining traditional times for eating on weekends and during the annual harvest festivals, when Quichua cultural forms are asserted. More than maintenance of tradition, the practice of these women, she argues, is political, though it may not be seen as such by those not in the community: "the language of the debate within the parish over the racial implications of cultural practices is constituted in a form that, while clearly understood by parish residents, renders it invisible to outsiders as political discourse" (308–309). While she argues that the women are resisting the forces of assimilation and white supremacy, Weismantel also sees dangers for women and indigenous culture in reifying festivals that are no longer grounded in material realities of an agrarian economy when women's work was highly valued. Men working in the towns and children going to school internalize metropolitan ideologies about time and work, redefining work to include only that which is remunerated with wages. In this framework the work women do in the home to maintain family and culture, once considered vital to survival, may be devalued, and ethnicity defined as feminine, traditional, and unnecessary. Men's work, on the other hand, may be defined as productive, modern, and associated with whiteness, undermining both women's lives and indigenous culture.

Also exploring the impact of colonialism and resistance to it, Jeffrey Pilcher (1997) argues that community cookbooks, authored primarily by women, maintained indigenous cuisine and were a resistance to pressures to incorporate imposed European standards of healthy and "proper" meals, and by extension, European culture. Comparing these cookbooks to their commercial counterparts, Pilcher traces the development of Mestizo cuisine as the national cuisine of Mexico through the nineteenth and twentieth centuries, and demonstrates that attempts by commercial cookbooks to transform Mexican diets from the corn-based food of the lower classes to the wheat-based diet of Europeans were unsuccessful even among elites, who might have eaten European food in public, but ate Mexican food at home. Using Benedict Anderson's notion of the modern nation being an imagined community constructed partially through print literature, Pilcher argues that the women authors of community cookbooks participated not only in resisting European cultural imperialism, but in the construction of a national cuisine which contributed to a Mexican national identity.

History/Popular Culture

Over the last decade a number of works of social history have focused on women and food. Mary McFeeley's (2000) and Sherrie A. Inness's (2001) books are both roughly chronological and topical approaches to the twentieth-century history of U.S. women and food. Inness's research is based on the messages directed at women in popular media, including cookbooks, advertisements, and articles in magazines about cooking. She argues that these images construct gender by depicting "kitchen work as 'naturally' rewarding to women both emotionally . . . and aesthetically" (12). She examines cooking literature for children, the representation of electric appliances as freeing women from drudgery while allowing them to be creative, the depiction of "ethnic" foods during the two world wars while racial and ethnic hierarchies were maintained, the shoring up of gender roles during the crises of the depression and World War II, and representations of women happily going back into their kitchens in the 1950s. While some of McFeeley's narrative is also based on media representations of women and food, she also uses other historical documentation and autobiographical narrative. Her topics include early twentieth-century farm kitchens, experiments with cooperative housekeeping, Fannie Farmer's introduction to scientific cooking, women's survival techniques during the depression, rationing during the Second World War, cooking in the 1950s, the Julia Child food revolution, the vegetarian movements of the 1960s and 1970s, and cookbooks by chefs.

In a 1992 article, Cindy Dorfman presents an analysis of the place of the kitchen in contemporary American culture while providing an excellent historical overview of the American middle-class kitchen. Through descriptions of the actual space allocated within the home for cooking, and representations of the kitchen and cooking in cookbooks, domestic science literature, and the media, she demonstrates that while the kitchen "has undergone a wonderful metamorphosis through this century, from a formless room full of hodge-podge appliances to a streamlined, coordinated, multifunction room that can express its owner's taste" (37), it continues to define the place where women ought to be. Contemporary filmic images of the kitchen as a place of emotional and even sexual intimacy, she argues, are attempts to manipulate women back into the kitchen, a newly defined but no less limiting space for women.

Amy Bentley's (1998) volume on rationing during the Second World War also focused on the persistence of gender roles through women's place in the kitchen, arguing that gender hierarchies were maintained even while boundaries between public and private were blurred. Gender roles were challenged by men going off to war and more women going to work outside the home, and some even doing traditionally male work. In consequence, the family meal, Bentley posits, "became a weapon of war, and the kitchen a woman's battlefront" (5), a way to reassure Americans that not so much had changed because women's primary place was still in the kitchen. Looking closely at the gendered aspects of the food in that meal, Bentley finds red meat became associated with masculine virility, while sugar was identified with femininity.

Jane Dusselier (2001) examines the gendered representation of candy in advertising. Initially only for wealthy and middle-class women and connected with the hedonism associated with the Gilded Age, candy was transformed between 1895 and 1920 into a food that was also appropriate for men. Candy marketed to men was projected as necessary for stamina, culminating in the connection between soldiers and Life Savers during World War I, a sharp contrast to the indulgence that eating candy represented for women. She also found that the very shape and texture of candy was gendered; women's candy was soft and round, confections such as bonbons, and men's candy was hard or the newly fashioned candy bars.

The 1950s, a time when people were spending a higher percentage of their incomes on food, is the focus of Erica Endrijonas's (2001) analysis of the messages directed at women through cookbooks. Postwar prosperity and the new emphasis on cooking elaborate dishes as a way to get Rosie the Riveter back into the kitchen, along with the marketing of processed foods, she argues, produced enormous contradictions:

"Buy processed foods but cook from scratch; be creative but follow directions precisely; accommodate all family members' preferences but streamline the food purchase and preparation process; work part-time but be a full-time homemaker; and do it all with little or no training" (157).

Constructions of Identity

One of the most basic assumptions of scholarship in both food studies and women's studies is that the daily life of ordinary people is not only worthy of study but necessary to any understanding of past and present worlds. Necessary for physical survival, daily meals are no less crucial to the construction of cultures and the people within them. Cultural studies scholar Deborah Lupton (1996) takes a poststructural approach to food and the construction of identity, arguing that food is centrally implicated in whom we become. Food discourse and the power relations embedded within it and which it produces, along with early bodily experiences of eating, she theorizes, construct who we are. Providing a sophisticated and complex version of *we are what we eat*, Lupton identifies "food and eating . . . [as] intensely emotional experiences that are intertwined with embodied sensations and strong feelings . . . central to individuals' subjectivity and their sense of distinction from others" (36).

Also taking a cultural studies approach, Elsbeth Probyn (2000) examines food writing, food representations in media, food personalities, interviews with people about food, films, and literature. Not concerned with food per se, Probyn is instead interested in what food and its representations can tell us about the culture that constructs our identities, and how eating can refigure these identities and their relation to each other. She posits that bodies "eat with vigorous class, ethnic and gendered appetites, mouth machines that ingest and regurgitate, articulating what we are, what we eat, and what eats us" (32). Arguing that since the HIV crisis sex is no longer a useful lens to examine culture, Probyn turned to food in conjunction with sex. Connected to the flesh, and identifying the point at which "knowing the self and caring of the other merge," eating and sex are seen as "practices that open ourselves into a multitude of surfaces that tingle and move," that break us "into parts that relate to each other following different logics, different speeds" (70). When eating and sex are commingled rather than added to each other, they may have the potential to disrupt assumptions, make new lines of connections, increase the possibility for pleasure, and promote new ethics. She focuses on various sites that conflate food and sex including a gay and lesbian food festival featuring sexy chefs and a lesbian "dominatrix of the kitchen" (65), and the Two Fat Ladies of the BBC cooking series, Clarissa Dickson Wright and Jennifer Paterson. While her discussion does nod to gender and sexual orientation, she is primarily interested in sex and eating because it "offers a way of returning to questions about pleasure within restraint, sympathy understood as a means of respecting the situatedness of lives and identities . . . to the very practical figuring of an everyday ethics of living" (75).

Focusing on African American women, Doris Witt (1999) uses food to explore the "mutual exclusions of psychoanalysis and Marxist political economy" (16). Informed by Julia Kristiva's psychoanalytic reinterpretation of Mary Douglas's work on pollution rituals, and influenced by Ann McClintock's work on the complicity of white women in imperialism, Witt aims to do "culturally contextualized psychoanalysis that is simultaneously psychoanalytically informed history" (15). She argues that the connection between Black women and food is the "central structuring dynamic of 20th century U.S. life" (5). Black women are represented both as nurturers and givers with no appetite themselves, and as women with huge appetites. The central concern of the book is the "tension between these two poles, with how the binary through which Black women have been designated as both provider/producer and castrator/consumer has structured U.S. culture . . . with the disjuncture between the minimal power that African American women have wielded in the United States and the often exaggerated perceptions of their power" (24). While her work is focused on representations of African American women and men through literature and popular culture, her project is to determine the construction of subjectivities in the United States.

Recipes and Cookbooks as Creative Expressions

In 1997 Margaret Randall published a book of poems about women and food that contain actual recipes or refer to food preparation. A respected poet, Randall asserts that these works may be read as literature or used to cook food, but scholars of food and literature must do more. Some of the recent work on women and food makes precisely the argument that recipes and cookbooks can be read as literature. Linguist Colleen Cotter (1997) uses comparative linguistic discourse analysis of pie crust recipes from commercial and community cookbooks to establish that recipes are narrative forms. Recipes in both genres of cookbooks may be narratives, she argues, but those in community cookbooks also function to construct community. Unlike precise recipes in commercial cookbooks, directions in community cookbooks may be minimal, assuming readers already have some knowledge. Those who have no firsthand knowledge of the community are outsiders, while for those who have presumably seen their mothers or grandmothers make pies, a list of ingredients is sufficient.

Also arguing that food writing has literary merit, Anne L. Bower (1997) reads cookbooks as fictions because they have settings, characters, and plot–all the necessary components of literature. Like most of women's art, she posits, recipes and cookbooks are a distinct genre that has not been recognized by a patriarchal literary establishment. The articles in this collection use literary theory to make this point, many authors referencing Susan Leonardi's 1989 piece which first made the argument that recipes and cookbooks are a form of women's literature. Anne Goldman (1992) critiques Leonardi's analysis for its essentialist notion of women's lives, and that critique could be applied to most of this work. Goldman contends that recipes and cookbooks are not constructed in a universal "women's culture," but within particular cultures. Her analysis of cookbooks is based not only in a gendered context, but in the political and cultural histories of the authors' communities. Colonialism is as central to Goldman's analysis of two cookbooks by the Mexican authors Cleofas Jaramillo and Fabiola Cabeza de Baca as patriarchy. These books, she posits, "demonstrate how political circumstance—the struggle for control of Mexican culture that succeeds the struggle for proprietorship of Mexican land–in this case helps to shape both the way people conceive of themselves and the manner in which they speak this sense of self-assertion. . . . self-reflection in both narratives is accordingly complicated by political and literary history, the demands of publishing and of the languages available to Hispana writers during the first half of the twentieth century" (175). Her comparison of these two texts with non-native Mexican cookbooks focuses on cultural appropriation. Goldman's analysis of a 1934 book of recipes from New Mexico by Edna Fergusson shows that Mexican food was taken by the United States just as the land had been. Citing Fergusson's assertion that since the annexation of Mexico the cuisine "belongs to the U.S.," Goldman concludes, "Cultural appropriation is thus justified by a political event, the U.S. military takeover of Mexico" (181). Arguing that the line between autobiography and ethnography is blurred in Jaramillo's and de Baca's works, Goldman posits that they resist both the unique individuality of the autobiography and the representative "ethnic type" of colonialist ethnographies, asserting instead that they make "ethnicity concrete, representing it as it is experienced by the individual, rather than invoking Culture as an abstraction" (189). Affirming that this cultural work is the difficult and conscious work of women,

Goldman is also clear that gender is central to this experience, but only within the context of Mexican history, politics, and culture.

In another analysis of women's food writing, Traci Marie Kelly (2001) categorizes three forms of storytelling through recipes. The first is what she calls the culinary memoir, primarily a memoir with food as a recurring theme, with recipes as an option. Kelly's examples of culinary memoir are Elizabeth Ehrlich's *Miriam's Kitchen* (1997) and Ruth Reichl's *Tender at the Bone* (1998). The second form she identifies is autobiographical cookbooks, such as *The Alice B. Toklas Cookbook* (1954) and Pearl Bailey's *Pearl's Kitchen* (1973), in which recipes are intertwined with memoir. Norma Jean Darden and Carole Darden's *Spoonbread and Strawberry Wine* (1994) is a prime example of Kelly's third category, autoethnographic cookbooks, a form which seeks both to represent the group within its own sense of its history and culture and to contradict dominant representations. Ntozake Shange's *If I Can Cook/You Know God Can* (1998) is another excellent example of this type of autoethnography. While the stories and recipes focus on her experiences, the themes of the work are the history of slavery, the contemporary condition of Black America, and the cultural connections among Black diasporan communities resulting from the enduring connections to Africa. Rafia Zafar (1999) maintains that Black women cookbook authors have to work against the legacy of racist representations of Black women cooks—of the enduring images of mammy and Aunt Jemima. In her review of *Spoonbread and Strawberry Wine* and *Vibration Cooking: Or the Travel Notes of a Geechee Girl* by Vertamae Smart-Grosvenor (1970), Zafar argues these cookbook authors "enact a gastronomic Black Reconstruction" (451) by putting their families and themselves into the history and contemporary community life of African Americans. None of these autoethnographic works could be categorized as merely women's literature.

Arguing that Chicana and Native American women reclaim their ethnic and gender identities through writing about food, Benay Blend (2001) reads their recipes and other food writing "as political commentary" that is a resistance to the "commodification of their culture" (146). Food writing, she theorizes, may also be autobiographical, but in the case of Chicana and Native American writers, the "I" is always embedded in the context of the cultural and political "we." It creates women's cultural space, and "destabilizes certain predominant values that support the dominant culture[;] the culinary metaphor provides women writers with a discourse of resistance in which the self in relation to an ethnic group is empowered" (162).

Also examining the use of food writing to maintain community borders, Janet Theophano (2001) argues that cookbook writers are "constructing, defending and transgressing social and cultural borders . . . as points of departure for reflection" (139). In an analysis of Buwei Yang Chao's 1945 cookbook *How to Cook and Eat in Chinese*, Theophano demonstrates how the author guards the borders of the Chinese community and challenges white assumptions about Asians, while creating allegiances with her American readers. Whites can learn to make the Chinese food in Chao's book, but Theophano argues that she repeatedly indicates that the cultural differences between the two groups are so deep that Americans could never learn to eat the food Chinese eat at home. The recipes in the book, Chao states, are not authentic Chinese cuisine but what she has adapted for Americans. One example of this cultural gulf is the difference between Chinese and American cultures in acceptable levels of intimacy. Because they are comfortable with intimacy, Chao says, Chinese eat from a common bowl, while Americans not only eat on separate plates but must talk incessantly during a meal to cover up their lack of genuine connection (148). Chao's cultural commentary is autobiographical, and she uses this medium to again challenge white assumptions by discussing the negative effects of her missionary education on her sense of self (149). Theophano's analysis of Chao's cookbook clearly shows how she used food writing to convey much more than instructions on how to prepare Chinese food.

Eating Problems/Disorders

The issue that comprised nearly all of the work on women and food until the 1990s is still a serious concern to feminist scholars. In a sociological study of women with what she calls eating *problems* rather than disorders, Becky Thompson (1994) argues that binging/purging or starving oneself begin as coping or survival strategies in response to both childhood sexual abuse and societal injustices. Characterizing the sexual abuse of children as an epidemic, Thompson argues that binging or starving is an attempt to deal with the pain of physical or psychic bodily intrusions. Consciously multiracial in her analysis, Thompson critiques feminist scholars for their exclusive focus on white middle-class women and the exclusion of race, class, and sexual orientation from their analysis. She points out that standards of beauty in Latina and African American communities do not favor thinness, so that analyses that cite the images of ultra-thin models as the cause of young women starving themselves cannot be applied to women whose communities give them another message. Similarly, feminist arguments that blame eating disorders on the expectation that women will be able to manage both careers and their domestic responsibilities are found to ignore African American married women's history of labor force participation. Common assumptions that lesbians do not care about their personal appearance because they are not interested in attracting men have rendered lesbians invisible, denying both the possibility that they may have eating problems and the spearheading role they have taken in politicizing fat oppression and constructing alternate models of female beauty. Thompson's approach to eating problems roots them in intersecting social formations. Citing race, class, gender, and sexual oppression in the society and the abuse of women and girls in families as important causes of eating problems, she maintains that eating problems will be cured only when the society cures itself of injustice.

Philosopher Susan Bordo (1993) also focuses on the cultural meanings of the prevalence of eating disorders among women, theorizing that anorexia nervosa is the "logical (if extreme) response to manifestations of anxieties and fantasies fostered by our culture" (15). Maintaining that the "natural" body is a fiction, Bordo takes a social constructionist perspective to the body, including in her analysis the effects of both patriarchy and white supremacy. Anorexia, she argues, is not an individual disorder but the result of the convergence of cultural "currents or streams" or "axes of continuity" inscribed on women's bodies (142). The Western philosophical dualism of mind and body in which the body is alien from the self, a limitation and an enemy that must be overcome because it threatens the loss of control, is the first axis Bordo identifies. This dualist axis manifests in anorexics' extreme alienation from their bodies. Their hunger, Bordo posits, is not a response to lack of food, but is seen by them as a force from outside themselves, the demands of disconnected bodies. Purity and intelligence are functions of the mind which are counterposed to the body. A desire for thinness, Bordo holds, is a logical response to the West's "historical heritage of disdain for the body" (139–140). The second axis is the desire to control this alien body. Unable to control other aspects of their lives, women go to extreme measures to control their bodies through dieting and exercise, gaining a sense of accomplishment by their ability to achieve a perfect body, bending their bodies to their wills, gaining mastery *over* their bodies. Finally, Bordo defines the gender/power axis as having two levels, both rooted in the duality of body versus mind and fear of the body. The first is the "fear and disdain for traditional female roles and social limitations," and the second is the "deep fear of 'The Female' with all its more nightmarish archetypical association of voracious hungers and sexual instability" (155). Young anorexic women's fears about growing up to inhabit traditional gender roles are expressed in their revulsion at female anatomy and bodily functions. Citing the epidemic of female invalidism in the mid nineteenth century and the contemporary dramatic increase in anorexia, Bordo holds that these responses of both groups of women, seen by some feminist scholars as a protest, must be understood as cultural anxieties "written on the bodies of anorexic women, not embraced as conscious politics" (159). Bordo distinguishes these relatively mundane fears about what they must do as adult women from the fear of "The Female," "hungering . . . voracious . . . extravagantly and excessively needful . . . without restraint . . . always wanting . . . always wanting too much affection, reassurance, emotional and sexual contact, and attention" (160; ellipses in original). Rooting constructions of the body in history, Bordo maintains that fear of "The Female" is in ascendance during times of extreme social stress and when women are asserting their independence. Nineteenth-century corsets that severely inhibited women's physical movement and contemporary injunctions to thinness are attempts to rein in women's bodies, instances of power relations between women and men expressed and maintained through constructions of woman's body.

In a provocative essay that looks at cross-cultural constructions of the body and eating disorders, Carole Counihan (1999) finds that "tribal" societies in New Guinea and a number of societies in the Amazon consider male and female bodies to have many similarities, a construction which is in sharp contrast to the gender dichotomies that exist in the West. In New Guinea and the Amazon, men actually fear women's penetration of their bodies and the resulting loss of their male identities. In the West, on the other hand, male bodies are seen as impermeable while female bodies are vulnerable to penetration. The bodily penetrations of eating and sexuality pose a threat to Western women because of this vulnerability, and women see fasting as a viable option to protect themselves. Counihan's other work on eating disorders (1999) also brings important cross-cultural material to the discussion, showing that in the West patriarchy, Judeo-Christian ideology, Cartesianism, and identification of women with food create the possibility of lethal fasting, a practice fundamentally different from ritualistic fasting in non-Western societies where systems of gender complementarity rather than gender dominance prevail.

This new scholarship on women and food addresses the basic issues raised by women's studies more than two decades ago and yields new insights into both women's lives and the contexts in which they are embedded.

Notes

1. Claude Lévi-Strauss's *The Raw and the Cooked* (London: Jonathan Cape, 1970) is the classic in this genre.

2. Recent books or chapters in books include: a history of ethnic food by Donna R. Gabaccia, *We Are What We Eat: Ethnic Food and the Making of Americans* (Cambridge: Harvard University Press, 1998); a study of identity and food by sociologist Deborah Lupton, *Food the Body and the Self* (Beverly Hills: Sage, 1996); a chapter on colonialism, culture, curry, and the construction of Indian women by political scientist Uma Narayan, "Eating Cultures" in Narayan, ed., *Dislocating Cultures: Identities, Traditions, and Third-World Feminism* (New York: Routledge, 1997); Harry Levenstein's histories of the American diet, *Revolution at the Table: The Transformation of the American Diet* (New York: Oxford University Press, 1988) and *Paradox of Plenty: A Social History of Eating in Modern America* (Oxford University Press, 1993); a collection of essays edited by philosophers Diane Curtin and Lisa Heldke, *Cooking, Eating, Thinking: Transformative Philosophies of Food* (Bloomington: Indiana University Press, 1992); Anne Murcott, ed., *The Sociology of Food and Eating* (Aldershot, U.K., Gower, 1983); Doris Witt, *Black Hunger: Food and the Politics of U.S. Identity* (Oxford University Press, 1999); Phyllis P. Bober, *Art, Culture, and Cuisine: Ancient and Medieval Gastronomy* (Chicago: University of Chicago Press, 1999); Peter Garnsey, *Food and Society in Classical Antiquity* (New York: Cambridge University Press, 1999); James Schmiechen and Kenneth Carls, *The British Market Hall: A Social and Architectural History* (New Haven: Yale University Press, 1999); Richard Pillsbury, *No Foreign Food: The American Diet in Time and Place* (Boulder: Westview, 1998); Don R. Brothwell and Patricia Brothwell, *Food in Antiquity: A Survey of the Diet of Early Peoples* (Baltimore: Johns Hopkins University Press, 1998); Martha Carlin and Joel Rosenthal, eds., *Food and Eating in Medieval Europe* (London: Hambledon Press, 1998); Carole Counihan and Penny Van Esterik, eds., *Food and Culture: A Reader* (New York: Routledge, 1997); Stan Griffiths and Jennifer Wallace, eds., *Consuming Passions: Food in the Age of Anxiety* (Manchester: Manchester University Press, 1998); and Barbara Harriss-White and Sir Raymond Hoffenberg, eds., *Food: Multidisciplinary Perspectives* (Cambridge: Blackwell, 1994).

3. *Social Research: An International Quarterly of the Social Sciences* 66, 1 (Winter 1998).

4. The ASFS newsletter is sent to members. To join the email discussion list send a message as follows: Address: listproc@listproc.umbc.edu Subject: leave blank. Message: subscribe asfs.

5. Andre Simon, *The Art of Good Living: A Contribution to the Better Understanding of Food and Drink, Together with a Gastronomic Vocabulary and a Wine Dictionary* (New York: Knopf, 1930), J. George Frederick, *Cooking as Men Like It* (1939), and A. J. Liebling, *Between Meals: An Appetite for Paris* (New York: Simon and Schuster, 1962).

6. Elizabeth Spelman used this phrase in her groundbreaking book *Inessential Woman: Problems of Exclusion in Feminist Thought* (Boston: Beacon, 1988).

References

Avakian, Arlene Voski. 1997, 1998. *Through the Kitchen Window: Women Writers Explore the Intimate Meanings of Food and Cooking*. Boston: Beacon.

Bailey, Pearl. 1973. *Pearl's Kitchen: An Extraordinary Cookbook*. New York: Harcourt.

Barndt, Deborah, ed. 1999. *Women Working the NAFTA Food Chain: Women, Food & Globalization*. Toronto: Second Story Press.

———. (1999) "Whose Choice? Flexible Women Workers in the Tomato Food Chain." In *Women Working the NAFTA Food Chain*.

Belasco, Warren. 1989. *Appetite for Change: How the Counterculture Took on the Food Industry, 1966–1988*. New York: Pantheon.

Bentley, Amy. 1998. *Eating for Victory: Food Rationing and the Politics of Domesticity*. Urbana: University of Illinois Press.

Beoku-Betts, Josephine A. 1995. "We Got Our Way of Cooking Things: Women, Food and Preservation of Cultural Identity among the Gullah," *Gender and Society* 9, 5 (October): 535–555.

Blend, Benay. 2001. "In the Kitchen Family Bread Is Always Rising!" In *Pilaf, Pozole, and Pad Thai: American Women and Ethnic Food*, ed. Sherrie A. Inness. Amherst: University of Massachusetts Press.

Bordo, Susan. 1993. *Unbearable Weight: Feminism, Western Culture and the Body*. Berkeley: University of California Press.

Bower, Anne, ed. 1997. *Recipes for Reading: Community Cookbooks, Stories, Histories*. Amherst: University of Massachusetts Press.

Cotter, Colleen. "Claiming a Piece of the Pie: How the Language of Recipes Defines Community." In *Recipes for Reading*, ed. Bower.

Counihan, Carole. 1999. *The Anthropology of Food and Body: Gender, Meaning, and Power*. New York: Routledge.

———. 1999. "Food, Power, and Female Identity in Contemporary Florence." In *The Anthropology of Food and Body*, ed. Counihan.

———. 1999. "An Anthropological View of Western Women's Prodigious Fasting: A Review Essay." In *The Anthropology of Food and Body*, ed. Counihan.

———. 1999. "Food Sex and Reproduction: Penetration of Gender Boundaries," In *The Anthropology of Food and Body*, ed. Counihan.

Counihan, Carole, and Steven L. Kaplan, eds. 1998. *Food and Gender: Identity and Power*. Newark: Gordon and Breach.

Counihan, Carole, and Penny Van Esterik. 1997. *Food and Culture: A Reader*. New York: Routledge

Darden, Norma Jean, and Carole Darden. 1994. *Spoonbread and Strawberry Wine: Recipes and Reminiscences of a Family*. New York: Main Street Books.

David, Elizabeth. 1977. *English Bread and Yeast Cookery*. London: Allen Lane.

———. 1998. *South Wind through the Kitchen: The Best of Elizabeth David*. North Point, CA: North Point Press.

DeVault, Marjorie. 1991. *Feeding the Family: The Social Organization of Caring Work*. Chicago: University of Chicago Press.

Dorfman, Cindy. 1992. "The Garden of Eating: The Carnal Kitchen in Contemporary American Culture." *Feminist Issues* (Spring): 21–38.

Douglas, Mary. 1966. *Purity and Danger: An Analysis of Concepts of Pollution and Taboo.* New York: Praeger.

Dusselier, Jane. 2001. "Bonbons, Lemon Drops, and Oh Henry! Bars: Candy, Consumer Culture, and the Construction of Gender, 1895–1920." In *Kitchen Culture in America: Popular Representations of Food, Gender and Race,* ed. Sherrie A. Inness. Philadelphia: University of Pennsylvania Press.

Ehrlich, Elizabeth. 1997. *Miriam's Kitchen: A Memoir.* New York: Viking.

Erica Endrijonas. 2001. "Processed Foods from Scratch: Cooking for a Family in the 1950's." In *Kitchen Culture in America: Popular Representations of Food, Gender and Race,* ed. Sherrie A. Inness. Philadelphia: University of Pennsylvania Press.

Fisher, M. F. K. 1954. *The Art of Eating: The Collected Gastronomical Works of M. F. K. Fisher.* Cleveland: World.

Friedman, Harriet. 1999. "Remaking Traditions: How We Eat, What We Eat, and the Changing Political Economy of Food." In *Women Working the NAFTA Food Chain,* ed. Barndt.

Goldman, Anne. 1992. " 'I Yam What I Yam': Cooking, Culture, and Colonialism." In *Decolonizing the Subject: The Politics of Gender in Women's Autobiography,* ed. Sidone Smith and Julia Watson. Minneapolis: University of Minnesota Press.

Harris, Jessica. 1989. *Iron Pots and Wooden Spoons: Africa's Gifts to New World Cooking.* New York: Atheneum.

———. 1995. *The Welcome Table: African American Heritage Cooking.* New York: Simon & Schuster.

Helkde, Lisa. 1993. "Let's Eat Chinese: Cultural Food Colonialism." Paper presented at the Midwestern Conference of the Society for Women in Philosophy.

———. 2001. "Let's Cook Thai: Recipes for Colonialism." In *Pilaf, Pozole, and Pad Thai: American Women and Ethnic Food,* ed. Sherrie A. Inness. Amherst: University of Massachusetts Press.

Inness, Sherrie A. 2001. *Dinner Roles: American Women and Culinary Culture.* Iowa City: University of Iowa Press.

Kanafani-Zahar, Aida. 1997. " 'Whoever Eats You Is No Longer Hungry, Whoever Sees You Becomes Humble': Bread and Identity in Lebanon." *Food and Foodways* 7, 1: 45–71.

Kelly, Traci Marie. 2001. "If I Were a Voodoo Priestess: Women's Culinary Autobiography." In *Kitchen Culture in American: Popular Representations of Food, Gender, and Race,* ed. Sherrie A. Inness. Philadelphia: University of Pennsylvania Press.

Kirshenblatt-Gimblett, Barbara. 1997. "The Temple Emanuel Fair and Its Cookbook, Denver 1888." In *Recipes for Reading,* ed. Bower.

Leonardi, Susan J. 1989. "Recipes for Reading: Pasta Salad, Lobster à la Riseholme, and Key Lime Pie." *PMLA* 104: 340–347.

Levenstein, Harvey. 1988. *Revolution at the Table: The Transformation of the American Diet.* New York: Oxford University Press.

———. 1993. *Paradox of Plenty: A Social History of Eating in Modern America.* New York: Oxford University Press.

Lévi-Strauss, Claude. 1970. *The Raw and the Cooked.* London: Jonathan Cape.

Lupton, Deborah. 1996. *Food, the Body and the Self.* London: Sage.

McFeeley, Mary. 2000. *Can She Bake a Cherry Pie?: American Women and the Kitchen in the Twentieth Century.* Amherst: University of Massachusetts Press.

Mennell, Stephen. 1985. *All Manners of Food: Eating and Taste in England and France from the Middle Ages to the Present.* Oxford: Basil Blackwell.

Mintz, Sidney. 1985. *Sweetness and Power: The Place of Sugar in Modern History.* New York: Viking.

Narayan, Uma. 1995. "Eating Cultures: Incorporation, Identity and Indian Food." *Social Identities* 1, 1: 63–86.

Pilcher, Jeffrey. 1997. "Recipes for Patria: Cuisine, Gender and Nature in Nineteenth-Century Mexico." In *Recipes for Reading,* ed. Bower.

Probyn, Elsbeth. 2000. *Carnal Appetites: Food, Sex, Identities.* New York: Routledge.

Randall, Margaret. 1997. *Hunger's Table: Women, Food, and Politics.* Watsonville, CA: Paper-Mache Press.

Reichl, Ruth. 1998. *Tender at the Bone.* 1998. New York: Random House.

Shange, Ntozake. 1998. *If I Can Cook/You Know God Can.* Boston: Beacon.

Shapiro, Laura. 1986. *Perfection Salad: Women and Cooking at the Turn of the Century.* New York: Farrar, Straus, and Giroux.

Shiva, Vandana, 1992. "Development Ecology and Women." In *Cooking, Eating, Thinking: Transformative Philosophies of Food,* ed. Diane W. Curtin and Lisa M. Heldke. Bloomington: Indiana University Press.

Theophano, Janet. 2001. "Home Cooking: Boston Baked Beans & Sizzling Rice Soup as Recipes for Pride and Prejudice." In *Kitchen Culture in American: Popular Representations of Food, Gender, and Race,* ed. Sherrie A. Inness. Philadelphia: University of Pennsylvania Press.

Thompson, Becky W. 1994. *A Hunger So Wide and So Deep: American Women Speak Out on Eating Problems.* Minneapolis: University of Minnesota Press.

Toklas, Alice B.. 1984. *The Alice B. Toklas Cookbook.* New York: Perennial.

Visser, Margaret. 1986. *Much Depends on Dinner: The Extraordinary History and Mythology, Allure and Obsessions, Perils and Taboos of an Ordinary Meal.* Toronto: McClelland and Stewart.

Weismantel, M. J. 1996. "Children and Soup, Men and Bulls: Meals and Time for Zumbagua Women." *Food and Foodways* 6, 3–4: 307–327.

Witt, Doris. 1999. *Black Hunger: Food and the Politics of U.S. Identity.* New York: Oxford University Press.

Zafar, Rafia. 1999. "The Signifying Dish: Autobiography and History in Two Black Women's Cookbooks." *Feminist Studies* 25, 2: 449–469.

THE MARKETPLACE

Representations of family meals even now when most married women work outside the home are often nostalgic evocations of warmth and safety—the haven presided over by father at the head of the table and mother serving some version of comfort food. As intimate as the experience of eating still may seem, our relationship to food in a capitalist economy is determined in large part by the food industry, and our relations of race, gender, and class are shaped by the social construction of cooking and eating. The essays in this section argue that in the late nineteenth- and twentieth-century United States what came to be accepted as proper meals, even what mothers fed their babies, was constructed by large corporations.

Laura Shapiro's essay demonstrates that Betty Crocker, a creation of General Mills, helped to sell the company's products along with particular notions of femininity and masculinity. Gerber Infant Foods, Amy Bentley shows, changed not only preferred diet for infants but "modern motherhood" through their successful campaign to introduce solid food much earlier than had previously been usual. Of course, the most "modern" of foods was not what the mother might produce in her kitchen, but what she bought in those little jars with the picture of the quintessential white baby on them. In addition to what we ate and what we fed our babies, corporations also changed ideas about the equipment we used to prepare our food. The standard kitchen stoves that we now take for granted are not necessarily the most convenient or efficient design for cooking, but as Leslie Land demonstrates, uniform design was most efficient for maximizing profits for General Electric and Standard Gas, corporations that came to dominate stove manufacturing. Eating out is the food activity most associated with the marketplace, but as Jan Whitaker shows, the bland menu offered in restaurants at the turn of the twentieth century constructed white Anglo-Saxon cuisine as "healthy" food in opposition to the diet of the Eastern and Southern Europeans who were flocking to eastern cities in search of a better life. Ironically, it is precisely this diet, rich in vegetables, garlic, olive oil, and whole grains, that is now hailed by many as the most beneficial for good health.

Most of us no longer look to General Mills and Gerber as paradigms of American values, and Betty Crocker no longer reigns supreme as she did in the 1950s. But the food industry continues to wield enormous power and constructs gender relations in its representations of women, albeit necessarily more subtlely than it did before the women's movement.

"I Guarantee": Betty Crocker and the Woman in the Kitchen

LAURA SHAPIRO

In the spring of 1954, some of America's most popular magazines, radio shows, and television programs ran a food advertisement trumpeting "one of the great recipes of the year."[1] Great or not, Dutch Pantry Pie certainly summed up many of the nation's culinary preoccupations at the time. It called for melting American cheese in Carnation Evaporated Milk, adding potatoes, and putting the mixture in a pie shell made with Gold Medal Flour. Then the mixture was covered with cubes of Spam and a top crust was added. For the sauce, the instructions were to mix more evaporated milk with a can of soup. Even for the early '50s, an era when cookery was proud to be commercial, Dutch Pantry Pie led home cooks on a remarkable march through the food industry.

But what was equally striking about the recipe, at least as it appeared in the April issue of *Woman's Day*, was the person offering it up. She was Mary Blake, well known as a spokeswoman for Carnation. Magazine readers may or may not have been aware that Mary Blake, per se, didn't exist: Carnation's home economists wrote her copy, signed her mail, and made her speeches. At Libby's, home economists did the same for Mary Hale Martin; at Dole, she was called Patricia Collier; Ann Pillsbury presided over Pillsbury's recipes, and there were dozens more, typically portrayed in the ads with pen-and-ink portraits of smiling women. These women weren't real, exactly, although real women stood behind them. They were authority personified, lending a human face to food corporations bidding for the attention of female shoppers. But in the ad for Dutch Pantry Pie, Mary Blake did more than wear a human face, she made a strangely human gesture. The recipe, she told readers, was created "by my good friend Betty Crocker of General Mills."[2]

Her good friend? These two fictional figures were trading recipes? Betty Crocker, longtime spokeswoman for General Mills, was a credible source for any recipe calling for its Gold Medal flour. But a second glance at Dutch Pantry Pie hints at why this particular dish may have needed a more pointedly domestic backstory than even its name implied. The cheese was heavily processed, the milk came from a can, the meat did have animal origins but they lurked far in the past—plainly, if this meal was to qualify as home cooking, two human faces were none too many.

Mary Blake predicted that Dutch Pantry Pie would sweep the nation, and the ad did show up widely. But what really swept the nation were figures like Mary Blake and Betty Crocker, who forged a crucial link between old habits and new foods. Ever since the end of the Second World War, chemistry labs and assembly lines had been taking over more and more of the nation's cooking. Now the food industry was overhauling the very concept of "cooking." In ads and other promotional materials, such traditional kitchen chores as cleaning vegetables, chopping ingredients, measuring, and mixing were dismissed as old-fashioned drudgery. The new "cooking" meant opening boxes, defrosting foods, combining the contents of different packages, and decorating the results. When Kraft was promoting miniature marshmallows in 1955, for example, the company ran enormous newspaper ads featuring a "Kraft Kitchen Recipe." Set up in standard cookbook format, the recipe started with a list of ingredients: one box of lemon pudding and one cup of miniature marshmallows. Then came the instructions: "Prepare the pudding according to directions on the package. Cool. Fold in the marshmallows."[3]

Right at the forefront of this effort to reeducate homemakers was the food industry's busy sisterhood of pen-and-ink home economists. In person and in print, they taught women how to use new electric stoves, mixers, and blenders, how to cook blocks of frozen peas, how to garnish canned ham with pears dipped in food coloring, and how to make crepes suzettes with pancake mix. Known in the business world as "live trademarks,"[4] these figures were designed to project specific, carefully researched characteristics to women shopping for their households. "Ideally, the corporate character is a woman, between the ages of 32 and 40, attractive, but not competitively so, mature but youthful-looking, competent yet warm, understanding but not sentimental, interested in the consumer but not involved with her," explained a business publication in 1957.[5] To a historian tracking them, these women seem both ubiquitous and elusive, flourishing in a surreal universe that left purely optional the distinction between fiction and reality. In the pages of *Forecast*, a home economics magazine where real and invented home economists mingled especially comfortably, Mary Alden of Quaker Oats was given a byline for an article on nutritious oatmeal breakfasts,[6] and Frances Barton of General Foods presided over a luncheon attended by the magazine's real-life editor.[7] When Irma Rombauer, author of *The Joy of Cooking*, published a cookbook emphasizing convenience foods in 1939, she listed and thanked all the "home economists" who had helped her but made no distinction between, say, Jeanette Kelley of Lever Brothers (real) and Martha Logan of Swift (fictional).[8] On one notable occasion, Mary Barber, the real-life spokeswoman for Kellogg's, took a cruise to Honduras courtesy of United Fruit, accompanied by its real-life representative, Ina Lindman. In an ad published in *Forecast*, Mary Barber acknowledged Ina Lindman but saved her most enthusiastic praise for another home economist at United Fruit: Chiquita Banana. "I came home with a new understanding of what makes Chiquita Banana the successful teacher she is!" wrote Mary Barber. "It's Chiquita's warmth, her sympathy, her *showmanship*."[9]

The most famous by far of these figures was, of course, Betty Crocker. A treasured property of General Mills, Betty Crocker has outlived her sisters by several decades. Over the years her job has varied—today she's more symbolic than genuinely authoritative—but during the immediate postwar era she was a sure, steady voice guiding homemakers through a time of tension and change in the kitchen. Millions of Americans listened to her on the radio, read her column in the newspaper, and watched her on TV. In part she flourished because General Mills, unlike many of the other companies with live trademarks, recognized the value of her widely trusted persona and poured considerable resources into promoting her. But she also took up a permanent place in the nation's culinary consciousness because of the food with which she was most powerfully identified—the classic, frosted layer cake. Few products emerging from the middle-class American kitchen have had the emotional heft of this iconic dessert, universally recognized as a triumph of love as much as skill. Betty Crocker knew very well the enormous resonance of a cake baked at home. "Cakes from every land have been introduced to America—but none is so glamorous as the typically American cake developed in this country—the gorgeous concoction of richly tender layers, crowned with luscious, creamy icing!" she wrote in a 1942 Gold Medal flour recipe booklet. "No wonder that more cakes are made in American homes than any other type of baked food. They are a real achievement in the art of cooking. And cakes have become the very symbol of home life in our country."[10]

Home cooks didn't need to be reminded that the stakes were high. Baking a cake is, in fact, a precarious undertaking: much can go wrong even in an oft-used recipe, depending on such factors as the weather, the size of the eggs, or the freshness of the baking powder. And when the cake is meant for a birthday or a company dinner, failure hits hard. Questions and lamentations about cake-baking had long predominated in forums where women had a chance to ask for help with cooking. *Household* magazine, published during the 1940s and '50s in Topeka, Kansas, for a largely midwestern readership, ran a regular column in which a cooking expert answered readers' questions; and month after month, their questions were about cakes. "I never had any trouble making cakes of any kind by hand. Since receiving my new electric mixer I do not have good cakes." "After my angel food cakes stand a while the surface gets moist and sticky." "What causes my chiffon cake to be heavy on the bottom?"[11] In the columns of the Confidential Chat, a long-running readers' question-and-answer forum in the women's pages of the *Boston Globe*, letters on baking and cakes appeared constantly. "Will some experienced cook tell me why cakes fall on the bottom though they rise on top?" "Do you know how to measure shortening exactly, with the aid of water?" "When my beloved husband reached home this evening he as usual gave me a big hug and kiss and asked: 'Did you make a cake or pie today?' I'd just taken your wonderful 'two-egg cake' from my oven."[12]

Not surprisingly, it was trouble with baking that gave birth to Betty Crocker. In 1921 Washburn Crosby, the Minneapolis flour company that would become General Mills, ran a magazine promotion inviting people to complete a jigsaw puzzle and send it in to the company. Those who did so would receive a pincushion in the shape of a flour sack. Thousands of people sent in the jigsaw puzzles, and many took the opportunity to include letters to Washburn Crosby, seeking advice on their breads, biscuits, and cakes. The company saw this as a good chance to communicate with customers, so home economists on staff answered every letter, signing them all "Betty Crocker"—"Betty" for its homey quality, and "Crocker" in honor of a longtime company executive. Betty Crocker was little more than a signature at first, but she gained a voice in 1924 when "The Betty Crocker Cooking School of the Air" began broadcasting from a Minneapolis radio station, with a Washburn Crosby employee as Betty Crocker. The show ran for nearly three decades, registering more than a million "students."[13] Other radio programs followed, with different women over time personifying Betty Crocker, but the public had no problem fixing her identity. By the early 1950s, General Mills surveys showed that 99 percent of American housewives were familiar with Betty Crocker's name, more than two-thirds correctly identified her with General Mills and its products, and some 20 percent spontaneously said "Betty Crocker" when asked to name the home economist they found "most helpful."[14]

Betty Crocker's presence in print advertising was widespread, and millions of people requested copies of her recipe booklets, but she had her greatest impact on the public through radio. The radio, declared *Fortune* magazine in 1945, "made" Betty Crocker.[15] Not only did it have a national reach that no print publication could match, it was also a peculiarly appropriate home for a figure whose relation to the real world was so intangible. To hear her voice was to add a dimension to her persona that print could not provide, but for a listener to complete the picture required imagination—itself a good medium for someone who was, in fact, imaginary. "And here she is, America's first lady of food—your Betty Crocker," the announcer used to proclaim on "Time for Betty Crocker,"[16] underscoring the fact that Betty Crocker could be whatever her public wished or believed.

Betty Crocker's radio shows, developed before broadcasting enforced any important distinction between editorial content and advertising, conveyed a remarkably fluid version of reality. They seemed to emanate from a world without boundaries, where real people conversed easily with made-up colleagues, and genuine discussions melted into commercial fantasies. "Time for Betty Crocker," for instance, was a five-minute show that played nine times a week in the '50s and reached more than eight million homes. The real-life Win Elliot—Betty Crocker's long-time announcer and interlocutor—always introduced the fictional Betty Crocker. "Hello, everybody," she would say cordially. Betty Crocker was portrayed from 1950 to 1964 by Adelaide Hawley Cumming, who had been a radio and TV commentator specializing in fashion and women's news during the 1940s. Cumming's voice was pleasant and confident, never intimate, and never coy. Her Betty Crocker was a grown-up and a professional, someone to be trusted for her expertise. "You know we've found that noodle casseroles are popular with most families," she informed her listeners on a typical show. "But they can become pretty humdrum unless we're careful to vary them. And our Noodles Cantonese recipe from my new *Good and Easy Cookbook* does just that." Win Elliot, by contrast, spoke in warmer, less formal tones. "Hey, from all I gather, Betty Crocker, the gals are really going for *all* the recipes in that new cookbook of yours." When the talk turned to 4-Square Fudge Cake, the vehicle for discussing Gold Medal flour, it was Win Elliot who created the domestic context. His wife Rita, he said, had just made the cake for company. "The women all wanted the recipe, and the men—well, they wanted second and third helpings. What a success! The crunchy nuts in that moist, chocolatey, rich, tender . . . *deli*cious cake . . . ummmm mmmmmm." Betty Crocker then chuckled and told him, "Win, you've just been describing what we like to call 'that good Gold Medal texture!' " And she went on explaining the merits of Gold Medal until Win Elliot said, "Well, Betty Crocker. It looks like time's up." "So it is, Win," she agreed.[17]

Strikingly, while she calls him Win, he invariably addresses her as Betty Crocker. There's an implicit hierarchy in Betty Crocker's radio world, one that subtly reverses traditional sex roles. Betty Crocker is the professional, Win is the homebody; she's the source of information, Win is the enthusiast; she's authoritative, and Win is supportive. In her books and in print advertising, Betty Crocker often made a point of praising the housewife's importance; but this message gained tremendous power by going undercover, in a sense, on the radio. Rather than overtly patting housewives on the back, she simply ran the show with confidence, described her work and travels, and emphasized that good cooking was an achievement in which women could take a great deal of pride. This kind of unsentimental esteem for housewives had begun with Marjorie Husted, one of the first Betty Crockers, who built up the home service department at General Mills through the 1940s and became a company executive. As she explained in a speech to advertising copywriters in 1948, her research among modern homemakers had convinced her that they felt "*uncertain—anxious—insecure*" about their work and its status. When she asked what they would need in order to feel satisfied with their domestic careers, the answers echoed one another: "Encouragement and appreciation . . . Appreciation and recognition . . . Family appreciation. . . ."[18] Hence nobody in Betty Crocker's vicinity was in danger of being identified as "just a housewife," not even Rita, whose chocolate cake—"What a success!"—was applauded prominently by all. In any home where Betty Crocker reigns, her radio shows promised, the woman in the kitchen finally reaps the respect she's due.

General Mills could see that Betty Crocker was unparalleled when it came to reaching homemakers and building trust in the company. The phenomenal success of *Betty Crocker's Picture Cook Book*, published in 1950 with a then record-breaking first printing of nearly a million copies, showed just how much home cooks wanted the simply phrased reassurance and reliable advice they associated with her name. By the end of the 1940s, however, her traditional home base in radio was starting to seem dowdy. Americans were in thrall to the new medium of television, and radio was fast losing ground as an advertising vehicle. Many of the country's favorite radio personalities were moving to TV; why not Betty Crocker? Her radio shows continued, but in 1950 General Mills gave Betty Crocker her own TV series, filmed on location at company headquarters in Minneapolis. Now the nation would meet her in person.

This move to television coincided with one of the company's most important new ventures. According to General Mills, American homemakers served more than a billion cakes a year,[19] and the company knew from its own mail just how nervous many of those homemakers were about baking them. Along with its competitors, General Mills had been hard at work for years developing a cake mix. In 1948 the company launched its first one, called Ginger*cake*—italics in the original—and followed it with Devils Food Cake and Party Cake mixes. (Party Cake, explained a company newsletter, offered something for everyone. "With egg yolks, it produces a golden cake, with whole eggs, a yellow cake, with egg whites, a white cake and whole eggs plus spices, a spice cake. In combination with icing recipes that come with every package, it will make 64 different cake and icing combinations.")[20] Pillsbury and other companies also introduced their first cake mixes around this time, and ads for what Swans Down called "Miracle-perfect! Miracle-easy! Miracle-quick!" baking sprang up in magazines and newspapers.[21]

Despite the trauma associated with cake-baking, the new mixes were not an easy sell. For women who believed, with Marjorie Husted, that family love was best symbolized by "the fragrance of good things baking in the oven,"[22] a cake mix was guilt in a box. "Many women have resisted the innovations designed to make their job easier because they feel it makes their role seem less necessary and worthwhile," reported advertising expert Janet Wolff.[23] Much of the early publicity about cake mixes justified them by dwelling on the huge expenditures of time and strength that went into old-fashioned baking. Making traditional gingerbread, according to General Mills, called for "13 distinct steps, several of which involve two or more individual operations. . . . Only a homemaker who has gone through the ordeal can appreciate grandmother's near heroism."[24] But if cake mixes were so very easy to use, the challenge and the sense of achievement dropped right out of baking—and by extension, homemaking. Moreover, survey after survey showed that of all their household tasks, women tended to like cooking best, perhaps because it did have the potential to be involving, demanding, and creative.[25] Consequently, many ads urged women to think of a cake mix not as an end in itself but as the starting point for a burst of imagination. "One of the best ways a woman can express her personality is through the foods she serves," counseled Ann Pillsbury. "Mixes are not designed to destroy that creative instinct—but for the busy home-maker, they are the base. The basic product is supplied—the frosting, filling or topping is left to her."[26]

General Mills was counting on mixes of all sorts to dominate the American kitchen in years to come. By 1950 the company was produc-ing cake mixes and piecrust mixes as well as the familiar Bisquick, and more products were in the pipeline. Television would be the key to persuading women that these emblems of speed and certainty deserved pride of place in modern housekeeping. Here, after all, was a selling medium so new that Americans came to it without preconceptions. Through television, they could be persuaded that what counted in bak-ing were triumphant results—not genuine effort, not even genuine con-tact with the ingredients. Betty Crocker would guide women as she always had, but this time embodying a more dignified, almost imper-sonal relationship to the kitchen. Only one show from her TV series survives, the very first, and it hints at a persona and mission for Betty Crocker very different from any she had before.[27]

Broadcast on CBS-TV in the fall of 1951, the inaugural program opened with a dramatic tableau staged far from sink or stove. A woman, anonymous, stood on a promontory against the sky, two young children clinging to her hands. Her chin was lifted, her gaze was unflinching, and her purpose was grave, if not precisely definable. She seemed to personify a valiant young America, defender of truth and protector of the helpless. Then, as she paused with her little family on their arduous though unspecific journey, a firm, masculine voice made clear to viewers just what it was she stood for. "Homemaking," he announced. "A woman's most rewarding way of life." And with the theme thus pro-claimed, the hostess of the show appeared—giving the nation its first view of Betty Crocker as a live person. This transubstantiation from fantasy to flesh was handled with great care. Adelaide Cumming's name was not spoken, nor did it appear in the credits. Instead, the announcer welcomed viewers into the unmediated presence of Betty Crocker her-self. And there she was, looking just like her famous portrait; Cum-ming's dress and hairstyle had been chosen to resemble it. Her greeting was familiar, too: the well-modulated "Hello, everybody." But Betty Crocker did not take human form for the first time surrounded by baking pans and measuring cups. When the camera zoomed in, she was seated, with perfect poise and a gracious smile, behind a desk.

The show had what was known as a "service" format, providing de-tailed information about cooking and baking with constant reference to

General Mills products. Interspersed with these segments, which were filmed in the General Mills kitchens, there was a patriotic soap opera in two scenes about a woman who invites an immigrant family for Thanksgiving dinner. Her need for a mince pie recipe gave Betty Crocker all the transitions she needed to get from the American way of life to piecrust mix. But during the frequent segments of the show devoted to rolling out pastry or making instant biscuits, Betty Crocker was never seen cooking. She did show up in the kitchen, but she shared it with a (real-life) General Mills home economist introduced as Ruth. It was Betty Crocker who gave the advice and instructions, and Ruth who did the work, swiftly and efficiently. Even more starkly than on the radio, Betty Crocker's world was free of old-fashioned female drudgery. In fact, it was free of old-fashioned females. Ruth's work was depersonalized, and Betty Crocker's was managerial. Betty Crocker herself, though very much in the kitchen, was not of it. Tall, handsome, and perfectly at ease in front of the camera, Cumming had such beautifully molded diction she could barely say "Stir-N-Roll" pastry with the requisite slur. It came out "Stern Roll."

This highly professional stance made a pointed contrast to the sentiment-drenched Thanksgiving dinner in the dramatic section of the show. With her new persona, Betty Crocker seemed to be distinguishing between home cooking and home cooks. Yes, the meal was still the heart of the holiday, she emphasized, but in these modern days the meal would practically cook itself with the help of the right products. What was truly important—and "rewarding"—were the intangibles of home life, summed up in the opening imagery of female courage and commitment. At the end of the show, seated once more at her desk, Betty Crocker urged viewers to pause during the holidays to remember the blessings of "family living and loving." Then she read aloud a Sunday school hymn, one that thanked God for all the good things of everyday life, and bid farewell.

The series flopped. In 1952 General Mills tried again with another format, this one featuring Betty Crocker as the hostess of an entertainment show with guest stars. That flopped, too.[28] Americans could listen to Betty Crocker on the radio, they wrote her thousands of letters a week, they bought her cookbooks in record numbers, but they were never comfortable with a real, live Betty Crocker who sat down in their living rooms once a week for a visit. Apparently the cognitive dissonance was just too overwhelming. The portentous message of the first program too was unpersuasive: women never wholly submitted to the notion that homemaking was their most rewarding way of life. Married women had been entering the workforce in steadily increasing numbers since 1940. The decade that began with Betty Crocker's TV debut ended with nearly 30 percent of married women working outside the home.

But Betty Crocker did continue appearing on television, and her new emphasis on depersonalized cooking settled in for a long run. For the rest of the decade she was featured in short commercials,[29] where she pitched General Mills products—an unambiguous role that viewers apparently found less disconcerting than her experiment as a guest in their homes. Most of her work was confined to cake mixes, and her message was pared to their chief selling point: mixes were easy to use and infallible. Often in TV commercials she showed up in Gracie Allen's house, just as Gracie was telling George Burns that she couldn't think of what to make for her club meeting or a holiday dinner. "Why don't you ask your friend, Betty Crocker?" George would say. In a moment, the two women were admiring a marble or spice cake that had been produced with almost no visible effort. "It's so easy, even I can bake a Betty Crocker cake!" Gracie would exclaim with relief at the end. Perhaps because Gracie, like Betty Crocker, was a seamless blend of the real and the imaginary, the two women seemed thoroughly comfortable together. But unlike Betty Crocker's radio world, where a woman's voice took the lead and women's accomplishments earned full recognition, she and Gracie had virtually nothing to do in the TV kitchen. It took no skill to come up with this particular marble or spice cake—indeed, that was the point of their delighted self-congratulation. Betty Crocker, who had started her career by sharing a vast store of culinary expertise, now wielded little more than an air of conviction. By the mid-'50s her persona in print ads followed the tone set by TV. "In strawberry season—or any time—you have it all over mother's generation," she told readers in a 1954 angel-food cake mix ad. "Much of the guesswork is gone from cooking. Kitchen time is cut way down. By the ready-to-eat and ready-to-cook foods. By magical appliances that practically *think* for you. . . . These days, you can even *bake* without experience."[30] During this period her TV commercials introduced a tagline that would become famous. "I guarantee a perfect cake, every time you bake—cake after cake after cake," she assured viewers, conjuring an image of identical, flawless cakes rolling off an assembly line. With this, the woman in the kitchen effectively became redundant. In 1960 Betty Crocker herself disappeared from both radio and television (though she continued to thrive in print). In one of the TV cake-mix commercials that followed her departure, nobody cooked at all—a cartoon spoon merrily mixed batter in a cartoon bowl.

By the end of the 1950s, packaged foods had gained a permanent place on the nation's tables, and most of Betty Crocker's sisters were out of business. Even cake mixes, which had been poor in quality at first, improved enough over time to lure many home cooks. "There are some good mixes on the market," James Beard wrote to his friend and fellow cookbook author Helen Evans Brown in 1960. "I like the hot roll mix of Pillsbury and the buttermilk pancake mix of Duncan Hines, and their cake mixes aren't so bad either."[31] But to many women, including some who cooked from boxes and jars, the hands-off approach to making dinner was fundamentally unsatisfying. It didn't have enough to do with food, or genuine work, or the pleasure of eating. Analyzing the emptiness at the heart of "the housekeeping role" in the age of convenience, the psychologist Lois Hoffman observed that "many a housewife is *saddened* to learn that with a package mix she can make an angel food cake two inches higher than the one she had previously made from one cookbook and twelve left-over egg whites."[32] Her essay was published in 1963—the very year that Julia Child first appeared on television, up to her elbows in flour, butter, and garlic. Here was a culinary authority different from any who came before. There was nothing corporate about her image, nothing packaged about her message; when she stirred the sauce you could practically smell the shallots. But what distinguished her most sharply from her predecessors was the way she spoke to home cooks. Julia Child offered no guarantees, and she never promised she could make cooking easy. Instead, she promised to make it understandable—and to make the woman in the kitchen strong. Homemakers watched and listened, hungrily. More than four decades later, her daughters number in the millions.

Notes

1. *Woman's Day*, April 1954, 113.
2. Ibid.
3. *San Francisco Chronicle*, August 18, 1955, 19.
4. "The Current State of Live Trademarks," *Tide*, March 22, 1957, 28–30.
5. Ibid.
6. Mary Alden, "Breakfasting Well . . . *and Economically*," *Forecast*, January 1952, 16–17.
7. "Diary of an Editor," *Forecast*, October 1948, 8.
8. Irma Rombauer, *Streamlined Cooking* (Indianapolis: Bobbs-Merrill, 1939), n.p.
9. *Forecast*, April 1948, 71.
10. General Mills, *Betty Crocker Cook Book of All-Purpose Baking* (General Mills, Inc., 1942).
11. "Kitchen Questions," *Household*, February 1950, 21; October 1951, 75; March 1955, 58.

12. *Boston Globe*, September 19, 1948, A35; November 16, 1950, 19; January 5, 1956, 28.

13. General Mills, *The Story of Betty Crocker* (General Mills, Inc., 1992), n.p.

14. General Mills, "Appendix 'A'" in *Betty Crocker . . . 1921–1954* (General Mills, Inc., n.d.), n.p.

15. "General Mills of Minneapolis," *Fortune*, April 1945, 117.

16. "Betty Crocker on Net Radio: Ultimate in Integrated Sell," *Sponsor*, December 27, 1954, 35.

17. Ibid.

18. Marjorie Husted, "Women, Our Most Important Customers" (speech delivered at the Copywriters' Meeting, Minneapolis, June 21, 1948), 8–9.

19. General Mills, "Eat Your Cake and Have It, Too," *Progress Thru Research*, Fall 1949, 10.

20. Ibid., 9–10.

21. *Boston Globe*, July 29, 1948, 19.

22. Husted, "Women, Our Most Important Customers," 9.

23. Janet Wolff, *What Makes Women Buy* (New York: McGraw-Hill, 1958), 16.

24. General Mills, "General Mills Research Brings a 'Delicacy of the Ages' Up to Date," *Progress Thru Research*, Fall 1948, n.p.

25. See, for example, the Gallup Poll, February 10, 1951, in George Gallup, *The Gallup Poll: Public Opinion 1935–1971* (New York: Random House, 1972), 964–965.

26. Ellen Pennell [Ann Pillsbury], "Food Secrets from the Experts," *Forecast*, February 1948, 24.

27. I am grateful to the staff of the Corporate Archives at General Mills for making it possible for me to see a videotape of this show, which is not normally available for viewing.

28. *Sponsor*, 82–83.

29. Once more, I am grateful to General Mills for the opportunity to see a sample of these commercials on videotape.

30. *Life*, May 17, 1954, 16.

31. Beard to Brown, January 1, 1960, *Love and Kisses and a Halo of Truffles*, ed. John Ferrone (New York: Arcade, 1994), 255–256.

32. Lois Hoffman, "The Decision to Work," in *The Employed Mother in America*, ed. F. Ivan Nye and Lois Hoffman (Westport, CT.: Greenwood Press, 1963), 26–27.

Counterintuitive: How the Marketing of Modernism Hijacked the Kitchen Stove

Leslie Land

As a long-time cook, food writer, food editor, and short person, I have spent most of my life wondering: Why are all home kitchen stoves exactly 36 inches tall, in spite of the widely accepted dictum that work surfaces should be tailored to the height of the user? Why is the oven both low and in front, so it blasts you with heat while breaking your back? Why, in other words, is the most important appliance in the American kitchen so poorly designed, and why is this poor design so pervasive?

What's especially galling is that 'twas not always thus. From their commercial introduction in the early nineteenth century until the turn of the twentieth, stoves came in a wide assortment of heights, and they offered ovens under, over, and beside the cooktop in a mind-boggling array of variations. Consolidations in the stove industry and the disappearance of hundreds of small foundries had narrowed the options by the end of the 1920s, but buyers still had plenty of different heights to choose from. The Sears, Roebuck catalog of 1927, for instance, offered stoves with cooktops anywhere from 29 ⅓ to 33 ¾ inches tall.[1] And most of them had elevated ovens. But just after entering its most gloriously useful era, the kitchen stove turned its back on progress, devolving into a rigidly conformist box that was—and is—uncomfortable for almost everybody.

The raised oven was far from unknown in the nineteenth century, but it had its heyday in the early part of the twentieth, when freedom from the need to stoop was a major selling point. As the catalog copy for the 1907 Climax Estate gas stove pointed out, ranges with elevated ovens "must appeal to any one as being practical, common sense, and convenient. Access is easily had to the broiler, bake oven and cooking top without stooping or bending. Full view of the baking and broiling is a great advantage to the cook."

The trend picked up steam as time went on. Most mid- and high-priced stoves built in the teens and twenties offered multiple ovens—a high one for every day, and a large, low one under the burners, known as a "holiday oven" because it was big enough to roast a really big turkey (and only needed on state occasions). Among the rest, chances were the whole works started at table height and the high oven was the only one you got. That was the case with the Hughes Electric, a pioneering model offered by the Edison Electric Appliance Company in 1920. It was common with the less expensive gas models, and a given with stoves that burned oil, which needed the space below the cooktop for the columnar burners. By 1928, the high oven was everywhere, from the oil-burning Perfection "modern as the swift-winged liners of the air," to the offerings of the American Stove Company, which claimed to be the largest in the field and had high ovens on all six of its gas stove lines. As late as 1934, GE was showing high oven stoves in its demon-

stration kitchens,[2] but by then it was all over except the stooping and bending.

Starting near the turn of the decade and gaining force as the '30s progressed, the vogue for streamlining swept through the kitchen, leveling everything in its path. The great majority of ovens sank below the cooktop, never to rise again, and variable heights vanished, victims of continuous countertops and the assorted cabinets and appliances that fit beneath them. Essentially, the stove became a box so that it would fit tidily between other boxes, and it had to be one standardized height so the maximum number of other box-tops would match up.

The idea of the continuous countertop is frequently traced all the way back to Catharine Beecher, who described something resembling one in her 1869 book, *The American Woman's Home*. But just as much—or more—early credit is due the Hoosier company, which began marketing its multipurpose kitchen units in 1899. Beecher's plan did include a work surface or "cook form" level with the sink, but she didn't suggest making other surfaces level with the cook form, and the stove wasn't just separate, it was in another room. The Hoosiers, on the other hand, though still not butted up to the stove were supposed to be placed near it, and they did introduce the idea of modular kitchen furniture; you could buy multiple units and have the work surfaces line up. Furthermore, the cabinets above and below that work surface were precursors of those that arrived in the '30s and still dominate today.[3]

Hugely successful, the Hoosiers and their many imitators became

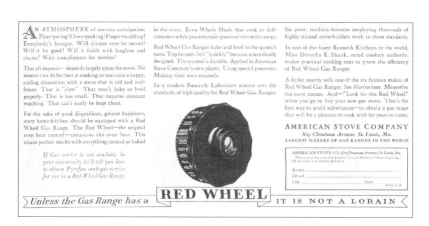

The sell was the "Red Wheel" thermostat, but every one of these nifty new stoves had a high oven. At this point, they could let the pictures say "gas is better than coal or wood," but they still had to reassure potential buyers that gas was available. Ad for American Stove Company, from *Woman's Home Companion*, June 1929, p. 113.

more and more numerous in U.S. kitchens through the first decades of the century. But they remained freestanding items, just as the kitchens that housed them remained assemblages of discontinuous elements, right through the 1920s. Meanwhile, in Germany, home of the most influential architecture of the age, there were clear warnings of the shape of things to come. The Haus am Horn, a Bauhaus model single-family home displayed at Weimar in 1923, had a single-level sink and sideboard along one kitchen wall. There was a level L-shaped work surface in the experimental Weissenhof settlement, in Stuttgart, in 1927, and the Frankfurter Küche, also unveiled in 1927, took the idea to its illogical conclusion. All work surfaces in this kitchen were the same height, a triumph of simplified line much admired by architectural theorists.

Sigfreid Giedion described the Haus am Horn and Weissenhof kitchens in *Mechanization Takes Command*, a frequently quoted history of mass production that came out in 1948. The Frankfurter Küche is cited by Raimonda Riccini in "The Rationalized Kitchen," a pair of essays in the huge, wide-ranging *History of Industrial Design* published in Italy in 1990. For these authorities, and others like them, the continuous countertop is an unmitigated Good Thing. Riccini, for instance, whose title speaks volumes, finds a lot to fault in the circa 1850 free-standing kitchen range: "The construction material, the amount of space it took up, and the smoke and heat given off made it impossible to place the stove alongside such pieces of furniture as old fashioned dressers or even worse, the early attempts at continuous work surfaces." Giedion, for his part, refers to the Haus am Horn effort as "the earliest example of the kitchen in which organization is joined to form" and speaks approvingly of "the cooking centers, favored by surfaces and appliances at equal heights."[4]

Favored or not, the continuous counter was admired mostly by a small group of avant-garde architects, and if that had stayed true right through the thirties and forties, there's a good chance that only patrons of the arts would still be stuck with the thing. But the German theorists turned out to have the zeitgeist on their side, and nowhere more strongly than in the United States. Inspired by the simplifications for which the Bauhaus was famous, American industrial designers removed the decorations from every consumer product from toasters to automobiles, radios to refrigerators; and they leveled uneven surfaces—including those in the kitchen—whenever they got the chance. Going the Bauhaus one better, they also rounded off sharp corners in a homage to aerodynamics known as the streamlined look. Though products like bathroom scales and pencil sharpeners weren't measurably improved by the reduction of air drag, the sense of modernity and forward progress streamlining conveyed turned out to have considerable sales appeal to people mired in the Depression.

The stage had already been set. Major advances in manufacturing and transportation that had started in the last quarter of the nineteenth century were fully assimilated. Locally produced necessities—wheat for porridge, lye soap for cleaning, horses for getting from here to there—were well on their way to being supplanted by brand-name consumer goods: Grape Nuts, Ivory Snow, Ford cars. There were more, and more various, factory-produced items for sale than there had ever been before, and as a result, advertising grew from being an adjunct of something else (manufacturing, publishing, retailing) into a full-fledged industry, complete with the forerunners of psychological profiling. The earnest, if often hyperbolic, descriptions of a product's merits that had characterized late Victorian sales efforts gave way to what came to be called "Consumer Engineering," an approach that appealed as much to buyers' sense of style—and fears of failure—as it did to their desire for bargains.[5] Simply selling people things they needed was no longer enough; it was necessary to persuade them that they needed things they'd never dreamed of. Since most household purchases were made by women, the newly created ad agencies targeted women particularly, and "promised to create a new market of consumers, indeed to systematize desire."[6]

But if advertising was becoming more convoluted, design was straightening out. Art Nouveau gave way to Modernism. "Clean" lines and simplified forms replaced sinuous curves and decorated surfaces in everything from furniture and textiles to dinnerware, while the idea of thematic unity in home décor gained greater and greater currency.[7] Decorating itself moved toward widespread popular legitimacy, and for the first time since the prescient Beecher, kitchens were designed as wholes by professional "household engineers" such as Christine Frederick and Lillian Gilbreth (about whom more in a minute).

Even without these changes in fashion, some kind of radically new stove was probably inevitable; the industry was suffering an untenable overcapacity. During the 1920s, rising prosperity had combined with major improvements in both sheet-metal fabrication and gas and electric technology to fuel a major boom in stove sales. Appliance makers expanded. But almost before they could get to the bank, first recession, then depression hit. Companies such as General Electric and Standard Gas were desperate for ways to keep moving durable goods such as stoves and refrigerators, equipment which was all too likely to be retained rather than replaced since it was not only expensive but, well, durable. A gas stove bought in 1925 was probably still working just fine in 1932, and hard times no doubt exacerbated the conservative tendencies of stove buyers, already a somewhat reluctant group when it came to adopting the latest thing.[8]

With a nation full of useful old stoves and a depression on, the only way to stimulate consumption was to persuade buyers that the old models were seriously outmoded. But since the stoves were, by and large, perfectly adequate to their purpose, the only way to make them seem outmoded was to make them look outmoded, and that meant bringing in industrial designers, most famously Norman Bel Geddes, who eventually made his name one of the selling points of his designs.

Unlike old-fashioned industrial engineers, the designers came from the world of visual persuasion, and for them, outward appearance was just as important as functionality. Bel Geddes, for instance, had started out in theatrical design and then moved into advertising before he found what proved to be his true calling. It took a while for manufacturers to be persuaded of the designers' usefulness, but they were almost all on board by the time the decade was half over.[9]

No wonder. The designers sold themselves even better than their designs moved merchandise, and once the momentum was on their side no business could afford to be left behind looking old-fashioned. Between 1929 (when Frank Alvah Parsons, commissioned by the American Stove Company to design a range that would be seen as a piece of kitchen furniture, came up with a couple of flat-topped beauties called the Jonquil and the Patrician) and 1938 (when *The Stove Builder*, "Official publication of the Institute of Cooking and Heating Appliance Manufacturers," declared "Streamlining now dominates all phases of the industry")[10] kitchen design entered the modern age. By decade's end, the continuous counter was a *catastrophe accomplie*; the stove was locked at counter height; and that height was an equally locked 36 inches.

At that time the average American woman was about five feet three[11] and the importance of proper working heights—roughly 32 inches, in this case—had been well known and quite widely trumpeted for almost thirty years. (Frederick W. Taylor's highly influential *Principles of Scientific Management*, source of the term "Taylorization," and seed for a forest of time and motion studies, was published in 1911.)

There were two distinct groups that might have been expected to point out that these tall counters and the stoves that matched them were no boon to the average woman: feminists and the aforementioned household engineers. Unfortunately, the feminists by and large assumed that what women wanted was out of the kitchen, and while the household engineers were equally determined to keep them in it, their care-

A "complete Electric Kitchen" from GE, showing a transitional model of range: still up on legs and still with a high oven but a continuation of the countertop, which is itself continuous. From *The New Art of Buying, Preserving and Preparing Foods*, Presented by General Electric Kitchen Institute (1934), p. 7.

fully considered proposals for improvements in kitchen design did not include criticism of companies they relied on for employment.

The feminists, as described by historian Dolores Hayden in *The Grand Domestic Revolution*, "demanded the transformation of the private domestic workplace, the kitchen," into something large, centralized, and, preferably, cooked in by someone else. Marie Stevens Howland "passed over domestic work . . . as a job for 'trained people.'" Charlotte Perkins Gilman was an advocate of the kitchenless home, where housework would be done "by experts instead of amateurs." And Henrietta Rodman also envisioned "trained help from the domestic science departments of the high schools."

As Hayden points out, the problem was succinctly stated by Laura Fay-Smith, who wrote in a *New York Times* article of 1915, "The feminist wants to climb high above the harsh labors of the house, on the shoulders of the women whose hard necessity compels them to be paid servants." This disinterest in the actual physical labor—and enjoyment— of cooking left the field of consumer advocacy wide open for the "self-proclaimed 'efficiency experts' such as Lillian Gilbreth or Christine Frederick who claimed that technology could achieve these same goals (less labor, less isolation) without transforming the traditional home or the woman's role as housewife."[12]

Christine Frederick (1883–1970) was a home economist who became an efficiency expert by learning from her industrial-consultant husband, T. George Frederick. She built her own consulting business by turning their Long Island kitchen into "the Applecroft Home Experiment Station" and was, early in her career, a household editor both for the *Ladies Home Journal* and *The Delineator*. She spent most of her working years as an unashamed hybrid of consumer advocate and copywriter, lecturing and writing books about homemaking and home design while consulting on—and writing sales pamphlets for—a range of manufactured goods from Hoosier cabinets to Campbell's soups.

But Frederick's heart was really in advertising. Her best-known work, a guide for perplexed merchandisers called *Selling Mrs. Consumer*, published in 1929 and dedicated to Herbert Hoover, reveals her as an enthusiastic supporter of industry whose assessment of the average woman—sharp enough about what she wanted, but overly susceptible to emotional and visual appeals—was neatly matched by her opinion of the average manufacturer—a testosterone-blinded oaf who had better listen to her if he ever wanted to sell anything.[13]

In contrast to Frederick, who had no outstanding academic credentials, Lillian Gilbreth (1878–1971) had a doctorate in psychology, and though she also came into the business through an efficiency-expert husband, she went on to became an engineer in her own right. The first woman elected to the National Academy of Engineering, she was also an advisor on women's issues to every president from Hoover to Johnson. Along with her husband, Frank Bunker Gilbreth, she developed a theory of management they called "The One Best Way," which posited that there was a single ideal method for every activity, and that every goal from business efficiency to personal happiness would be achieved if this ideal were found and followed.

However different their backgrounds, Frederick and Gilbreth shared similar views on the basics of kitchen design. Both were bewitched by the idea of equating cake-baking and dishwashing with widget-fabrication; and both were perhaps over-beguiled by the ease of moving objects on—and cleaning—a level plane. But both of them knew perfectly well that the best counter height for kneading dough is not the best for making sandwiches, and they certainly knew that fixing all kitchen counters in the country at any one height would be the antithesis of efficiency—at least as far as the user was concerned.

Along with step-saving, which got its first impassioned defense in *The American Woman's Home*, making sure work surfaces were the correct height for the person using them was one of the cardinal tenets of the efficiency movement, at home as well as at work. The importance of individual tailoring was staple information in newspaper features, magazine articles, and books about home design. For example, Martha Van Rensselaer and Flora Rose Helen Canon's 1919 book, *The Manual of Home-Making*, addressed the subject frequently, and was one of the few that mentioned the stove specifically: "This [the importance of correct height] applies to cook stoves as well as to tables and sinks. It may be necessary to raise the stove on blocks to bring it to this level." *House and Garden*'s Ethel R. Peyser stayed on the height message for years. In September 1920, speaking of the kitchen table (and bringing in the servant question, which was seldom mentioned in these prescriptions), she wrote "ordinary heights are from 32 to 28 inches. Get the height that fits your workers." Three years later, in November, in an article titled "Laying It on the Kitchen Table," she repeated, "In order to use the work surface with convenience the top should be about 32 inches from the floor. But if you always employ 'shorties,' 28 inches may do."[14]

Gilbreth put height first on her list, quite possibly because at five feet seven she was unusually tall. When she designed a model kitchen for the New York Herald Tribune Institute in 1930, only two of the many labor-saving principles on display were described as crucial: "1. Working surfaces adapted to fit the height of the worker. 2. The circular work space" [in essence, a close placement of stove, sink, and refrigerator now commonly called "the kitchen triangle," though there were additional refinements].[15]

The *Tribune* offered free copies of the model kitchen floor plan to anyone who asked for them, and it invited readers to "have one of our experts measure you by Dr. Gilbreth's chart . . . and tell you just how high your kitchen tables and other working surfaces should be to prevent unnecessary fatigue."[16]

Christine Frederick was equally adamant, and sooner. On July 6, 1913, not long after her career had taken off, a *New York Times* article headlined "The Woman Who Invented Scientific Housekeeping" reported her observation that "the ordinary houseworker, whether mistress or servant, . . . works at a surface too high or too low. One need not enlarge upon this to the woman with aching back, yet how few think of changing the conditions even in their own houses. To obviate this, Mrs. Frederick has worked out a table of measurements for women of various heights."

49

This table, as laid out in Frederick's book, *Household Engineering* (1915), stipulated heights galore: to the base of sinks, for standing work surfaces and for sitting work surfaces. The standing work surfaces, presumably including stoves, ranged from 31 ½ inches, for a woman five feet tall, to 34 ¼ inches, for a woman who was five feet six. All this was in spite of the fact that, as she pointed out only two pages later, "No absolute rule can be given for invariable heights because not only the height of the worker must be taken into consideration but also the length of her arm, and whether she is short or long waisted, etc."[17]

In other words, Frederick had a firm grip—deathgrip might not be too strong a word—on the idea that it was important for each individual cook to have her work surface at an equally individual height. But she didn't hold on. By the end of her career she had no trouble blithely announcing, "Today we have settled on 36 inches as the most comfortable counter height for most workers,"[18] though she did allow you might be able to raise or lower the toe space of the base cabinets if necessary.

Other home economists were equally accepting, even when they knew the standard height was likely to cause problems. Consider Louise Peet and Lenore Thye, who covered the subject of kitchen layouts in a very thorough book called *Household Equipment*. True to accepted ergonomic wisdom, they pointed out: "The practice in modern kitchen layouts of having all surfaces on a level, using the 36 inch height of the range as the unit of measure, places more emphasis on appearance than suitability. Different tasks performed in the kitchen frequently require work surfaces of different heights."[19]

In spite of this understanding, Peet and Thye didn't protest the height of the range, perhaps because they knew there was nothing their readers could do about it. And they seem to have taken for granted that the stove dictated the height of the counter. But the long history of variable stove heights, combined with their sudden jolt to rigidity just when the continuous counter became the sine qua non of American kitchen design, suggests that originally it was the counter that dictated the height of the stove, rather than the reverse.

Then why 36 inches? Just about everyone who was looking at women in the kitchen seems to have agreed that work surface height should be proportional to the height of the user, so even if you accept the idea that only an "average" woman could be considered, the proper height for her counter would have been quite a bit less than a yard.

It's tempting to blame Lillian Gilbreth. Her demonstration kitchen for the *Tribune*, which had 36-inch counters, was "planned for a housekeeper 5 feet 7 inches tall, since that is the height of one of the home economists on the Herald Tribune Institute staff,"[20] and she did go on to design similar installations for General Electric.

Yet Gilbreth was so insistent about customized heights (tall women were advised to raise their counters on blocks, short ones to saw the legs off of anything too high) that it's hard to imagine she would have proposed a universal standard so far off the average . . . hard, that is, until you remember that a continuous countertop cannot be all things to all tasks. If you don't want to break your back when it's time to do the dishes, all measurements derive not from the top of the counter but from the bottom of the sink.

In the women's advice literature of the time, all routine domestic activities were seen as things to get through as quickly and efficiently as possible, but washing was the one that got the hideous drudgery prize. Though the creative aspects of cooking were given short shrift and meal preparation was seldom described as fun, the household engineers spent a great many more—and more eloquent—words on the back pain caused by too much bending over the sink than they did on any other flaw in old-fashioned kitchen layouts.

In the 1913 *Times* article, for instance, Mrs. Frederick's remarks on height started with the words "architects or carpenters have decided that the standard kitchen sink shall be so many feet and so many inches high. Therefore at this sink works the woman who is only five feet two, the woman who is five feet ten, and all those in between. There is just one height of woman who works at it with ease. The others are under constant and unnecessary physical strain, with its consequent loss of time and energy."

Gilbreth's pamphlet-writer was equally ready to single out the sink. "No woman who has ever labored for even five minutes in an inefficient kitchen needs to be told that the most exhausting part of dishwashing, ironing and any other task usually done standing is the constant bending over."[21] It was a sore point that had staying power, as shown by this analysis from *The House, Its Plan and Use* (1948), by Tessie Agan. Describing the steps involved in making a Waldorf salad, she explains, "Cutting the apples, the celery and the walnuts and mixing and arranging on plates can be comfortably accomplished at a height anywhere near the center of the torso. But washing dishes is a longer and oft repeated activity so that a more exact location has been determined. For the bottom of the sink, which is the lowest point reached in this activity . . . the preferred height of the bottom of the sink which is 5 inches or more deep is 31 inches from the floor. *If the sink is properly set and if it has work counters on each side, as is often the case, the height of these counters is 36 inches from the floor.*"[22]

51

The italics are mine because they are, in a sense, the smoking sink. In the early '30s, countertops were generally about 31 inches tall, while the tops of the—freestanding—sinks were a sensible 36 inches. Proper working heights were old news by that time; as early as 1922, advertisements for the Standard Plumbing Fixture company were boasting: "'Standard kitchen sinks,' yard stick high, provide comfort and prevent back-strain. How high is yours?" When the mania for continuous coun-

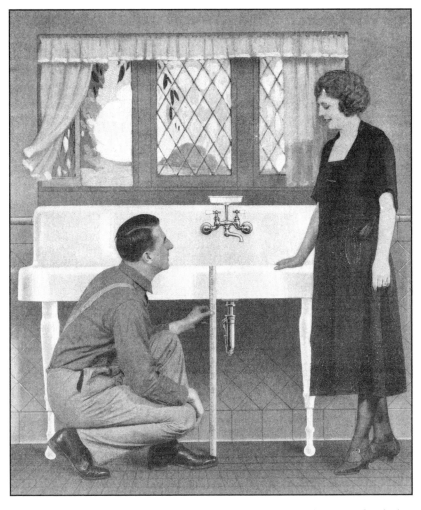

Right idea, wrong homemaker. They couldn't show her looking dumpy, so they had to cheat. By the yardstick conveniently provided, this woman is almost 6 feet tall. Ad for Standard Plumbing Fixtures, from *Good Housekeeping*, September 1922, p. 197.

ters decreed that everything from the breadboard to the stove burners to the sinktop must be the same height, the sinktop won, and the 36-inch stove was born.

After describing even deeper sinks and the even higher counters that should surround them, Agan admitted, "some activities in connection with the preparation of food are not done comfortably" at sinktop-counter height. Pastry-making, for instance, required a height similar to that of the sink-bottom, so "obviously, a special lower surface for mixing and rolling of doughs is desirable." It was equally obvious that the stove ought to be lower, too, but the stove wasn't mentioned. Something more than ergonomics was plainly at work, and that something was fashion, a fashion that was thoroughly entrenched by the time Agan wrote her book, a fashion so friendly to commercial exploitation that adjustable stoves never had a chance.

"Stoves are rapidly reaching the style consciousness which we are accustomed to in the Automobile Industry," wrote designer Onnie Mankki in a 1934 article for *The Stove Builder* called "Coming Trends in Stove Design." He went on at some length about the importance of form and color, then added, "The introduction of the cabinet type range also has brought certain features which are still controversial. Whether or not we are justified in lowering the oven door to the somewhat inconvenient low position necessary to produce a low table top, will find many people strongly defending both points of view."[23]

Not for long, at least not among stove makers. The streamlined look of the tabletop range was too powerful a selling point to be questioned for very long. "The modern range is demonstrated as an attractive piece of furniture to replace the homely and obsolete stoves of yesterday," the magazine proclaimed two years later, describing the products displayed at the Great Lakes Exposition in Cleveland in 1936.[24] By then, the transition was just about complete. The high oven was gone and so, in many cases, were the legs that might have made the stoves easily adjustable.

"Whereas we used to have woeful black, squatty, graceless ranges, today we have the console models," gushed Ethel Peyser in *House Beautiful* in May 1931. "One outstanding new type is the cabinet—by some, we think wrongly, called the console-range . . . [it has] a flat top that can be used as a table when not in use for cooking," various drawers, for both broiling and storage, and "The legs are adjustable and can be raised or lowered to suit the cook!" The exclamation point suggests Ms. Peyser was delighted by the adjustability feature; at last, here was a stove that could be the right height for any number of different women.

This good idea also occurred to Norman Bel Geddes, designer of the prototypical modern stove-as-box (for the Standard Gas Equipment Corporation, in 1930). Geddes revamped Standard's entire line, eliminating what had been almost a hundred designs and replacing them with a set of twelve modules that could be mixed and matched "to create quite different stoves . . . but the company found it cheaper to manufacture 'a single piece stamped steel front frame' for each model," eliminating the possibility of adjustable height.[25]

A customer survey had flagged ease of cleaning as a prime consideration for stove buyers, and that may be why Bel Geddes's design had a flat front instead of legs. He might also have been in efficiency mode; bringing the stove down to the ground made room for storage drawers. But there's also a chance that the choice was primarily a visual statement, a way of setting the new stove apart—every previous stove had legs (leftovers from the days of solid fuel); this radical new model didn't.

Regardless of the reason for amputation, refrigerators were next. Henry Dreyfuss took the legs off the GE in 1934, then Raymond Lowey lowered the Sears Coldspot. "When we began our design," he later wrote, "the Coldspot unit then on the market was ugly . . . perched on spindly legs high off the ground."[26] Possibly taking a cue from Bel Geddes's stove, Lowey used the space beneath the 'fridge cabinet for storage. But while a flat front instead of legs is no hardship with a refrigerator—the time one spends standing in front thereof is brief—it was no favor to the users of stoves, who lost the generous toe kick that let them stand comfortably close to the work surface.

What they gained—if that's the word—was an aesthetically unified set of streamlined appliances, all of which looked modern and proclaimed their owner an up-to-date possessor of the latest thing. Yet the puzzle remains. Legs would have made adjustability easier, but they weren't essential. It wouldn't have been all that expensive to stamp out bases of different heights, and stove makers certainly didn't mind offering several versions of what was basically the same sheet metal box. The Hotpoint stove catalog of 1938, for instance, offered numerous "Special Features. . . . Add them to Hotpoint's basic features and you have a modern range specially designed to meet your own specific needs." You could have a "choice of ovens" (the Royal and Deluxe ranges offered more wattage) and a "choice of broilers"(fancier ones were aluminum, standard was porcelain); there were choices in work surface arrangement, number of burners, number of ovens, and numbers of storage drawers. You could opt for extra outlets, get spiffier hardware, even, if you paid more, avoid burning your arms by getting the controls on the front of the stove instead of on the backsplash. The one thing you could not get was—you guessed it. Under "Choice of dimensions," which offered depths of either 23 or 25 inches, and lengths of 21, 39, 39 ⅗, 42, and 54 inches, there was the discouraging announcement: "Height of cooking top—all models are 36 inches from floor."

Admittedly, most of those "special features" were little more than cosmetic, but not all of them. Hotpoint could at least have offered adjustability to those who were willing to pay for it. But if they did, it would have blown away the modern-looking continuous countertop, and along with it the chance to sell the modular kitchen cabinets produced by furniture manufacturers, the electric sink, complete with disposal and dishwasher, made by Hotpoint itself, and by extension the increased use of electricity that the fully modernized kitchen would consume.

The continuous countertop, child of the Bauhaus and the assembly line, rapidly grew up to be a mighty engine of cross-marketing. Once you were sold on the idea of the continuous counter, once you were safely locked in with the stove, the one essential piece of equipment that you could not hope to build or alter at home, none of your old kitchen furniture fit. But thanks to its locked, uniform height, all of the new stuff on the market was just the right size. The opportunities for cooperative advertising were enormous, and they were not overlooked. Earl Lifshey innocently described one way this worked in *The Housewares Story*, a history written for the National Housewares Manufacturers Association:

> The trend toward more up-to-date kitchens got a big boost in 1935 when the National Kitchen Modernization Bureau was established jointly by the Edison Electric Institute (now the Electric Energy Association) and The National Electrical Manufacturers Association to actively promote kitchen modernization throughout the country.
>
> Tied in with the Federal Housing Bureau on general modernization of the home . . . the new bureau launched an extensive program that included the creation of model modern kitchen displays; radio programs; distribution of modern electric kitchen plan books; a feature motion picture entitled "the Courage of Kay" in which the subject was dramatized with numerous tie-ins with retailers, appliance and kitchen equipment manufacturers, builders and others.[27]

Faced with a juggernaut like that—the project was stopped only by the onset of the World War—it's not surprising that high ovens and uneven workspaces were the odd utilities out. Women never stopped

BEFORE . . . The old-fashioned kitchen full of work, crossed and re-crossed with countless steps. The scene of hundreds of lost hours loaded with routine drudgery . . . the result is lost youth and beauty, and impaired health.

AFTER . . . The modern General Electric Kitchen—a lifetime investment that pays for itself. Easily one-by-one, each unit can be added one at a time, and each helps pay for the next through actual savings effected. The G-E Kitchen Institute, through the G-E representative in your community, will show you how to attain this desirable goal. There is no obligation to you.

Cross-marketing in action. The modern GE kitchen has modular cabinets, a dishwasher, all electric appliances, *and* a bigger window. (Why the gas stove in the "before" picture needed a big black pipe is not revealed.) From *The New Art*, p. 9.

wishing for elevated ovens, though, and "Shopping for a Good Stove," Joy Parr's essay about how the business worked in Ontario in the early '50's, could as easily have been written about the United States:

> Historically, the most common Canadian solid-fuel-burning ranges had had ovens beside rather than below the burners. Early gas and electric stoves followed this form. Buchanan [Donald W. Buchanan, head of the National Industrial Design Council], skeptical when he could find only one Canadian electrical range, a McClary, with the oven at what the housewives claimed was the right height, referred the matter to an authority, Dr. J. B. Brodie, head of household science at the University of Toronto.
>
> Dr. Brodie made common cause with the housewives, arguing that plans "to 'streamline' everything and have a working space around the kitchen at one level . . . are evolved by those who do not work in a kitchen and we know that they are not efficient." Her words were well chosen[.] Buchanan, a proponent of British Good Design principles, regarded streamlining as a heresy hatched by American salesmen.[28]

In spite of considerable pressure from consumer groups, most Canadian manufacturers were unwilling to try reintroducing high oven stoves, at least in part because American market tests had failed. The one model built didn't sell, and that may well have been because it just didn't look right. Henry Dreyfuss, who disavowed the later excesses of streamlining while proudly claiming his part in having hatched it in the first place, offered the following analysis in his 1955 autohagiography, *Designing for People*: "Our grandmothers used [the high oven range] twenty-five years ago, but it virtually disappeared when the industrial designer came along and created a revolution in the kitchen by making everything counter height, including the stove. Several years ago, however, research indicated a preference for a high-oven range and a manufacturer offered an improved model. Women liked its greater convenience . . . but they didn't buy it. The table-top stove flush with the other cabinets in the kitchen had become such a style factor that the ladies refused to be budged away from it."[29]

Regrettably, Dreyfuss seems to be right. The continuous counter still rules, probably at least in part because deconstruction finally solved the high oven problem at just about the time he was writing. By the end of the 1950s, wall ovens were a such a cliche of "contemporary" kitchen design that English music hall comedians Flanders and Swann could sing, "I'm delirious about our new cooker equipment with the eye-level

What a difference a decade makes (though cold storage remains aesthetically problematic and—not being for sale—isn't shown.) In 1929, the kitchen is a cosy, social space. Ten years later, it's a shrine to visual order at the expense of all else. Ad for Congoleum Rugs, from *Woman's Home Companion*, June 1929, inside front cover; ad for Pabco Lineoleum, from *Woman's Home Companion*, April 1939, p. 34.

grill. This means that now, without my having to bend down, the hot fat can squirt straight in my eye."[30]

Wall ovens are now commonplace in middle-class homes and almost a given in those of the rich. But the separate oven has done nothing to solve the counter problem, and though Modernism has been out so long it's enjoying a revival, streamlining never stopped defining this aspect of kitchen design. Why would it? The continuous countertop is the best thing that ever happened to a multibillion dollar industry. All mass-produced kitchen cabinets are still built to the 36-inch standard; so are most dishwashers; and for those who must buy a kitchen range, the tyranny of the yardstick is as absolute as it was sixty years ago.

Notes

1. The 1927 Sears Roebuck catalog offered an assortment of stoves: 2 electric, 2 gas, 2 gas and coal, 5 wood and coal. Not all heights-to-cooktop were listed, but this group included models at 29 ¼, 31, 32, 33, and 33 ¼ inches.

2. *The New Art*, a promotional cookbook "presented by General Electric Kitchen Institute" (Cleveland, Ohio) in 1934, offered full-color illustrations of a couple of the latest GE kitchens, in each of which—for the last time—the stove had an elevated oven.

3. Earl Lifshey, *The Housewares Story* (Chicago: National Housewares Manufacturers' Association, 1973) 129.

4. Sigfried Giedion, *Mechanization Takes Command: A Contribution to an Anonymous History* (New York: Oxford University Press, 1948), 523–525. Raimonda Riccini, "The Rationalized Kitchen," in *History of Industrial Design* (Milan: Eketa, 1990), 2: 300.

5. This trend is described at length in chapter 4 of Jeffrey L. Meikle's *Twentieth Century Limited, Industrial Design In America, 1925–1939* (Philadelphia: Temple University Press, 1979). It's also succinctly run through on pages 22–23 of *The Streamlined Decade*, by Donald J. Bush (New York: George Braziller, 1975).

6. Kathy L. Peiss, "American Women and the Making of Modern Consumer Culture," *Journal of MultiMedia History*, 1988 (electronic text, unpaginated).

7. Meikle, *Twentieth Century Limited*, 7–18.

8. The first American gas stoves were made shortly after the Civil War, and had been considerably improved by the last quarter of the century, but the first edition of the *Boston Cooking School Cookbook*, published in 1896, gave the new fuel only a couple of brief mentions while devoting two full pages to a careful description of how to build a coal fire. Almost three decades later, in the 1927 edition, electricity (introduced for cooking in 1891, though it was almost 1920 before the first stoves were widely advertised) got the single sentence, and gas had been promoted to a short paragraph that began: "A gas range is used wherever gas is available." Gas was by no means available everywhere, however. Careful instructions for building a coal fire were still central to the chapter on heat sources.

Both gas and electricity made great strides in the '30's and '40's, with some cities almost completely converted by the mid-'30's. But as late as 1948, it still made sense for a treatise on home design to say, "the finish [of the stove] may be a smooth polish on the material, as is common on coal or wood ranges. Other ranges and some coal or wood ranges are finished with porcelain enamel" (Tessie Agan, *The House, Its Plan and Use* [New York: J. P. Lippincott, 1948], 351). The first edition came out in 1939, but this one is described on the title page as "completely rewritten and reset," so Agan clearly had the opportunity to remove dated information if she felt it was no longer useful.

For a brief history of the spread of new stove technologies, see *Never Done, A History of American Housework*, by Susan Strasser (New York: Pantheon, 1982). She found that "95 percent of Cleveland homes cooked with gas or electricity in 1935, although a quarter of them continued to use wood and coal heating stoves" (264).

9. Meikle, *Twentieth Century Limited*, 83: "*Product Engineering*'s annual survey in 1932 revealed that only 48 percent of domestic appliance manufacturers concerned themselves with improving design appearance. By 1935 the figure had risen to 91 percent."

10. Unsigned article, "Trends of the Chicago Markets," *The Stove Builder*, February 1938, 66.

11. Five foot three was the height of Henry Dreyfuss's everywoman "Josephine," in his guideline for designers, *The Measure of Man*, which was first published in 1955. Dreyfuss explained he had spent years gathering anthropometric data from the widest range of sources available in order to arrive at this figure, but that there were no truly universal statistics available. That's doubly true for the 1930s (the armed forces did a lot of measuring while recruiting for the war). But given the gradual increase in the heights of Americans that was still taking place in mid-century, it seems reasonable to suppose the average woman was no taller in 1940 than she was in 1955.

12. Dolores Hayden, *The Grand Domestic Revolution: A History of Feminist Designs for American Homes, Neighborhoods, and Cities* (Cambridge: MIT Press, 1981), 113, 200, 264–265.

13. Mrs. Christine Frederick, *Selling Mrs. Consumer* (New York: The Business Bourse, 1929). See particularly chapters 3, 5, 17, 18, and 29. In fairness, it should be pointed out that *Selling Mrs. Consumer* was not a compendium of manipulative tricks for advertisers—although they could have used it as one—but rather a genuine attempt to make manufacturers more responsive to the needs of their customers. Mrs. Frederick yielded to no one in her zeal for capitalism; the responsiveness was unblushingly in aid of selling as much as possible to as many people as could be persuaded to buy. But she decried the exploitation of factory workers by makers of cheap products and, at least at the beginning of her career, spoke out frequently against installment buying, which she feared led to crushing debt and knew was not based on friendliness to the poor. "Some of our industrial and financial leaders, who make their millions from installment selling . . . also talk, among themselves and not for public consumption, . . . about how labor must think thrice before striking if it has installment payments to meet" (386).

14. Martha Van Rensselaer and Flora Rose Helen Canon, *The Manual of Home-Making* (New York: Macmillan, 1919), 208. Ethel R. Peyser, "Furnishing Your

60

Kitchen," *House and Garden*, September 1920. "Laying It on the Kitchen Table," November 1923, 69

15. Unsigned pamphlet, *New York Herald Tribune*, 1930, 6.

16. Ibid., 2.

17. Mrs. Christine Frederick, *Household Engineering: Scientific Management in the House* (Chicago: American School of Home Economics, 1919), 39–41.

18. "The Seven Steps to a Good Kitchen," *South Coast News* (Laguna Beach, CA), March 14, 1950.

19. Louise Peet and Lenore Thye, *Household Equipment*, 5th ed. (New York: John Wiley and Sons, 1961), 215. These women were, respectively, a "professor of Household Equipment" at Iowa State University, and the Chief at the Housing and Equipment Research Laboratory, Institute of Home Economics in the Agricultural Research Service of the USDA.

20. *Tribune* pamphlet, 6.

21. Ibid.

22. Agan, *The House, Its Plan and Use*, 337. The first suggestion that the counter problem might originate at the base of the sink came from Jane Langmuir, who at the time of our conversation was an Associate Professor of Interior Architecture at the Rhode Island School of Design.

23. "Coming Trends in Stove Design," by Onnie Mankki (a designer with Designers for Industry, Cleveland, Chicago, and New York), *The Stove Builder*, March 1934, 26.

24. Unsigned article, *The Stove Builder*, September 1936. The description encompasses offerings from 27 manufacturers of cooking stoves.

25. Meikle, *Twentieth Century Limited*, 102, quote attributed to an unpublished letter to Bel Geddes from W. Frank Roberts (president of Standard Gas Equipment), September 5, 1933.

26. Raymond Lowey, Industrial Design (New York: Overlook Press, 1979), 98.

27. Lifshey, *The Housewares Story*, 132–133.

28. Joy Parr, "Shopping for a Good Stove," in *A Diversity of Women, Ontario, 1945–1980*, ed. Parr (Toronto: University of Toronto Press, 1995), 88.

29. Henry Dreyfuss, *Designing for People* (1955, rev. ed 1967; New York: Viking Press, 1974), 67.

30. Michael Flanders and Donald Swann, "Design for Living," London, 1957 (from the musical revue *At the Drop of a Hat*).

Feeding Baby, Teaching Mother:
Gerber and the Evolution of Infant Food and Feeding Practices in the United States

AMY BENTLEY

The consumption of food is an extraordinarily social activity laden with complex and shifting layers of meaning. Not only what we eat, but how and why we eat, tell us much about society, history, cultural change, and humans' views of themselves. What, when, and how we choose to feed infants and toddlers—the notion of "baby food" as opposed to "adult food," and whether these foods are nourishing and satisfying—reveal how mass production, consumption, and advertising have shaped our thinking about infancy and corresponding parenting philosophies and practices. Because women have long been the primary caregivers, food procurers, and preparers, it is natural that women, as both mothers and consumers, are at the heart of this discussion of the development and naturalization of commercial baby food in the United States.

In this article I explore the naturalization of mass-marketed baby food through an examination of the origins, development, and early marketing of the Gerber Products Company. Specifically, I examine how in one generation, from Gerber's beginning in the early 1930s to the 1950s' postwar baby boom years, mass-produced solid infant food, especially fruits and vegetables, was transformed from an item of rarity into a rite of passage—a normal, naturalized part of an infant's diet in the United States—and in becoming so helped to displace breast-feeding.

While much has been written on the shift from breast- to bottle-feeding in the United States and elsewhere, the important historical,

The author thanks the Winterthur Museum and Library and the College of Human Ecology, Cornell University, for research fellowships enabling the collection of data for this article. Another version of the essay appears as "Inventing Baby Food: Gerber and the Discourse of Infancy in the United States," in Warren Belasco and Phillip Scranton, eds., *Food and Drink in Consumer Societies* (New York: Routledge, 2001).

cultural, and nutritional implications of solid infant food in this shift have not been adequately explored.[1] An in-depth historical examination of the subject is important, as late-twentieth-century studies show that before the age of four months, an infant's gastro-intestinal system is ill equipped to receive anything but breast milk or its equivalent (though there is much debate over the adequacy of formula substitutes as well). Too early an introduction of solids can put undue stress on kidney functioning. Moreover, children who are breast-fed develop fewer bacterial and viral illnesses, food allergies, and incidences of diarrhea, ear infections, and perhaps even cancer. Anything displacing breast milk (solid food as well as formula) limits the ingestion of important antibodies, enzymes, hormones, and other substances that assist in a child's optimal development. Thus prevailing wisdom at the turn of the twentieth century admonishes breast-feeding to age twelve months—with the American Academy of Pediatrics advocating the nursing of infants to two years of age if possible—and the introduction of foods at four to six months.[2]

In the space of about a hundred years (from the mid-nineteenth to mid-twentieth centuries) normal feeding patterns of infants in the United States changed from near-exclusive consumption of breast milk (whether by mother or by wet nurse) and an introduction to solids later in the infant's first year, to bottle-feeding and the introduction of solids at six weeks postpartum. These changes from breast to bottle and late to early introduction of solids, themselves related, are both products of the many well-known social and economic components of the late nineteenth and early twentieth centuries: industrialization, mass production and advertising of the food supply; changing consumption patterns; the discovery and promotion of vitamins; evolving notions of the body and health; the promotion of science as the ultimate authority; and the medicalization of childbirth and infancy with the increased prominence and power of the medical establishment. While mothers and health professionals alike welcomed commercially mass-produced baby food as a convenient, affordable way to provide more fruits and vegetables year round for American babies, the creation and marketing of Gerber baby food, which from its inception has dominated the U.S. market, helped spur the introduction of solid foods into babies' diets at increasingly earlier ages. Gerber baby food thus functioned as a supplement to, but also a substitute for, breast milk, playing an important role in the dramatic decline of breast-feeding in the twentieth century. To explore these issues, I will examine the discourse of late-nineteenth- and early-twentieth-century "pre-Gerber" infant feeding patterns, detail the origins and development of Gerber baby food, and analyze early marketing campaigns in the 1930s directed toward women as both professional dietitians and mothers.

A word about sources and their interpretation. My ideas and arguments here are informed by my readings of (among other types of data) over two dozen household and childcare advice manuals. These materials, as well as the Gerber advertising campaigns and corporate literature that I examine, are documents largely prescriptive in nature, and thus problematic. While they divulge much about the ideas of the "experts," they are less successful in helping us understand what and how women actually fed their infants: how they used the foods, what meanings women inscribed upon them, and how women received and made use of the advertising information and images. Historian Jay Mechling rightly views with skepticism any demonstrable connection between advice manuals and actual practice. Arguing that people gain most of their notions of "correct" child rearing from their parents as well as the larger culture in which they were raised, he regards any instruction through childcare manuals as supplemental at best. "Childrearing manuals are the consequents not of childrearing values," Mechling argues, "but of childrearing manual-writing values,"[3] which is to say, the values of those people writing the manuals, embedded in the existing culture. During the period explored here, the late nineteenth and early twentieth centuries, according to Mechling, the "source of advice is connected with the rise of a specialized subuniverse of knowledge, language, and power [and] communicate quite clearly that childrearing knowledge was specialized knowledge" possessed by a growing number of "experts," whether they be in home economics, nutrition, or the medical profession.[4] "To whatever extent there appears to be a sharing or at least a complementarity of these internal states across several authors," Mechling concedes, "the historian can generalize further about some sector of the belief system of a historical American society."[5]

While this belief system may or may not coincide with mothers' actual infant feeding practices, it is possible to tease out information from the experts' publications regarding how, what, and when mothers fed their infants.[6] Fortunately, for our purposes, we can use these sources of information for what they do best—to uncover a newly emerging discourse regarding infant food and feeding practices from such "experts." While the manners in which women actually did feed their infants become visible here through a limited number of primary documents, a full understanding of actual practices must be saved for another day. Nevertheless, a focused examination of the "expert" discourse becomes the first step in unfolding the very important story of women and solid infant feeding practices in the United States.

Women and "Artificial" Infant Feeding in the (Pre-Gerber) Nineteenth Century

To understand fully the effects of mass-produced baby food it is important to revisit the development of artificial infant formulas, the forerunners of mass-produced solids such as Gerber. Existing scholarship indicates that in the pre-industrial Western world 95 percent of children were breast-fed, either by their mothers or by wet nurses. Breast-feeding, often called "wet-nursing" whether performed by the infant's biological mother or by another woman, was in contrast to the remaining small percentage of infants who were "dry-nursed" or "brought up by hand," that is, fed mixtures of boiled flour and water or cow's milk, variously called pap or panada. While the existing literature does not make clear the age and extent to which infants were simultaneously breast-fed and fed pap mixtures (the earliest known infant feeding devices date back to the second or third centuries, but we know little about how they were used[7]), until the twentieth century, most infants fed artificially usually failed to thrive, because of either inadequate nutrition or contaminated animal milk or water.[8]

In the mid-nineteenth century, experts admonished (and there is evidence to suggest at least it was mainstream thinking) that infants live on a liquid diet of breast milk or modified cow's milk for most of their first year.[9] Women passed around home recipes for breast milk substitutes or, for those with the means or access, found them in published household advice manuals common to the period. A pediatrician writing later in the twentieth century described this practice as "the grandmothers' aphorism, 'only milk until the eruption of molars' (twelve to sixteen months)."[10] According to one researcher, "Milk alone was believed sufficient until the baby showed signs of failure, and often the young child's diet was confined to little more than milk until he was two years of age. Meat was considered damaging."[11] Advice manuals recommended that cereals or meats (not necessarily in that order) be introduced when teeth began to appear, between six and nine months of age, at first as thin gruel mixtures, or beef broth or juices. "The food for children should be light and simple," advised Mrs. Sarah Josepha Hale in 1857, "gruel alone, or mixed with cow's milk; mutton broth, or beef tea; stale bread, rusks, or biscuits, boiled in water to a proper consistence, and a little sugar added."[12] Hale recommended that complete weaning could take place as early as seven months, but more commonly after twelve months.[13]

While mothers fed infants the "strength-producing" meats and cereals in the first year, advice manuals recommended that children not be given fruits and vegetables until two or three years of age. This was in part the result of the wary attitude in general toward fruits and vegetables. Medical opinion, as well as folk practice in the United States, was still influenced by the centuries-old Galenic theories of health and disease, which dictated that eating fruit made people, especially children, susceptible to fevers.[14] Properties inherent in the fruits and vegetables were thought to cause severe diarrhea and dysentery, especially in the summer. An 1880s newspaper illustration, for example, depicts a skeleton disguised as a fruit seller offering produce to little children, indicating that raw, unboiled fruits and vegetables led to cholera.[15] While there is no question that fruits and vegetables could cause harm, especially in such turn-of-the-century urban metropolises as New York City whose water and sewer systems were imperfect and overloaded, the actual culprit was most likely contaminants residing on the outside of the produce, or contaminated water or milk that happened to be ingested, rather than anything innate in the produce itself.[16] Given the laxative effect of fruits and vegetables if consumed to excess, however, it is easy to understand how people made the assumption. Moreover, in this era before the discovery of vitamins, most people felt that fruits and vegetables provided excessive bulk and roughage, and contributed little in the way of nourishment helpful to infants.[17] Advice manuals of the mid-nineteenth century reflect and even attempt to challenge this prevailing ideology. "The growing creature requires food that contains the elements of the body . . . food that abounds in albumen, fibrine, gelatine, and the earthy salts," wrote Joseph B. Lyman and Laura E. Lyman in their 1867 advice manual. "What substances do we find richest in the constituents of perfect food? *Flesh*, *milk*, *eggs* and *wheat bread*" (italics original).[18] However, the authors went on, "There is in the minds of thousands of anxious mothers a great dread of fruits of all kinds as being dangerous for the young."[19] Attempting to dispel these commonly held notions, the Lymans advised that the problem was children's consumption of fruits to excess, not the produce itself.

By the late nineteenth century, the industrialization and advertising of the food supply laid important groundwork for changing recommendations concerning infant care and feeding. Before the turn of the century, most Americans' diets were fairly monotonous regimes of soups, stews, bread, dairy products, fresh meat when available, salted or smoked when not, and seasonal fruits and vegetables only, unless preserved through pickling, jams and preserves, drying, and some home canning. Improvements in stoves and food preparation devices made food preparation easier, iceboxes and refrigerators kept foods fresher. All, in many ways, made cooking a less arduous task for women—although there were most certainly tradeoffs, as many scholars have pointed out. Canned goods, especially canned produce, though commonly available in the late 1800s, were too expensive for most. By the 1920s, however, manufacturers produced canned goods in sufficient quantity as to become more affordable, allowing Americans to consume (among other things) more fruits and vegetables year round. With this industrialization of the food supply Americans' diets became more varied and their nutrition subsequently improved, though it can be argued that canned goods and other processed foods diminished taste and nutrients, leading to Americans' acclimation to salt and sugar in heavy quantities.[20] To sell these mass-produced items the early twentieth century witnessed the proliferation of advertising firms creating increasingly sophisticated advertising. The increased number and circulation of magazines and newspapers, and the growth in population and literacy rates ensured audiences for corporate advertising.[21]

Along with industrialization and advertising, fin-de-siècle Americans turned increasingly to science as the ultimate authority.[22] An effect of this was the increased stature, whether self-generated or not, of the medical community. Doctors supplanted midwives in the delivering of babies, and more of these were delivered in hospitals than in homes. Employing wet nurses as an alternative to mothers' breast-feeding, a common practice among wealthier women, became frowned upon. Instead, during this "chemical period" in infant feeding, medical authorities took charge, partially by devising complicated "percentage" formulas as breast milk replacements only they could administer.[23] As Rima Apple and others have amply demonstrated, the result was the "medicalization of motherhood." Profoundly influenced by prevailing behaviorist theories of psychology, authorities advised that parenting instincts and common sense must take a back seat to science. Infants were to be fed on strict schedules, for example, and were not to be picked up when crying, which would only reward the negative behavior, women were told.[24]

Doctors and childcare experts still considered breast-feeding best, no doubt in part because of the high infant mortality rates occurring in the burgeoning cities that had limited access to fresh, clean cow's milk. Marion Mills Miller in 1910 advocated that "no other milk, however skillfully modulated, no 'infant's food,' however scientifically prepared," could fully replace mother's milk.[25] But, the advisers often qualified, only if a woman's breast milk supply was adequate. In their 1920 advice manual Martha Van Rensselaer, Flora Rose, and Helen Cannon, eminent Cornell University home economists, gave recipes for artificial formula, but called it "the next best thing" if a "baby cannot be fed by its own mother."[26] "It is a great pity when a young baby cannot have his mother's milk as his main food," Carlotta C. Greer advised in her 1928 book, *Foods and Homemaking*. "A doctor who is familiar with the needs of a little baby is able to write a prescription of formula for modified milk."[27]

With the medicalization of motherhood there were more and more reasons why breast milk became inadequate. Improved technology helped artificial formulas and cow's milk to become a safer and more healthful alternative for infants. Optimistic faith in science required little reason why formula feeding was equal to—if not better than— breast milk. Formula feeding was easier for doctors to measure and regulate, allowing them to tinker with the makeup of artificial formulas when necessary. Anxious mothers, becoming less and less confident of their parenting abilities and common sense, wanted what was best for Baby and voluntarily relinquished their authority. Hospital deliveries that whisked babies away to the nursery fostered a sterile and awkward climate for mother-infant bonding and discouraged breast-feeding. Taking their cues from the medical community, home economics experts recommended not only that an infant's mouth be swabbed and rinsed with fresh water after every feeding, but that a woman's breast be cleaned with a boric acid solution before and after nursing as well.[28]

Mothers became more and more convinced that they did not have sufficient milk to nurse their newborns. Although most certainly some women could not physically breast-feed and significant numbers who performed paid employment outside the home found it logistically difficult to do so, it is not surprising that around the turn of the century the numbers of women breast-feeding their infants declined for other reasons as well. No doubt many simply did not want the bother of nursing their infants. Wealthier women, who had always breast-fed less often than other women, now turned to using artificial formulas instead of employing wet nurses. Middle-class women followed suit, with working-class women ceasing to breast-feed accordingly. Further, what little historical data exist indicate that women's cessation of breast-feeding took place in stages not only with regard to economics, but by ethnicity and degree of urbanization: African American and Latina women and those in rural areas breast-fed much further into the twentieth century than Caucasian women and urban dwellers.[29]

By the late 1880s several brands of "proprietary foods," mass-produced, mostly grain mixtures to be added to milk or water—the forerunners of today's infant formulas—appeared on the market, including Leibeg's, Nestle's Milk Food, Imperial Granum, Wells, Richardson, and Company's Lactated Food, Wagner's Infant Food, Mellin's

Food, as well as Borden's Eagle Brand condensed milk. Some included cereal grains as part of their "formulas," some did not, but all characterized their products as "food" rather than "liquid," as formulas later became categorized. Brightly colored and elaborately etched trade cards, the popular turn-of-the-century advertising medium which women and children in particular delighted in collecting and trading, illustrate this demarcation of infant formula as food. Advertising slogans included: "Nestle's Milk Food: Baby's Friend"; "Imperial Granum: The Incomparable Food for the Growth and Protection of Infants and Children"; "Wells, Richardson, and Company's Lactated Food: A Scientific Food for Infants and Invalids"; "Wagner's Infant Food: Infants and Children fed on Wagner's Infant Food are remarkable for muscular strength, firmness of flesh, and a lively and intelligent appearance"; and "Mellin's Food for Infants and Invalids: The only perfect substitute for Mother's Milk."[30]

Home economists and nutritionists—women in these newly emerging fields that employed the latest scientific discoveries about food and nutrition—did not much like proprietary, or patent, foods. "They cannot compete successfully with carefully made milk mixtures in substitute or artificial feeding," advised Flora Rose of Cornell University's recently established Home Economics Department: "Perhaps the strongest case against the patent foods is their lack of the food-stuff known as mineral matter or salts, which is so essential to healthy growth and development. Many cases of malnutrition result directly from the use of such of these foods as are deficient in fat and mineral matter. A common ailment among babies thus fed is rickets, an ailment that is serious and may be lasting in its effects."[31] She conceded, "When a patent food is made with milk, its bad effects are minimized and it may serve a useful purpose."[32] What Rose called "mineral salts" were indeed important. Confirming what many chemists and nutritionists suspected, within the next decade researchers discovered vitamins in foods, including vitamin D, which prevents rickets. What evidence exists indicates that most mothers, at least in rural areas, did not feed their infants mass-produced proprietary foods. While Cornell University home economics students in the 1920s added a small amount of Mellin's Food to their month-old charge's formula, a 1933 study of over 700 infants in upstate New York indicated that only 6 percent of mothers had ever fed their babies patent foods, half using brands which were to be mixed with milk and half with water.[33] Still, the increasing availability and promotion of such products, along with the rise in safer, cleaner cow's milk thanks to certification programs and pasteurization, contributed to the falling number of women who breast-fed their infants.

It makes sense that manufacturers and advertisers constructed these liquid formulas as solid rather than liquid. This was the infant food of the time, after all, the nourishment on which babies survived, as there was not yet a tradition of feeding infants under nine months real solids, especially fruits and vegetables. While there was available a very small supply of canned fruits and vegetables for infants, they were sold at apothecaries, and used as medicine. They were clearly not designed for everyday use.[34] Without a mass-produced baby food such as Gerber there was no opposite solid baby food with which to contrast the infant formula. As parents and doctors became more acclimated to artificial infant formulas, however, it was only a small step to the earlier and earlier introduction of solid foods. In just a few short decades authorities' opinions about the subject changed dramatically.[35]

Women and Infant Feeding in the (Pre-Gerber) Twentieth Century

The first two decades of the twentieth century, a time characterized by historians and others as the arrival of the culture of modernity, was a period of great change not only for women, but in the realms of economics, politics, the arts, science, and social and religious thought. In the 1910s and 1920s, still before the arrival of Gerber, infant feeding practices had begun to change noticeably, and most prominently in the larger role fruits and vegetables were to have in an infant's diet. Still, experts recommended a relatively late introduction of solids, and grassroots evidence indicates that most mothers did not begin their infants on solids until after six months of age or later.

As earlier mentioned, during these decades scientists had begun to identify as "vitamines" (the spelling was later modified) the specific nutrients previously called "mineral salts" that existed in foods. Vitamins, scientists learned, existed not only in meat, grains, and dairy products, foods they had always considered vital to nourishment and growth, but also in fruits and vegetables, which had previously been regarded as benign at best and with suspicion by many, although there were several nineteenth-century groups that espoused the virtues of a vegetarian diet.[36] The promotion of fruits and vegetables as vital to human growth and nourishment was heightened during the Great War, as the federal government found it difficult to recruit able-bodied young men and maintain their health while in the service. The new knowledge of vitamins was immediately employed and propagated to help solve this problem of the ill health of recruits.[37] By the 1920s home economists and dietitians were introducing Americans to the notion of vitamins, and advising them not only to consume more fruits and vegetables themselves, but to feed more such foods to their children as well.

Early-twentieth-century household advice manuals, though at times contradictory in their recommendations (as such manuals continue to be almost a century later), reveal this increased emphasis on fruits and vegetables, while still advocating the introduction of solids in the second half of the infant's first year. A 1914 manual, with the delightfully straightforward title *How to Cook and Why*, by Elizabeth Condit and Jessie A. Long, for the first time enthusiastically endorsed fruits and vegetables specifically for their "mineral matter." "As in all questions of feeding," related the authors, "it is the food given the children which is of the greatest importance. Serious results follow in the unhealthy development of their bodies when their food lacks mineral matter and the acids found in fruits."[38] They recommended introducing a barley flour and water mixture and strained diluted orange juice at between six and nine months of age, but (still) did not advocate the introduction of solids until between nine and twelve months. Flora Rose recognized the importance of vitamins, referring to them as "fat-soluble" and "water-soluble growth-promoting substances."[39]

In 1928, on the eve of the development of Gerber baby food, Carlotta C. Greer in her *Foods and Home Making* gave both vitamins and vegetables a prominent place in advice about infant feeding. Experts advocated orange juice for infants, Greer informed her readers, "because it contains vitamins and minerals."[40] "Scientists working on the effect of food on the body are proving that fresh vegetables are needed to make us healthy."[41] "Both babies that are fed on mother's milk and those that are fed on modified cow's milk should have certain food other than milk," Greer advised, although "the young baby must not be given solid foods."[42] Greer recommended a teaspoonful of orange juice introduced at three weeks of age, cereals at five to six months, vegetables at six months, toast or zwieback at seven months, and egg yolk at twelve months.[43] While she advocated the introduction of certain foods, fruits, and vegetables, much earlier than previous advice manuals, striking is the relatively later introduction of cereals and meat, the latter of which Greer did not recommend during the first year at all.

In the 1920s, there were still well-known authorities advising that a one-year-old infant's diet be composed only of whole milk or whole milk with a cereal dilutant, orange juice, and perhaps simple cereals and beef broth and beef juice, but increasingly these recommendations were called "conservative" or "old-fashioned." More likely experts advocated a diet more along the lines of Greer's: the early introduction of orange juice and cod liver oil, and solids, specifically egg yolk and cereal, at five to six months of age.[44]

Grassroots evidence—what and how women were actually feeding their babies in the pre-Gerber decades of the twentieth century—seems to indicate that while some women no doubt introduced solids at an early age, the mainstream in consensus and practice was not to rush the introduction of solids, especially fruits and vegetables. For example, a collection of letters written in the 1910s to Cornell Home Economics Department professor Martha Van Rensselaer reveals glimpses of both early and later introduction of solids. The letters were written mostly in response to Flora Rose's series of pamphlets *The Care and Feeding of Children*. The pamphlets, part of the Cornell Farmers' Wives Reading Courses (later called the Cornell Study Clubs), contained study questions which women were to fill out and send back to the Home Economics Department. While most letter writers praise the courses and the information, some are testimonials to the good advice contained in the pamphlets, and a few take stern issue with the information.[45]

Mr. W. J. Gilchrist's January 30, 1911, letter, for example, indicates that he and his wife followed Flora Rose's advice to breast-feed exclusively until at least nine months: "We have now a fine healthy child of 9 months. No little credit is due to the information contained in the above mentioned tract. As the baby is about to start on artificial foods, would you kindly inform me where we can procure part 2 of [*The Care and Feeding of Children*]?" Another 1911 letter from a German immigrant whose English is self-taught, reveals the opposite.[46] "Dear Miss Van Rensselear," begins Mrs. Marie Christ. "I [raised] 6 babies myself and have got them all. 3 strong boys, and 2 girls, one girl got drowned, 7 years old." Responding to the study question, Is it as common as it used to be for mothers to nurse their infants?, Christ replies, "I think no and these is lots of reasons for it":

> Some have to work to hard, and that was my reason, because I could not nurse a one. Some are to[o] [weak] in their whole system and some do not want the bother. . . . I think there is not hardly a one among thousands in the european country who thinks that just the nursing of the mother should be enough after a babie is 3 months old, and some start earlyer than that, to feed them something besides the nursing. The[y] look at they nursing just as we do, to the tea and coffee given to a five year old one. Nobody would think that would be enough for a whole meal. The[y] all feed them something besides the nursing, thousands of mothers just simple[y] cook a porridge from half watter, half milk and sugar and god wreath flour. The older

the[y] get, the less water the[y] put in. I know babies and my oldest boy never got a drop of water after he was 4 months old.

"What the american babies needs," Christ concluded, "is more nourishing food, less [waking], less candy, and cookies, and [cakes], and a little toughening."[47]

While the letters indicate women were introducing solids to their infants at various ages, the 1933 Cornell study (still in the early years of mass-produced baby food) of the feeding practices of over 700 infants in upstate New York revealed on average the late introduction of solids. While 60 percent of infants were fed orange juice during their first 3 months and infants received cod liver oil at 5.2 months on average, the average age at which solids were introduced included: cereal at 7.5 months; vegetables at 9.4 months; fruit at 8.1 months; egg at 10 months; fish, 12.1 months; and meat, 11.6 months—much later than the practices that occurred only years later.[48]

Gerber: Creation Narratives and Icons

Thus in the late 1920s, with the discovery and promotion of vitamins and changing attitudes toward fruits and vegetables, the market was ripe for the introduction of mass-produced canned produce for babies, and Gerber stepped up to fill the niche. According to company legend, a narrative prominently featured in late 1990s Gerber public relations, the Gerber Products Company grew out of not a corporate-driven search to develop a new product and generate a consuming public, but out of the genuine need and inventiveness of a mother trying to prepare mashed peas for her seven-month old child. While in the early twentieth century some mass-produced canned fruits and vegetables for infants were available, as previously mentioned, they were expensive, manufactured in limited quantities, and available only at drug stores. Women largely cooked and strained fruits and vegetables for their toddlers, an often tedious and time-consuming process. Thus, in the summer of 1927, Mrs. Dan Gerber, wife of Fremont Canning Company owner Dan Gerber, "following the advice of a pediatrician," we are told, was trying to strain peas for her infant daughter. Finding the job tedious and time-consuming, she asked her husband to try his hand at the task. According to the company history, "After watching him make several attempts, she pointed out that the work could be easily done at the Fremont Canning Company, where the Gerber family produced a line of canned fruits and vegetables. Daniel Gerber, covered in strained peas, thought his wife had a good point." From this, we are told, came the idea to market strained vegetables and fruits along with the company's regular line of canned produce. By late 1928, strained peas, prunes, carrots, spinach, and beef vegetable soup were ready for the national market.[49]

We do not know whether this creation narrative is "true," especially since in its 1930s advertising Gerber related a much different version discussed later. However, the facts could most certainly be accurate. Since women at the time performed most of the work surrounding childrearing, it makes sense that one mother, frustrated at the time it took and messes it created to prepare the now-vital fruits and vegetables for infants, would seek time- and labor-saving methods. That the husband of "Mrs. Dan Gerber"—we never learn her given name—processed canned fruits and vegetables already makes it more plausible. Whether factual or not, the story creates a compelling, personalized portrait of the beginnings of Gerber—a homey, "authentic" happening far removed from the cacophony of noise and the mire of grease, steel, steam, and smoke of the industrial factory. The story of a woman's ingenuity transforming childrearing in the United States enhances the purity and trustworthiness of the product, a key factor to Gerber's success, and also conceals the profit motive of the company.

The baby food products were so successful that within a matter of years the Fremont Canning Company changed its name to the Gerber Products Company, and abandoned its line of regular vegetables to become the exclusive maker of baby foods. First producing pureed vegetables and fruits (the process was termed "strained" at the time), it soon opened a line of cereals, and within a few years introduced chopped produce and dinner combinations for older toddlers. Despite competitors' quick development of their own mass-produced strained baby foods, Gerber managed to maintain its dominance of this new market. Evidently Gerber had hit a chord with consumers, mothers, and health professionals. Conditions were such that commercially canned baby food provided mass quantities of pre-prepared strained fruits and vegetables to a public primed to accept them: canned goods were becoming more affordable to more Americans; advertising was hitting its stride; fruits and vegetables were more commonly recommended for infants; and doctors and health professionals were becoming more and more involved in (and controlling of) infant health and everyday care. Women at home full time as well as a considerable number of working mothers—employed as domestics, factory workers, seamstresses, teachers, secretaries, clerks, or telephone operators—no doubt embraced and benefitted from already-prepared solid infant food. Moreover, Gerber baby food was not the only new phenomenon emerging at the time that significantly altered childrearing. Commercial diaper services, more homes wired for electricity, washing machines, refrigerators, and other innovations of technology in the home altered women's work in general as well as childcare in particular.[50]

Few Americans today are unfamiliar with the winsome, compelling Gerber Baby that has graced the labeling and advertising of the Gerber Products Company since the early 1930s. Indeed, since its first full-scale production and marketing of commercially canned solid baby food, Gerber has dominated such competitors as Clapp's, Stokeley, Libby, Heinz, and Beech-Nut in United States market share. The Gerber name is synonymous with baby food, and the icon of the Gerber Baby traditionally has symbolized quality and trustworthiness, so much so that a 1998 survey found Gerber to have the highest consumer loyalty in the United States.[51] In 1928 the Fremont Canning Company solicited illustrations of a baby face for the advertising campaign to introduce its newly developed baby food. Dorothy Hope Smith, an artist who specialized in drawing children, submitted a simple, unfinished, charcoal sketch, indicating she could finish the sketch if it were accepted. Again, according to the company narrative, Gerber executives were so taken with the simple line drawing of an infant's head that they acquired it as it was. The illustration proved so popular that Gerber adopted it as its official trademark in 1931, and offered consumers copies for ten cents. At the turn of the twentieth century, the Gerber Baby continues to appear on all Gerber packaging and advertising, including in its recently redesigned labels and new line of organic foods.[52] The sketch's immense popularity has generated much speculation through the decades about the actual identity of the Gerber Baby. Rumors held that Humphrey Bogart, Elizabeth Taylor, or even Senator and presidential hopeful Robert Dole posed for the sketch as an infant. According to the company, the real Gerber Baby is retired English teacher and sometime mystery novelist Ann Turner Cook. Cook, still living in the 1990s, was heavily advertised as being present at the unveiling of the redesigned Gerber labels in 1996.

The Naturalization of Gerber: Decline of Breast-Feeding, Earlier Introduction of Solids

At the same time Gerber baby food took off in popularity, the average age infants were first fed fruits and vegetables decreased dramatically. In the late 1920s, just as Gerber began its national advertising and distribution of canned baby foods, prevailing wisdom advocated introducing strained fruits and vegetables around seven months. By the

1930s, however, pediatricians advocated the introduction of fruits and vegetables between four and six months of age. Adhering to the "if a little is good a lot must be better" school of thought, by the 1950s the average age doctors recommended these foods be first fed to infants was four to six weeks, with some doctors advocating—and women feeding—infants strained cereals and vegetables within days of birth.[53] At the same time there came a dramatic shift, from mothers breast-feeding their infants to the vast majority bypassing nursing altogether and starting out their infants on mass-produced formula.[54] Evidence suggests the two phenomena are related; Gerber solid baby food functioned not only as a supplement to breast milk but as a substitute for it as well. To understand how this came about it is helpful to turn to early advertising campaigns of the 1930s.

Shortly after the Fremont Canning Company began to manufacture its baby food, it began to advertise. Mass-producing any industrial product, especially during the Great Depression as consumer purchasing slowed to a minimum, meant establishing and expanding a steady market of buyers by acquainting the public with products through advertising campaigns. Gerber, as well as other manufacturers of new products, found it necessary not only to educate and persuade the public to buy baby food, but to acclimate and familiarize them with the manner in which baby food was packaged and presented, the steel cans as well as the labeling. Only recently had fully automated canning factories been in operation, allowing foodstuffs to be canned and sold to consumers for reasonable prices, and Americans still held lingering suspicious about the quality of canned goods. Though it had been two decades since Congress had passed the Pure Food and Drug Act, some remembered well the days of adulterated and spoiled foods concealed by opaque packaging.[55] Further, Americans in the first part of the twentieth century were still becoming acquainted with mass advertising designed to create new needs where none had existed before, or to promote products, such as Gerber baby food, which responded to and allowed for a more fast-paced life brought on by technological innovation.[56] With the mass production and advertising of goods, packaging and branding became an essential part of the product, "an integral part of the commodity itself."[57] The Gerber Baby from early on became just that: an integral part of the commodity, allowing the Gerber Products Company to bypass such traditional middlemen as grocers and through advertising appeal directly to women as dietitians or as mothers.

By playing on parents', especially mothers', anxieties about the well-being of their infants, presenting medical doctors as the ultimate baby experts, and positing the uncontested assumption that commercially prepared foods are superior to those cooked at home, Gerber advertising in the 1930s successfully imbued its products with qualities of exceptional purity and wholesomeness, convenience and modernity, and scientific efficiency. While not an exhaustive study of Gerber promotion pitches, a survey of 1930s issues of the *Journal of the American Dietetic Association* and *Ladies Home Journal* reveals how Gerber quickly undertook an ambitious national campaign to convert health professionals and consumers to its baby foods. In its earliest years of advertising Gerber focused on helping consumers and dietitians become comfortable with the idea of using canned goods in general and Gerber baby foods in particular, and persuading women that it was in their best interest, and in their babies' interest, to use Gerber baby foods.

Convincing the Dietitians

In the late 1920s and well into the 1930s Gerber placed full-page advertisements in each monthly issue of the *Journal of the American Dietetic Association*, the official publication of the American Dietetic Association (ADA). The ADA, founded in 1917, was the professional organization for the fast-growing, overwhelmingly female field of dietetics and nutrition. Whereas there were 660 ADA members in 1925, for example, by 1938 the number had grown to 3,800. The ADA in the 1920s and 1930s became influential in coordinating and promoting dietary policy and guidelines for optimal health and nutrition.[58] Promoting Gerber baby food as scientifically prepared and thus free of contaminants, vitamin filled, and healthy and wholesome food for infants was clearly the primary goal of the company's ADA journal advertising. "Care in every detail makes the Gerber products better for Baby," began one 1932 advertisement.[59] Two 1934 advertisements, each complete with photos of workers dressed in white operating sparkling clean machinery, began respectively, "Oxygen is excluded in the Gerber straining process [to conserve vitamins],"[60] and "Careful sorting—rigid inspection, another reason why Gerber's are better for Baby."[61] In the same issues the American Canning Company ran regular advertisements designed to resemble scholarly articles on the safety and healthfulness of canned foods. "The Canning Procedure,"[62] "Vitamins in Canned Foods: Vitamin A,"[63] and "Canned Foods for Infant and Early Child Feeding"[64] were three such ads, each providing scientific information on the benefits of canned foods. Such ads, along with the Gerber ads, were attempting to combat suspicion toward canned foods. While many middle-class women in the United States used commercially canned goods with some regularity by this time, food professionals in particular still held some justifiable suspicion about whether canned produce was as nutritious and safe as fresh. In what would become standard practice, some 1930s ADA journal issues also included bona fide research, funded by Gerber, touting the safety, health, and full vitamin content of canned baby foods. Flora Manning, in the Division of Home Economics at Michigan State College, published two such articles in the 1930s, "Canned Strained Vegetables as Sources of Vitamin A," and "Further Studies of the Content of Vitamins A and B in Canned Strained Vegetables."[65] Both, not surprisingly, found little difference in the vitamin content of canned and strained foods.

Another set of Gerber ADA journal advertisements situates dietitians as the intermediary between women and their children's doctors. Revealing the company's faith in the power of persuasion through advertising, ads began with such openings as "Gerber advertises . . . so that mothers will cooperate with you";[66] "Yes, Doctor, we do talk to your patients . . . and we tell them facts which help you and help us (ellipses original)";[67] and "Thanks, Doctor, this helps me carry out your instructions."[68] The copy situates the reader, as female dietitian, conversing with the (male) medical doctor about how to persuade women to feed their children Gerber baby food. The ads and articles function to naturalize the idea that Gerber's canned fruits and vegetables for baby are just as nutritious as fresh as home-prepared foods, and even more appropriate since they are so scientifically prepared.

Convincing the Mothers

Like those for many other new mass-produced and advertised products in the early twentieth century, Gerber's first advertising campaign in 1929 focused on selling its products directly to women, since many grocers did not carry Gerber baby foods.[69] The ads were placed in such women's magazines as *Ladies Home Journal*, subscribed to by over a million women.[70] In what was common practice at the time, the advertisements urged women to send in one dollar for a set of Gerber foods, and asked them to provide the name of their grocer, whom Gerber would then persuade to carry their products. Doctors, however, could request the products free of charge. Emphasizing its products as scientifically prepared and thus trustworthy, Gerber informed women that its foods "Provid[ed] in a scientific, wholesome manner . . . the important vegetable supplement to baby's milk diet." It also focused on the products' ability to impart to women freedom and mobility, a notably modern concept: "The new Gerber Products make Mother and Baby alike independent of the kitchen's restrictions. Baby can really travel now."[71]

Later advertising focused on this theme of freedom for Mother and Baby. Not only did Gerber provide freedom from kitchen drudgery, but ads informed that preparing baby foods by hand was essentially a disservice to the woman herself, her baby, and her husband. "For Baby's Sake, Stay Out of the Kitchen!" read the headline of one 1933 advertisement. "It isn't fair to baby—really—to spend long hours in the kitchen. . . . For baby's sake and for your own—learn what doctors tell young mothers just like you" (ellipses original). Moreover, the ads stated, women could not provide the same quality no matter how hard they tried: "You can't, with ordinary home equipment, prepare vegetables as safe, as rich in natural food values, as reliably uniform as ready-to-serve Gerber products!"[72] The opening of another Gerber ad read, "Square Meals for Baby . . . and better for him than vegetables you could prepare yourself with ten times the work!" (ellipses original). "Don't serve Gerber's for your sake," the ad went on, "*serve them for Baby's sake!*" (italics original). "They're the finest vegetables Baby can eat—and Baby deserves the best!"[73]

Most strikingly, the advertisements focus on a woman's relationship with her husband. An early Gerber ad in *Ladies Home Journal* opens with a photo of a concerned-looking man's face. Surrounding the male face is the text, "To puzzled fathers of rather young children. If you've had to exchange a charming wife for a tired mother who spends endless hours in the kitchen dutifully scraping, stewing and straining vegetables for your child—you'll be glad to read this story." The ad then continues with a version of the Gerber creation story different from the late-twentieth-century one, one that focuses on a male persona entirely. "Five years ago, Mr. Dan Gerber faced the same situation, and knowing a great deal about vegetables he set out to solve this problem."[74] Although there is an accompanying photo of a woman feeding a baby identified once more as "Mrs. Dan Gerber," there is no mention of her involvement in the creation whatsoever. The narrative implies that it was Dan Gerber's frustration and dissatisfaction at "having to exchange" his now un-charming, tired, and haggard-looking wife that led to Gerber baby food being invented. Although the advertisement carries a masculine persona, it was clearly designed for women's consumption, appearing as almost an ominous warning to mothers of small children. The advertising as a whole functions not only to increase women's confidence in the wholesomeness of the product, but also to reduce their confidence in their ability to care for their infants—and also that hardworking provider—without the help of these experts and these products.

In addition, both sets of advertising indirectly or directly advocate the earlier and earlier introduction of these foods. Many ads mention the use of solids at three months or earlier. Under the above-mentioned photo of "Mrs. Dan Gerber" and her daughter Paula, for example, the caption notes that "Paula began to eat Gerber Strained Cereal at 3 months, and had her first Gerber's Strained Vegetables at 3 ½ months" (again, this is in contrast to the 1990s creation story that mentions that the mother is feeding peas to her "seven month old," an age no doubt assigned in light of the contemporary standards of introducing fruits and vegetables only after six months of age).[75] Gerber's competitors contributed to this trend as well. A 1937 ad for Clapp's baby food introduces us to photos of three-month-old baby John Curlett being fed his Clapp's Baby Cereal. "At 4 months," the copy informed women, "he'll be introduced to all of Clapp's Strained Vegetables." The final photo shows John at eleven months of age, "flourish[ing]" because of his Clapp's diet.[76] The most blatant ad, however, is a 1938 Libby's baby food ad picturing a baby who can barely hold up its head. The caption reads: "Hurry, Mother, it's Libby time! Tiny babies love the vegetables that Libby prepares so carefully."[77]

Not only did specific ad copy and photographs encourage the notion that infants under four months need solid food, but the icon of the Gerber Baby itself contributed. The drawing that has graced every Gerber product and advertisement since 1931 looks by several estimates approximately two to four months old: earlier than advice rendered just a decade previous, earlier than the four to six months advocated by most United State doctors and infant care guides for introducing solids, and well under the six months of age sanctioned by the United Nations International Code of Marketing of Breastmilk Substitutes guidelines. The Gerber Baby itself, then, gave (and gives) the implicit impression that babies this young should be eating solid foods. It makes sense that Gerber and other baby food manufacturers would advocate early introduction of their foods. They of course sought to create and expand market share: by getting more mothers to buy the products; by convincing mothers that babies at early ages should be started on solids; and by eventually developing products that kept babies and toddlers consuming their foods for as long as possible.

Coda: Women and Baby Food at the Turn of the Twentieth Century

The development and widespread success of the Gerber Products Company can be understood as a mixed blessing. There is no doubt that canned fruits and vegetables, for infants and adults, increased year-round availability and thus consumption of these foods vital to human health and well-being. Before the advent of readily available canned foods, prevailing feeding practices prevented infants from getting enough of these foods in their diet. Moreover, as any parent or childcare provider knows, there is a welcome efficiency to canned baby foods, especially when working, spending time outdoors, or traveling.

But are canned fruits and vegetables as nutritious as fresh, home-prepared ones, as Gerber continually claimed? Often not, especially in earlier decades of the twentieth century. Contrary to its advertising claims, canned foods such as Gerber's have traditionally been over-cooked, and have contained added salt, sugar, starches, fillers, artificial preservatives, and occasionally some dangerous contaminants (such as lead and pesticides). Canned vegetables and fruit also contain less fiber. Moreover, unless the precise percentage of each ingredient is listed on the label, the consumer has no way of knowing the percentage of water or fillers versus fruit or vegetable. A jar of pureed peas, for example, which lists as its ingredients "peas, water," could conceivably contain 51 percent peas and 49 percent water.[78]

What is the status of Gerber baby foods at the beginning of the twenty-first century? With almost 70 percent of the U.S. market, Gerber remains the leader in solid baby foods, but it has been losing market share in recent decades and is trying to figure out how to maintain its dominance. Part of the loss has to do with a political, economic, and social climate that differs markedly from its counterpart one hundred years ago. The marked skepticism of the 1970s spurred a consumer-oriented, business-suspicious public ethos, becoming the catalyst for larger public discourses about science versus nature, patriarchal authority versus women's knowledge, and faith in industry versus distrust of corporate America. The return to breast-feeding and the popularity of such alternatives as organic baby foods in the infant food industry are evidence of this cultural shift, in part a reaction to the aggressive push by multinational corporations to sell powdered infant formula in developing countries, and Beech-Nut executives knowingly substituting sugar water for apple juice, for which Gerber suffered by association.

Gerber does have its share of trouble that challenges its reputation as the arbiter of purity and nutrition. In the 1980s glass shards were found in some jars of baby food—a distinct blow to its reputation.[79] More recently the FCC charged Gerber with misleading advertising. A 1995 campaign claiming "4 out of 5 doctors recommend Gerber baby food" was found to be highly inaccurate. (The study actually showed that 88 percent of doctors polled had no opinion about choice of baby food. Of the remaining 12 percent, 4 out of 5 recommended Gerber.)[80] Further, the Center for Science in the Public Interest (CSPI) and other groups claim that Gerber baby foods contain unacceptable amounts of pesticides (which Gerber strenuously denies), mislead consumers as to the actual percentage of food versus water and fillers, and contain unhealthy chemically modified starch (called "tapioca"), and unnecessary salt and sugar. In 1996 Gerber eliminated sugar, salt, and modified starch from most of its products, but is still criticized for not eliminating them in all of them, and for creating baby "desserts" that are arguably unnecessary and harmful for infants.[81]

To maintain and even increase market share, Gerber is trying to break into European markets where it has never done as well. Analysts positively regarded its buyout by Sandoz (which was then absorbed by Novartis) as a way to penetrate these markets. It has focused on introducing foods for older children (Gerber Graduates), and by capturing more of the Latino market (whose birthrate is higher than Anglo Americans') by introducing a tropical line of fruits, and by targeting African American women, who buy more baby food for their infants.[82] As a means to maintain market share Gerber in 1996 opened its own line of organics called Tender Harvest, and after years of resistance has pledged not to include any genetically modified foods in its products.[83] Most controversially, Gerber is aggressively pushing its products in developing nations, where birth rates are higher and, as economies strengthen, there is much room for growth. The Middle East, Asia, Africa, and Latin America are all targets.

Gerber's strong-arming of the Guatemalan government over the use of the Gerber Baby illustrates the ethical political economy of the infant food industry as it develops outside the United States, and demonstrates the power of the Gerber Baby as icon. In 1992 Gerber, seeking to enter the infant food market in Guatemala, was told by the government it could not use the Gerber Baby on its products or in its advertising, as the baby looked too young to pass the International Code of Marketing of Breastmilk Substitutes set up by the United Nations after the Nestle formula debacle.[84] One very clear rule of the code prohibits advertising of foods with pictures of very young babies, which give the appearance (especially to illiterate women) that such products are acceptable substitutes for breast milk.[85] Gerber fiercely fought restriction, persuading

U.S. Congress members and the American Embassy in Guatemala to help get the Guatemalan government to change its policy. Although the matter was taken to court, Gerber has been able to spend huge sums of money lobbying its case and tying the matter up indefinitely. In the meantime it continues to do what it pleases, which is to use the Gerber Baby on its products and advertising materials. The Guatemalan government has not the resources Gerber has to fight it out.[86]

Since its first foray into national advertising Gerber has employed the same charcoal sketch of the original Gerber Baby as a main feature in its product advertising and label design. For good reason. An enormously compelling icon that is nationally and internationally recognized, it is an image on which mothers have depended and on which Gerber has relied to spur greater sales and market share. Yet once a symbol of American purity, abundance, and scientific expertise, at the advent of the twenty-first century the famous Gerber Baby, seen on every jar of baby food, had been scrutinized much more closely.

Notes

1. The scholarship on breast-to-bottle feeding includes: Rima Apple, *Mothers and Medicine: A Social History of Infant Feeding, 1890–1950* (Madison: University of Wisconsin Press, 1987); Penny Van Esterik, *Beyond the Breast-Bottle Controversy* (New Brunswick: Rutgers University Press, 1989); Valerie Fildes, *Breasts, Bottles, and Babies: A History of Infant Feeding* (Edinburgh: Edinburgh University Press, 1986); Janet Golden, *A Social History of Wet Nursing in America: From Breast to Bottle* (Cambridge: Cambridge University Press, 1996); Patricia Stuart-Macadam and Katherine A. Dettwyler, eds., *Breastfeeding: Biocultural Perspectives* (New York: Aldine de Gruyter, 1995); Marilyn Yalom, *A History of the Breast* (New York: Alfred A. Knopf, 1997); Meredith F. Small, *Our Babies, Ourselves: How Biology and Culture Shape the Way We Parent* (New York: Anchor Books, 1998); and Linda M. Blum, *At the Breast: Ideologies of Breastfeeding and Motherhood in the Contemporary United States* (Boston: Beacon Press, 1999).

2. Jane E. Brody, "Breast Is Best for Babies, But Sometimes Mom Needs Help," *New York Times*, March 30, 1999; Elizabeth Cohen, "New Two-Year Breast-Feeding Guideline Irks Busy NYC Moms," *New York Post*, October 1, 1998: 29; Frances J. Rohr and Judith A. Lothian, "Feeding throughout the First Year of Life," in *Nutrition and Feeding of Infants and Toddlers*, ed. Howard and Winter, (Boston: Little, Brown, 1984), 65–130; Lewis A. Parness, ed., *Pediatric Nutrition Handbook, Third Edition* (Elk Grove Village, IL: American Academy of Pediatrics, 1993). See also Michael C. Latham, "Breast Feeding Reduces Morbidity," *BMJ*, May 15, 1999: 1303–1304; and Michael C. Latham, "Breastfeeding—A Human Rights Issue?" *The International Journal of Children's Rights* 18:56, 6 (1998): 1–21.

3. Jay E. Mechling, "Advice to Historians on Advice to Mothers," *Journal of Social History* 9, 1 (Fall 1975): 55.

4. Ibid.

5. Ibid., 56.

6. And, further, I might disagree a bit with Mechling and argue that, at least in the post–World War II era, most middle-class new parents are far enough removed from extended family, and thus inexperienced enough with infants (especially when it comes to post-1970s return to breast-feeding) that the manuals do reflect practice more than they might otherwise.

7. Valerie Fildes, "The Culture and Biology of Breastfeeding," in *Breastfeeding: Biocultural Perspectives*, ed. Stuart-Macadam and Dettwyler, 101–126. Thomas E. Cone, Jr., "Infant Feeding: A Historical Perspective," in, *Nutrition and Feeding of Infant and Toddlers*, ed. Howard and Winter, 1–7.

8. Catharine E. Beecher and Harriet Beecher Stowe, *The American Woman's Home Companion* (New York: J. B. Ford, 1869), 268. "Artificial" is the term in the literature used for foods given to infants other than breast milk. This includes prepared liquid formulas and "beikost," a term meaning any nonmilk food. See Sara A. Quandt, Ph.D., "The Effect of Beikost on the Diet of Breast-fed Infants," *Journal of the American Dietetic Association* 84 (1984): 47–51; see also S. J. Fomon, *Infant Nutrition*, 2nd ed. (Philadelphia: W. B. Saunders, 1974); and Felisa J. Bracken, "Infant Feeding in the American Colonies," *Journal of the American Dietetic Association* (1953): 1–10.

9. Interestingly, not until the nineteenth century did cow's milk, usually diluted with water and sweetened with sugar, become the breast milk substitute of choice. See Alice L. Wood, "The History of Artificial Feeding of Infants," *Journal of the American Dietetic Association* (1955): 21–29.

10. Herman Frederic Meyer, *Infant Foods and Feeding Practice: A Rapid Reference Text of Practical Infant Feeding for Physicians and Nutritionists* (Springfield, IL: C. C. Thomas, 1952), 143.

11. Wood, "The History of Artificial Feeding of Infants," 24.

12. Mrs. Sarah Josepha Hale, *Mrs. Hale's Receipts for the Million* (Philadelphia: T. B. Peterson and Brothers, 1857), 219.

13. Ibid. 220.

14. Patricia M. Tice, *Gardening in America, 1830–1910* (Rochester, NY: The Strong Museum, 1984), 53–54; Sidney Mintz, *Sweetness and Power: The Place of Sugar in Modern History* (New York: Viking, 1985), 75–76.; J. C. Drummond and Anne Wilbraham, *The Englishman's Food: A History of Five Centuries of the English Diet* (London: Pimlico, 1939, 1991), 68; Wood, "The History of Artificial Feeding of Infants," 22.

15. Tice, *Gardening in America*, 53–54.

16. See, for example, Edwin G. Burrows and Mike Wallace, *Gotham: A History of New York to 1898* (New York: Oxford University Press, 1999): chap. 67; Cone, "Infant Feeding," 12.

17. Cone, "Infant Feeding," 14; and Suzanne F. Adams, "Use of Vegetables in Infant Feeding through the Ages," *Journal of the American Dietetic Association* 35 (July 1959): 692–703.

18. Joseph B. Lyman and Laura E. Lyman, *The Philosophy of House-keeping: A Scientific and Practical Manual* (Hartford: Goodwin and Betts, 1867), 303.

19. Ibid., 304.

20. Susan Strasser, *Never Done: A History of American Housework* (New York:

Pantheon, 1982); Ruth Schwartz Cowan, *More Work for Mother* (New York: Basic Books, 1983).

21. See, for example, Roland Marchand, *Advertising the American Dream* (Berkeley: University of California Press, 1985); Stuart Ewen, *Captains of Consciousness: Advertising and the Social Roots of Consumer Culture* (New York: McGraw-Hill, 1976); and Jackson Lears, *Fables of Abundance: A Cultural History of Advertising in America* (New York: Basic Books, 1994).

22. Charles Rosenberg, *No Other Gods: On Science and American Social Thought* (Baltimore: Johns Hopkins University Press, 1997); Susan Reverby and David Rosner, eds., *Health Care in America : Essays in Social History* (Philadelphia: Temple University Press, 1979).

23. Wood, "The History of Artificial Feeding of Infants," 25.

24. Katharine K. Merritt, M.D., "Feeding the Normal Infant and Child," *Journal of the American Dietetic Association* 14 (April 1938): 264–268; Apple, *Mothers and Medicine*; Van Esterik, *Beyond the Breast-Bottle Controversy*.

25. Marion Mills Miller, Litt.D., *Practical Suggestions for Mother and Housewife*, ed. Theodore Waters (New York: The Christian Herald Bible House, 1910), 89.

26. Martha Van Rensselaer, Flora Rose, and Helen Cannon, *A Manual of Home-Making* (New York: Macmillan, 1920), 435.

27. Carlotta C. Greer, *Foods and Home Making* (Boston: Allyn and Bacon, 1928), 498–499.

28. Flora Rose, "The Care and Feeding of Children: Part 1" (October 1, 1911), 15, Kroch Library Archives and Manuscripts, Cornell University.

29. National Academy of Sciences, *Nutrition during Lactation* (Washington DC, 1991), 28–46. Interestingly, after breast-feeding reached its nadir in the early 1970s the pattern reversed itself: African American and Latina women, and those in rural areas resumed breast-feeding much more slowly and in smaller numbers. See also Sarah A. Quandt, "Sociocultural Aspects of the Lactation Process," in *Breastfeeding: Biocultural Perspectives*, ed. Stuart-Macadam and Dettwyler, 134; Fildes, "The Culture and Biology of Breastfeeding," 108–109.

30. Trade card collection, Winterthur Museum and Library, Winterthur, DE; article on trade cards, Ellen Gruber Garvey, *The Adman in the Parlor: Magazines and the Gendering of Consumer Culture, 1880s to 1910s* (New York: Oxford University Press, 1996), chap. 1. See also Susan Strasser, *Satisfaction Guaranteed: The Making of the American Mass Market* (New York: Pantheon Books), 164–166; and Harvey Levenstein, *Revolution at the Table: The Transformation of the American Diet* (New York: Oxford University Press, 1988), chap. 10.

31. Rose, "The Care and Feeding of Children," 24–25.

32. Ibid.

33. "Report of Richard, April 15 to June 15, 1920," Records of the Home Economics Department, Cornell University, Collection #23/2/749, Box 19, Folder 44. Rachel Sanders Bizel, "A Study of Infant Feeding Practices as Found by a Survey of 702 New York State Babies," Ph.D. diss., Cornell University, March 1933, 66–68.

34. Strasser, *Never Done*.

35. In fact, I would also like to know when the terms "artificial food" and "proprietary food," used in all childcare and pediatricians' manuals, were dropped, indicating that the use of such breast milk substitutes was now entrenched, if not the

norm. I know that the terms are used in the 1952 edition of Meyer's *Infant Foods and Feeding Practice*, but by the next edition, 1960, the terms are dropped.

36. Levenstein, *Revolution at the Table*, chap. 7.

37. Ibid., chap. 9.

38. Elizabeth Condit and Jessie A. Long, *How to Cook and Why* (New York: Harper and Brothers, 1914), 102.

39. Rose, in Van Rensselaer, Rose, and Cannon, *A Manual of Home-Making*, 412.

40. Greer, *Foods and Home Making*, 34.

41. Ibid., 265.

42. Ibid., 501.

43. Ibid.

44. Nancy Lee Seger, "A Study of Infant Feeding Practices as Used with Cornell's 45 'Practice House' Babies from 1920–1944," Master's thesis, Cornell University, February, 1945, 115–117.

45. Collection of letters to Martha Van Rensselaer in the 1910s, found in the Home Economics Records 23/2/749, Box 24, Kroch Library, Cornell University.

46. 4/3/[1911] letter to MVR from Mrs. Marie Christ.

47. Ibid.

48. Bizel, "A Study of Infant Feeding Practices," 137, 160.

49. Gerber Company History, Gerber website. A similar version, one that gives Mrs. Gerber's name as Dorothy, is recounted in Ellen Shapiro, "The Consultant Trap," *Inc.* 17 (December 1995): 31–32.

50. Cowan, *More Work for Mother*.

51. Mercedes M. Cardona, "WPP Brand Study Ranks Gerber 1st in U.S. Market," *Advertising Age*, October 5, 1998, 3.

52. Judann Pollack, "Gerber Starts New Ads as Agency Review Narrows," *Advertising Age*, December 16, 1996, 6. Gerber Company History, Gerber website; "A Jarring Experience: Ann Turner Cook, Now 70, Is Still the One and Only Gerber Baby," *People*, November 10, 1997.

53. Cone, "Infant Feeding"; Adams, "Use of Vegetables in Infant Feeding through the Ages."

54. Blum, *At the Breast*, 38.

55. Strasser, *Satisfaction*, 33–35.

56. Ibid., 89, 95.

57. Gerald B. Wadsworth, "Principles and Practice of Advertising," *A&S* (January 1913): 55, as quoted in ibid., 32.

58. Lynn K. Nyhart, "Home Economists in the Hospital, 1900–1930," in *Rethinking Home Economics*, ed. Sarah Stage and Virginia B. Vincenti (Ithaca: Cornell University Press, 1997), 128.

59. *Journal of the American Dietetic Association* 8 (July 1932): 199.

60. *Journal of the American Dietetic Association* 10 (July 1934): 183.

61. *Journal of the American Dietetic Association* 10 (May 1934): 79.

62. *Journal of the American Dietetic Association* 11 (January 1936): 493.

63. *Journal of the American Dietetic Association* 12 (September 1936): 271.

64. *Journal of the American Dietetic Association* 15 (April 1939): 305.

65. Flora Manning, "Canned Strained Vegetables as Sources of Vitamin A,"

Journal of the American Dietetic Association 9 (November 1933): 295–305; Flora Manning, "Further Studies of the Content of Vitamins A and B in Canned Strained Vegetables," *Journal of the American Dietetic Association* 12 (September 1936): 231–236.

66. *Journal of the American Dietetic Association* 11 (September 1935): 293.

67. *Journal of the American Dietetic Association* 15 (June–July 1939): 513.

68. *Journal of the American Dietetic Association* 16 (January 1940): 85.

69. Strasser, *Satisfaction*, 11, 126.

70. Ibid., 91.

71. *Ladies Home Journal*, July 1929.

72. *Ladies Home Journal*, August 1933: 77.

73. *Ladies Home Journal*, October 1933: 127.

74. *Ladies Home Journal*, July 1933: 51.

75. Elsewhere I have seen the baby's name given as "Sally." See Shapiro, "The Consultant Trap."

76. *Ladies Home Journal*, September 1937: 60.

77. *Ladies Home Journal*, December 1938: 99.

78. Daryth D. Stallone and Michael F. Jacobson, "Cheating Babies: Nutritional Quality and the Cost of Commercial Baby Food," Center for Science in the Public Interest (CSPI) Report, April 1995.

79. "Gerber Products Company Recall 55,000 Jars of Fruit Juice for Infants after Pieces of Glass Are Found in Four Jars," *Wall Street Journal*, October 19, 1984: 12; "Reports of Glass Inside Jars of Gerber Products Probed," *Wall Street Journal*, February 20, 1986: 4; "Gerber Decries State Order Taking Product Off Shelves," *Wall Street Journal*, February 24, 1986: 48; "Gerber Is Suing over Maryland's Ban on Baby Food," *Wall Street Journal*, February 25, 1986: 14; "FDA Finds Glass in Jars of Gerber Food Products," *Wall Street Journal*, March 3, 1986: 15; "Gerber Takes Risky Stance as Fears Spread about Glass in Baby Food," *Wall Street Journal*, March 6, 1986: 27.

80. Bruce Ingersoll, "Claim by Gerber for Baby Food Was Simply Mush, FTC Alleges," *Wall Street Journal*, March 13, 1997: B5.

81. Unpublished documents in author's possession: "Cheating Babies"; "Pesticides in Baby Food," The Environmental Working Group/The Tides Foundation, July 1995.

82. "To Block or Not to Block," *Progressive Grocer* 75 (May 1996): 96–97; Stephanie Thompson, "Gerber Aims at Latino Birth Explosion," *Advertising Age*, March 6, 2000: 8; "Gerber Life Revamps Direct Mail Effort," *Advertising Age*, March 6, 2000: 27.

83. "Gerber Unit Introduces Organic Baby Food Line," *Wall Street Journal*, October 31, 1997: B5; "New Product Review," *Supermarket Savvy* (March/April 1998): 1; "Gerber Will Stop Adding Sugar, Starch to Products," *Wall Street Journal*, June 26, 1996: 7; Lucetter Lagnado, "Gerber Baby Food, Grilled by Greenpeace, Plans Swift Overhaul," *Wall Street Journal*, July 30, 1999: A1; Henry I. Miller, "The Biotech Baby Food Scare," *Consumers' Research Magazine*, 82, 10 (October 1999): 12–13.

84. Van Esterik, *Beyond the Breast-Bottle Controversy*.

85. The United Nations World Health Assembly has expressed concern about

the marketing of complementary foods in ways that undermine breast-feeding. Any food given to an infant during the period recommended for exclusive breast-feeding (until the age of about six months) will actually replace breast milk. Thus when it is marketed as suitable for feeding infants within that range, it can be considered to be a breast milk substitute. "Cracking the Code: Monitoring the International Code of Marketing of Breast-Milk Substitutes" (London: World Health Organization, 1977).

86. June 13, 1997 correspondence from David Clark, Legal Officer, UNICEF, in author's possession.

Domesticating the Restaurant: Marketing the Anglo-American Home

JAN WHITAKER

The art—and the allure—of home-cooked meals helped Anglo-American women to break into the restaurant business in the first third of the twentieth century. As outsiders in a field of business filled with immigrant males, they used domestic values to compete for success in the marketplace. By catering to a largely female clientele, they brought change to the nascent restaurant industry, domesticating a male-dominated sphere of production and consumption and introducing a middle-class dining culture into a marketplace previously bifurcated into high-class and low-class eating places. The home ideal on which they based their restaurants, though presented as universal, was rooted in a privileged and ethnocentric middle-class standard that did not grant working-class immigrant homes equal value. By the 1940s, however, it had become an industry norm.

Social and economic changes in the early twentieth century enlarged women's opportunities to carry home-based skills and values into the sphere of business. As America industrialized, the urban workforce grew and more meals were eaten outside the home. No longer did eating out mean that the diner was a wealthy bon vivant, on the one hand, or virtually homeless, on the other, as had been true in the nineteenth century. The number of restaurants grew, and new types of eating places emerged as restaurant patronage expanded. The movement to prohibit alcohol increased demand for eating places free of liquor, and sandwich shops, cafeterias, and tea rooms appeared and flourished. Increasingly in the 1920s, the new types of alcohol-free restaurants began to attract a middle-class patronage which was learning to appreciate the convenience and pleasure of eating out.[1]

In the 1910s and 1920s more women and whole families began to eat away from home. Sociologist Frances Donovan, engaged in a participant observation study of restaurants in 1916, found it remarkable that suburban Chicago families had begun to patronize restaurants. This was significant for several reasons. For one, it suggested that middle-class women felt free to eat away from home without fear of being judged negligent or careless about their families' meals. Second, it meant restaurants had begun to attract a new clientele who came to eat, not drink. It was precisely these kinds of patrons who gave women restaurateurs an influential role, particularly because the emerging restaurant industry believed the women had special insights on how to cater to the new clientele.[2]

The number of unescorted women eating in public was also growing rapidly due to an increase in women in the workforce around World War I, and to relaxed attitudes about what was respectable behavior. Around the turn of the century many restaurants had operated as men's clubs in all but name. As places where men were free to drink heavily, smoke, and engage in rough talk, they were considered off limits to middle-class women. Nor were genteel women themselves eager to patronize restaurants, which many regarded as "the tail end of the saloon business." Prior to National Prohibition in 1920, many restaurants underscored the idea that they were not proper places for ladies by refusing service to lone women or by segregating them in curtained-off areas, in separate dining rooms, or on upper floors.[3]

Only a few types of eating places—such as restaurants in downtown shopping districts and ice cream and confectionery shops—catered principally to women around 1900. However, as more women took jobs outside the home, their restaurant options widened. In the late 1890s, several women's organizations in Chicago formed lunch clubs for working women. They were usually bare halls in the basements of office buildings, staffed by volunteers who provided soup and sandwiches to customers who served themselves. Seeing the popularity of these eating places, some women opened similar cafeterias as money-making ventures. Also in the early twentieth century, women introduced another new type of eating place, the tea room, which, like the early cafeterias, appealed mainly to women customers.[4]

Between 1890 and 1930 the number of women running restaurants in the United States increased almost seventeenfold, from about 2,400 to 40,000. Although women made up only about 18 percent of all restaurant-keepers in 1920, their influence was growing. In large part this was because Anglo-American women were entering the business. Frequently college-educated, trained in home economics, and inspired with zeal to improve the public's eating habits, they brought new energy and ideas to the industry. Their choice of career often baffled their friends and family, who felt it was somewhat disgraceful. It is difficult to appreciate how unusual it was for college-educated women to enter the restaurant business, but it would be analogous to women graduates of elite colleges today deciding to run motels or casinos.[5]

The more prominent women in the business asserted that by operating a restaurant they were providing valuable social services in keeping with women's historical role. Some compared their work in the restaurant business to that of women social reformers whose mission had been to make the whole world homelike. Although such statements were meant to justify women's presence in the male business world, they also seemed to bespeak a genuine calling. Some women spoke of the restaurant business as a way of recovering an ancient female vocation that had been wrongfully usurped by men. "This business of feeding humanity is logically women's field," concluded Clara Mae Downey, owner of the Olney Inn in Maryland. "It satisfies her inborn desire to serve the race," she said. Mary Dutton, proprietor of the Chicago Ontra cafeteria chain begun in 1910, declared that the public restaurant was "a home dining room on an enlarged scale." For this reason, she said, a woman in this field would "become so interested in seeing that everything is provided for the comfort and enjoyment of her guests, that she will forget the long and unusual hours which restaurant work necessitates."[6]

Others believed that women belonged in restaurants because they were naturally superior to men in the culinary arts. But perhaps they meant that Anglo-American women were superior. For men had no monopoly in operating substandard eateries. Many immigrant women ran lowly restaurants that scarcely provided for their own subsistence and often violated health codes. Yet the new women in the business typically defined their competition as male and tended to ignore the many foreign-born women who ran little neighborhood eateries and boarding house dining rooms. Thus, when searching for historical female forebears in the hospitality business, they skipped back a century or two and discovered a handful of female colonial innkeepers.[7]

In disregarding their sister restaurant operators as peers and forbears, the newcomers reflected conventional middle-class opinion, which judged most ethnic restaurants as substandard. Even if ethnic proprietors used their own family kitchens as their workplace, as was sometimes the case, Anglo-Americans would not have regarded the meals they served as "home-cooked." Home cooking tacitly referred to meals prepared in Anglo-American homes, not to food cooked in just any home. Cities were filled with small French and Italian table d'hôte restaurants which served low-priced meals of seven or eight courses. (*Table d'hôte* is French for table of the host, reflecting the practice of opening one's home to paying diners who historically sat at the family table.) Tables d'hôte were viewed as foreign, not as purveyors of home cooking. Not only did critics complain that everything on their menus tasted the same, they also thought that tables d'hôte were unsanitary. They were convinced, for example, that the reason napkins were elaborately folded was to hide stains and that sauces were meant to disguise spoiled meat. Even the relatively adventurous journalist Christine Terhune Herrick, who recommended that readers of her book *In City Tents* give tables d'hôte a try, reported that ethnic restaurants in America sometimes assembled meals from "the leavings of hotels and high-priced restaurants."[8]

Not that there weren't many unsanitary practices in restaurants. Inspectors often found spoiled food served to diners. Sanitation was primitive in many restaurants, as a 1911 University of Illinois home economics restaurant checklist showed. Common problems observed in restaurants included proximity to stables, absorbent walls, unhealthy employees, worn china, uncovered food, "rank" flavors, and over-handling of food materials. But although these were real health issues, it was uncommonly easy for the middle-class imagination to associate them with foreign cooks and staffs. Thus adulterated restaurant food was often represented as a problem intrinsic to the European "chef's art" (i.e., trickery), while unclean waiters were called "blackcoated," a negatively nuanced reference to the customary European uniform.[9]

By contrast, the Anglo-American home was portrayed as a place where highly trained and organized women were in command, where motives were pure and selfless, where no deceit took place, and where the latest scientific discoveries would be employed for the benefit of the family. Food produced in this environment, therefore, could only be sanitary and wholesome. Even if a middle-class family hired a foreign-born cook, the fact that the woman of the house supervised and directed her would insure that the family's meals were authentically American.[10]

Home cooking was not an objective description but, rather, a sumptuary ideal which prescribed how all Americans ought to live. Rather than reflecting prevailing meal customs, the new middle-class restaurants run by Anglo-American women modeled how the dining room should look, how the table should be appointed, how a diner should comport herself, as well as what food was proper to eat and how it should be prepared. The restaurant was as fully a model of the "all-American" home as were the advertisements in women's magazines—a point not lost on major food manufacturers who were eager to introduce new products via public eateries. The home-cooking ideal ordained that food be prepared plainly and simply, and that the dining environment be restful, harmonious, and subdued. Above all, it demanded thoroughgoing cleanliness.

The Young Women's Christian Association (YWCA), whose cafeterias provided an occupational training ground and springboard for home economists interested in improving public eating places, was a leading proponent of sanitation. A 1917 YWCA manual gave detailed instructions for maintaining cleanliness by scrubbing cafeteria walls, woodwork, and flooring. "Insist on each [garbage] can being washed inside and outside as clean as a plate, each time it is emptied," specified the manual. It instructed servers to deliver food to patrons with gloved hands, in an environment "without noise or bustle, in quarters as clean as a new pin, flooded with the light of day." Another exponent of the hygienic kitchen was Alice Bradley, a cooking teacher who ran Miss Farmer's School of Cookery in Boston for many years. She advised tea room managers that guests should be invited "to inspect the kitchen, refrigerator, or back yard if they wish." Similarly, the Mayflower Tea Room in New York City advertised in *Vanity Fair* magazine in 1918 that it was "spotlessly clean in its dainty Puritan primness."[11]

Many women who were squeamish about eating food outside the home felt that only their own gender could be trusted to keep a restaurant clean. Men, they believed, were naturally slovenly and too impatient to clean thoroughly. "The restaurant needs the sharp eyes of 'mother' to look for dirt or worse things in the corners," advised one female restaurant consultant. Many women who ran restaurants said they would not hire men to work for them because they believed that women cooks and kitchen managers held a higher standard of cleanliness. Sociologist Frances Donovan confirmed women's higher standards in her study of Chicago restaurants. After spending months working as a waitress, she reported in 1920 that the only clean restaurant kitchens she had seen were those managed by women. Cooking expert Anna J. Peterson, in an address to the National Restaurant Association in 1924, told of a struggle she had waged with an Italian restaurant chef with bad habits. In a war of wills, she eventually triumphed and won him over to her clean and "scientific" approach to cooking, she said.[12]

Women educated in home economics were also eager to introduce plain food to restaurant menus. Many of the restaurants operated by the new women entrepreneurs featured food that tended to be bland by today's standards, with many pale or white food selections prepared with an abundance of butter and cream. Overall the cuisine found in many cafeterias and tea rooms was reminiscent of nineteenth-century invalid and nursery dishes, a particular specialty of women caterers. Meatless recipes, and dishes in which meat was minced and combined with other ingredients, were believed to be less taxing to the system of a fragile individual (that is, a sick person, a woman, or a child). Restaurant consultant Gertrude Sanborn observed in 1912 that there was a need "in public eating places everywhere . . . for good, plain, home-like cooking" such as scalloped fish, spinach and egg salad, meat and potato cakes, and creamed eggs. Cooking expert Alice Bradley recommended dishes such as creamed chicken on toast, which became a favorite on tea room menus.[13]

Tea rooms, women's restaurants par excellence, made invalid cookery a specialty, though they did not use this term. Women's Exchanges were a type of tea room which offered affluent women a clublike environment, while raising money for indigent women by selling hand-sewn and craft items they made. The New York City Women's Exchange was something of a shrine to plain cookery, exemplified in its baked apples, waffles, and fried mush. Lest they miss out, regular patrons were sent notices when waffle season began. One wealthy patron returning from her summer house in the Adirondacks reportedly confessed that the shock of returning to the city was eased by the anticipation of eating fried mush at the Exchange. Another success story built on plain fare was found in restaurateur Grace E. Smith, who built a thriving empire in Toledo, Ohio, serving 5,000 diners a day with roast beef hash, rice pudding, tapioca, and mashed potatoes.[14]

Women advocated plain food for reasons which, while ostensibly health-based, reveal an undercurrent of moral judgment. In a 1911 *Good Housekeeping* article, for example, young working women were warned not to add sugar, salt, catsup, or pickles to their food, as these seasonings and condiments might induce mood swings. Women reformers worried that young shopworkers were too fond of rich food like clam patties and cream puffs, recommending instead that lunch should consist of a cheese sandwich on whole wheat bread and a glass of milk. Criticism of cream puffs, for example, was based more on their effects on character than on health, possibly because eating for enjoyment was regarded as dubious.[15]

A liking for plain food was lodged deep in Anglo-American cuisine, which did not favor strong seasonings. The odor of onions was considered socially embarrassing, and garlic was rarely used in middle-class Anglo-American kitchens well into the twentieth century. A 1925 spaghetti sauce recipe from a cookbook by a YWCA manager reveals what happened when immigrant food was Americanized; the recipe calls only for tomato puree, sugar, salt, and pepper. Poet Octavio Paz has criticized traditional North American cuisine for its lack of sauces and seasonings, observing that "a Yankee meal is saturated with Puritanism, is

94

made up of exclusions." He then asserts, "The maniacal preoccupation with the origin and purity of food is the counterpart of racism and discrimination." As a class, women restaurant operators were scarcely "maniacal," but they did come from a milieu which had taken up the causes of food purity and the Americanization of immigrant diets, and it would scarcely be surprising if their conviction that plain food was better sprang from a sense of cultural superiority.[16]

Another cultural factor behind the preference for plain food was the prevalent Puritan-like belief that appetite should result from honest exertion. Sauces, for instance, were believed to be appetite inducers for the jaded palates of debauched socialites. Earnest middle-class reformers were fond of saying, "Hunger is the best sauce." According to this logic, if a diner did not earn her appetite through hard work then she should skip a meal.

Simplicity also ranked high as a virtue in Anglo-American cookery. Simple food preparation meant using readily available fresh ingredients (no imports!) and manipulating those ingredients as little as possible. The opposite of simple food was fancy food, a category which included the products of French cuisine. At times the proponents of simple food came close to equating a taste for fancy food with degeneracy. Helen Ewing, a columnist for the trade magazine *The American Restaurant*, suggested that attraction to "elaborate concoctions" was un-American. This can be seen as a translation into culinary terms of a belief, widespread among social reformers such as Jane Addams and her associates, that Europe was old, tired, and corrupt, and had little to offer young America.[17]

French cuisine was no more popular with women restaurant operators than with American culture at large. Although it had been fashionable in the 1870s, like all things French, it became associated with nouveau riche tastes and with social ostentation in the 1890s. The excesses of wealth displayed in that decade doomed French food, linking it with decadence in the eyes of the reformist middle class of the early twentieth century. Cookery reformer Ellen Richards, creator of the New England Kitchen, a lunchroom in Boston, in 1917 affirmed a belief that there was a causal connection between rich food and "the increase of crime, of insanity, of certain forms of disease, of moral recklessness."[18]

City tea rooms, generally more upscale and expensive than sandwich shops or cafeterias, carefully rode the line between fancy and simple food. They were not about to serve their patrons cheese sandwiches on whole wheat bread. They found a way to rehabilitate French cuisine by Americanizing it, in much the same way as had been done by The Boston Cooking School and presented in its magazine *American Cook-*

ery. Although tea room food was simply prepared, it was expected to be more artful and dainty than what would be served at a lunch counter. Without the seasonings and sauces (except for white sauce, which was highly approved), items such as patties and puffs were staples on tea room menus. When presented on the menu of a tea room, a clam patty was no longer foreign, but American food. Patrons could trust its wholesomeness, and it satisfied the requirement enunciated by New York restaurateur Alice Foote MacDougall that "eating should be a fine art."[19]

Tea rooms also excelled at creating a homelike environment which put women at ease and convinced them to trust the quality and preparation of the food they were served. Hash might be served in the tea room and hash house alike, but in the tea room it represented home cooking, while in the grease-filled atmosphere of the noisy hash house it suggested dyspepsia and food poisoning. Supposedly the hash house entirely lacked home atmosphere. A homelike eating place, according to temperance advocate Frances Willard in the late 1890s, was "quiet" and its food was "dainty." A restful dining room to many women such as Willard around the turn of the century would very likely have light gray walls and carpeting. Voices would have been kept to a hush. It simply did not occur to native-born American women of the middle class that a good meal at home could be spicy, noisy, and lively or that the room in which it was consumed could be messy or lacking a genteel decorative scheme.[20]

Middle-class restaurants run by women, especially tea rooms, were renowned for their ability to evoke "atmosphere." Typically this was achieved by soft lighting, attractive table appointments, and tastefully artistic furniture and decor generally of the understated Arts and Crafts or Colonial Revival styles. Even cafeterias were models of good homes, albeit in the lower ranges of the middle class. Although many cafeterias were starkly plain in the early days, by the 1920s they had become more inviting, with decorated entryways, fountains, mirrored walls, potted plants, and live piano music.[21]

Restaurants that excelled in creating the cuisine and the ambience held dear by the new restaurant women were Schrafft's and Mary Elizabeth's in New York City. Perhaps no other restaurant fulfilled middle-class women's notion of home-away-from-home as successfully as did Schrafft's. Although it was owned by a man, William Shattuck, it was from the start managed by his sister Jane. Its expansion to a chain of twenty-one restaurants by 1925 was credited to her and to the all-women staff she employed, many of whom were college-trained in domestic science. Schrafft's strove to convey an air of middle-class

The Richards Treat cafeteria, a landmark for decades in downtown Minneapolis, was owned and operated by Lenore Richards and Nola Treat.

feminine gentility in its personnel, its decor, its crustless tea sandwiches, and its ubiquitous paper doilies. Mary Elizabeth's, on the corner of Fifth Avenue and 36th Street, had a white front with a big window decorated with flower boxes and emblazoned with the Mary Elizabeth signature. Inside, its windows were curtained with dotted Swiss, and its large fireplace, inglenooks, and "scrubbed look" color scheme of yellow and white gave the impression of a cozy cottage. An article in a 1923 trade magazine noted that Mary Elizabeth's decorations, "though simple, are in the best of taste, nothing ornate or elaborate." Put in other words, it looked nothing like the typical immigrant home in which anything ornate, elaborate, or Victorian would probably have been cherished as a beautiful treasure.[22]

The gentility of Schrafft's and Mary Elizabeth's was equaled by many department store tea rooms, inns, and small dining rooms managed by women. They succeeded in supplying the quality that 1920s restaurateur and coffee wholesaler Alice Foote MacDougall described as "the intimate feeling we used to have when we gathered around the dining-room at home." The homelike atmosphere was typically evoked with candles, flowers, and noninstitutional tableware and furniture. Mac-Dougall was one of the many women restaurateurs who used peasant pottery rather than restaurant-supply china. Many women restaura-

Schrafft's Alexander Room, on the fourth floor of the restaurant's Fifth Avenue location in New York City, defined the meaning of domestic gentility for countless thousands of patrons.

teurs furnished their dining rooms with gateleg tables and Windsor chairs complemented with cupboards full of teapots and dishes. Tea rooms often covered their windows with curtains and lighted their interiors with floor and table lamps and wall sconces. In suburban and rural areas, restaurants run by women were often located in residential buildings. If the house possessed a fireplace, its mantel would invariably display an arrangement of teapots or pewter plates.[23]

Colonial decor represented the summit of the American home ideal, and was often found in tea rooms and other eating places run by Anglo-American women. The popularity of the Colonial Revival movement has been linked to the reaction of established classes to the influx of immigrants in the late nineteenth and early twentieth centuries. Whatever the inspiration, the late teens and twenties ushered in a taste for rag rugs, bare wood floors, deacons' benches, pewter accessories, spinning wheels, and pre-Victorian antiques of all kinds. Many of these items adorned Smith College graduate Mary Aletta Crump's homespun Crumperie tea room in Greenwich Village. Greenwich Village bohemians were, after all, mostly Anglo-Americans from New England, the South, and the Midwest. The appeal of colonial decor to women customers was noted by male restaurateurs, who discovered at Prohibition's end that women would patronize barrooms if they were designed to look like early American taverns.[24]

Remaining true to home values, the new women in the restaurant business often decried the profit motive. Although they sought financial success, many said they found their gratification in terms of self-expression. This was particularly true of tea rooms, which were seen as a demonstration of the owner's taste and an extension of her individuality. Proprietors who ignored business realities failed, of course, yet tea rooms in particular minimized the appearance of commercialism by keeping money out of sight, catering to patrons' special needs, and offering second helpings without charge.

They also tried to hire help who appeared to want to serve rather than to gain big tips. Some tea rooms with women managers, notably those in department stores, did not permit waitresses to accept tips. Much middle-class opinion in the early twentieth century was set against European-born waiters, who were perceived as too mercenary and inclined to fawn over and manipulate their patrons in order to win a larger tip. Some women also distrusted waitresses in popular-priced restaurants who increased their tips—and risked their virtue—by flirting with male customers. Restaurants run by women almost always had female help, not only because they were supposedly neater and cleaner, but because men would not take orders from women. Older women or female college students with "breeding" made ideal workers in tea rooms and cafeterias, and helped to make patrons feel as though they were at home. It is likely that patrons accustomed to having domestic servants would have responded well. Being waited on at home was a disappearing luxury around the First World War as many former servants left domestic service to work in factories, hotels, and restaurants. Alice Foote MacDougall, a woman of means whose husband's illness had forced her to support herself, discovered one day that a waitress in her restaurant had once been a servant in her own home.[25]

But there were limits to how well the home could serve as a model for the restaurant. A home, quite obviously, is not run to make a profit. Tea room correspondence courses, such as Alice Bradley's "Cooking for Profit," often extolled the thriftiness of homemakers and implied that this would serve them well if they ran a restaurant. But no matter how well tea room or cafeteria managers conserved and stretched their resources, no matter how many stale cakes they recycled, their success depended on many factors not in the usual repertoire of the homemaker. Amateurism took a high toll in business failures among women proprietors. Those who truly ran their restaurants like homes failed, while those who succeeded learned that a restaurant can resemble a home only in appearance.

Patricia Murphy, proprietor of Patricia Murphy's Candlelight, is a case in point. When she opened her first restaurant in Brooklyn Heights, New York, in 1930, she imagined herself a "housewife planning a family meal." She was a keen bargain shopper, but had no idea of how to keep accounts. She figured that if she netted a dime on each meal she could stay afloat. Although she turned a profit, she had to work weekends, late nights, and holidays. Her restaurant literally was her home. She reported she was willing to make it her life because she was a "frustrated housekeeper" who never had a home of her own.[26]

Murphy's formula of good food and atmosphere proved successful, and she opened a second restaurant in 1939. Meanwhile she had learned a thing or two about business. She installed a bar as soon as Prohibition ended, and when her Christian Scientist landlords objected to liquor being served, she bought them out. Later she opened a restaurant in suburban Manhasset, grossing nearly $1.5 million the first year. Murphy's success led her to hire executive chefs, institute employee incentive plans, and eventually build her own restaurants in Westchester and Florida. Although she continued to portray her activities as "entertaining guests," she had mastered the psychology of selling. She designed her new establishments to accommodate large crowds and to engineer waits in the bar or the gift shop (on some busy days at the Westchester Candlelight in the 1950s, as many as one thousand patrons waited for seating), yet she retained an intimate homelike feeling with small dining rooms, outdoor gardens for strolling, candlelight, floral arrangements, and the provision of individual loaves of bread.

Murphy's career demonstrates how inappropriate homemaking was as a model for a business enterprise. Joseph Dahl, editor of a number of restaurant industry publications, expressed the contradiction like this: women using the home as a model have improved the industry in terms of food quality, sanitation, decor, and a cozy atmosphere, yet their success has unleashed a flood of amateurs (i.e., women) who have "pathetic" expectations of success.[27]

Increasingly, many of the successful women restaurateurs of the 1930s adopted a rationalized approach to running eating places. Home cooking, with its variability, was one of the first casualties, replaced by the standardized recipe which allowed the cook no culinary choices. The Ware sisters, restaurant owners in New York City, proclaimed that standardized recipes took decisions out of the hands of cooks who were "generally uneducated, untrained people." Another expert, Linda Spence Brown, said standardized recipes assured patrons of a "uniform product" and that their use was the "most successful substitute I know for the practice and skill of the mothers in our homes, or for the experience and knowledge of the old-time chef." Mother, clearly, was no longer wanted in the restaurant kitchen.[28]

It is hardly surprising that the new women restaurateurs adapted so easily to managerial authority. The domestic social role of many of the women of this class was supervisory, directing the labor of women of other classes and ethnic groups who did the hard and dirty work of the household. In this sense the restaurant modeled on the home accurately reflected reality. For example, when white women supervised the cooking of Black women, they found the situation comfortably familiar. The mother and daughter proprietors of the Gingham Shop explained in *Woman's Home Companion* in the early 1920s that their tea shop's special waffles cooked by their home servant, "faithful Dinah," were exactly like those she prepared for them at home. In Elizabeth Eager's Chimney Corner in Baltimore, a woman's magazine reported, "Negro waitresses of a high grade give deferential service, and an old family servant . . . gives the cooking the home flavor that is so rarely found in a public restaurant." It seems doubtful that the old family servant cooked what she ate in her own home (if she was lucky enough to have one). If she worked for Alice Foote MacDougall, for instance, her cooking had to please the mistress. MacDougall instructed her Black cooks on how to prepare food like that served in MacDougall's home.[29]

The "home-cooking" slogan in restaurants soon became a gimmick. In the 1920s Kansas City cafeteria owner Myron Green ran a billboard advertising campaign which claimed, "The pies I serve are made by real housewives." How could they be real housewives, the public might have wondered, if they were employed in a restaurant? The advertisement assuaged—even as it validated—widespread fears that women were deserting homemaking for paid employment. Throughout the 1920s the home was seen as imperiled as more women entered the workforce and showed little desire to cook. A 1927 questionnaire at the University of Kansas revealed that only seven out of the 1,513 women students surveyed wanted to be homemakers after graduation. Many women with families relied on packaged food or took the family out to dinner as never before. In 1927 an estimated 25 to 30 percent of all meals in larger cities were eaten in restaurants, according to industry analyst Joseph Dahl, who attributed this to more women working, smaller homes and kitchen facilities, difficulties in hiring servants, a higher standard of living, and a desire for recreation.[30]

The credibility of restaurants which claimed to have home-cooked meals grew weaker by the 1930s. "Its virtue has been completely destroyed," complained Helen Ewing, columnist for *The American Restau-*

rant. "It is like [an] over-emphasis which announces a lie," she declared in 1931. Preserving home values in the public marketplace proved impossible. In the process the home was crafted into an advertising tool while the further winnowing away of homely arts and crafts continued unabated.[31]

In the restaurant industry, women failed to win a predominant share of the business, contrary to what some experts, such as Dahl, had predicted. By 1940, 24 percent of restaurants were operated by women, showing only a small increase from 1930. Nor did women's influence continue to increase within the trade. Once the industry had learned how to draw women patrons into restaurants, it tended to lose interest in what women restaurateurs had to offer. The trend, in any case, was toward larger restaurants and chains that demanded the kind of capital few women had access to. Nevertheless, by World War II, the middle-class restaurant was a firmly established institution, attracting women alone or in groups, the fastidious of either gender, and families with children. Not until the 1960s, however, would mainstream Americans learn to appreciate ethnic restaurants.

Notes

1. On changes occurring in the restaurant industry, see Harvey Levenstein's *Revolution at the Table: The Transformation of the American Diet* (New York: Oxford University Press, 1988). On the positive influence of Prohibition on the growth of restaurants, see "Has Prohibition Hurt the Restaurant? No!," by Joseph Burger, in *The Restaurant Man* 1 (April 1926): 20–21.

2. On families eating out see Frances Donovan's *The Woman Who Waits* (Boston: Richard G. Badger, 1920; New York: Arno Press Reprint, 1974), 113–114. Describing women's influence on the male-dominated restaurant industry, J. O. Dahl observed, "The average restaurateur did not learn to cater to this new business [women's] until thoughtful women started to compete for this business and take it from him." See Dahl's *Restaurant Management* (New York: Harper & Bros., 1927), 243.

3. An example of the impropriety attached to dining in restaurants that served alcohol is revealed in Florence Wenderoth Saunders's *Letters to a Business Girl* (Chicago: Laird & Lee, 1908). Describing the high-priced cafe as "seductive," Saunders paints a scene of moral danger in which young women drink too much and fall prey to male companions (135–137).

4. On lunch clubs and early cafeterias, see "The Origin of the Cafeteria," *Journal of Home Economics* 17 (July 1925): 390–393. It took men a while to warm up to the idea of serving themselves, and they did not accept the new cafeteria idea at first. On this, see "These Things We Have Learned about Cafeteria Service," *Cafeteria Management*, December 1924: 11. My *Tea at the Blue Lantern Inn* (New York:

St. Martin's Press, 2002) describes the types of tea rooms found in the first half of the twentieth century.

5. See "Occupation Statistics" in the 12th, 13th, 14th, and 15th Census of the United States. In 1900 approximately 30 percent of all restaurant-keepers were foreign born, and another 20 percent were of foreign-born parentage.

6. For the Downey quote, see "College Graduates and Restaurant Management," *Journal of Home Economics* 26 (December 1934): 621. The Dutton quote is found in "Restaurant Management" in *An Outline of Careers for Women*, ed. Doris Fleischman (Garden City, NY: Doubleday, Doran, 1929), 436.

7. On the operation of boarding house restaurants, see Albert B. Wolfe, *The Lodging House Problem in Boston* (Cambridge: Harvard University Press, 1913), 47–50, 101–104.

8. On the distrust of ethic restaurants and European cuisines generally, see for instance "The Triumph of the American Idea," by E. H. Nies (*Cafeteria Management*, November 1923: 11). Nies exalts cafeterias where "the food they sell is American food devoid of *à la*'s or *mit*, undisguised and unafraid. . . . There is no need here for that school of cookery which aims to disguise those skeletons and ghosts upon which the hungry population of Europe regales itself." American food by contrast he hailed as "sanitary and sane." See also Christine Terhune Herrick, *In City Tents* (New York: G. P. Putnam's Sons, 1902), 174.

9. See "A Score Card for Eating Houses," *Journal of Home Economics* 3 (December 1911): 470–471. The tendency to equate unsanitary restaurant conditions with immigrants is revealed in the term "greasy spoon," which Greek Americans knew was aimed especially at them. See Charles C. Moskos, *Greek Americans*, 2nd ed. (New Brunswick, NJ: Transaction, 1989), 125.

10. See Laura Shapiro's *Perfection Salad: Women and Cooking at the Turn of the Century* (New York: Farrar, Straus & Giroux, 1986) for a depiction of model scientific cookery in the home.

11. The sanitation practices of the Y are described in Blanche Geary's *Handbook of the Association Cafeteria* (New York: YWCA, 1917), 64. Alice Bradley advised prospective tea room managers in her correspondence course entitled *Cooking for Profit*, rev. ed. (Chicago: American School of Home Economics, 1922), 228. The Mayflower advertisement is found in "The Shops of Vanity Fair," *Vanity Fair*, January 1918: 21.

12. Advice on sanitation was offered by Linda Spence Brown, as quoted in J. O. Dahl's *Restaurant Management*, 85. See also Donovan, *The Woman Who Waits*, p. 119, and "The Truth about Quantity Cooking," as told by Anna J. Peterson, *Cafeteria Management*, October 1924: 21–22.

13. Sanborn's suggestions are found in "The Lunchroom in Business," *Journal of Home Economics* 4 (February 1912): 10. She observed that in most public lunchrooms "the chef has not as high a standard as the housekeeper at home."

14. Food favorites at the New York Women's Exchange are given in "The Maid and the Menu: Can a Woman Order a Dinner?," *New York Times*, October 30, 1904: 6. Smith's most popular dishes were identified by Alberta M. Macfarlane in "They Know Their Onions," *Independent Woman* 21 (September 1942): 266.

15. In "The Young Business Woman's Lunch" by Bertha Stevenson, *Good Housekeeping*, November 1911: 696. Stevenson asks "How can a girl who feeds

herself on cream puffs be anything but mercurial?," perhaps foreshadowing Dan White's "Twinkie defense" in his trial for the murder of Harvey Milk.

16. The spaghetti sauce recipe is in Mabel E. Schadt's *Cafeteria Recipes* (New York: The Woman's Press, 1925), 28. Paz contrasts North American food with Mexican food in "Eroticism and Gastrosophy," in *About Man: An Introduction to Anthropology*, ed. Arthur A. Berger (Dayton, OH: Pflaum/Standard, 1974).

17. See Helen Ewing's "What about This 'Home Cooking'?" in *The American Restaurant*, March 1931: 45. Ewing reflected a belief earlier institutionalized in the work of the Federal Food Administration, whose goals included teaching immigrants to "eat American." See Helen Christine Bennett's "American Food Makes Americans," *Pictorial Review* 20 (August 1919): 46. Addams herself had opened an alcohol-free coffeehouse restaurant at Hull House in 1895. See *Hull House Bulletin*, January 1896, p. 4, in folder 243, Hull House Collection, University of Illinois at Chicago Circle.

18. See Ellen Richard's *The Cost of Food*, 3rd ed. (New York: John Wiley & Sons, 1917), 3.

19. MacDougall said her disgust with the average restaurant led to her determination to provide high-quality food in an atmosphere refreshing to the "soul" as well as the body. See her "Eating Aesthetically" in *The Forum*, September 1928: 394–397.

20. See *Occupations for Women*, ed. Frances Willard (Cooper Union, New York: The Success Company, 1897), 120–122.

21. The California family cafeterias are described in "That Plaguy Dinner: Have a Cafeteria," by Ysobel Farowe, *Delineator* 97 (September 1920): 39.

22. On Schrafft's see "Schrafft's to Expand Restaurant Chain in 1925," *The Restaurateur*, January 3, 1925: 3–4. For a nostalgic remembrance, see Julie Baumgold's "Schrafft's," *New York*, December 21–28, 1987: 72–73. Mary Elizabeth's is profiled in "The Story of Mary Elizabeth's," *The American Restaurant* 6 (July 1923): 40–42.

23. The Alice Foote MacDougall quote is found in her *The Secret of Successful Restaurants* (New York: Harper Bros., 1929), 126. Many descriptions of domestic decor in eating places operated by women are found in *The Tea Room Booklet* (New York: Woman's Home Companion, 1923).

24. Colonial decor was recommended to tea room proprietors in Clifford Lewis's correspondence course *The Tea Room Training Course* (Washington, DC: Tea Room Institute, 1923). Documents on The Crumperie are found in the papers of Mary Aletta Crump, Sophia Smith Collection, Smith College.

25. Cafeteria owner Lenore Richards explained that in order to create a homelike atmosphere, she was careful not to hire "the so-called experienced girl," but instead sought out the "simpler, more wholesome type." Quoted in Dahl's *Restaurant Management*, 93. MacDougall related this incident in Alice Foote MacDougall: *The Autobiography of a Business Woman* (Boston: Little, Brown, 1928), 200.

26. Murphy tells her rags-to-riches story in her *Glow of Candlelight* (Englewood Cliffs, NJ: Prentice-Hall, 1961).

27. See Dahl, *Restaurant Management*, 250–251.

28. The Ware sisters recommended standardized recipes in "The Tea Room Business," *Journal of Home Economics* 16 (October 1924): 569. Brown is quoted in

Dahl, *Restaurant Management*, 134. Home-style baking came into restaurants in World War I along with untrained help who could not produce fancy European pastries. See "Pastries Developed by the Cafeteria," by Emil Burk, *Cafeteria Management*, May 1926: 21.

29. See Lois Borland's "The Gingham Shop" and Eager's "The Chimney Corner" in *The Tea Room Booklet*, 32 and 10, respectively. "I work with [the cooks] until the dishes suit me and are similar to those I have in my own home," said MacDougall in "Alice Foote MacDougall Talks about Control," *Catering Management*, October 1930: 10.

30. Myron Green's slogan is in "75 Years of Food Service History," *Restaurant Business* 75 (May 1976): 95. The Kansas questionnaire is reported in "Home Cooking Stands No Chance with Co-Eds," *The Restaurant Man* 2 (January 1927): 20. Across the United States about 14 percent of all meals were served in restaurants, according to Dahl, *Restaurant Management*, 2.

31. By 1924 *Cafeteria Management* was complaining "this 'mother's cooking' claim is intensely overdone." See "'Mother's Cooking'—But Can You Really Boast It?," *Cafeteria Management*, April 1924: 17. See also Ewing's "What about This 'Home Cooking'?," 45.

Histories

Providing food for family and friends has always been the traditional work of women. Privileged women were not exempt from overseeing family meals, although they could pass on these duties to hired help—usually women. Even now those who work outside the home are expected to cook and fulfill other domestic responsibilities while male family members generally relax once they leave their jobs. As the essays here show, women's age-old relationship to food ranges from being creative and enjoyable, to a dull chore, financially necessary, or much worse, a desperate, sometimes futile, attempt to keep families alive.

Nancy Jenkins's portrayal of Martha Ballard gives us a picture of a woman living in the early years of the American republic who suffered from the modern condition of juggling a career with family responsibilities. Her work as a midwife often kept her away from home for days at a time, but ever mindful of the needs of her husband and adult son, Ballard would arrange for her daughters or hired girls to prepare the men's meals, a job she found burdensome. In "Cooking to Survive," Barbara Haber contrasts the lives of two women who cooked for a living: one a working-class Black woman from Oklahoma and the other an upper-class white woman from New York who had fallen on hard times. Cleora Butler cooked with exuberance for employers, family, and friends, always finding the work creative and gratifying. On the other hand, Alice Foote MacDougall, though she became a successful restaurateur and had much to be proud of, never got over her loss of status caused first by her father's business failures and then by the death of her husband. Darra Goldstein's essay on the siege of Leningrad brings a grim reality to the meaning of providing food. With food supplies shrinking as the siege went on, seeking sustenance became the purpose of women's day-to-day existence. The population ate bread made with sawdust and other fillers—if they were lucky enough to get it—and stripped rooms of wallpaper in order to eat the glue. Most poignant is the daily dilemma women with children faced: whether to sustain themselves with some of the food they managed to gather so as to be able to do the physically demanding work of finding more food, or to give it all to their starving children. All of these essays show the seriousness of the connections between women and food, a subject that in the past has often been trivialized as being mainly about the baking of cookies.

Martha Ballard: A Woman's Place on the Eastern Frontier

NANCY JENKINS

April 1, 1807: "Snows & Blows but we are able to Make a fire and have food to Eat, which is a great Mercy for which I wish to thank ye Great Doner."

The Diary of Martha Ballard

Cookbooks can tell us much about the food of past times, but the views they present of historic kitchens, and of women's roles therein, are necessarily limited. Cookbooks are prescriptive, rather than descriptive, describing not so much what people actually ate, what women (for it is to women that most cookbooks are addressed after about 1650) actually cooked, as what the authors hoped they would eat and cook. And historically cookbooks were restricted in their audience to an elite segment of society that was literate and that found in the printed word an accessible and legitimate source of information. In researching what Americans ate, and how they procured it and prepared it, in the early years of the republic, I've found that diaries, journals, and correspondence can enormously enrich more formal culinary literature. At the same time, such personal documents give us great insight into women's lives at a time in our history when from young girlhood the primary obligation of women of almost all social classes was to guarantee the food supply of families and communities.

One particularly rich and relevant source for information about women's lives and food on what historians call the Eastern Frontier, that is, the pioneering settlements of Maine in the late eighteenth and early nineteenth centuries, is the diary kept by Martha Ballard, which was the subject of Laurel Thatcher Ulrich's masterful study *A Midwife's Tale*. The book won Ulrich a Pulitzer Prize for history and was later made into a public television documentary. The diary itself has recently been published in its entirety for the first time.[1]

Martha Ballard was just shy of fifty years old in January 1785 when she began, apparently for the first time, to keep a diary. From then till her last diary entry on May 7, 1812, shortly before she died, not a day seems to have passed without a comment of some kind, even if it was merely a note about the weather or a birth or death in the Maine frontier community that she served as midwife and what we would today call a visiting nurse or paramedic.

Mrs. Ballard came to Maine's Kennebec valley in 1777 from Oxford, Massachusetts. Her husband Ephraim, a miller and surveyor, had arrived in Maine two years earlier, part of a broad movement out of the older, more settled parts of Massachusetts that was interrupted only briefly by the Revolution. After his wife and five children joined him, Ephraim settled his family along the banks of Bowman's Brook where it empties into the Kennebec in Hallowell. There he rented land with a gristmill and saw mill, and Martha raised their children (the youngest, Ephraim Jr., was born in Hallowell in 1779), planted her gardens, gathered herbs and simples like balm o' Gilead, buckthorn, and mallow, and composed her diary. In the spring of 1791, the Ballards moved down river a ways, and later they went to live on land that was part of their son Jonathan's farm, but essentially they were residents of this growing river community throughout the twenty-seven years of the diary.[2]

Maine was still a backwater of Massachusetts when the Ballards came to live there, and Hallowell was a frontier village of log houses, although it was beginning to be well settled with a meeting house, wharves, a couple of stores, and by 1777 a population of some one hundred families on both banks of the river. Ephraim Ballard was not alone in seeking out cheap land and abundant resources in the Maine backcountry. As the 1790 census showed, the population of the District of Maine had increased by 40,000 since the end of the war; two hundred new towns were established between the Revolution and 1820, when Maine became a state. Thus, the years covered by Martha's diary were extraordinarily busy and productive, for Martha herself as much as for the growing community that she served. Along with the births and deaths that she assisted, she also paid discreet attention in her diary to local scandals (noting, for instance, the male parentage of illegitimate babies, as the tradition of midwifery obliged her to do), crimes and misdeeds, and arrivals and departures from as far afield as Boston and New York. But events of the greater world beyond the Kennebec intruded only rarely in the pages of her diary, and even then it is necessary to read between the lines to understand that when, for instance, she writes of her husband's surveying team beset by "men they knew not" and robbed of compasses and documents, the reference is to an ongoing struggle between, on the one hand, landed proprietors who controlled vast stretches of Maine wilderness and, on the other, settlers or squatters attempting to lay claim to territory.[3]

Food historians examining Martha's diary may also find it necessary to read between the lines. There is not a recipe to be found, nor any instructions that give a hint about how she or any other woman prepared the cornmeal and flour that were ground in Ephraim's mill, the fruits and vegetables that came from her garden, the veal calves and swine that were slaughtered on a regular basis. But she notes what she planted, when she harvested, days of brewing and baking, of churning and cheese-making, and, although cooking was apparently a minor interest in her busy life, when guests arrived for tea, coffee, or chocolate, "roast chickins," or a "line [loin] of veal."

This work, like the wool she spun and the cloth she wove, or that was done under her direction, was not incidental to what we would call her "real" job as a midwife. Indeed, although midwifery was an important source of cash and barter income, the "real" work of Martha Ballard and women like her throughout North America, was in providing sustenance for their families twelve months a year at a time when outside sources of provisions were hard to come by, especially in winter when the ground was frozen iron hard and the ice-clogged river was no longer a trade route. As in other frontier communities, Hallowell had to be self-sustaining, and within Hallowell, individual families had to be self-sustaining too. And most of that sustenance was the result of women's work. It is difficult to put an economic value on that work until we remember that without it, families might well have starved.

"The girls Baked & Brewed," Mrs. Ballard says on many occasions, indicating either her own two daughters or, after they had married and moved on, the hired girls who helped out, and from this we understand the intimate yeasty connection between baking bread and brewing beer—but we don't know whether the girls were making corn bread, wheat bread, or—most likely—the mixture that thrifty New England housewives called thirded bread, a third cornmeal, a third rye, and a third wheaten flour.

Once her own daughters, Hannah and Polly (her eldest, Lucy, had married before the diary begins), had set up housekeeping on their own, Martha relied on a series of young women from within the community, nieces and daughters of friends and neighbors, most of whom came to live with the Ballards during their time of service. The immediate reason for this, of course, was the need for an extra pair of hands with household tasks like brewing, baking, or setting up the warp for a piece of homespun cloth. But beyond the obvious, it was also a way of extending and strengthening bonds within the community, and it was a way to train young women in the multitude of skills they would need as they too grew up, married, and established households of their own. In no sense were these "girls" treated as servants. Juniors in the household, yes, but otherwise in the same position vis-à-vis the senior Ballards as their own daughters had been. Why, then, didn't they stay home and train with their own mothers? The answer, I believe, lies in the development of the concept of adolescence and post-adolescence. At a time in their lives when young women are testing their own independence, the mother-daughter relationship, even when most loving, can be fraught, and this is no modern phenomenon.[4] Quite possibly, sending a girl to live with a trusted neighbor or relative was the equivalent of sending her off to boarding school, a way of defusing the situation for both mother and daughter and helping both to arrive at a comfortable situation that would maintain the closeness of the family bond while permitting the girl to grow into a more independent role.

The economy of frontier communities like Hallowell was a complex mixture. Subsistence farming supplied most family needs; at the same time, small export crops, wood products, for instance, or grain, provided cash money, and an assortment of small-scale skills and crafts, such as midwifery in Martha's case and surveying in her husband's, also brought in extra cash or commodities. An intricate bartering system governed the exchange of goods and services among neighbors. For her assistance at a birth or an illness, Martha was often paid in foodstuffs, sometimes as common as a couple of pumpkins or a barrel of rye flour, but sometimes exotic or difficult to obtain—rice, a packet of India tea, chocolate, a brace of pigeons, or a bottle of brandy or rum. (Once, as a special present for a special service, Martha was given "an oreng.") Like Ephraim Ballard, many farmers dealt in lumber, cutting timber and ripping logs not just for home and building construction but for ship-building, soon to become a major industry on the Maine coast, and for export to the Caribbean. Cordwood was shipped to fuel city fireplaces, tanbark was important for the leather industry, and woodash went to make potash or pearlash for various uses, including soap-making and, a more recent discovery, as a leavening for baked goods.

Ephraim and his sons kept the saw and grist mills going, but this was an economy in which women played an equal, if officially subservient, role to men. Martha, and her daughters as they married and established homes of their own, kept poultry for meat, eggs, and feathers (to stuff pillows, mattresses, and quilts), milked and pastured cows, made butter and cheese for the family larder and for sale outside, spun flax and wool and wove fabric, kept vegetable and herb gardens, and converted produce into pickles and pantry staples for the winter. But the Ballards were not entirely self-sufficient, and both cash and barter went to obtain coffee and tea, molasses, pepper and salt, garden seed, tobacco, sugar, and fish. (Though upriver, Hallowell was still within the tidewater of the Kennebec, and the Ballards had good access to cod, both fresh and salt, smelts in season, and smoked herring.) Purchases of commodities like flour, apples, potatoes, wheat, and corn (whether for seed or for home use) were common, despite the fact that these were all produced by the family or their neighbors. Martha frequently mentions making cheese, but almost as frequently she speaks of buying it at one of the stores at "the Hook," the commercial center of the community.

There is no evidence that Martha Ballard, or anyone in her community, acquired or even knew of the slim 47-page booklet of recipes and household hints that was published in Hartford, Connecticut, in 1796. Amelia Simmons's *American Cookery* was apparently the first American cookbook, although American editions of English cookbooks had been published in the colonies. As such, it was a modest attempt to define, for the first time ever, the content of a new, thoroughly American branch of the domestic arts, and it was apparently greeted with great success, for two editions were published in 1796, a revised edition came out in 1800, and successive editions were published in the years that followed.[5]

Cookbooks, as I noted above, are not always the best evidence for what people eat or how they prepare it. Instead of recording the way people live, cookbooks represent an ideal that the author hopes, for one reason or another, will be achieved. Nonetheless, putting together the information from Martha Ballard's diaries and Amelia Simmons's cookbook, we can see some way into this world of two hundred years ago. In a brand new country, with a brand new and highly developed sense of commonwealth, of national identity, of civic and patriotic pride that at times bordered on outrageous jingoism, it was natural that a national cuisine, a style of cooking unique to this seaboard collection of former colonies, should, like American music and American speech, be an integral, identifying part of the evolving national culture.

What makes the Simmons cookbook unmistakably American is the presence of food products and processes that were also part of Martha Ballard's kitchen and garden, of her food world if you will, products such as corn, pumpkins, squash, potatoes, and cranberries in particular—all products of the New World that were still little known in much of Europe. Cooking techniques using the open hearth and the bake oven were still the same ones that had evolved over centuries in northwest Europe, but they too were beginning to change. The black cast-iron kitchen range, the stove that warmed country kitchens and dominated the memories of anyone who grew up in rural America before about 1935, was still some years over the horizon, although the first patent would be issued in Philadelphia during Jefferson's administration in 1808.

Wheat had long been the favorite bread grain of the English; as such, it was grown, or attempted, throughout the colonies. But in the northeast yields were low, especially compared to corn, and pests and diseases were always a problem; already by 1800, wheat cultivation was on the decline, replaced by cornmeal as the staple, even for breads. The Ballards still grew wheat, and bought it, and Martha often baked wheat-flour ("Flower") bread, but that may reflect their status as millers with access to grain. Corn occupies a far more prominent place in the diaries, both as a garden crop and as a pantry staple.

But what did Martha Ballard do with the corn and cornmeal, which was purchased by the bushelful when their own supplies ran low? Can we assume it was an ingredient in the Brown Bread she baked so often? Lydia Child's recipe for Brown Bread, published a few decades later, calls for half Indian and half rye, though some, she says, prefer one-third Indian and two-thirds rye.[6] Did Martha also make Indian pudding with her Indian meal? Amelia Simmons gives us three recipes for this— a rich one with eggs, raisins, butter, and sugar; another with molasses and spice; and finally one that is simply Indian meal steamed in a quart of sweetened milk. As for Johnny cake, that nearly archetypal American cornmeal product, there's not a mention of it in the diaries, although Martha does make herself Hasty Pudding once when she feels unwell, and Hasty Pudding, Mrs. Child reminds us, is best made with Indian meal.[7]

Along with apple and mince, pumpkin pies were favorites in the Ballard household. Not a baking day went by, it seems, without pies being put in the oven. One wonders if they were eaten only as a dessert at the end of the meal or if perhaps they were sometimes a main course for supper, with a piece of cheese on the side—as they still were in old-fashioned homes in my Maine childhood. Miss Simmons's pumpkin recipes are listed under puddings, but she is really talking pies since the "pudding" is baked in a crust—and very familiar pies, too: the combination of pureed pumpkin with cream, eggs, molasses, allspice and ginger would happily grace a Thanksgiving table to this day.

(Incidentally, although Christmas is mentioned but three times in twenty-seven years and always en passant, without any sense of feasting, Thanksgiving is always noted in Martha Ballard's diaries, sometimes very simply: "It is Thanksgiving day." The holiday is invariably marked by a gathering at the meeting house, and it was often the occasion for a family feast as well. On December 1, 1803: "We roasted a goos, boil[d] Beef, Pork and fowls for Diner." And on November 30, 1809, when Ephraim and Martha apparently dined alone: "My Child[n] Sent us in pies."

Many of the staple, standard vegetables and fruits mentioned in *American Cookery* would have been as familiar to any continental European cook of the day as they are to modern Americans: seven kinds of green peas, six kinds of kidney beans, broad beans (listed as Windsor beans or horse beans) and chickpeas ("calivanse" or garbanzos), asparagus, cauliflower, carrots and parsnips, potatoes, onions, beets, cucumbers, lettuces and cabbages, radishes, artichokes (meaning Jerusalem artichokes, an American native), horseradish, watermelons and muskmelons, grapes, currants, pears and apples. "Garlicks" are mentioned but, Simmons says, though they are much used by the French, they are "better adapted to the uses of medicine than cookery."

At one time or another, Martha grew most of the vegetables described by Simmons. But she also grew peppers (possibly only for medicinal use—she says they are an antidote to colic) and garlic (for cooking or medicine—probably both), and she mentions plums, quinces, gooseberries, damsons, and cherries, whether her own or from the orchards of her neighbors. Rhubarb was another familiar fruit that grew well in this northern climate, though it too may have been more for medicinal than for culinary purposes. And twentieth-first-century gourmets who claim credit for "discovering" new varieties should note that Martha mentions blue potatoes and both purple and sweet corn flourishing in her garden. Because she was a midwife, which meant that she also served as something of a paramedic, particularly for the women of her community, Mrs. Ballard grew a great variety of medicinal herbs, some of which may also have been used in cooking—she planted coriander, anise, mustard, and camomile, and several times speaks of harvesting saffron or providing it as a medicine.[8]

Baking was a regular activity in the Ballard household, often accompanied by brewing, since similar yeasts were used for both bread and beer. Mrs. Ballard's oven was probably built, like most New England ovens, into the brick wall of the fireplace. If the fireplace was located on an outside house wall, the oven could be accessible from both inside and outside the house in order to make baking day more comfortable during the hot summer months. Even the humblest European-American home had a hearth of some sort—it would not have been considered a home otherwise—but not every home had a bake oven. Many of Martha's neighbor's—Mrs. Forbes, Mrs. Savage, Mrs. Williams, and Mrs. Vose—baked in her oven from time to time, exchanging the use of the oven for other goods and services, and Martha earned cash money one summer when she baked for a neighbor, Captain James Purrinton. (That was in 1803, several years before he shocked the little frontier community one night by murdering all his family saving son James, who "fled in his shirt only," as Martha recorded it.)

Cakes of compressed yeast did not become available until the late nineteenth century. Cooks might rely on a type of sourdough, keeping back part of the dough from each baking to start the next batch, but in households where beer was produced, barm, the frothy residue kicked up when brewing, was also used to raise bread. There were other nostrums made with hops or potatoes or both that would entice the wild yeasts drifting on the air. (One such combination required that potatoes be boiled and strained and their water reboiled and used to steep dried hop flowers. Then the potatoes were mashed and the strained hop liquor poured over. The mixture was thickened with a little flour, salt, and sugar or molasses, then set aside to host wild yeasts and start the process all over again.)

By the time Amelia Simmons's cookbook was published, another form of leavening was coming into general use, one that, as Mary Tolford Wilson has pointed out, was to "revolutionize European cookery as well."[9] Pearlash, a refined form of potash, was added to doughs and batters to lighten them and produce a faster rise—an early indication of the persistent American motif of fast food, food that was quick and easy for busy women to assemble and put on the family table. *American Cookery*, the first cookbook to mention pearlash, recommends it to leaven cookies and gingerbread. A form of potassium carbonate obtained by leaching wood ashes, pearlash or potash was a valuable commodity produced throughout colonial America and exported for use in glass-making, among other industrial purposes. It was also a critical ingredient in soap-making and for bleaching finished cloth, two uses that were familiar to Mrs. Ballard. She made soap periodically as a matter of course, soap being vital in all aspects of home and personal maintenance. And as a weaver, she was adept at whitening her fabric by soaking it in a potash solution. It would be false to conclude from this that, knowing the uses of potash, she "must have" used it in baking too, but the mention of pearlash in Simmons's cookbook means it is not without possibility in Martha Ballard's kitchen as well.

Mrs. Ballard was almost single-handedly responsible for her vegetable gardens, a responsibility that seems only to have increased as she grew older. It was Martha who cleared the ground in spring, Martha who pulled the winter banking away from the warm east side of the house to prepare the soil for the first little seeds to go in, Martha who planted potatoes, sowed seed, transplanted cabbage "stumps" (plants that had been wintered over in the cellar and set out in early spring to provide fresh greens and seed for the succeeding year's crop), Martha who saved seed and even sold seed to other gardeners. And of course Martha was responsible for the harvest and for putting it by, pickling it, salting it, drying it, to provide for the long months of winter. Ever the frugal housewife, she speaks in one entry of making vinegar from pumpkin parings.

Day by day, in the month of May 1809, here is what Martha did in her garden: set turnips and cabbage stumps; planted cucumbers and three kinds of squash; again, planted squash and cucumbers; prepared a bed and planted more squash seeds; again, planted squash, also cucumbers, muskmelons, and watermelons; planted "long" squash; dug holes and planted three quince trees; planted two more quince trees and an apple tree; planted potatoes; set out lettuce plants and strawberries (the squash and cucumbers planted on May 15 were already up a week later, she noted); sowed "string peas"; planted "crambury," brown, and hundred-to-one beans; set out—that is, transplanted—squash plants; again, set out squash plants and cucumbers. Mr. Ballard helped with the digging and set the poles for Martha's hop plants, whose flowers were a source of yeast for brewing and baking, but Martha did everything else. While doing so in that month of May she also tended a sick neighbor, delivered four babies (including one of her own granddaughters), brewed ale, baked bread, boiled soap, ironed, and did the normal run of housework. That year she was seventy-four years old.

Ulrich, Martha's biographer, calls attention to "the intricate horticulture that belonged to women, the intense labor of cultivation and preservation that allowed one season to stretch almost to another."[10] In this day and age, when we have lost, suppressed, and abandoned so many of the skills of our past, we would do well to remember the importance of gardening, especially in women's lives and in reckoning women's sense of their own worth and worthiness as providers rather than mere consumers. Not only do we not cook much anymore, we no longer know much of anything about growing our own food. Put to the test, most of us would fail. Yet the good food that we know was so prevalent in America until perhaps the middle of the previous century was the product of more than just skilled hands in the kitchen. It was the outcome of skill, patience, care, and attention paid in the garden too.

Martha's skill and diligence in the garden and the kitchen meant that the Ballards were never without food on the table, as the epigraph to this essay indicates. Sometimes it was plain food, but there is only one indication in the diary that it was ever without abundance. That was late in April 1785, when the river had remained frozen far later in the season than normal: "A Great Cry for provision. no Vesils arived yet. ye ice run this Day," she writes, reflecting the community's dependence on river traffic to maintain supplies.

We don't often know the details of what Martha Ballard put on her table; there are no recipes in the diary, not even the kind of notes about seasoning or cooking time that can help a skilled cook reconstruct a recipe, despite the many notations about cooking and sharing food and the extra mouths at the table, guests who came for a meal or to spend a few days. Was Martha a good cook? Did friends and family look forward to her table, to a chicken pie like the one, rich with butter and gravy, described by Amelia Simmons, followed by a custard of eggs and cream, warm from the oven and fragrant with nutmeg and cinnamon? Alas, we'll never know because not once does she provide us with anything like a reference to cooking procedures, a suggestion of flavoring, let alone a recipe. Yet it's impossible to read Martha Ballard's diaries without coming away with a sense of the importance of food in women's lives—its importance in establishing and strengthening bonds within the community and at the same time in giving recognized worth and dignity to the lives of women, not just in frontier communities but throughout the young republic.

Notes

1. *The Diary of Martha Ballard, 1785–1812*, ed. Robert R. McCausland and Cynthia MacAlman McCausland (Rockport, ME: Picton Press, 1992); Laurel Thatcher Ulrich, *A Midwife's Tale* (New York, 1990).

2. In 1797, north Hallowell, where all the Ballard homes were located, broke away to become Augusta, now the state capital.

3. Diary, November 15, 1795, discussed in Ulrich, *A Midwife's Tale*, 209.

4. James Henretta and Gregory Nobles, *Evolution and Revolution: American Society, 1600–1820* (Lexington, MA, 1987) (quoted in Harvey J. Graff, *Conflicting Paths: Growing Up in America* [Cambridge, 1995]), speak of the early nineteenth century as precisely a time of "the appearance of a recognizable experience of adolescence" along with the development of age-related peer groups and peer culture. The reasons, too complex to go into here, are discussed in Graff, 26 et seq.

5. Amelia Simmons, *American Cookery*, facsimile of the first 1796 edition published as *The First American Cookbook* (Oxford University Press, 1958; rpt. New York: Dover, 1984), with a very useful introductory essay by Mary Tolford Wilson.

6. Lydia Maria Child, *The American Frugal Housewife*, 12th ed. (1832); facsimile (Cambridge: Applewood Books, n.d.), 76–77.

7. Simmons, *American Cookery*, 26; Child, *American Frugal Housewife*, 65. Indian

pudding was so called *not* because it was an Indian recipe, but because the main ingredient was Indian meal, or cornmeal.

8. I should call attention to another Maine herbalist, nearly a century later, Almira Todd of Dunnet's Landing, so beautifully described by Sarah Orne Jewett in her story "The Country of the Pointed Firs," published in 1896.

9. Wilson, in Simmons, *American Cookery*, xiii.

10. Ulrich, *A Midwife's Tale*, 324.

Cooking to Survive: The Careers of Alice Foote MacDougall and Cleora Butler

BARBARA HABER

What could these two women possibly have in common—Alice Foote MacDougall, a high-born New Yorker who opened a chain of popular Manhattan restaurants in the 1920s and '30s, and Cleora Butler, a Black cook from Oklahoma who mostly worked for others during the same period and for another fifty years? As different as they were in class and race and regional origin, they were yet representative of a number of American women who called upon their skills in cooking and selling food to support themselves and their families, and who won some measure of success and fame for their efforts. Both wrote autobiographical works that tell their stories—Alice Foote MacDougall, *The Autobiography of a Business Woman* (1928), and Cleora Butler, *Cleora's Kitchens: The Memoir of a Cook & Eight Decades of Great American Food* (1985). The lives of such women are only now being claimed by scholars and other serious writers, but for a while their stories were the stuff of popular culture—and especially of romantic novels and movies that created distorted and often demeaning images of women who made careers in food.

Perhaps the best-known fictionalization of such women's lives was one that appeared during the Depression and was actually inspired by the life and career of Alice Foote MacDougall. This was Fanny Hurst's *Imitation of Life* (1933), about the struggles of two widowed mothers, one a white business neophyte who opens an Atlantic City diner, the other an African American cook she befriends and whose recipes she uses to start an international chain of home-style waffle shops. The book was twice made into a movie, first in 1934 with Claudette Colbert as the white entrepreneur whose restaurants make her a multimillionaire and Louise Beavers as her undemanding Black partner who is content to draw a modest salary and supply an Aunt-Jemima image for the company. The same characters and plot reappeared in a 1959 remake of the movie, except that the successful waffle-shop magnate was transformed into a famous actress played by Lana Turner. (Evidently the food business was not considered glamorous enough for a star like Turner, whose coifed hair and elegant wardrobe would never have held up in a restaurant kitchen.)

Both Hurst's book and the Hollywood weepers it spawned include a subplot that contrasts the privileged life experienced by the daughter of the wealthy white heroine and the misery felt by the African American woman's light-skinned daughter who tries in vain to pass for white. Nor does money bring much happiness to the main characters in either the novel or movie versions of *Imitation of Life*. If anything, their stories send out a depressing message about women's lives that permeated popular American fiction and films in the first half of the twentieth century. Simply stated, the message was that women who pursue careers outside of the home can rarely if ever find love and fulfillment, and that those who do must first expect to suffer loneliness and despair. Hurst's successful businesswoman never remarries—a man she finally falls in love with winds up engaged to her daughter—and the African American mother and daughter in the novel experience more than their share of sorrow and regret. With these two characters, the author evidently wanted to condemn racism and discrimination in America, showing how hard it was for Black women to overcome their color and become more than faithful mammies, maids, and cooks. Yet so offensive did the poet Langston Hughes find the book's portrayal of African Americans that he wrote a dramatic parody of the novel entitled "Limitations of Life."[1]

Such criticism notwithstanding, popular culture of the period steadily perpetuated images of unhappy career women who can't hold on to their men and long-suffering but cheerful Black servant women who "know their place" and never aspire to more. These were stereotypes that would stop showing up in movies and television only in the aftermath of the civil rights and women's rights movements in the 1960s and 1970s. By that time, Louise Beavers had made a lifelong profession of playing comical African American domestics in well over a hundred movies. (One of her last but best-known enactments of the racial caricature came in the early 1950s, when she played the title character, a family cook, in the TV sitcom *Beulah*.) Joan Crawford had similarly become typecast as a dissatisfied female careerist in a number of movies, most notably in *Mildred Pierce* (1945), where she played another rich but unhappy restaurant-chain owner, this one burdened with a ne'er-do-well, spendthrift boyfriend and a hopelessly spoiled daughter.

These racial and sexual stereotypes were almost certainly a reaction to the threat that strong, independent, and successful women posed at the time to the sensitivities of men, if not also to women who were committed to marriage and domesticity. For the fact is that well before the Depression and certainly during hard times in the thirties and early forties, numbers of enterprising American women were striking out on their own to support themselves and their children when they could no longer count on men to be sole breadwinners. And some of these women, Black and white, were achieving success and some measure of personal fulfillment in their work, a few even becoming rich or famous or both by trading on their cooking skills or competing in the male-dominated fields of food distribution and restaurant ownership.

This was the case with Alice Foote MacDougall. By the time she became the model for Fanny Hurst's successful restaurant franchiser, MacDougall was already a minor national celebrity whose story was widely publicized during the 1920s.[2] In *The Autobiography of a Business Woman* MacDougall described how she was born into a wealthy New York family and later married a promising coffee wholesaler, but was left a widow at forty with no money to speak of and three very young children to support. Her riches-to-rags-to-riches story describes how this upper-class woman who had no work experience and no marketable skills nevertheless managed to create a career for herself in a segment of the New York commercial world that no other woman had hereto-fore dared to enter. MacDougall began by succeeding where her husband had failed, in the male-dominated wholesale coffee business, and then went on to establish popular coffeeshops in the city and still bigger, more ambitious restaurants that were known as much for their exotic European ambiance as for their food.

Until recently, the achievements of African American cooks like Cleora Butler were lost to history, leaving only racist images that found their way into cookbooks as well as novels and movies. Typical of the condescension that reduced Black women cooks to anonymity was a foreword to Alice Foote MacDougall's first cookbook, *Coffee and Waffles* (1926), by Charles Hanson Towne. "The old Southern mammies who were unable to write down their priceless recipes had an almost divine intuition concerning the dishes they concocted," wrote Towne. "Through their own kind they passed their good things on to us; but they were inarticulate as to how they accomplished those menus which were fit for the banquets of Lucullus."[3] Such sentiments echoed in countless southern cookbooks that likewise conjured up nostalgic im-ages of bandana-headed African American kitchen workers but never named a single Black cook and often never conceded that such women created the recipes contained in the cookbooks. "Publicly I acknowledge an everlasting debt," wrote John Fox, Jr., in his introduction to *The Blue Grass Cookbook* (1904), "and to the turbaned mistress of the Kentucky kitchen gratefully this Southerner takes off his hat." But neither Fox nor the recipe compiler, Minnie C. Fox, quite made it clear that many of the recipes were created by the "turbaned mistresses" and not the named white contributors to the cookbook.[4] The same is true of Celestine Eustis's *Cooking in Old Creole Days* (1903), whose introduction by S. Weir Mitchell also invokes the familiar stereotype of the African American cook: "a fat woman of middle age, with a gay bandana kerchief about her head—proud of her art, somewhat despotic, and usually known as Aunty."[5]

Even when cookbooks began to credit African American women as originators of their recipes, white compilers rarely failed to mention how hard it was to extract precise directions from Black contributors when their approach to cooking seemed so innate and unscientific. In *200 Years of Charleston Cooking* (1930), editor Lettie Gay exemplified this tendency to belittle African American cooks as inarticulate primitives, women who felt their way through a recipe and would hardly know what to do in a modern kitchen.

> The difficulty in getting a Charleston recipe, we found, is not always due alone to the unwillingness of the cook to part with her secret. Her cooking instinct knows no rules, no measures. She is far more likely to conjure her oven than to use a heat control device. She wouldn't know what to do with a thermometer, but by hunches she knows when to take a boiling syrup off the stove. To translate hunches, a fine mixture of superstitions and a real knowledge of cookery, into intelligible recipes is no easy task. . . .[6]

It is only within the last twenty years or so that cookbooks have finally been compiled by articulate Black women like Cleora Butler. More than supplying recipes, Butler rescued African American cooks from anonymity and demeaning stereotypes when she told her story and that of her family in *Cleora's Kitchens*. For generations, Butler and her mother, Maggie Thomas, gained a reputation for their skills by working for wealthy white families in oil-rich Oklahoma, where they regarded themselves and were regarded as respected paid professionals, no matter how close and friendly they became to their employers. Throughout the Southwest, moreover, their cooking became practically legendary among African Americans, so that mother and daughter were regularly called upon to cook for celebrations in their own community and for famous Black entertainers like Cab Calloway and his band whenever they visited the region. Butler also went on to establish her own successful pastry shop and catering business in the course of a long eventful career that she vividly described in a cookbook that is also an illustrated family history.

Born more than thirty years apart and into radically different social milieus, Alice Foote MacDougall and Cleora Butler nevertheless deserve comparison as determined, self-reliant women who simultaneously embodied and defied the prevailing stereotypes of women who made careers in cooking and food. In spite of her success and the satisfaction she took in her achievements, MacDougall remained true to her "anti-suffrage, anti-feminist proclivities," a self-declared "mid-Victorian" who believed that neither she nor any other woman should have the vote or aspire to be anything but a wife and mother. In making such statements, MacDougall never took into account the many American women who never had the luxury of being fully supported by a protective male or even expected that that would ever be the case. Such a woman was Cleora Butler, who knew from her parents' and grandparents' experience that whether or not she married, she would have to earn a living, and who did so with joy and professional pride for most of her long life. She also found ways to deal with racial discrimination in Oklahoma in the years before the civil rights and women's rights movements began to fight on behalf of all Black women. It was on their own terms and not as part of any militant collective effort that both MacDougall and Butler found ways to survive and succeed, overcoming obstacles they chronically faced on account of their race or sex or the economic conditions of their day.

The frontispiece for *Alice Foote MacDougall's Cook Book* (1935) is a photograph of the author as a dowager sitting primly in her Victorian living room where she is surrounded by an elaborate silver tea setting and platters of delicate cookies and scones. She might have stepped out of an Edith Wharton novel. The photograph perfectly captures this New York socialite long bereft of her birthright of old money and upper-class entitlements but still possessed of hauteur and noblesse. One would never know that at this stage of her life, she was fighting to save her restaurant empire from the ravages of the Depression.

In her autobiography, MacDougall described how she was born for better things in 1867 in the Washington Square home of her great-grandmother, whose husband was a former mayor of New York City. MacDougall's equally well-born father, to whom she was blissfully devoted ("my first and perhaps my only great love"), was a Wall Street financier and bon vivant who regularly stuffed the young girl's purse with money and took her with him as he fraternized with other members of New York's social elite.

> Papa took great pride in his wine cellar. He was accustomed to having wine at dinner always, not so much for himself as for the many English and French gentlemen who were his constant guests. After our drive, Commodore Vanderbilt, Frank Work, Charles Lanier, Mr. Harbeck, or some other gentlemen would return with Papa to our home on Eleventh Street. Then Papa would set out his choicest wines for their delectation—brandy fifty years old, filling the room the moment it was uncorked with a delicious, indescribable aroma, whisky, sherry, port, all choice and very old. Conversation sparkled and the open fire glowed, but not more warmly than did my father as he thus entertained his friends.[7]

MacDougall's father also took his family on his many business trips abroad, where they hobnobbed with prominent Europeans and dined in Old World restaurants whose atmosphere MacDougall would later attempt to duplicate in her Mediterranean-style restaurants, to which she gave names like Firenze and Piazzetta. Her mother, on the other hand, provided a model of good housekeeping that contrasted with her husband's and daughter's impulsiveness but came in handy when Alice MacDougall later took on the mantle of restaurant owner: "You could tell the time of day by what the maid was doing. If Jenny was brushing the fourth step of the front stairs, you could lay your last dollar that it was ten-thirty a.m.; and as sure as it was Thursday night, so did we feast on chicken. Order and method carried to its nth degree—a little of a strain for irregular Papa and me, but excellent of the smooth running of the house."[8]

The first stage of the family's social decline began when her father's overconfidence somehow caused him to fall from financial grace.

> The wolf came to our highly respectable door, and Papa went from one mad venture to another in the get-rich-quick hope, only to be baffled, beaten at every turn. And I, his constant companion, shared this misfortune in the blind, uncomprehending way of a young girl, suffering the tortures of a profound sorrow over the incomprehensible trouble of my darling father. Night after night I lay awake, weeping and worrying, unable fully to understand, magnifying the danger, powerless to help, impotent to avert the approaching catastrophe.[9]

Worse was to come when her husband, Allan MacDougall, a handsome and successful New York coffee broker fourteen years her senior, also suffered failure that his wife felt was caused by some "inherent weakness of his nature" but which looks from her description like clinical depression. "No longer was there the smile, the alert address toward the duties of life—rather a slinking, pathetic fear and a slow relinquishment, not alone of responsibility, but of all happiness and joy."[10] As with her father's downfall, Alice MacDougall vividly describes her all but overwhelming feelings of fear and desperation, including a momentary impulse toward suicide, but discreetly forbears to tell how her husband died save for saying that he left her badly in debt with three young children. Only elsewhere do we learn that he succumbed to throat cancer in 1907.

Throughout her *Autobiography*, self-pity alternates with self-congratulation, as when MacDougall describes her reasons not to seek employment as a secretary or retail sales clerk but to start her own business, using what little she already knew about the coffee business from her husband's career.

> I was forty, and the years had taken their toll. Hysteria and insomnia racked me day and night. I had no business training or business knowledge of any kind. My entire capital was $38. My expenses were $250 a month. My assets were three little children.
>
> Why, then, did I choose business instead of a salaried position?
>
> I chose coffee because it was a clean and self-respecting business. No friend, however much he might love me, would buy or drink bad coffee. Therefore I would be free of the stigma of charity.[11]

MacDougall's husband and his family had been in the coffee business as jobbers, dealing in green coffee only. However, she remembered that shortly after her engagement, Allan MacDougall had roasted small amounts of rich aromatic South and Central American coffees whose taste contrasted favorably with the standard Java-and-Mocha mix that was then being sold by New York's major wholesale grocers. It was from her husband's superior blend that MacDougall began her own coffee supply business.

> It was so rich and delicious in flavor, so economical and satisfying, that even before we were married I begged Allan to go into this branch of the business and distribute roasted coffee direct to the consumer. He laughed at the idea, but the conviction remained that there here was a means of livelihood. When necessity demanded some activity on my part, I decided upon the roasted-coffee business.[12]

In November 1907, Alice MacDougall rented a small, dark room that months earlier had been offered to her husband on Front Street, then the commercial center of the city. Here she learned to taste and test coffee and master the rudiments of doing business among merchants who resented her presence and fully expected her to fail. "There was much antagonism to me on the Street," she recalled: "I was a dreadfully ill woman, and the men gave me 'six months.' At the end of that time they expected me to disappear as unexpectedly as I had arrived, and one can scarcely blame them."[13] In spite of these dread predictions, Mac-Dougall managed to get credit, buy and blend her coffee, and distribute five hundred letters advertising her new enterprise to friends and relatives. Then, when orders came, she ground the coffee by hand and delivered it herself in ten- and twenty-pound packages, sometimes slogging through rain and snow, and occasionally entering through the back doors and basements of homes that formerly welcomed her as a social equal.

Though she took pride in not asking for help beyond buying her wares, MacDougall got some timely financial assistance from one of her father's friends, a prominent banker who early on in her struggle gave her a thousand-dollar bill that she used to pay her outstanding debts. More often than not, however, MacDougall was served by little more than her indomitable will and self-confidence, as when, knowing nothing about cocoa, she took on a large order of both coffee and cocoa from the director of fresh-air camps run by a New York newspaper for poor urban children.

> From that day and for many after, cocoa salesmen led a weary life and my digestion all but passed away, for I tasted cocoa sweet and cocoa bitter; cocoa fair and cocoa most indubitably foul; cocoa made with xxxx sugar, and cocoa less proud, sweetened with God knows what. But by June large drums of cocoa, as well as bags of coffee, went to the Fresh Air Fund, and I had the satisfaction of knowing that I had lowered the price, bettered the quality, and supplied the little children of the New York slums with a pure and helpful drink.[14]

MacDougall not only succeeded in handling a growing mail-order business, but she took risks as a female commercial traveler and successfully sold her coffee to a variety of customers at some distance from New York City, including hospitals, hotels, clubs, and colleges in the New England area. That she often had better luck at men's colleges like Williams than Smith College and Bryn Mawr only confirmed Mac-Dougall's contempt for the idea of female emancipation and the suffrage and feminist movements of her day. She blamed her rejection by female buyers at the women's colleges on their susceptibility to the flattery of salesmen and their timidity in purchasing from an untried vendor of their own sex: "my admiration of college intellect outside of scholastic matters had a severe blow, and my opinion concerning women in general and a certain type of college woman in particular was strengthened."[15]

MacDougall subsequently turned her anti-suffrage convictions to her own account by gaining a reputation as a "conservative among women" among her customers, most of whom she knew to be similarly inclined. At the same time, she decided to cash in on the sentiments surrounding the movement to give women the vote, and did so by the simple expedient of changing her company's name from "the obscure A. F. MacDougall" to "the glory of Alice Foote MacDougall." Subsequently, she got an order for ten pounds of coffee from a suffragist leader and was still happier to find that "there were many kindly souls, men and women, who, not occupied by big reforms, could assist a woman struggling for another kind of independence, and with the establishment of my identity as a woman the business leaped forward to definite success."[16] Still later, in 1920, MacDougall was able to appeal to men and women equally when she changed the name of her company to Alice Foote MacDougall and Sons, Inc. By that time she had recruited her two sons, Allan and Donald, to serve as president and vice president respectively, and made herself chairman and treasurer of the company.

The year before, MacDougall had opened what would become the first of her uptown restaurants, the Little Coffee Shop in Grand Central Station, as a place to advertise and sell her company's products, which by then included cocoa and tea as well as her mainstay, coffee. The shop got off to a slow start until customers asked to taste her coffee and MacDougall set up tables and chairs for the purpose, turning the place into a small bistro. She also decorated the shop with brasses and blue-white china that she also began to sell, along with attractive pottery, glassware, leather gifts, and basket ware that she imported at low cost from postwar Europe. In addition, she made Wednesdays her "at home" days when she served customers directly, creating a friendly informal atmosphere. The turning point for the success of the shop and for MacDougall's career as a restaurateur came on a bleak, winter day in 1921 when she decided to make and offer free hot waffles to busy commuters. The story is told in several places but most characteristically in *Alice Foote MacDougall's Cook Book*:

> That funny first bowl of batter! Never can I forget my erratic impulse and its surprising result. Remembering the misery of some of my early days when, totally unprepared for storm, I tramped through a raging blizzard and spent the day wet and chilly as a result,

or when, poverty-stricken, I made my own lunch of a hearty glass of cold water, I decided on a blizzardy day one February to practice a little bit of the Golden Rule and do as I had *not* been done by. The waffle iron came by taxi to the Little Coffee Shop in the Grand Central. The batter was made and cooked—and the waffles *given* away that cold wintry day. Entirely unpremeditated was the impulse. Startling was the result. A bowl of batter in a place 12 feet by 16 feet in February. 1921—six large Restaurants and a business amounting to about $2,000,000 in February, 1927![17]

It is hard to tell from her account whether her decision to make and give away waffles was truly a spontaneous act of charity and good will or a shrewd marketing idea that was certain to win new customers for her coffee. Either way, the waffles worked, for she claims that soon her establishment was serving coffee and waffles every day and "turning people away by carloads."

The following year, the father-in-law of one of her sons provided a large loan that allowed the company to open a second and even more successful coffeeshop a block from Grand Central. Here, the necessity of installing a ventilating system gave rise to another marketing ploy and the expansion of the new shop's menu.

When we opened Forty-third Street we had a pantry but no kitchen, for we intended to serve nothing but coffee and waffles, and these were cooked in front of people's eyes on tables made especially for waffle irons. The ugly hood used to deflect steam and smoke from these tables was quickly turned into what we called a waffle house—a latticed, three-cornered-cabin affair under which a colored maid stood, suggesting the Southern-waffle, colored-mammy, log-cabin idea. Within a short time, however, we expanded our original plan of serving merely waffles and coffee, adding first sandwiches and then all of the delicious foods we could think of. In March, four months after our opening, we served eight thousand people with three full meals a day, and by August 1923 we took on more space, doubling our seating capacity less than a year after opening.[18]

It is easy to see from this passage where Fanny Hurst found the prototype for her waffle-shop franchiser in *Imitation of Life*. Mac-Dougall's own empire building began in earnest in 1923 not long after she returned from a recuperative visit to Italy, where she was inspired to change the décor of her southern-style coffeehouse on Forty-third, turning it into a indoor replica of Mediterranean courtyards and naming it The Cortile. Two more Italianate establishments followed in the same part of the city, called The Piazzetta and Firenze, and, finally, there came the Sevillia, a Spanish-motif restaurant with Moorish trappings and waitresses wearing mantillas and crimson Iberian costumes. Some two thousand customers were served the Saturday after the opening of this largest of the Alice Foote MacDougall Restaurants, which featured an Alhambra Room, an Early Renaissance Room, and a Wine Shop when Prohibition ended in 1933.

The ambiance of her restaurants notwithstanding, their menu remained as American as the maple syrup that adorned the tables. Hardly a recipe contained in either of her cookbooks includes anything close to Italian and Spanish cuisine. Instead, she offers directions for making canapés with peanut butter and chopped bacon, black bean soup, corn chowder, chicken fricassee, hamloaf, and for dessert such standbys as gingerbread, pineapple upside down cake, and tapioca pudding. As much as their menu, it was the atmosphere of MacDougall's eating places that appealed to her mostly female clientele, who were drawn to the ambience of far-off places while all the while stuck in the middle-class neighborhoods of Greater New York.

Among the ladies' luncheon set, MacDougall became a New York icon whose personal appearances at her restaurants were greeted with the same expressions of excitement and appreciation received nowadays by celebrity chefs. But beyond making waffles, her cooking skills were practically nil, as the former socialite was almost proud to admit. "Now I am not a cook," she declared in *Coffee and Waffles* (1926), anticipating former President Nixon's denial of criminality: "I am first of all a mother. When I became one I could make delicious salted almonds. That was all."[19] In *Alice Foote MacDougall's Cook Book*, the author's inability to bake is likewise seen as a badge of honor: "No one in my family can ever boast of the cakes, or bread, or pie, that 'Mother made' as I have never made any. Love of my family, if nothing else, would prevent me." In the same spirit, after a visit to Italy and its famous pastry shops, MacDougall further admitted that where cooking was concerned she had little knowledge or curiosity:

> Glad would I be if I could explain to you the process by which this or that dolce is made. By what combination of wine and water; of flour and sugar; of essences and seasoning the wonderful result is obtained, but since my days in Italy have been fully occupied with other interests, I must content myself with those dainties of home-bred type that have long satisfied a family each of whom has, as they say, "a sweet tooth."[20]

In lieu of cooking and baking expertise, MacDougall had a feeling for what kind of food her customers felt most comfortable with and how to serve it attractively in a romantic atmosphere that blended European elegance and American cleanliness and efficiency. She knew instinctively that running restaurants had as much to do with show business as with fine cooking and proper management. In 1929, MacDougall demonstrated that she had learned much about the food service business when she published *The Secret of Successful Restaurants*, a book addressed to women but offering any prospective restaurateur a practical and detailed approach to every aspect of opening and operating a profitable restaurant. MacDougall's guide even includes an appendix that recalls her mother's punctilious housekeeping by providing the hour-by-hour schedules she set for her kitchen managers, service managers, and hostesses.

Even as MacDougall offered to show women the way to duplicate her success, she characteristically advised them to think twice about going into the business, suggesting that such an ambition can be confused in women's minds with a more normal desire for homemaking. At the same time, at the peak of her own success, she claimed to have a special sympathy for the conflicting claims of careerism and domesticity that she saw in women of her time and no doubt in herself. And just as characteristically, she assumed that all women had the luxury of making such a choice.

Unfortunately for MacDougall, her attempt to reach that ineffable goal that she herself seemed to be striving for as a woman was curtailed by the Wall Street Crash that took place the same year *The Secret of Successful Restaurants* was published. What caused the collapse of her restaurant enterprise was not only the general economic downturn but a long term million-dollar lease she had signed for her last and largest restaurant, the Sevillia. The catastrophic effects of this business decision are alluded to at the very end of *Alice Foote MacDougall's Cook Book*.

> For twenty and more years, through sheer necessity, I have battled in the arena of so-called business life. By God's mercy, I met with a certain success. Then came crushing disaster, and now once again I am climbing that steep and arduous business ladder, step by step, rung by rung. It's a big fight. It's full of zest. But it is cruel. Each day I envy that woman whose "place is in the home." That is why, perhaps, toward the end of a strenuous life, I am offering to other women A Cook Book [*sic*].[21]

By the time, she wrote these words, her restaurants had gone into receivership, and MacDougall, at the age of sixty-five, was obliged to resume personal control. Within four months, she managed to increase business by 50 percent and was able to repurchase her first two restaurants, the Little Coffee Shop and the Cortile, but the Alice Foote MacDougall Restaurants finally succumbed to the Depression, and MacDougall herself was left to be supported by her older son, Allan, who abandoned the coffee business and became a buyer of wines and spirits for National Distillers.

Despite her frequent proclamations that she would have preferred a life of elegant leisure as the wife of a wealthy man, someone like her father, she took pardonable pride in building her business and gave others hard-won good advice about how to run their own restaurant operations. As early as the 1920s, she had the prescience to see what changes were being wrought in national dining habits and what new roles restaurants were beginning to play in the lives of busy Americans in the cities and suburbs, observing that restaurants were taking their places as substitutes for the home as places of leisurely gatherings. Her ability to supply a feeling of intimacy in well-run eating places where American home cooking could be mixed with a sense of the foreign was the key to her brief success and considerable personal celebrity as an American businesswoman.

To the modern reader, Alice MacDougall often comes across in her floridly written books as supercilious and self-dramatizing, sometimes even somewhat bigoted and prejudiced against her own sex. In the end, however, she deserves credit for her courage, hard work, and creativity in building a business that supported her family and hundreds of employees whom she evidently treated well and fairly even though her strict rules and regimented restaurants must have been demanding.

Cleora Butler could also lay claim to a family tradition in food, one in which the women gained a measure of fame for their cooking, unlike earlier generations of Black cooks who remain mostly anonymous. Butler came from an African American heritage that included former slaves who became landowners first in Texas and later in Oklahoma. Before the Civil War, her great-grandmother, Lucy Ann Manning, served for many years as a house cook on a large plantation near Waco, Texas, where she and her husband Buck had migrated with their owner from Mississippi. Following emancipation, her great-grandfather was given a tract of land by his former owner and in turn gave fifty acres to each of his seven children. (Only parenthetically does Cleora Butler mention that Buck Manning's former owner was also his father, suggesting how common was the practice of plantation owners begetting illegitimate children by their household slaves.) Besides working his land, Cleora Butler's grandfather, Allen Manning, had to put to use some of the kitchen skills he had learned from his mother while his wife attended to their eleven children, the oldest of whom, Mary Magdalena or Maggie, would become Butler's mother. "It was natural that, as the oldest, Maggie was required to assist in the Manning kitchen and, in time, to take full responsibility for it," her daughter observed. "Maggie was quick in developing the talent that established her as one of the finest cooks in northeast Oklahoma."[22]

While cooking for so many may have added to her mother's skills, Butler believed that it may have come as a relief for Maggie to accept the proposal of a local farmhand, Joseph Thomas, though in fact Allen Manning would not give up his daughter (and her cooking) for another five years. The couple's marriage took place in 1898, at which time they moved into a three-room house provided by Thomas's employers, a young Waco doctor and his new wife, and Maggie Thomas began doing the cooking for the couple. "The closeness in age of Joe and Maggie to their employers soon led to a friendship that transcended the normal employer/farmhand relations of the day," Butler remarked. In fact, her mother and the doctor's wife exchanged cooking and sewing skills, so that Maggie Thomas also became a fine seamstress and was able to pass this additional talent on to her daughter.

Cleora Thomas was born in 1901 into a new era when children of her race in America had no personal recollection of slavery and when the newly opened Indian Territory held promise for African Americans of free land and further independence in totally Black townships. The young girl left Texas with a large wagon train that included her parents, her widowed grandfather and his new wife and remaining children, sisters and brothers of her father, and a number of other farmhands, all hopeful of opportunities in what would soon become the state of Oklahoma. "Dad was confident," she recalled, "as was Mother, who knew her cooking and sewing skills would always be on hand if outside income was needed."[23]

Most of the migrators settled in Muskogee where Maggie Thomas did in fact make dresses and other garments for wealthy families in the area. However, she stubbornly refused to turn the money she earned from her sewing into a family coffer presided over by her father, with the result that the Thomases built and lived in their own house. There at the age of five and a half, Cleora Thomas made her first attempt at cooking dinner from leftover slices of pork liver while her mother was giving birth to a baby brother. Later, at ten, the young girl successfully baked her first batch of biscuits using a new baking powder and cookbook supplied by Calumet, and two years later she began a series of kitchen forays inspired by witnessing her mother's success in baking and selling cakes.

When I was twelve, the time spent in the kitchen at my mother's side was the most precious to me. I watched as she magically mixed liquids and powders, added dashes of pepper and salt (plus assorted and crumbled leaves that I learned were called spices), placed them inside or atop the stove and produced marvelous concoctions that invariably tasted yummy. The apparent ease with which she cooked convinced me that turning out cookies and cakes must be a pushover.[24]

Her mother's inspiration notwithstanding, the child's first attempt at baking a cake was judged by her brothers to be a failure and was buried in the back yard in what she would call "the dough patch," a graveyard for failed experiments that subsequently included "the molasses caper."

My efforts at blending sorghum molasses and flour to make cookies resulted in a solid sheet of gummy residue. My tasters, Walter and Joey, refused outright to even smell it. So adamant were they that they snitched to my mother about the secret dough patch. Mother was furious. She started out giving me a tongue lashing, but some-where in the middle of it began to laugh and laughed till she was weak. She told me to stick to making good biscuits and to experiment only when she was there to guide me.[25]

Among the affluent people for whom her parents worked was Harriet Weeks, the sister of Oklahoma's first governor, and the Weeks family generously left their house to Joseph and Maggie Thomas when they left Muskogee. The northeast section of Muskogee in which the Thom-ases lived had belonged to a Black man before it became the site of mini-farms with livestock in the early 1900s and later a purely residen-tial area. Here Joseph Thomas farmed his own land, took care of the family livestock with his sons, and milked cows for other families in the neighborhood, while his daughter helped her mother perform house-hold tasks that included work in the kitchen and delivery of Maggie Thomas's valued baked goods.

We were pretty self-sufficient. Dad's work at the Weeks' provided cash for store-bought items and, to help along these lines, Mother baked and sold bread to families in about a five-block area around our house. Starting on Friday evenings and throughout most of Saturday, we'd all pile into the wagon and make deliveries. As we pulled up to each house, my brothers and I would run up to the door, make the delivery, and collect twenty-five cents for each loaf. This, mind you, was when a loaf of bread could be purchased for a nickel in the store.[26]

Maggie Thomas also staged "cook-ins" during the winter months in which she would ask her children what kinds of cookies or desserts they wanted and then see to it that sister and brothers alike were taught how to make the treats properly. "Learning to be self-sufficient, especially in the kitchen, was something Mother insisted upon for all of her children," Cleora Butler recalled "We didn't mind it a bit. After all, it was a family tradition."

Though the young girl also learned from her grandfather, who had a special talent for preparing hog meat and making pork sausages, her special bond was with her mother, whose cooking began to win awards in Oklahoma and caused her to be hired by some of the best hotels in Muskogee.

> My mother was not only my first teacher, but, without reservation, the best. I always marveled at how she turned out so many delicious dishes on a wood-burning stove. Mother mastered things like popovers, cream puffs, all kinds of cakes—from plain pound to angel food—and won blue ribbons at the state fairs. Of course, I used the same kind of stove when I started, but would hesitate to do so today, now that I have become accustomed to the plethora of devices designed to help out in the kitchen. When I use my blender, mixer, or Cuisinart, I think of what a thrill my mother would have gotten using them. Late in life, long after she had established her reputation as an exquisite cook, she did use some of the appliances that became available on a limited basis when she worked as a pastry chef at Sever's hotel in Muskogee and in the same capacity at the Ambassador Tea Room when the family moved to Tulsa in 1925.[27]

Cleora Butler never stopped feeling privileged at having her mother as her teacher: "Throughout my young life, she filled me with confidence and taught me that cooking was a fine art. Foodstuffs were but raw materials—the sculptor's stone, the artist's paint, the musician's instrument. Mastering the art of cooking rested on following the basic directions of a recipe (reading it four or five times if necessary), then improvising where desired. I learned early that 'dumping and stirring' could be hazardous to your results."[28]

At the age of fifteen, the future cook and caterer also received formal instruction in cooking at Muskogee's Manual Training High School, where her class was chosen to prepare a meal for members of the Muskogee Board of Education. The success of the meal insured the job of her young instructor, Lucy Elliot, the sister of a prominent local clothier who was president of the Oklahoma State Negro Business League.

(Years later, when Cleora Butler looked back over her seventy years as a cook, she recalled that the most memorable affair she ever catered was the silver anniversary of her former high school teacher. She recollects that the affection and appreciation she felt for that teacher, and not the menu, was what meant the most.) Upon graduation, Butler left with an affluent friend for Oberlin Junior College but had to quit after her first year when, as it seems, her family could no longer afford the tuition. She was overjoyed when her friend married the son of a well-to-do rancher of Creek Indian and African American heritage but worried about her own future when for a time she wound up cleaning floors at Muskogee's Central High School instead of cooking for a living, as she wanted to do.

In 1923, at the recommendation of an aunt, she found her first job as a cook for a family in Tulsa, which by the mid-1920s had become the social and commercial center of Oklahoma. "It was *the* place to be." Butler recalled. "One black entrepreneur had reportedly moved to Tulsa and opened a bank account with $75,000 *in cash*! Everybody was caught up in the high style of living that was characteristic of the entire nation."[29] Four of her closest friends followed the young woman to the city, and in 1925 her parents also moved to Tulsa, to which her father had been commuting as a cook, he too following the family tradition. Once settled in, Maggie Thomas, who had been coming to the city occasionally and sewing for her daughter's employers, began to work as pastry chef for the newly opened Ambassador Tea Room.

The first sign of the crash to come occurred when the family for which Butler was working had to dismiss her following the failure of a Mexican silver mine in which they invested all their cash reserves. For a time, the young woman freelanced as a caterer, serving at many farewell parties for Tulsans whose fortunes were lost, before she found work with the family of a busy oil worker. In spite of the nation's need for oil, jobs had become scarce in Tulsa and breadlines started to form, but her parents continued to find work and receive support from their daughter and sons, one of whom had begun playing saxophone for the Cab Calloway band. "Times may have been tough," Cleora Butler remembered, "but the Thomas/Manning clan was holding its own."

The collapse of the stock market also caused changes in the way that Tulsa's African Americans entertained themselves.

Tulsa's black community had felt the effects of the financial crash long before October of 1929. Money had already become scarce on the north side of town, where most blacks lived, and unemployment had been growing since 1927. Still everyone loved parties and a good time as much as they ever did, even though few could afford to throw a bash for even four or six friends. Our way around this was for everyone to bring something. We'd get together and brew our own beer. Then each would bring his or her share of ingredients for the planned menu. It always turned out to be an exciting evening.[30]

Cleora Butler observed that such BYOB parties also became popular even among the wealthier white population. "Their parties were perhaps more grandiose than those we had, but I know they were never more fun."

As their fortunes rose, the oil worker's family for which Butler was working purchased one of the most elegant houses in Tulsa where, by coincidence, her mother had been working for the former owners. Between 1932 and 1940, the younger woman cooked hundreds of meals and prepared or supervised countless parties, including the elaborate reception for a young bride who had married into her employer's family. Cleora Thomas was herself married at the end of this period to George R. Butler, a hotel worker who had been courting her for several years. However, her most vivid memory of this time was the visit of the Cab Calloway orchestra in June 1937, which occurred simultaneously with the World Heavyweight Championship fight in Yankee Stadium between Joe Louis and Max Schmeling, when Louis knocked the German boxer out in the first round. "The blacks of North Tulsa literally danced in the streets," Butler remembered. "This was a most special occasion. We didn't often get a chance to cheer about anything, let alone a hero of our own." Following the radio broadcast of the fight, the victory was celebrated with fried chicken and homemade ice cream by family and friends of the Thomases and Mannings and members of the visiting Calloway band. Nor was this the first time Cleora Butler and her mother cooked for visiting Black musicians. Whenever bands came to town conducted by the likes of Cab Calloway, Duke Ellington, Count Basie, and Jimmy Lunceford, the groups played separately for whites and African Americans and stayed in Black hotels and homes. Butler's saxophonist brother Walter customarily brought Calloway to his parents' home, after which the band leader never stopped raving about the cooking skills of his saxophonist's mother and her daughter.

For a while, Butler's marriage prevented her from working full-time, but the advent of the Second World War created new opportunities:

In 1942 Tulsa was gearing up for war. There were parties galore, especially beginning when most everyone thought the whole thing would be over in a matter of months if not weeks. When sons and daughters, fathers, uncles and aunts were going away, people said,

"Let's have a party!," so I did a lot of catering during that period. I've always felt it was a little like returning to the roaring twenties. There were parties all over the place. Parties for departing soldiers and sailors and a lot of parties for no specific reason at all.[31]

In 1944 Cleora Butler again began working for a prominent Tulsa family but left after a few years, this time to take care of her father-in-law, who had developed cancer and required constant care. In the early fifties, apart from occasional catering, her cooking career took a back seat to nursing duties, but she took up another career that had begun a decade before when she experienced racial discrimination at a hat sale in an exclusive downtown Tulsa department store.

> While society in the 1940s had changed to the point where blacks could shop in a few white establishments, it was not usually permitted for one to try on clothing, especially hats and shoes. Occasionally, you might be permitted to try on a hat, but you were given a hand mirror and shown to a back room where "preferred" customers could not see you trying on your selection.
>
> The hat I wanted was exquisite, so despite the horrible treatment, I purchased it. In fact, I bought two, but left the store infuriated and totally resolved never to buy another hat as long as I lived. Because of my continuing passion for hats, however, I found a way out of my problem. Research turned up a millinery correspondence school in Chicago, in which I immediately enrolled.[32]

Butler's solution was typical of her can-do attitude, and in no time she mastered the millinery craft and was able to supply her North Tulsa friends with hats that she could sell for as much as $50 each.

Even after Tulsa department stores began to abandon their pattern of segregation and discrimination, Butler continued her home millinery business, along with occasional catering since cooking and especially baking were always closest to her heart and she was always being called upon to cook for Tulsa's social elite. In the mid-fifties, she also took a job as a stock clerk in a dress shop, where she learned the rudiments of running a business and became friendly with people at every level of Tulsa society. When the store closed in 1961, Cleora Butler decided to start her own business so that in April of the following year, with a loan from the Small Business Administration, she and her husband opened Cleora's Pastry Shop and Catering. Like her millinery enterprise, the idea of a pastry shop had been hatching since the 1940s when she supplemented her family's income by selling small pies for five cents apiece in her father-in-law's billiard parlor. With her mother's help, she had been baking some 150 pies a day in her own kitchen, and later, just before she opened her shop, a contact from the dress shop resulted in orders for her to bake batches of tarts each week for a lunchroom in South Tulsa. With this experience in production baking, Cleora Butler felt ready to run a pastry shop of her own.

The couple expected that the work would be hard but were not prepared for running a business with limited help. Their work day began at six a.m., and after a full day of making doughnuts, pies, and cakes, they would finally return home at nine p.m.

Take-out chili and hamburgers were added to the shop's bill of fare, and bread soon followed at customers' insistence. Sourdough French bread became a favorite after one customer supplied Butler with the ingredients for making a starter and taught her all she knew about baking the bread. The sourdough recipe proved particularly successful and was especially favored by a customer who bought the bread as part of a weekly ritual:

> One of my North Tulsa friends would come into the shop every Thursday evening, just as our bread for the next day' sale was coming out of the oven, to purchase a loaf of our sourdough bread for the family for whom she worked. Each week she would also buy a second loaf for herself, but before she would let us wrap it, she'd break open the top of the loaf with her fingers. Reaching into her purse, she would withdraw a stick of butter, push it down into the still warm loaf and hand the bread back to us for wrapping. This, she allowed, was her weekly treat, to herself.[33]

At the same time that large orders of food were coming in from work crews building the Turner Turnpike through Oklahoma, the catering side of the business began to expand rapidly with calls from the Tulsa Opera Guild and the Tulsa Philharmonic auxiliary to serve at special parties and brunches. Only when it became obvious that her husband, who suffered from diabetes, could not keep up with the pace did the enterprise close down in 1967 and Butler began to nurse him, as she had his father, until he succumbed to his disease in 1970. After her husband's death, Butler began slowly to rebuild her catering business, serving food first to a local school and church, and eventually remodeling her kitchen to accommodate the increased business that her reputation had attracted over the years in Tulsa and Muskogee. Her best memories of this period, other than the silver anniversary of her old teacher, was the picnic she prepared for the family and friends of the childhood friend she had gone to college with and who had married into a family of successful African American oil industrialists. She took pride in the fact that her friend's husband had served for years as president of the Oklahoma NAACP and had drilled the first successful oil well in Africa.

The differences between Alice Foote MacDougall and Cleora Butler go deeper than class and race and regional origin. They have as much to do with the fact that one was a talented businesswoman who almost never cooked or wanted to, and that the other was a talented cook who made cooking her business and her means of self-fulfillment. As much as their memoirs, the recipes they left behind are evidence of their essential approaches to life, the kind of people they were, and the way they connected with others.

"While I had never cooked a meal myself, I taught others to do so," MacDougall proudly claims in *Coffee and Waffles*.[34] For all her trips to Italy, she found garlic to be "insinuating" and declared that "many a happy day in Europe . . . has been ruined by that little vegetable." (Salt and pepper were her favorite seasonings, with paprika and bay leaves making an occasional guest appearance in her dishes.) She does, however, extol the virtues of olive oil, but only in connection with green salads if you don't count her recipe for "Sauce Napolitana," which does contain olive oil, a little garlic, and Parmesan cheese but is Americanized with a cup of tomato catsup.

Concern with the attractiveness of food and the need for frugality during the Depression led MacDougall to offer recipes for canapés that make use of almost any scraps one can find in the refrigerator so long as they are served on bread cut into fancy shapes. At the same time, her first three canapé recipes call for caviar, paté de fois gras, and Roquefort cheese—not quite what one would expect to find in middle-class refrigerators of the day. The contradiction is most apparent in the first chapter of MacDougall's *Cook Book* called "Reflections on Waste but Not Wasted Reflections" where she offers money-saving suggestions for roast beef leftovers—re-warm it, serve it chopped on toast, slice it in a salad—that are salvaged from nothing less than a ten-pound rib roast, first cut! Clearly, MacDougall wants to have it both ways—to show us that she too has had to scrimp and save but also that she still knows her way around haute cuisine and could afford expensive cuts of meat.

In contrast, Cleora Butler saw food as a sensual pleasure and cooking as a way of sharing love with the many people who mattered in her life. She was also able to grow and develop as a cook, so that her account of the eight decades of great American food includes not only traditional regional dishes of the Southwest but stylish dishes of the 1970s and '80s that introduced new ingredients and combinations of food into American kitchens. Her earliest recipes were for dishes she learned from her mother such as hickory nut cake (with nuts that were gathered on the mountain behind her grandfather's house), burnt sugar ice cream, grated sweet potato pudding, and corn fritters. In later years, she was cooking rice pilaf with pine nuts, buckwheat cakes with chicken livers, tomato-mozzarella salad with red onion and anchovies, jalapeno corn bread, and a macadamia nut chess pie.

When Cleora Butler describes her food memories, she speaks about how dishes tasted and smelled as well as how they looked. She vividly describes the yams she ate in childhood, which oozed syrup as they came from the oven. Her most vivid recollections of food are inevitably tied to family and friends, as when she described the wedding she catered for her childhood friend. "That summer afternoon was sheer intoxication for me," she recalled. "I gave my utmost to the preparation of the baked ham, filet of beef and fried chicken, of course, but the opportunity of putting my talents to use for the children of my old friend gave me a complete sense of fulfillment."[35] Most telling was Butler's willingness to sacrifice her career to the care of the people she loved, inevitably making do with less during critical times.

Alice Foote MacDougall and Cleora Butler not only achieved a measure of local fame but managed also to make some lasting contributions to the world of food and the history of their times. Still worth reading today is *The Secret of Successful Restaurants*, MacDougall's detailed guide to running an efficient and profitable eating place. And even her unsurprising recipe collections tell us much about New York dining in her time, and about the difficulty restaurants had in reconciling fine dining and Depression austerity. Cleora Butler's book likewise preserves an important part of the culinary and cultural heritage of the American Southwest by giving us many African American regional recipes and a unique account of more than a century of Black family life in Texas and Oklahoma. More than anything else, however, their writings recall two remarkable women who managed to make creative, fulfilling lives for themselves in the world of food, although that world represented such different experiences for each of them.

Notes

1. Langston Hughes, "The Limitations of Life," in *Black Theatre U.S.A.*, ed. James V. Hatch (New York: The Free Press, 1996), 331.

2. Helen Josephine Ferris, *Girls Who Did: Stories of Real Girls and Their Careers* (New York: E. P Dutton, 1927).

3. Alice Foote MacDougall, *Coffee and Waffles* (Garden City, NY: Doubleday, 1926), viii.

4. Minnie C. Fox, *The Blue Grass Cook Book* (New York: Duffield, 1904).

5. Celestine Eustis, *Cooking in Old Creole Days* (New York: R. H. Russell, 1903), xiv.

6. Lettie Gay, ed., *200 Years of Charleston Cooking* (New York: J. Cape & H. Smith, 1930), xv–xvi.

7. Alice Foote MacDougall, *The Autobiography of a Business Woman* (Boston: Little, Brown, 1928) 10.

8. Ibid., 26.

9. Ibid., 40.

10. Ibid., 43.

11. Ibid., 51.

12. Ibid., 52.

13. Ibid., 55.

14. Ibid., 74–75.

15. Ibid., 84.

16. Ibid., 87.

17. Alice Foote MacDougall, *Alice Foote MacDougall's Cook Book* (Boston: Lothrop, Lee, and Shepard, 1935), 201.

18. MacDougall, *Autobiography of a Business Woman*, 125.

19. MacDougall, *Coffee and Waffles*, 26.

20. Alice Foote MacDougall, *The Secret of Successful Restaurants* (New York: Harper & Brothers, 1929), 37

21. MacDougall, *Alice Foote MacDougall's Cook Book*, 268.

22. Cleora Butler, *Cleora's Kitchens; The Memoir of a Cook & Eight Decades of Great American Food* (Tulsa: Council Oak Books, 1985).

23. Ibid., 21.

24. Ibid., 24.

25. Ibid.

26. Ibid., 29.

27. Ibid., 34.

28. Ibid., 35.

29. Ibid., 40.

30. Ibid., 43.

31. Ibid., 48.

32. Ibid., 52.

33. Ibid., 55.

34. MacDougall, *Coffee and Waffles*, 26.

35. Butler, *Cleora's Kitchens*, 58.

Women under Siege: Leningrad 1941–1942

DARRA GOLDSTEIN

Who can measure the trauma of differing wartime experiences? Suffering is relative and unquantifiable, and comparisons can seem tasteless, even disrespectful. Yet even if suffering cannot be quantified, human deprivation can be. Starvation is a matter of simple subtraction: Below a certain number of calories per day, the body begins to consume itself, and several universal physiological consequences ensue. First come listlessness and apathy. As the body grows emaciated, the skin assumes an unhealthy pallor and stretches tight against the bones. Often the body becomes bloated, with fingers and toes so swollen that even buttoning a coat is difficult, and walking an ordeal. Gums bleed; the body is covered with open sores that refuse to heal. Certain psychological symptoms are also universal enough to be considered chemical. Starvation tends to reduce us to a primitive, "dehumanized" state in which our only concern is to find food.

The experience of the siege of Leningrad shows that even when facing starvation, people will fight to keep their humanity intact. And though their heroism was not always voluntary, women were the acknowledged saviors of Leningrad. Admittedly these women had a physical advantage over men: their better-insulated bodies enabled them to endure greater privation, at least initially. But something else was at play, which had more to do with nurture than with nature. Women's traditional familial and social roles made the crucial difference in their ability to negotiate through the seemingly endless days of the siege. Their primary impulse to focus first on their families helped them to overcome the forces of inertia, both physical and psychological, during the nine hundred days of extreme deprivation when continuing to live seemed pointless and irredeemably bleak. While it would be erroneous to imply that all women behaved nobly during the siege—numerous cases document the selfish, even savage, behavior of some—women made sacrifices that often proved life-saving, both for themselves and for others. The very fact of their femaleness arguably helped the women of Leningrad to survive the terrible blockade of the city.

In the United States and Great Britain the preferred wartime attitude of women was an admirable pluckiness coupled with an enthusiastic embrace of innovation: If sugar and eggs are in short supply, we'll still bake our cake, we'll simply use substitutes! This positive ideal presupposes the availability of a certain basic amount of foodstuffs, with which people can afford to be creative. Leningrad women had to be creative beyond measure. Tested by want, they searched their apartments for edibles in the forms of tooth powder, Vaseline, glycerine, cologne, library paste, and wallpaper paste, which they scraped from the walls. They tore books apart and gave their children the glue off the bindings. Hardship demanded innovation, but it was hardly light-hearted. In wartime Britain, butter and eggs may have been scarce, and flour dark and heavy, but people did not starve. Such cookbooks as Ambrose Heath's *Good Food in Wartime* insist that many prewar recipes "by some very slight adaptation to present needs, can still appear with success upon our war-time tables, not quite up to their pre-war form perhaps but certainly more than merely presentable."[1] The British Ministry of Food worked hard to educate housewives in wartime economy, providing information about unfamiliar products like dried egg powder and recipes for belt-tightening meals. Thus the Ministry's Food Facts No. 331 suggests a "Swiss Breakfast," a highly nutritious muesli touted as "a delicious change from porridge."[2] One might argue that Britain's wartime exigencies actually broadened people's palates by introducing them to a wider range of foods once they had to forgo their beloved bacon and eggs.

Though it is a commonplace that the nurturing of the family falls largely to women, the extent to which women will sacrifice their own well-being for their family's has not been fully examined. One wartime study in Britain showed that mothers regularly gave their husbands and children the best food from their own plates,[3] and the women of Leningrad largely did the same. But amid widespread hunger, against the absolute limits of human endurance, such acts of maternal self-sacrifice become something other than noble. During the German siege of Leningrad, which lasted for nearly nine hundred days, over one million people died of starvation and related causes; nearly 200,000 died in February 1942 alone.[4] The resourceful women of Leningrad painstakingly retrieved old flour dust from the cracks in the floorboards and licked decades of spattered grease from the kitchen walls, savoring it slowly.

The question of how much food to share was problematic, and in ways we can't fully imagine. If a mother had children who were slowly wasting away, her inclination was to feed them first, above all. But it was also imperative that the woman keep up her own strength in order to take care of them, especially if they were young. If she didn't survive, how would they? Hunger weakened one's ability to think logically, to calculate in any meaningful way. The world seemed blurry; the small piece of bread on the table represented all that was tangible. Should the mother give her children extra food from her own meager ration, or should she try to conserve her strength to hold the family together?[5] The women of Leningrad were forced to face these questions daily, and the simple answers were all deadly. Two-thirds of the city's civilian population during the siege was made up of female office workers, housewives, children, and the elderly[6]—groups whose food allowances were considerably smaller than those of factory workers or front-line soldiers; consequently, a decision concerning 50 grams of bread could (and did) mean the difference between life and death.

Before examining the ways in which women fought to survive, we must understand the constraints under which they lived. The siege effectively began on September 8, 1941, when German forces cut off all land access to Russian-controlled territory; it ended only on January 27, 1944, with the breaking of the German blockade. Like other Russians, Leningraders had been on war rations ever since the German invasion began on June 22. As in England, these rations created hardship without much urgency. Factory workers were entitled to 800 grams of bread a day,[7] while office workers received 600 grams, and dependents and children under twelve were allotted 400 grams—somewhat less than one pound. Still, most people were able to supplement the bread rations with meat, grains, fats, and sugar. On September 2, however, as the German forces closed in on the city, the bread ration for factory workers in Leningrad was reduced to 600 grams a day, with office workers receiving 400, and dependents and children only 300 grams of bread, or about three-quarters of a pound.

In the first week of September, the Germans began to shell Leningrad. An emergency inventory of the city's food supplies revealed that there were only enough grain and flour reserves to last the civilian population for thirty-five days.[8] The situation worsened on September 8 with the bombing of the Badaev warehouses, where stores of flour and sugar were kept. Although workers managed to salvage much of the molten sugar, the flour was a total loss. Authorities responded by cutting the bread ration further, to 500 grams for factory workers, 300 grams for office workers and children, and 250 grams for dependents, including housewives, whose tasks were arguably more strenuous than those of office workers.[9] But it soon became clear that even this curtailment was insufficient to feed the population with the flour remaining in the city's storehouses. And so the allowances were reduced even more drastically, culminating in the November 20 ration of 250 grams of bread a day for factory workers, and only 125 grams of bread—a mere two slices—for all others.[10]

Technically these bread rations should have been supplemented by other foods, but in that first fall and winter of the blockade nothing else was available, or available only sporadically. Thus the bread ration was the only guaranteed source of nourishment. If you were too weak to go to the designated store to receive your daily ration, and if you had no one to trust with your card, you got nothing to eat. In an effort to conserve food supplies, the authorities strictly controlled the issuing of ration cards. If your card was lost or stolen, it could not be replaced. The reality was as simple, and as harrowing, as that. A small piece of cardboard determined your fate.

Even when the bread ration was safely brought home and divided among the family, what sort of nourishment did it provide? Traditional Russian rye bread is famous for its rich, sour flavor, its dense texture, and its high nutritional value. But because ingredients were so scarce, the proportion of flour used in the siege loaf was continually revised. In mid-September, oats that had formerly been reserved for horse fodder were added to the commercial bread recipe, as was malt, which previously had been used in the production of beer (the breweries were now closed). By late October the percentage of malt used in commercial loaves was increased to 12 percent, and moldy grain that had been retrieved from a ship submerged in Lake Ladoga was dried out and added to the dough.[11] The taste of this loaf was extremely unpleasant. Yet even these fillers were not sufficient, and in late November, when minimum rations dropped to 125 grams of bread, the composition of the standard loaf was set at 73 percent rye flour, 10 percent "edible" cellulose, 10 percent cottonseed-oil cake (*zhmykh*), 2 percent chaff, 2 percent flour sweepings and dust shaken out of flour sacks, and 3 percent corn flour.[12] The seemingly high proportion of rye flour masks the fact that the dense fillers made this siege loaf 68 percent heavier than a normal loaf of bread. Thus from their 125-gram ration people effectively got only 74.4 grams of nourishing rye flour. And while the cottonseed-oil cake originally intended for cattle fodder did contain protein, the "edible" cellulose was not digestible. Dmitri Pavlov, who oversaw Leningrad's food supplies during the siege, writes that "the bread was attractive to the eye, white with a reddish crust. Its taste was rather bitter and grassy."[13] But others who survived on this bread are less gentle in their assessments. The bread was so damp and heavy that "when you took it in your hand water dripped from it, and it was like clay."[14] It appeared "greenish-brown ... , half wood shavings."[15] "Nothing was issued but bread, if you could call it that. Those four ounces on which life depended were a wet, sticky, black mash of flour waste products that fell apart in your hands."[16]

In 1997, when visiting St. Petersburg's new Museum of the History of Breadbaking, I had the experience of tasting siege bread. The museum director, Liubov Berezovskaia, accommodated my request to find out more about wartime bread by asking a survivor to bake me a loaf. Unlike the traditional round Russian loaf, siege bread was rectangular in shape. In order to incorporate as many additives as possible, the bread had to be baked in pans, since free-form loaves would not hold together.[17] The bread was heavy and pale in color, its texture rather crumbly, yet gummy on the tongue. Most memorable were the sensation of chewing on sawdust and the splinter of wood that pierced my mouth. Swallowing even a small piece required considerable effort.

Picture a mother with two children, whose husband is away at the front. As is typical for most Russian families, her elderly mother lives with them. This woman is one of the lucky ones—she has a factory job that affords her the highest category of rations, while her children and mother receive only the third, or lowest, category. Yet she lives in fear that her strength will give out and she'll lose her good ration along with her job. It is late November 1941. For a week now her family has had almost nothing to eat but two slices of coarse bread a day. They survive on the factory dinner she brings home. Each day she goes to the canteen at work and receives an ample portion of thin soup. She drinks the liquid from the top of the bowl, then carefully transfers the bits of grain and cabbage left in the bowl into a jar she's brought from home. This hot liquid doesn't relieve her hunger, and it makes her legs swell, but at least she has something left for her family.[18] Her mother has grown too weak to move; in fact, she is like another child who needs tending.

Her children spend all day in the apartment, waiting listlessly for her return. She tries to focus on her work, but it's difficult. She has to get up at six in the morning because most of the trams have stopped running. She stands in a long line at the bakery for the family's bread ration and brings it home, then drags herself several miles to work on swollen legs through streets that have not been cleared of snow. Every day she sees heavily swaddled figures swaying along the narrow footpaths. She can recognize the goners from their shuffling gait, and every day she worries whether to follow them or pass them by. The moment that they fall is the worst. They crumple and drop. She wants to stop—it's the humane thing to do—but she has no strength to help them. So she tries to make her way past them, stepping around them, not over them, and never looking at the pile of cloth itself, lest an arm reach up or a pair of eyes implore. Bodies lying in the street no longer concern her; it is the ones still in motion that cause her pain. The woman concentrates on each step, trying not to think about the people inside the other bundles of clothes, or even about her family at home. It is the darkest time of year, with only five hours of daylight, when even daytime seems like twilight because the sun hangs so low in the sky. The apartment is very dark. Ever since September the windows have been covered with plywood to protect against air raids; weak blue lights have replaced normal bulbs in an effort to conserve energy.

Then on December 9 the electricity is shut off throughout Leningrad; there isn't enough fuel for the power stations. Only a few commercial bakeries and factories are kept running. People pin phosphorescent patches onto their coats so that they won't bump into each other in the dark. The woman's factory has closed down; she has lost her worker's rations. Now her family of four must make do with only 500 grams—a little over a pound—of bread a day, with no supplemental soup from the factory canteen. Even though she no longer has to walk miles to work, continuing to live feels impossible. With no electricity, there is no heat. The pipes have frozen and burst. The plumbing no longer works. Panic flutters in her chest. The woman reminds herself that her family is luckier than most: they at least have a *burzhuika*, a primitive wood stove, and they still have a few books to burn, and a few more pieces of furniture. Some kerosene is left over from September, so they can eat their bread by lamplight. Now, instead of going to work, each morning she joins hundreds of other women who head to the Neva River, where holes have been cut in the ice. She fills two buckets with water and struggles back up the icy embankment, trying hard not to spill too much. She puts sticks in the water to keep it from sloshing and ties the buckets onto her child's sled. By the time she gets home the water has frozen. She's not surprised: the thermometer has not risen above $-30°$ F for a week.[19] In the dark she can barely manage to haul the buckets up the four flights of ice-glazed stairs to her apartment. Finally, she is inside. She lights the stove and melts the ice, using some of the warm water to wash her children's faces, sooty from the kerosene. She tells herself that at least she doesn't have to try to wash diapers like her neighbor down the hall, who struggles to change her infant daughter under layers of blankets so that she won't freeze to death. She pours the rest of the hot water into mugs for her family. They drink it, relishing the warmth, trying not to focus on the sweet, musky taste of the water, the taste that comes from the hundreds of corpses that have been thrown into the Neva by people too weak to bury their dead in the frozen ground.[20] The walls of the apartment are covered with a thick layer of frost. The family huddles together, wrapped in winter coats and blankets.

It was the men who died first. Olga Grechina, a survivor, writes:

The men were the first to go. There was no sight more pitiful and terrible than a siege man! It was then that women understood how well nature had made [us]—[we] had huge reserves of inner strength, which, it turned out, men did not have. The lack of meat, fats and tobacco severely sapped their strength, and they somehow immediately fell apart. At first they began to grow weak, to let themselves go—they stopped washing and were covered with gray stubble. There were very few of them in the city in comparison to the number of women, but their inability to adapt to the tragic conditions of life was striking. They began to fall down in the street, they didn't get out of bed, they were dying and dying. . . .[21]

It is true that the male metabolism requires more calories to survive; nevertheless, the claim by journalist Harrison Salisbury that men died because they "led more vigorous lives"[22] is objectionable as well as incorrect. In fact, the burden of getting water, scavenging for firewood, and searching for food—all "women's work," even in these most extreme circumstances—required huge expenditures of energy. Retrieving water from the frozen rivers and canals was difficult enough, but getting firewood was far more strenuous. The river was filled with logs that had washed downstream and been trapped in the ice. Weak with hunger and fatigue, women used axes to chop the ice around the logs until they were released. Once free, the logs still had to be tied onto sleds and dragged back home, then sawed into pieces small enough for the stove. Paradoxically, despite the extra expenditure of calories, these grueling tasks helped to keep women alive. It was the elemental nature of their duties that gave women an advantage.[23]

It was especially difficult for new mothers. Most babies born during the blockade were small and weak from lack of nourishment in the womb. (It wasn't until June 1944 that the government finally issued a decree to increase the ration for pregnant women.)[24] Infants officially received only 3 ½ ounces of soy milk a day. Mothers like Elena Kochina drank a pot of water every night to try to keep their milk flowing, but it rarely helped. Kochina's baby daughter screamed and tore at her dry breasts.[25] Here is how Lidia Okhapkina nourished her baby:

> My Ninochka cried all the time, long and drawn out, and she couldn't go to sleep. Her crying, like moaning, drove me out of my mind. So to help her fall asleep, I gave her my blood to suck. I hadn't had milk in my breasts for a long time, in fact I didn't have any breasts left, everything had just disappeared. I pricked my arm with a needle just above my elbow and placed my daughter on this spot. She sucked noiselessly and fell asleep. But I couldn't fall asleep for a long time. . . .[26]

The city authorities intermittently provided the populace with food-stuffs salvaged from industry, and along with the new terminology for the different stages of dystrophy, their harsh-sounding names became part of the everyday language of the blockade. Especially distasteful and hard to digest were *shroty* (also known as *zhmykh* and *duranda*), hard cakes of pressed seed hulls left over from the processing of oil from sunflower, cotton, hemp, or linseed (*duranda* most often referred to linseed cakes). These seed cakes, commonly used as cattle fodder, sustained many lives. Often they were too hard to break into pieces by hand; instead a knife or axe blade was used to plane them like wood, and the shavings were fried like pancakes.[27] Other industrial products included *olifa*, boiled linseed or hempseed oil. Used in classical oil paints, *olifa* could be metabolized like edible oil, with the same nutritional value, but the flavor was vile. Still, it was preferable to machine oil, which people stole from factories that had ceased production. Although machine oil generally went right through the system and had no nutritional value, there was always a chance that it was based on animal fats or vegetable oil rather than petroleum. Similarly, coarse, wet bread seemed more palatable when fried in paint thinner,[28] and *mezdra*, the inner side of pig- or calfskin, could be boiled for hours to make a kind of soup. If you could endure the nauseating smell, the liquid afforded some protein, and it was better than the old leather straps people otherwise boiled. One woman cut up her gopher fur coat, boiled it, and ate it.[29] Sometimes the grain ration provided a coarse, grayish-black macaroni made of rye flour and linseed cake,[30] and in the late fall of 1941 a murky white yeast soup derived from cellulose began to replace grain. To make the soup, water and sawdust were allowed to ferment into a foul-smelling liquid, which contained some protein.[31] Soup is an important component of Russian cuisine, an integral part of the daily meal, and therefore women often made soup out of the family's bread

ration instead of just serving the bread plain. Although this soup consisted of nothing but breadcrumbs and water, the whole felt like something more than its parts.

As the siege continued, and hunger grew, the women of Leningrad
had to find sources of food beyond the official rations.[32] They brought
home the tough, dark green, outer leaves of cabbage they had previously discarded. Slowly braised and softened, the leaves were turned
into a dish known as *khriapa*.[33] Women scoured the city, braving artil-
lery fire in their search for food. At night, dressed in dark clothes,
crawling from row to row, they chopped at the frozen ground to dig the
potatoes that lay rotting in the fields. With true hunger, squeamishness
disappeared, and survivors tell of readily, even avidly, eating the wood
shavings, peat, and pine branches they scavenged. Often, though, the
metabolism proved more discriminating. Zoya Bernikovich nearly died
after eating pancakes made of dry mustard, which she was told were
delicious. Soaking was supposed to remove the mustard's volatile oils,
so Bernikovich duly soaked two packets of dry mustard in water for
seven days, then poured off the water and added enough fresh water to
make a thick, pasty batter, which she formed into two pancakes and
fried. Her doctor later remarked that she was lucky to have eaten only
one pancake before feeling the first burning sensations; others who ate
more pancakes didn't survive, their stomach lining eaten away by the
mustard.[34]

The more heartbreaking and horrifying issues surrounding food
were moral ones, and different people recognized different limits. For
many families, sparrows, pigeons, crows, canaries, cats, and dogs became acceptable food, despite reluctance and shame. But consume them
they obviously did, because virtually all animals, including pets and
house mice, disappeared from Leningrad within the first four months
of the siege (the mice, like the people, died of hunger).[35] The only
creatures left were rats, the scourge of the city, who fed on the bodies
of the dying and the dead. Except for the most depraved or those whom
hunger had deprived of reason, the people of Leningrad refused to
purchase the large chunks of meat sold by suspiciously well-fed vendors
at the market. Described variously as bluish or pale white in color, this
meat was undoubtedly human flesh. Memoirists frequently refer to the
sight of corpses lying on the street, their fleshy buttocks carved out.[36]
Bits of desiccated skin from the corpses were boiled into soup.

Perhaps the only salutary consequence of such conditions was the
generous community of women that evolved. Leningrad had always
maintained a conscious distinction between the intelligentsia and the
uneducated peasants who had flocked to the city from the countryside

following the 1917 Revolution. Now, standing for hours in a bread line, or helping someone cross a street under enemy fire or pull a heavy sled, women who ordinarily led separate lives began to converse with one another. And in many cases, the impractical *intelligentki* survived largely thanks to the wisdom of old peasant women who willingly shared what they knew. Women who had never given much thought to domestic exigencies learned how to dry tree bark and grind it into flour (the bark stripped from oak trees stopped the bleeding of gums), and how to extract vitamin C from pine needles for a scurvy preventative. Such folk knowledge far surpassed Tolstoy's celebration of the peasant arts. Beyond providing practical benefit, this advice reconnected intellectual city dwellers with a more elemental mode of life.

Conversations about food took on significant social meaning, transcending the sphere of women's relationships to encompass society at large. Unlike the great nineteenth-century Russian gastronomes who celebrated the art of dining well, the Soviet intellectual, nurtured on revolutionary idealism, disdained any talk of food as crass and bourgeois. For the intellectual, the higher life of the mind was all-important, and giving as little thought as possible to domestic concerns was a point of pride. But such lofty ideals inevitably clashed with the reality of siege existence. Even the most consummate intellectuals found themselves preoccupied with food, theorizing about it, rationalizing their actions surrounding it.[37] Suddenly they recognized the artistry involved in obtaining and preparing food. The lowly housewife was now ascendant, her daily occupations ascribed a greater value. The literary critic Lidia Ginzburg explains how siege conditions transformed the intellectuals' attitude toward food:

> This conversation [about food], which had previously drawn down the scorn of men and businesswomen (especially young ones) and which [the housewife] had been forbidden to inflict upon the thinking man—this conversation had triumphed. It had taken on a universal social meaning and importance, paid for by the terrible experience of the winter. A conversation on how it's better not to salt millet when boiling, because then it gets to be just right, had become a conversation about life and death (the millet expands, you see). Reduced in range (siege cuisine), the conversation became enriched with tales of life's ups and down, difficulties overcome and problems resolved. And as the basic element of the given life situation, it subsumed every possible interest and passion.[38]

At the same time that conversation became more elemental, so did the foods that people ate. Joiner's glue became standard fare for many.

Like the wallpaper and library pastes used before the introduction of synthetic adhesives, joiner's glue was based on animal proteins such as casein from milk, blood, and fish residues. Thus it contained proteinaceous material that provided some nutritional value. From a chance acquaintance on the street, Olga Grechina learned how to prepare an aspic from joiner's glue. The glue was soaked for twenty-four hours, then boiled for quite a long time, during which it gave off a terrible odor of burnt horns and hooves. Then the glue was allowed to cool and thicken. A bit of vinegar or mustard, if available, made it palatable.[39] Nearly all of the siege survivors express nostalgia for the "sweet earth" they consumed—soil from the site of the Badaev warehouse fire in which 2,500 tons of sugar melted onto the ground. Eating dirt may seem to us degrading, but those who ate it were grateful. The government had salvaged most of the thick, crusty, black syrup from the surface of the warehouse soil, using it to make candy,[40] but seven hundred tons were lost.[41] Starving Leningraders, however, did not consider the sugar a total loss. For months after the fire they used axes to chop away at the frozen earth and loosen the soil, still saturated with sugar. Retrieved down to a depth of three feet, the soil sold for one hundred rubles a glass; from more than three feet below the surface it cost only fifty rubles.[42] This "sweet earth" could be heated until the sugar melted, then strained through several layers of muslin. Or it could be mixed with library paste to make a kind of gummy confection. "This was 'candy' or 'jelly' or 'custard,' whatever the imaginative housewife decided to call it."[43] Some people simply ate the earth raw. Valentina Moroz describes its flavor:

> The taste of the earth has remained with me, that is, I still have the impression that I was eating rich curd cheese [full of fats]. It was black earth. Could it actually have had some oil in it? [You couldn't perceive] sweetness, but something rich [fatty-tasting], maybe there really was oil there. You had the impression that this earth was very tasty, genuinely rich [full of fats]! We didn't cook it at all. We would simply swallow a little piece and wash it down with hot water.[44]

In the spring of 1942, when the ice and snow melted after the first long winter of the siege (which proved to be one of the harshest winters of the century), the women of Leningrad extended their search for food, eagerly foraging for grass and weeds. Anything green contained vitamins, and many people, though clinging to life, suffered from scurvy, pellagra, and rickets. Grass disappeared from the city and its environs; trees were picked clean of their pale, new leaves. Grass could be mixed with *duranda* into pancakes, or savored fresh by the handful. Nettles and dandelion leaves made excellent *shchi*, the classic Russian soup traditionally based on cabbage or sorrel. Juicy dandelion roots were ground and made into pancakes.[45] Angelica (from the Botanical Gardens), orach, and other grasses all served as welcome food, giving Leningraders hope that, against all odds, they might yet survive. One factory canteen made inventive use of wild greens in the spring and summer of 1942, listing the following menu choices: Plantain soup (*shchi*), pureed nettles and sorrel, beet green cutlets, orach rissoles, cabbage-leaf schnitzel, seed-cake (*zhmykh*) pastry, seed-cake (*duranda*) torte, sauce of fish-bone flour, casein pancakes, yeast soup, soy milk (in exchange for coupons). After a winter of starvation, this menu seemed like a feast.[46]

Physical survival was one thing, and the daily quest for food certainly overshadowed all other concerns. But the diary entries of survivors afford glimpses into another difficult aspect of blockade life: the deterioration of relationships. Hunger caused tempers to be short, a physiological as much as a psychological condition. Husband and wife, mother and daughter—the siege unavoidably changed the way people treated one other. Love and hatred became mixed up: you wanted to share your food with your family, but at the same time you resented their needs.[47] Elena Skriabina describes the way hunger can affect personality:

> People are growing brutal right in front of our eyes. Who could have thought that Irina Kliueva, recently such an elegant, quiet, beautiful woman, was capable of beating the husband she's always adored? And why? Because he wants to eat all the time, he's never satisfied. All he does is wait until she's found some food. She brings it home, and he throws himself on it. Of course, she herself is hungry. And it's hard for a hungry person to give up the last bit.[48]

One's very style of eating could cause aversion in others. Merely watching someone else chew—even someone you loved—was agonizing if you had already finished your morsel. Those who ate quickly, swallowing everything in a few desperate gulps, felt anger toward those who lingered long over every bite. Elena Kochina writes of her struggles with her husband, who became so crazed from hunger that he even stole food from their infant daughter. He could not bear to watch his wife eat: "I happened to get a particularly hard piece of crust, which I chewed with delight. I sensed how he was looking with hatred at my evenly moving jaws."[49] This response was instinctive; Kochina's husband had lost the ability consciously to choose good behavior over bad, sacrifice over self-interest. In this way, for some people questions of morality all too easily slipped away.

Sexuality was also affected. Sexual relations mainly ceased. This had to do less with a lack of energy than with an increased alienation from one's diminishing body. The physical characteristics that mark gender largely disappeared. Shrouded in layers of heavy clothing, people all looked alike. It was impossible to tell who was male, who female. Hunger eroded the differences between old and young. Women traded their few good dresses for food and wore the clothes of their husbands, fathers, or sons.[50] Holding the baggy pants and quilted jackets together with belts and long scarves to keep out the cold, they wrapped their feet in cotton rags and made makeshift galoshes from old automobile tires to keep their feet dry. Women stopped menstruating; their breasts atrophied until only nipples were left. Like most people during the winter of 1941–1942, Olga Grechina did not even see her body for several months (it was too cold to undress for bed). Finally resolving to rid herself of the lice that plagued her, she got a coupon for one of the few working public baths. When she undressed she was horrified to find that she had neither a belly nor breasts. All of her bones stuck out; her legs were like sticks. Grechina felt a "disconnection" from her own body.[51] Lidia Ginzburg describes the sensation more fully: "In the winter, while people were discovering bone after bone, the alienation of the body proceeded, the splitting of the conscious will from the body, as from a manifestation of the hostile world outside. The body was emitting novel sensations, not its own."[52]

Under such conditions so far beyond our everyday understanding of "alienation," when one's very sense of self was undone, it was difficult to care about anyone other than oneself. The usual niceties of social interaction had long since disappeared. As bodies diminished, normal social structures also shrank and vanished. Food, once the pretext for friendly gatherings or their impromptu outcome, now ceased to be an element of social sustenance or succor. Although Russian culture holds that food has meaning only when it is shared, in blockaded Leningrad this practice was of necessity ignored. People simply ate what they had, when they had it, regardless. This unnatural role into which food was cast represented a particularly debasing aspect of siege life, and one which went to the core of what Russians hold most sacred; the loss of hospitality contributed to a sense of barbarism, of not belonging to a larger world than the one the body inhabited, and yet the body itself had become alien and strange.

Even so, when there was strength enough, some people engaged in small celebrations. Kira, a young hospital worker, sprinkled tiny squares of bread with a bit of hoarded sugar to treat her colleagues to "blockade pastries."[53] A simple crust of bread could become something special, if you only allowed it to: "Thickly sliced crusts, toasted on the outside and left moist on the inside went especially well with tea. If you left the bread in the frying pan and ate it with a knife and fork—then you had a *meal*."[54] On her birthday the critic Olga Freidenberg helped her mother set a special table, creating beauty in the midst of austerity:

> It is a parade of a home and a spirit that has been preserved; it was my own personal triumph. . . . To get my daily bread, I had sold the better part of [our china] for next to nothing. And yet there was still enough to adorn the table, and these old family members appeared on the white tablecloth in their former luster and coziness. Only Mama and I could understand the importance of this holiday table . . . like us, it lived and existed after terrors, deaths, siege, and hunger; and like it, we were still living and could still revive our hopes for our future arrival in real, living life.[55]

No matter that Freidenberg's stomach, unaccustomed to real food, vomited the meal; the emotional sustenance it provided outweighed any loss of physical nourishment.

Those who survived the siege were rewarded by the Soviet government. The presentation of the medal "For the Defense of Leningrad" was accompanied by much high-flown rhetoric about the courage and resilience of the women, who accounted for most of the survivors. Even Dmitri Pavlov's generally sober account of the siege underlines the heroism of Leningrad's women: "Their will to live, their moral strength, resolution, efficiency, and discipline will always be the example and inspiration for millions of people."[56] But at what price did such fortitude come? As Dmitri Likhachev has noted, their heroism is more accurately seen as martyrdom. Yet it is important to stress that unlike religious martyrdom, that of the women of Leningrad was not elected, at least not by them. In fact, the residents of Leningrad suffered largely because Stalin did not care enough about them to surrender the city. Stalin had always despised Leningrad with its large population of intellectuals, and perhaps now he chose to take his revenge. He did not attempt to save the citizenry; quite the opposite. Local collective farms that could have helped feed the population were quickly evacuated, their cattle and goods dispersed elsewhere.[57] And just days before the Germans encircled the city, large quantities of foodstuffs were ordered sent *out of* Leningrad.[58] This efflux ended only when the city was sealed off by the blockade. Though there have been other sieges in history, the blockade of Leningrad stands out for the government's refusal to spare its people.

Survivors of the Leningrad blockade report truly tasting bread for the first time, and savoring the essence of even the most rudimentary foods. And they gained a new awareness of texture: sunflower oil lush on the tongue, each grain of porridge a revelation as it burst in the mouth. Once-odorless foods like sugar or dried peas suddenly acquired an aroma that the pre-siege senses were unable to detect.[59] Along with the newly sensitive palate came a deeper appreciation of cuisine: "Siege cookery resembled art—it conferred tangibility on things. Above all, every product had to cease being itself. People made porridge out of bread and bread out of porridge. . . . Elementary materials were transformed into dishes."[60] The aesthetics of eating became newly attenuated. Such was the human cost of art.

Notes

1. Ambrose Heath, *Good Food in Wartime* (London: Faber and Faber, 1942), 5.

2. Reprinted in Marguerite Patten, *Marguerite Patten's Post-War Kitchen: Nostalgic Food and Facts from 1945–1954* (London: Hamlyn, 1998), 14.

3. An unnamed study of the British worker's diet found that "mothers give to fathers and children the lion's share of rationed foods. Other studies of family diets have revealed these deep-rooted habits, common to mothers everywhere, of which there is plenty of evidence at first hand. When there isn't enough chicken to go around, mother prefers the neck." In *The New York Times Magazine*, September 27, 1942: 32, cited in Amy Bentley, *Eating for Victory: Food Rationing and the Politics of Domesticity* (Urbana: University of Illinois Press, 1998), 91.

4. Leningrad's (now St. Petersburg's) Piskarev Cemetery houses a memorial to those who died during World War II. Their statistics state that 650,000 people died of hunger; but statistics from the Museum of the History of Leningrad place the number who died of starvation at one million. Russia's esteemed cultural historian Dmitri Likhachev estimates the total at closer to 1,200,000—and these were only the officially registered deaths, not those of displaced persons or other people living illegally in the city. See Dmitri Likhachev, "Kak my ostalis' zhivy" ("How We Remained Alive"), *Neva* 1 (1991): 31.

5. Likhachev writes: "There were very many women who fed their children by taking the last necessary piece from their own mouths. These mothers would die first, and the child would be left alone." In "Kak my ostalis' zhivy," 15.

6. See Dmitri V. Pavlov, *Leningrad v blokade*, 5th ed. (Moscow: Sovetskaia Rossiia, 1983). Pavlov was in charge of the Leningrad food supply during the siege. All citations are taken from the English translation of his book, *Leningrad 1941: The Blockade*, trans. John Clinton Adams (Chicago: University of Chicago Press, 1965), 77.

7. There are approximately 28 grams in one ounce. Thus 800 grams of bread is equivalent to roughly 1 ¾ pounds.

8. Pavlov, *Leningrad 1941*, 49. It is estimated that the population of Leningrad at that time numbered around three million.

9. This hierarchical Soviet system of rationing dates back to the Civil War period of 1919–1921, when Petrograd endured widespread hunger: "There were three categories of ration cards. Manual workers received the first; intellectuals, artists, teachers, office workers, etc., received the second; and the parasites of society—housewives and old people, especially of bourgeois origin—received the third." Pitirim A. Sorokin, *Hunger as a Factor in Human Affairs*, trans. Elena P. Sorokin (Gainesville: University Presses of Florida, 1975), xxxii. Sorokin's book offers a compelling analysis of the social and psychological effects of prolonged hunger.

10. With the opening of a transport road across the frozen Lake Ladoga, limited supplies could finally be brought into the city, and on December 25 the bread ration was increased to 350 grams for factory workers and 200 grams for all others. By February 11, 1942, the bread ration was restored to 500 grams for factory workers, 400 for office workers, and 300 for dependents and children. See Pavlov, *Leningrad 1941*, 79, for a chart detailing the fluctuating rations.

11. Ibid., 60.

12. Ibid., 63. I have taken Pavlov's figures as the most authoritative, but according to other sources the composition of the bread was even worse. Harrison Salisbury writes that as of November 13 it contained "25 percent 'edible' cellulose." See Salisbury, *The 900 Days: The Siege of Leningrad* (New York: Avon Books, 1969), 449. In her memoirs, the writer Vera Inber describes the bread exhibit at the Museum of the Defense of Leningrad. The descriptive label under the bread listed the following ingredients: "Defective rye flour—50%, Salt—10%, Seed cake (*zhmykh*)—10%, Cellulose—15%, and 5% each of soy flour, flour dust, and bran." See Inber, "Pochti tri goda (Leningradskii dnevnik)" ("Almost Three Years [Leningrad Diary]"), *Izbrannye proizvedeniia*, vol. 3 (Moscow: Gos. izd. Khudozhestvennoi literatury, 1958), 457.

13. Inber, "Pochti tri goda," 457.

14. Veronika Aleksandrovna Opakhova, in Ales' Adamovich and Daniil Granin, *Blokadnaia kniga* (*A Book of the Blockade*) (Sankt-Peterburg: Pechatyni dvor, 1994), 11.

15. V. S. Kostrovitskaia, in "Primary Chroniclers: Women on the Siege of Leningrad." I am deeply grateful to Nina Perlina of Indiana University and Cynthia Simmons of Boston College for making available to me this important manuscript, an unpublished collection of women's memoirs about the siege, which they have meticulously translated and edited.

16. Galina Vishnevskaya, *Galina: A Russian Story*, trans. Guy Daniels (San Diego: Harcourt Brace Jovanovich, 1984), 27.

17. Nikolai Antonovich Loboda describes these loaves, stating that "you can pour water or whatever else you want into pans, but a round loaf will fall apart." In Adamovich and Granin, *Blokadnaia kniga*, 81.

18. Ol'ga Grechina thus describes how she fed her dying mother. See Grechina, "Spasaius' spasaia" ("Saving Others, I Save Myself"), *Neva* 1 (1994): 236.

19. The relentless cold drove some to desperation: "I [remember] walk[ing] along Zhukovskii Street. A building is burning. A woman with long, wild, red hair is passing by. She sees the fire and says, 'Oh, warmth, fire!' She goes into the building and burns to death." Valentina Mikhailovna Golod, on "Tikhii dom" (The Quiet House"), a broadcast on the Russian television network ORT, February 10, 1999, 12:25 a.m.

20. Vera Inber states that even after filtering the water from the Karpovka River through eight layers of cheesecloth, it remained "terrible." Inber, "Pochti tri goda," 298–299.

21. Grechina, "Spasaius' spasaia," 238. See also Vishnevskaya, who writes: "We all went hungry together, but the men succumbed sooner than the women." *Galina*, 28.

22. Salisbury, *The 900 Days*, 436.

23. Lidia Ginzburg considers this instinct to endure atavistic. Writing of the long lines women waited in for food before setting off for work, she states: "Working women have inherited from their grandmothers and mothers time which is not taken into account. Their everyday lives do not allow that atavism to lapse. A man considers that after work he is entitled to rest or amuse himself; when a working woman comes home, she works at home. The siege queues were inscribed into an age-old background of things being issued or available, into the normal female irritation and the normal female patience." Lidiia Ginzburg, "Blokadnyi dnevnik," *Neva* 1 (1984): 84–108. All citations are from the English translation, Lidiya Ginzburg, *Blockade Diary*, trans. Alan Myers (London: The Harvill Press, 1995), 39.

24. Yulia Mendeleva, Director of the Leningrad Pediatric Institute during the siege, provides chilling statistics on infant health. Many babies born in 1942 were stillborn; the birth weight of those who lived was on the average over 600 grams (about 1 ½ pounds) less than that of prewar infants, and their overall length decreased by 2 centimeters. Less than 1 percent of the children admitted to the Institute during the siege were of normal weight; often they weighed three times less than they should have. Iuliia Aronovna Mendeleva in *Primary Chroniclers*.

25. E. I. Kochina, "Blokadnyi dnevnik," in *Pamiat': Istoricheskii sbornik*, vyp. 4 (Moscow, 1979, and Paris, 1981), 153–208. All citations are taken from the English translation, Elena Kochina, *Blockade Diary*, trans. Samuel C. Ramer (Ann Arbor: Ardis, 1990), 44.

26. Adamovich and Granin, *Blokadnaia kniga*, 290.

27. Elena Skriabina reports that *duranda* always caused heartburn. See Skriabina, *V blokade (Dnevnik materi)* (*In the Blockade [A Mother's Diary]*) (Iowa City, 1964), 43.

28. Ginzburg, *Blockade Diary*, 63.

29. Adamovich and Granin, *Blokadnaia kniga*, 36.

30. Pavlov, *Leningrad 1941*, 64.

31. See the description in Likhachev, "Kak my ostalis' zhivy," 17.

32. Pavlov provides daily caloric estimates for December 1941, which are predicated on the availability of some meat, fats, grains, and sugar in the diet. He readily admits, however, that more often than not only bread was available. Even with the optimal, full norm of rations, the daily caloric count for dependents (category 3, which included housewives) was only 466 calories. See Pavlov, *Leningrad 1941*, 122.

33. Information from Marianna Tsezarovna Shabat, Moscow, February 4, 1999.

34. In Adamovich and Granin, *Blokadnaia kniga*, 35.

35. Apparently, against all odds, a female zookeeper managed to keep the Leningrad zoo's beloved hippopotamus alive. See ibid., 179.

36. See, for instance, Grechina, "Spasaius' spasaia," 239; Likhachev, "Kak my ostalis' zhivy," 15; Salisbury, *The 900 Days*, 550; Vishnevskaya, *Galina*, 28; Skriabina, *V blokade*, 46; and Golod, "Tikhii dom."

37. Sorokin writes: "Under the influence of hunger the whole field of consciousness comes to be filled with notions and ideas, and their complexes, which are directly or indirectly associated with food. They intrude into the field of consciousness, unexpected and uncalled for, and displace other notions and ideas, crowding them out of the mind, regardless of our will and even contrary to it." *Hunger as a Factor in Human Affairs*, 73.

38. Ginzburg, *Blockade Diary*, 43.

39. Grechina, "Spasaius' spasaia," 239.

40. The clumps of sweet black earth were processed into hard candies. "In taste the candy was reminiscent of the famous pre-Revolutionary candy Landrin [named after a French confectioner], a popular candy with a slightly bitter taste." See Adamovich and Granin, *Blokadnaia kniga*, 30.

41. Pavlov, *Leningrad 1941*, 56.

42. Salisbury, *The 900 Days*, 546.

43. Ibid.

44. Adamovich and Granin, *Blokadnaia kniga*, 35.

45. Ibid., 179.

46. Ibid., 68.

47. Lidia Ginzburg writes perceptively about this. See *Blockade Diary*, 7–8.

48. Skriabina, *V blokade*, 38–39.

49. Kochina, *Blockade Diary*, 55.

50. Likhachev's wife, Zina, was able to trade a dress for 1200 grams of *duranda* to help keep the family alive. "Kak my ostalis' zhivy," 13.

51. Grechina, "Spasaius' spasaia," 269–270.

52. Ginzburg, *Blockade Diary*, 9.

53. Lidiia Samsonovna Razumovskaia in *Primary Chroniclers*.

54. Ginzburg, *Blockade Diary*, 66.

55. Ol'ga Mikhailovna Freidenberg in *Primary Chroniclers*.

56. Pavlov, *Leningrad 1941*, 134.

57. Grechina, "Spasaius' spasaia," 256.

58. Likhachev, "Kak my ostalis' zhivy," 9.

59. Kochina, *Blockade Diary*, 57.

60. Ginzburg, *Blockade Diary*, 65.

REPRESENTATIONS

Our assumptions about the world and our place within it are naturalized through social institutions. We are bombarded daily with representations from government, the academy, the media, popular culture, and the arts about who we are, how we should behave, and what we should dream. These representations are also reproduced in our daily social interactions in both our private and public lives. Because they are based on assumptions, they are not experienced as one perspective, but "the way things are, have always been, and will and should be in the future."

Alternative institutions and movements resist these messages often by revealing that they are, in fact, representations in the service of dominant groups. Feminist scholarship has been in the forefront of revealing and analyzing these messages. But as the critiques by women of color, poor women, and lesbians have shown, some of this work continues to perpetuate unacknowledged assumptions about race/ethnicity in representations of women as white, middle-class, and heterosexual. The blindness resulting from privilege is a testament to the power of dominant representations and the depth of their internalization.

The essays in this section span a range of scholarly approaches and topics, but all do the difficult work of deconstructing and analyzing various forms of representation. Reading two books on the impact of commercial food production on U.S. culture from the perspective of gender and race, Alice Julier critiques the authors for relegating them to variables of importance only as they refer to women and people of color. By not building these basic social formations into a structural analysis, the authors reproduce dominant representations of women and people of color. Both Sharmila Sen and Carole Counihan look at the place of food in self-representation, Sen in a literary analysis and Counihan in an ethnography. In her analysis of David Dabydeen's novel *The Counting House*, Sen argues that food is deployed to denote ethnic differences, rivalries, as well as shared colonial status between women from two groups forced into labor in the Caribbean, Africans and East

Indians. Employing what she calls "food-centered life histories," Counihan identifies the interaction of multiple ethnicities and racial and class representations of self.

These analyses of representation with three different methodologies in three very different sites underline the importance of being aware of the gender and racial aspects of analysis, particularly when they are absent or marginalized, the ways in which gender and race are central to identities, and the ways they may be enacted through food discourse and practices.

Hiding Gender and Race in the Discourse of Commercial Food Consumption

ALICE P. JULIER

> What is significant about the adoption of alien objects—as of alien ideas—is not the fact that they are adopted, but the way they are culturally redefined and put to use.
>
> Igor Kopytoff

> I met a guy who eats those chocolate-frosted Pop-Tarts. He breaks them up, puts them in a bowl and pours milk on them. I said geez, you might as well cook.
>
> Paula Poundstone

Like many people who teach at a college or university, I find that my weekly stack of mail usually contains a fair number of publishers' catalogs. As publishers discover my interests in the social aspects of food, more of my mail consists of advertisements for new food books.

For every book that comes across my desk describing large-scale changes in food consumption in American society, I get another book that deals with women and food, often concerning eating problems. The authors of the first are usually men. The authors of the latter are usually women. Today's mail contained a glossy ad for George Ritzer's newest volume, *Enchanting the Disenchanted World*, which expands his ideas about McDonaldization to take the reader on "a tour of the settings and structures that generate hyper-consumption." In another flyer I'm being encouraged to purchase *Fed Up: Women and Food in America* by Catherine Manton, which takes on "the place of food in women's history" from an eco-feminist standpoint. Why, I wonder, is "women's special relationship with food" positioned against "analyses of globalizing trends in consumption"? Aren't the two related? What does this dichotomy tell us about the study of food and eating? Why don't either of these texts consider a discussion of race relevant to their argument?

Rather than accept these divisions, I want to explore the consequences of dividing the study of food and eating into such categories. In particular, I am struck by the increase in books that examine the impact of industrial food on the diet and social experiences of Western peoples without centralizing the construction of difference and inequality. Using two recent texts of this sort, I highlight both the overt and subtle constructions of gender and race (and, to a lesser extent, class) that are unavoidably intertwined in these analyses.[1]

In general, the authors who write about global food processes want to explain trends in consumption, offering various theoretical treatises on the nature of food choice and eating patterns.[2] Given a long tradition of class analysis in Western social sciences, it's no surprise that they all contend with economic social inequality in some form. But when gender is included, it is often used to mean primarily "women." Race is even less present, often subsumed under discussions of ethnic variations and immigration patterns. In other examples, gender and race become variables, designating categories of consumers or even trajectories along which people consume. But what happens if we consider race and gender structural sets of arrangements that simultaneously operate to position people, construct meanings, and determine activities in relation to food?

Social scientists acknowledge that food, eating, and cooking are more than material or physiological processes; rather, they are ways in which people socially create and construct boundaries. At the same time, this insight is often restricted to particular topics that are considered "about" race or gender (e.g., talking about women in relation to the body or the family, or African Americans and prenatal nutrition). Race and gender are often deployed as labels that describe only the experiences of women or people of color, as if these were not reciprocal, structural, and relational terms that define life circumstances for dominant groups, too. What if we saw the construction of race and gender, of the "devalued Other" as a *defining feature* of both the production and consumption of food? What if this insight were applied on both the large, commercial, structural scale and the intimate everyday scale of smaller communities, households, families, and partners?

Commercial Food and Contemporary American Culture

Americans can eat garbage, provided you sprinkle it liberally with ketchup, mustard, chili sauce, tabasco sauce, cayenne pepper or any other condiment which destroys the original flavor of the dish.

Henry Miller

Richard Pillsbury's *No Foreign Food: The American Diet in Time and Place* and George Ritzer's *The McDonaldization of Society* both attempt to explain why people eat the foods they eat and how those food choices are related to an increasingly globalized market which expands commercial foodways and has a major impact on both diet and desire. I discuss these two books because they have received a fair amount of publicity. I believe it's particularly important to pay attention to books that explicitly try to popularize analyses of food and social life

Pillsbury's (1997) *No Foreign Food* is written in a style accessible to the general public, using boxed personal anecdotes to punctuate his lengthier analyses of changes in national and regional consumption. Pillsbury uses a "geography of American foodways" to argue that even as various cultural identities are being subsumed by commercial processes and mass culture, there is some evidence that regional cultural differences in food consumption remain. He charts a brief history of the American diet, turning then to the technologies and processes of production and distribution that have modernized our eating habits. In his view, large-scale economic and social changes are key to modern culture: the ability to grow and transport perishable foods is a defining feature of late capitalism and one that profoundly affects the cultural meanings available to individuals. Pillsbury then focuses on the ways advertising, restaurants, cookbooks, immigration, and commercial foods all disrupt "earlier" patterns.

Summarizing "the American diet," Pillsbury provides general information about changes in what people eat. Although he admits that it's difficult to characterize why people choose the foods they do, he ends up concluding that eating practices are "largely determined by the economics, regional affinity, and cultural heritage of the family" (Pillsbury 1997, 192). He accounts for competing trends between commercial standardization and an abiding regionality, but, in the end, he concludes that Americans are assimilationists, such that "an all-embracing [national] culture has meant that there can be no foreign foods" (1997, 208).

George Ritzer's (1996) *McDonaldization* thesis has received a fair amount of critical attention since he first coined the term in 1983.[3] He begins by asserting the continuing significance of Weber's classic theory of rationalization, which demonstrated how complex industrial society is dominated by bureaucratic principles. Institutional rules, means-ends structures of efficiency, and hierarchical ordering of activity dominate increasing areas of modern life. Such rational control simultaneously eases people's experience of modernity and limits their ability to act freely. Ritzer argues that a more contemporary version is modeled after

McDonald's rather than the bureaucratic organization. Although not focused on McDonald's per se, the analysis uses both the image of the fast food restaurant and its operating principles to suggest that more and more arenas of social and economic life are being governed by "efficiency, calculability, predictability, and control" (9). Along with the fast food industry and supermarkets, Ritzer applies his thesis to such varied topics as health care, shopping malls, higher education, family vacations, and workplaces.

Avoiding information about actual consumers, Ritzer speculates in depth about what drives people to accept and encourage a "fast food approach" to daily consumption. Within his analysis of the various dimensions of McDonaldization, he makes particular claims about both the shape of contemporary social lives and the motivations of individuals making such choices about consumption. The argument extends well beyond the realm of food choice in homes and restaurants.

Both books attend to the specific experiences of people through an exploration of larger structural trends, resting their analyses on some assumptions about the boundaries between spheres of social life and about the cultural norms people use in deciding what counts as good food. In the rest of this essay I explore two of these assumptions, one that focuses on gender and the family meal and the other on "American" food and white middle-class culture.

Gender, Commercial Food, and the Family Meal

In the fast-food industry, of course, family means people who spend quite a bit of money but don't wreck the furniture.

Calvin Trillin

How has commercial food changed our social practices? Why do people eat fast food? What changes have globalization and mass production wrought on the symbolic meanings and material conditions of people's daily food choices? Both books contend with these questions, most frequently by suggesting what global industrial trends mean for the routines of daily life. The site Ritzer and Pillsbury unquestioningly choose as the crucial space for local practice is the household, represented in these writings specifically as "the family."

Each text argues that standardized commercial food production and distribution have a direct and often deleterious impact on "the family." The arguments begin from the assumption that family is paramount, ubiquitous, and has a normative form that is, most often, a heterosexual couple with children. Historically, the family is a key site where social bonds are forged and socialization takes place, usually around food. In Western society, capitalism creates the conditions where family is no longer economically productive and self-sustaining but a basic unit of consumption. The boundaries between "outside" and "inside" worlds are actively created through the consumption practices of people in households. People "take in" the commercial world through their homes and close relationships.

Both authors establish that contemporary social structures (in particular the commercial production, distribution, and marketing of food) change the nature and frequency of family meals. Family meals are important because we can pinpoint them as one of the actual events where close emotional bonds are created and maintained. Mary Douglas (1972, 61) writes, "food acts as the medium through which a system of relationships within the family is expressed." Close ties are built on time spent together, preferences expressed and met, food shared, and emotional bonds realized. The dinner table is where family itself is actively constructed, both historically and ideologically. Marjorie DeVault's (1991) study of feeding work uses women's descriptions of creating family meals to demonstrate how "the material trappings of meals can become foundations for more emotional aspects of family life" (130). Many people's reminiscences about family love and support center on being fed both emotionally and physically at the dinner table.[4]

In contemporary society, laments about fast-paced social and economic changes in family life are often expressed through anxiety about families who do not sit down to "home-cooked" meals together. By imposing products and selling cultural meanings, commercial food changes the experience and function of family. For Richard Pillsbury, these changes have a negative effect on American cultural life. As he puts it, "The traditional 'normal' meal with Mom, Dad, and the kids sitting together at the kitchen table at the prescribed time and leisurely consuming a home-prepared meal while discussing the day's events has disappeared from most homes. . . . The concept of Dad always sitting at the head of the table and Mom at the foot is alien to many children, and the idea of using mealtime for relaxation and family bonding is almost inconceivable" (1997, 189).

These concerns about the decline in nuclear family meals center on what Stephanie Coontz (1992) describes as the "elusive traditional family," which, if it ever existed, did so for a short duration in American history (76).[5] Such complaints assume that there is a set of boundaries between the rational "outside" world of the industrial marketplace and the emotional "inside" world of home. This construction draws on a historical ideology of "separate spheres," where men and women have different relationships to the world based on their dominance of distinct social and economic arenas. Thus the logic of commercial production and consumption penetrates the sanctuary of private emotional life, the "haven in a heartless world," to impose cultural meanings and construct artificial needs for individuals within a household.

More specifically, capitalist culture encroaches upon the "female" sphere of nurturing, where women act as keepers of the culture, primary agents of children's socialization, and defenders of the private realm of family life. The implicit fear is that kids know more about Ronald McDonald than they do about their "own" regional, ethnic, or racial background. Pillsbury's analysis draws heavily upon these stereotypes of family and gender:

> Forty years ago the daughter of the family often spent hours in the kitchen with her mother learning the mysteries of how to cook all the family favorites. The arrival of Little League and then girls' sporting teams meant that less and less time was available to spend in the kitchen learning cooking techniques. All of the blame cannot be placed on after-school activities, however, as Mom probably wasn't there slaving away over the stove anyway; rather she was at work. The result has been a very significant decline in cooking knowledge in the typical household. Coupled with the attitude that cooking is boring, this has lead to ever greater demands for prepared foods. (1997, 97–98)

The powerful marketing of commercial food production and the changing family structure, particularly women in the workforce, increase people's use of restaurants, fast food, and "value-added" supermarket meals.

Ritzer pinpoints more particular culprits: "There is much talk today about the disintegration of the family, and the fast food restaurant may well be a contributor to that disintegration" (1996, 134). According to the logic of McDonaldization, eating out does not allow for the kind of leisurely slow-paced meal, complete with conversation and socialization of kids, that is supposedly so central to the formation of family relations and for training family members in their proper roles beyond the home.

Ritzer also indicts convenience in the home kitchen, where the microwave, frozen foods, and supermarket "value-added" products such as ready-to-go burritos or rotisserie chickens bring McDonaldization into the private home. Buying and using mass-produced food alters not only the amount but also the nature of labor within the household. By extension, it changes the meaning as well: "Those qualities of the family meal, the ones that impart feelings of security and well-being might be lost forever when food is 'zapped' or 'nuked' instead of cooked" (141). Lamenting kids who make their own meals with microwaves, Ritzer equates not having to cook with not having to care. Further, there can be no pleasure or satisfaction involved in feeding others or in eating when some of the work is done for the cook by an impersonal "outside" source.[6]

In this logic, reducing the labor involved in creating the family meal reduces the significance of family itself. This labor is discussed without either substantive or theoretical analysis of the way such work is generally the source of gender, race, and class inequality. Women are the ones who are ideologically and personally held accountable for doing cooking as caring work that constructs the family. By failing to do so, women "handicap" their children and spouses as they negotiate the "outside" world. For example, a typical parenting magazine suggests, "Kids whose families share meals are likelier to succeed in school and even to have better vocabularies" (Lapinski 1999, 7). People who cannot create "proper meals" for their families are to blame for all manner of social problems. This construction also leaves no room for any variations in the circumstances that structure the symbolic meanings of eating together.[7]

In effect, if the commercial marketplace provides the food, it inevitably becomes the source for cultural meaning. Barely hidden in this logic are ideological assumptions about who "should" be doing such work to construct family in an ongoing way: while women create family through their efforts, they are also "doing gender," reinforcing or re-creating differences between men and women (West and Zimmerman 1987; DeVault 1991). Fears about the decline in the family meal are really fears about the disintegration of "recognizable" gender boundaries. The assumption is that fast food, take-out, and commercial advertising are replacing women's function as nurturers and caregivers.

My critique questions the gendered and racial nature of such logic. Feminist researchers have challenged the ideological boundary between home and marketplace since research shows how both women's and men's daily practices cross such lines. The work of constructing family includes provisioning, deciphering ads and advice about what's good to eat, and finding appropriate places to buy the kinds of food that meet the physical and emotional needs of family members (DeVault 1991). Black feminist scholars demonstrate how the separate spheres ideology ignores the experiences of racial-ethnic women who have historically worked in and outside the home and defined themselves from both vantage points (Collins 1990; Dill 1988; Glenn 1985). The emphasis on family as a site of consumption also tends to obscure the conditions under which commercial food is produced and distributed. This is particularly important when we consider that women, people of color, and recent immigrants are often the ones doing the work of preparing and selling industrial foods.

By asserting that changes in the family meal equal a decline in family life, Pillsbury and Ritzer gloss over constantly shifting issues regarding family. In particular, these arguments would need to account for some of the following historical trends: how racial, ethnic, and working-class families have relied on women in the paid workforce; how wealthier white people have relied on paid and unpaid women of color to cook for their families; how "ethnic entrepreneurs" played a large part in creating products and defining commercial markets (Gabaccia 1998); and how "traditional" extended families who engaged in more household production generally depended on the labor of children (Coontz 1992). The ability to create and defend family as a private realm is not equally valued or equally available. Maxine Baca Zinn (1994) argues that "research on women of color demonstrates that protecting one's family from the demands of the market is strongly related to the distribution of power and privilege in society" (16). These conditions are all equally relevant to the ways in which commercial foods have changed people's eating habits within families.

If "family" is emblematic of types of consumption, the discussion needs to delineate how various kinds of families create and respond to current social and economic conditions. For example, Ritzer suggests that the reason why the McDonald's model and fast food have proven so "irresistible" is because contemporary Americans desire efficiency and this desire is a product of our current family and workplace arrangements. In particular, Ritzer often cites two different family "types" as important groups of consumers who determine practice: "Thus, the speed and the efficiency of a fast-food meal fits in well with the demands of the modern, dual-career or single-parent family" (1996, 146).

The rise in dual-income and single-parent families is a real social and economic feature of contemporary social life. On the surface, Ritzer's assertion of these appears sensitive to a wider view of what constitutes a household. But he is still constructing a normative center from which all others draw their ideological images. It also assumes that families themselves are the premier unit of consumption, creating the bulk of mass cultural meaning by eating Happy Meals in their minivans, even when statistics show that the majority of regular customers are individual men.[8] But the idea of family as a cohesive and supportive group is an ahistorical cultural construct, not necessarily reflective of people's real and changing experiences of family life. The important questions center on what is family and how are these various social groups (not all of which constitute family) affected *differently* by the structural forces of commercial production?

In his history of sugar, Sidney Mintz (1985) articulates the difference between "outside meanings" imposed by the forces of production, and "inside meanings." "Inside meaning" refers to the daily conditions of consumption, where people negotiate and impart significance to their acts, often in ways that complicate and abrade the forces of structural power. In effect, people approach commercial foods with a variety of purposes and create their own meanings within those structural constraints. For example, there are variations in cooking and eating that occur across stages in the life course of individuals. As already noted, teenagers and young single men tend to predominate as fast food consumers. At the same time, many groups of young adults in their twenties describe cooking at home with friends because it's an inexpensive social activity. Some married women reach a certain age and reject doing feeding work for others, finding liberation in letting the commercial marketplace do the cooking.

Whatever detrimental impact commercial foods have had on our lives, Jack Goody reminds us that they have "enormously improved, in quantity, quality, and variety the diet (and usually the cuisine) of the urban working populations of the western world" (1997, 338). Given this, we need to think and research, without prejudgments, about the ways people from various social and economic circumstances incorporate commercial foods into their lives. For families who live in more rural economically depressed areas outside of cities, "traditional methods of food acquisition (gardening, maintaining domestic animals, hunting and fishing) are still being used to supplement new foods" (Whitehead 1992, 106). All of these people do some food consumption through the public commercial sphere, and yet each constructs cultural meaning about food and about family in ways that go beyond Ritzer and Pillsbury's images of household life.

Igor Kopytoff (1986, 73) insists that all commodities have a biography and are best thought of as in the process of becoming, rather than in an all-or-nothing state of being. If relations of gender and race get enacted and created around home-cooked meals, it stands to reason that a comparative process operates with commercial foods like McDonald's, frozen dinners, and microwavable meals. Even so, this does not mean that we can assume that people passively accept the cultural meanings imposed upon them by outside forces. The power to bestow meaning is not always a function of the power to determine availabilities. Questioning the superficial gender-neutral nature of these analyses also entails questioning the universality of the effect of commercial food on choices made by individuals and small groups.

White Middle-Class Culture and American Food

White folks act like they invented food and like there is some weird mystique surrounding it—something that only Julia and Jim can get to. There is no mystique. Food is food.

Verta Mae Grosvenor

Conflicts about what is traditional and what is "American" are recurrent in both popular and academic food writing. Alan Warde (1997, 56) surmises that "the structural anxieties of our age are made manifest in discourses about food." As I've shown, some of these anxieties focus on a perceived loss of women's caring work within the family. But tied to these concerns are others about race and ethnicity, about the place of people within the structural and cultural landscape, and about the ability to construct a "national culture" amidst both pluralism and commercialism. Both Ritzer and Pillsbury play out these anxieties as they analyze the impact of commercial foods on regional and racial-ethnic food patterns.

Both authors agree that the forces of mass production and the marketing of industrial food inevitably obliterate many of the distinctions in consumption in American society. As evidence, Ritzer (1996, 95) quotes a *Saturday Review* article which claims, "Food in one neighborhood, city, or state looks and tastes pretty much like food anywhere else." Pillsbury evokes a previous era, where regional and ethnic boundaries created the variety that was the spice of American life: "The invasion of standardized signage, corporate retailers, and international manufacturers as well as a highly mobile population and the general placelessness of most urban society has meant that the connection with the past is just not as strong as it once was" (1997, 210–211).

At the same time, both writers suggest that the commercial marketplace is unequivocally the source of ethnic and regional variation in people's diets. They invoke the image of the food court in a suburban mall, where shoppers sit at centralized plastic tables surrounded by a ring of "global" fast food choices such as eggrolls, tacos, pizza, gyros, gumbo, and southern fried chicken. It is the commercial standardization of an urban street food experience. Certainly the nature of such foods is changed when they are mass produced for a large population. But to call such things "Americanized" suggests that there *is* a normative standard of American food, and implicitly food from a white European history, reminiscent of the kinds of diet and values that home economists attempted to impose on working-class, immigrant, and Native women in the early 1900s (Gabaccia, 125). It is no accident that the moral premise of such food instruction imposed by upper-middle-class white women was the same set of values (scientific order, efficiency) espoused by the developing commercial food industry.

Ritzer and Pillsbury's seemingly contradictory set of claims needs to be examined for the validity of its argument and for how it typifies both the idea of American culture and the average consumer through implicit assumptions about white middle-class experience.

Homogenizing Difference

In Ritzer's view, the commercial marketplace has the ability to level difference. The homogenizing effects of McDonaldization are more powerful than the historical activities of people who create and consume unique foods as a way of differentiating their region, race, or ethnicity. Thus, the foods produced and distributed by corporations, supermarkets, and most restaurants appeal to people more than "traditional home-made" foods for the following reasons: One, they're readily available and easy to access. Two, they require less effort to purchase and consume. Three, they are packaged and sold in ways that draw upon supposedly common cultural values.

The last reason is worth exploring for the way it suppresses differences between people in the name of shared national meanings. By consuming such products as a Big Mac, one consumes American culture. Indeed, this is often how people in other countries perceive such products. As Rick Fantasia (1995, 204) has pointed out, "fast food is identified abroad as a distinctively 'American' commodity[;] its cultural representations are likely to be strongly suggestive of what is viewed abroad as a distinctly American aesthetic, way of life, or experience."

However, the history of industrial food production in the United States and the variety of consumer experiences of and with commercial food products suggest that not all Americans approach commercially prepared foods in the same ways. Ritzer and Pillsbury's argument assumes that the cultural message of homogenization, developing a shared culture and assimilating, matters more in contemporary society than the culture people create from other aspects of their personal experience. But ample evidence exists to the contrary. For example, Tony

Whitehead's six years of food-related research with African Americans in North Carolina concludes the following: "Those who argue that the modern-day national diffusion of technological, communication, and transportation advances has effectively wiped out a distinctly southern culture . . . have mistakenly reduced the concept of culture to simple behaviors and ideas that can be completely destroyed by the introduction of powerful new ideas and material culture" (1992, 106).

For example, in Christi Smith's (1999) ethnography of white Appalachian out-migrants, people who have moved to cities describe eating at Cracker Barrel, a fast-food chain of "southern" restaurants, as a way of "tasting home" when one cannot easily get home-cooked versions.

As Sidney Mintz has pointed out, there are certainly cultural expectations about "newer" populations becoming integrated and assimilated into some version of mass culture that is packaged as "American." But the push toward homogenization is only one of the structural and personal forces people contend with in their daily lives. Mintz surmises, "That there are powerful pressures toward sameness, working particularly upon children, may be thought to increase the homogeneity of American food habits . . . but while learning to eat ice cream, and at fast food and ethnic restaurants has the effect of increasing homogeneity of a kind, this experience is not the same as learning or creating a cuisine. Strictly speaking, by learning such behavior people are becoming more sociologically alike, but it is not really clear that they are becoming more culturally alike" (1996, 113).

Differences based on gender, ethnicity, and race are intricately tied to class divisions in contemporary society. But Ritzer claims that commercial foods blanket such divisions. Since everybody has access to fast food and its popular cultural meanings, eating it becomes an easy way to participate in mainstream America. He contends that more people are affluent today and therefore can buy fast food and other McDonaldized products with their increased disposable income. While some groups of Americans may be experiencing greater affluence than before, many more are struggling harder with economic constraints. A large number of those who struggle are people of color and recent immigrants. Although theoretically most people have access to commercial food products, buying and consuming certain goods are inherently part of material and cultural stratification. While the upper middle class may consume commercial products, they have the material and symbolic resources to engage in other, more specialized forms of consumption.

Most important, in his desire to prove the power of cultural homogeneity, Ritzer misses the extent to which McDonaldization emerges, organizationally, in every setting, in relation to its opposite: production and consumption that is craft-based, artisanal, labor-intensive, and local or traditional.[9] Fast food exists in contrast with the boom in high-end haute cuisine. A supermarket that sells Velveeta probably also sells locally made specialty cheeses.

In fact, regional and ethnic racial differences are often strengthened in relation to McDonaldization. As Rick Fantasia (1999) points out, we need to pay attention to "the incredible marketing of creole, blackened, mesquite cooking processes and tastes . . . as well as the completely patterned progression of restaurant fashions that have moved from 'Chinese' or 'Asian' to increasingly specialized cultural fare (requiring an ever more finely-tuned 'cognoscenti' to determine the latest new taste) from Szechuan to Thai to sushi, each requiring a fairly elaborate infrastructure of specialized food distribution and marketing." Some of these competing trends in production and consumption are also about competing ideas about what is authentically "ethnic" in comparison to what is "American." Is it possible for only group members to create and consume "real" cuisines? Or are people with the cultural and economic capital of the upper middle class able to purchase such knowledge and engage in cross-boundary production and consumption? Is "eating the Other" an act of subjugation or empathy? (hooks 1998; Abrahams 1984). These debates, while vigorously pursued by some food scholars, are subsumed by Ritzer and Pillsbury's emphasis on homogenization.

Pillsbury does attempt to document the contributions of various racial and ethnic groups to a "national diet," but his version, which does not abandon the notion of a national cuisine, positions a model of culture and consumption that starts from a white European background and "adds in" ethnic and regional foods. He continually uses a normative center of white European fare in comparison to "immigrant" cuisine, stating in point, that "Chinese food has made few inroads into the traditional American kitchen" (1997, 162). Pillsbury's conflation of whiteness and Americanness is what Thomas K. Nakayama and Robert L. Krizek would describe as a "white rhetorical strategy" (1999, 99).

Normative assumptions about "American cuisine" erase ample historical evidence of generations of ethnic Americans at the center of defining foodways, using both native and imported foodstuffs to create new patterns of consumption even in colonial times. While dominant white European groups may have had the power to more strongly influence what gets defined as national culture, they did so in complex and contested ways, particularly around food. Donna Gabaccia (1998) demonstrates how, from the start, the Americas were a nation of "creolized eaters," drawing their basic foodstuffs from a variety of people's foodways. For example, culinary historians have recently begun to acknowledge the influence of African foods and cuisines on Europe and the Americas. Even so, they do not always recognize how African cooks in America came up with new and different ways to cook the same staples. According to Diane Spivey (1999, 239), "African American cooking itself encompasses numerous complex preparations that are considered to be standard 'American' recipes in this country today."

What lurks in Pillsbury's and Ritzer's analyses is the conflation of mass culture and national identity, as if one could completely determine the other. While critical of how capitalist mass production defines American culture, both authors accept its control over consumers. But, as Sidney Mintz has pointed out, "A 'national' cuisine is a contradiction in terms; there can be regional cuisines, but not national cuisines. I think that for the most part, a national cuisine is simply a holistic artifice based on the foods of the people who live inside some political system" (1996, 104). Such attempts at defining national culture—and in particular, national cuisine—are contested social and political battles. For example, Jeffrey M. Pilcher (1997) argues that the evolution of a Mexican national cuisine involved clashes between industrialization, Mexican elites who favored a European model, and the ultimately successful communities of women who incorporated Native American and campesino foodways into their cookbooks

People contend with mass culture in various ways, making it relevant and useful to their lives. Alan Warde suggests that scholars of consumption are often remiss in

> recognizing the way in which mass-produced commodities can be customized, that is appropriated for personal and private purposes. . . . Groups of people buy a common commercial product then work on it, adapt it, convert it into something that is symbolically representative of personal or collective identity. That it was once a mass-produced commodity becomes irrelevant after its incorporation into a person's household, hobby, or life. In one sense, all cookery is of this nature: labour is added, and by transforming groceries into meals social and symbolic value is created. That is the currently legitimate labour of love. (1997, 152)

Perhaps part of the problem comes from the way the authors divide contexts of production and consumption. Food production in both the "public" and "private" spheres depends on the labor of women and people of color, but these are treated as distinct topics for analysis.

When examining commercial food Ritzer and Pillsbury use race, gender, and class as variables and not as interrelated organizing principles for social life. In Ritzer's view, one of the potentially positive aspects of McDonaldization is that "People are more likely to be treated similarly, no matter what their race, gender, or social class" (1996, 12). Would he be able to maintain this claim if he centralized the construction of difference and focused more on the active ways that food gets produced and used by both industries and individuals? His analysis overlooks people who work in food service and food production. Most of these workers are at the lowest end of the wage pay scale and receive no benefits. The majority of people who hold these jobs are women, people of color, and recent immigrants. Thus, the "McDonaldized world" has inequality built right into the very nature of its production. Furthermore, fast food restaurants, supermarkets, and convenience stores vary depending on the neighborhood, region, urban or suburban setting. Customers are generally drawn from the demographic area surrounding the site. If we accept evidence of America's continued geographic segregation by race and class, it is highly likely that these commercial venues are equally segregated in the range of people who frequent one McDonald's over another. Studies of restaurants and fast food places suggest that, as in most workplaces, gender, race, and class are used as ways of differentiating and discriminating against workers and consumers.

Eating the Other

A walk around a typical supermarket today highlights products that were not standard available fare ten to twenty years ago. Ready-made hummus, instant couscous, soy sauce, and twenty varieties of salsa have equal shelf status with ice cream, pasta, ketchup, and mustard. Clearly, commercial food companies increasingly exploit the selling power of racial, ethnic, and regional variety. For Ritzer and Pillsbury, this "broadening of the American palate" is muted by the effects of commercial production on the quality and "authenticity" of such foods.

Ritzer (1996, 136) fears that "paradoxically, while fast-food restaurants have permitted far more of its people to experience ethnic food, the food that they eat has lost many of its distinguishing characteristics." Uniformity and predictability replace the craving for diversity. He claims that "people are hard-pressed to find an authentically different meal in an ethnic fast-food chain"(139). Pillsbury echoes this idea by arguing that ethnic and immigrant restaurants are "slowing Americanizing."[10] Such arguments make implicit assumptions about ethnicity, race, and the "ordinary American" consumer. Both writers assume that the majority of restaurants are patronized by white non-ethnics looking for an "exotic" meal. While some racial and ethnic restaurants have courted customers from the broad spectrum of American society, some have existed as part of ethnic enclaves where immigrants could partake of the foods of home.

Underlying these designations are two interesting assumptions. The first is that some foods can unquestioningly be defined as ethnic or racial.[11] Ethnic food, like ethnic culture, is assumed to be static, such that any change is viewed as assimilationist or a loss of tradition. The second is that food adaptations represent an inevitable corruption of authentic foods. Using interviews with Chinese Americans in the restaurant business, Netta Davis (1999) documents historical changes in the cuisine served, suggesting that such shifts are "a representation of Chinese and Chinese-American culture which is both 'unauthentic' fabrication and the product of an 'authentic' cultural adaptation. The accommodation of Chinese cuisine to the American market and palate are the result of a process of negotiation and transformation carried out by Chinese-American restaurateurs."

Leslie Prosterman (1984) uses a biographical account of a Jewish caterer to describe how changes in a standard kosher menu represented negotiations between the boundaries of religious culture, class-based concerns about sophisticated foods, and larger trends in American eating habits. Such changes illustrate the evolving rather than static nature of food traditions.

Pillsbury comments that the commercial marketing of certain foods "has encouraged those Americans fearful of 'foreign' cuisines to be a little more adventuresome" (29)[12] While it is important to emphasize how people choose foods outside their racial, ethnic, class, or regional experiences, the crucial questions should also focus on the conflicts around who gets to produce and define what is authentically ethnic or racial.[13] According to Donna Gabaccia, "Ethnicity in the marketplace was not the invention of corporate demographic marketing strategies" (1998, 160). She points to the belated corporate recognition of already thriving enclave markets and their attempts to compete with the already existing "enclave entrepreneurs." Big business food corporations "discovered" the selling power of ethnic and regional diversity after World War II, when there had already been a long history of successful smaller food producers, often from ethnic and racial groups, promoting products to both enclaves and the larger public market. Doris Witt (1999) and Rafia Zafar (1996) both use Verta Mae Grosvenor's culinary autobiographies to grapple with the symbolic and material uses of the term "soul food," concluding that it is not "a historical entity but as an evolving, flexible continuum: the food may change but the identity persists

. . . the 'boundaries' of culinary Black America may alter (in this case foods or styles of preparation) but the group itself remains identifiable by itself and to others" (Zafar, 81).

For example, the history of Aunt Jemima demonstrates the complex ways that African Americans have contended with a commercial representation of Black women and food. Witt sees "the trademark as a site where individual and collective boundaries have been mutually, albeit by no means equivalently, constructed and contested" (1999, 42). Significantly, each of these examples points to the way ethnic and racial groups participate in defining foods as part of their cultural experience. Those definitions are created both in tandem and in contention with those espoused by the commercial marketplace. Rather than focus exclusively on the impact of the capitalist market as it absorbs and sells various cultures, we need to examine how people in various groups act, collide, and collaborate in this cross-consumption.

Conclusion

If we understand race and gender as structural frameworks for social and economic life, then our analyses of global food trends and general patterns of consumption need to change. The first step is to move beyond the limits that consider gender and race only in relation to "feminized" topics like the body or only as symbolic markers for the experiences of nonwhite peoples. In particular, centralizing race and gender forces us to consider more than one level of analysis in studying food. Ritzer, Pillsbury, and other analysts of global capitalism do provide evidence that commercial foods do change the meanings and activities of people's daily lives. But it is equally true that people don't just accept the structural conditions and meanings of the material things they have access to; rather they construct their own critiques and new meanings which may or may not draw upon an already inscribed set of traditions.

I began by speculating about the divisions in the kinds of food books that come across my desk. I want to end by thinking about the scholarship on food and eating that I hope to see in the future. Most emphatically, it seems essential that studies of food and social life must explore how gender and race and class collide to create both the local and the global. Such research would focus on how specific food behaviors and roles regarding commensality are given gendered and racial meanings, how paid and unpaid food labor is divided to express gender and race differences symbolically, and how diverse social structures—not just families or ethnic groups—incorporate gender and racial values and convey advantages. These books would analyze the *construction* of such packages, simultaneously emphasizing the symbolic and the structural, the ideological and the material, the interactional and the institutional levels of analysis.[14] Perhaps then my appetite would be satisfied.

Notes

1. Although I prioritize gender and race, with some discussion of social class, I rely on conceptualizations of these terms that see them as intertwined with each other and various other forms of constructing difference and inequality in contemporary society. Ferree, Lorber, and Hess (1999) suggest that "gender, race, and social class are simultaneous social processes." Sexuality is also implicated in such arrangements, as another one of the "socially constructed, historically specific outcomes of the actions of and conflicts among dominant and subordinate groups [which] organize and permeate all the institutions of contemporary society in the United States" (xxi).

2. Examples of recent texts with similar aims include Bell and Valentine's (1998) *Consuming Geographies* and Gabaccia's (1998) *We Are What We Eat*. Although both of these books do a better job of contending with ethnicity, race, class, and gender, at a basic level they reproduce the same problems as Ritzer and Pillsbury. For Bell and Valentine, gender appears relevant only in relation to the home and the body. Even though Gabaccia presents a wonderful history of ethnic and racial entrepreneurship that defined local and national foodways, she minimizes the discussions of conflict and power inherent in such clashes of material and symbolic activity because she fails to theorize race and gender as organizing principles that set the stage for conflict.

3. *The McDonaldization of Society* was listed as one of the best-selling sociology books of the last twenty-five years (*Contemporary Sociology*, 1997). It was recently reissued along with two edited volumes, which include other writers' extensions of the McDonaldization thesis. There is often a McDonaldization panel at sociology conferences. Ritzer himself points out many instances of the way his term has entered popular usage (1996, xiii).

4. On the other hand, the family meal is often the site of conflict. Rhian Ellis (1983) documents stories from battered women who describe dinner as the catalyst for violent incidents. Bell and Valentine present research that shows children using dinner as a means of negotiating and asserting autonomy, which often results in conflicts (1997, 84–85).

5. Coontz (1992) argues for a historically informed analysis of family, concluding, "If it is hard to find a satisfactory model of the traditional family, it is also hard to make global judgements about how families have changed and whether they are getting better or worse. . . . Lack of perspective on where families have come from and how their evolution connects to other social trends tends to encourage contradictory claims and wild exaggerations about where families are going" (76–79).

6. Interestingly, Ritzer ignores the obvious comparison between households that rely on market-prepared food and households that rely on domestic help. Feminist historians describe the long legacy of wealthier white families who relied on African American or immigrant women and some Chinese and Japanese

men to cook for their families. By talking about how these families historically depended on cooking from an "outside" source, Ritzer would have to consider race and gender as organizing principles for the production and consumption of food. This changes the force of his critique about the nature of caring work. For example, although white women often relied on paid help in the kitchen, they were still the ones who held primary responsibility for the production of domestic hospitality and close social relationships in the family. A closer and more complex reading of such scenarios forces the analyst to view caring work as both physical and interactional labor that can be divided while still resting on structures of inequality that hold women and people of color more accountable. See Olesen (1993) and Rollins (1985).

7. Although the article asserts the absolute significance of primary socialization by family, what's interesting is that it goes on to try and alleviate the responsibility parents feel about providing home-cooked meals, suggesting that take-out food served at home can function as an equally successful way of creating family time and thus family itself.

8. "The 'superheavy users' in McDonald's parlance, mostly male and in their mid-teens to early 30s, come back at least twice a week. These are the people who make up 75% of the company's business" (Peter Drucker, *New York Times Magazine*, June 10, 1996).

9. Rick Fantasia provides evidence that "the reciprocally-determining process that creates 'McDonaldization' and 'distinctive' forms of culinary practice in the US has its perfect counterpart in the 1980's in France, where haute cuisine became an object of 'national (cultural) defense' (i.e. the emergence of Conseil Nationale des Arts Culinaire, and the fondation Brillat Savarin), just as the threat of the homogenizing 'other' (fast food) was in the midst of a significant boom" (personal communication, 1999). Further "it was not a coincidence that a serious market for 'Continental Cuisine' (the earliest American version of gourmet dining) emerged in response to the development of the fast food industry, as a way for American middle class elites to distinguish themselves from 'the masses'" (Fantasia 1995, 214).

10. For a better analysis of the relationship between commercial food corporations and ethnicity, see Warren Belasco, "Ethnic Fast Foods: The Corporate Melting Pot," *Food and Foodways* 2 (1987): 1–30.

11. Doris Witt (1999) does a terrific analysis of the shifting ways that Verta Mae Grosvenor describes soul food as racial or nonracial, particularly in comparison to the idea of "white foods" as mass-produced. To Witt, "by 'outing' peaches, watermelons, mangos, avocados and carrots, Grosvenor foregrounds the quixotic impossibility of white America's pursuit of racial purity via the consumption of chemically processed foods" (162).

12. Pillsbury's notions of what is "authentically" ethnic or racial are suspect throughout the text. In one instance he describes Caesar salad as the one kind of Greek food most Americans eat. Caesar salad was an American invention. Further, Mediterranean foods have, in fact, had a profound influence on American eating patterns. See Gabaccia (1998) and Belasco (1993) for examples.

13. In a comparative example, Anne Goldman's analysis of African American and Mexicana cookbooks concludes that they often constitute a form of culinary

autobiography, particularly for women, where gender and racial identity were issues to be explored in the text. The Mexicana cookbooks she analyzes often "evoke the flavors of the past in order to critique the cultural present" (1996, 17). What's interesting is that she finds ways that the label "genuine" can authenticate the writer and create distance for the reader, act as a way of dividing non-native readers from the community it celebrates. Reproducing recipes does not necessarily lead to cultural ownership (24).

14. This paraphrases Myra Marx Ferree's (1990) description of the difference between a sex-role analysis and a gender-relation analysis. I broaden her words to account for race and class, something she accomplishes in later writings with Judith Lorber and Beth B. Hess (1999).

References

Abrahams, R. 1984. "Equal Opportunity Eating: A Structural Excursus on Things of the Mouth." In *Ethnic and Regional Foodways in the U.S.*, ed. L. K. Brown and K. Mussell, Knoxville: University of Tennessee Press.

Baca Zinn, M. 1994. "Feminist Re-Thinking from Racial-Ethnic Families." In *Women of Color in U.S. Society*, ed. M. Baca Zinn and B. T. Dill. Philadelphia: Temple University Press.

Baca Zinn, M., and S. Eitzen, eds. 1989. *The Reshaping of America: Social Consequences of the Changing Economy.* Englewood Cliffs, NJ: Prentice-Hall.

Beardsworth, A., and T. Keil. 1997. *Sociology on the Menu: An Invitation to the Study of Food and Society.* New York: Routledge.

Belasco, W. 1987. "Ethnic Fast Foods: The Corporate Melting Pot," *Food and Foodways* 2.

———. 1993. *Appetite for Change: How the Counterculture Took on the Food Industry.* Ithaca: Cornell University Press.

Bell, D., and G. Valentine. 1997. *Consuming Geographies: We Are Where We Eat.* London: Routledge.

Collins, P. H. 1990. *Black Feminist Thought: Knowledge, Consciousness, and the Politics of Empowerment.* New York: Routledge.

Coontz, S. 1992. *The Way We Never Were: American Families and the Nostalgia Trap.* New York: Basic Books.

Davis, N. 1999. "We Don't Serve Chop Suey!: Chinese-American Resteranteurs Serving the 'Other.'" Paper presented at the annual meeting of the Association for the Study of Food and Society, Toronto.

DeVault, M. 1991. *Feeding the Family: The Social Organization of Caring as Gendered Work.* Chicago: University of Chicago Press.

Dill, B. T. 1988. "Our Mothers' Grief: Racial-Ethnic Women and the Maintenance of Families." *Journal of Family History* 13.

Douglas, M. 1972. "Deciphering a Meal." *Daedalus* 101, 1.

Ellis, R. 1983. "The Way to a Man's Heart: Food in the Violent Home." In *The Sociology of Food and Eating*, ed. A. Murcott. Aldershot, U.K.: Gower.

Fantasia, R. 1995. "Fast Food in France." *Theory and Society* 24.

———. 1999. Personal communication.

Ferree, M. M. 1990. "Beyond Separate Spheres: Feminism and Family Research." *Journal of Marriage and the Family* 52 (November).

Ferree, M. M., J. Lorber, and B. Hess, eds. 1999. *Revisioning Gender*. New York: Sage.

Gabaccia, D. 1998. *We Are What We Eat: Ethnicity and the Making of Americans.* Cambridge: Harvard University Press.

Glenn, E. N. 1985. *Issei, Nisei, Warbride: Three Generations of Japanese American Women in Domestic Service*. Philadelphia: Temple University Press.

———. 1999. "The Social Construction and Institutionalization of Gender and Race: An Integrative Framework." In *Revisioning Gender*, ed. Ferree, Lorber, and Hess.

Goldman, A. 1996. *Take My Word: Autobiographical Innovations of Ethnic American Working Women*. Berkeley: University of California Press.

Goody, J. 1982. *Cooking, Cuisine, and Class*. Cambridge: Cambridge University Press.

———. 1997. "Industrial Food: Towards the Development of a World Cuisine." In *Food and Culture*, ed. C. Counihan and P. Van Esterik. New York: Routledge.

hooks, b. 1998. "Eating the Other: Desire and Resistance." In *Eating Culture*, ed. R. Scapp and B. Seitz. Albany: SUNY Press.

Kopytoff, I. 1986. "The Cultural Biography of Things: Commoditization as Process." In *The Social Life of Things: Commodities in Cultural Perspective*, ed. A. Appadurai. Cambridge: Cambridge University Press.

Lapinski, T. 1999. Editor's Note. *Sesame Street Parents Magazine*, Fall.

Massey, D., and N. Denton. 1993. *American Apartheid: Segregation and the Making of the Underclass*. Cambridge: Harvard University Press.

McIntosh, W. A. 1996. *Sociologies of Food and Nutrition*. New York: Plenum Press.

Mennell, S., A. Murcott, and P. van Otterloo. 1992. *The Sociology of Food and Eating*. London: Sage.

Mintz, S. 1985. *Sweetness and Power: The Place of Sugar in Modern History*. New York: Penguin Press.

———. 1996. *Tasting Food, Tasting Freedom: Excursions into Eating, Culture, and the Past*. Boston: Beacon Press.

Nakayama, T., and R. Krizek. 1999. "Whiteness as a Strategic Rhetoric." In *Whiteness: The Communication of Social Identity*, ed. T. Nakayama and J. N. Martin. Beverly Hills: Sage.

Olesen, V. 1993. "Selves and a Changing Social Form: Notes on Three Types of Hospitality." *Symbolic Interaction* 17, 2.

Omi, M., and H. Winant. 1994. *Racial Formation in the United States: 1960–1990*. 2nd ed. New York: Routledge.

Pilcher, J. M. 1997. "Recipes for Patria: Cuisine, Gender, and Nation in Nineteenth Century Mexico." In *Recipes for Reading: Community Cookbooks, Stories, Histories*, ed. A. L. Bower. Amherst: University of Massachusetts Press.

Pillsbury, R. 1997. *No Foreign Food: The American Diet in Time and Place*. Boulder, CO: Westview Press.

Prosterman, L. 1984. "Food and Celebration: A Kosher Caterer as Mediator of Communal Traditions." In *Ethnic and Regional Foodways in the U.S.*, ed. L. K. Brown and K. Mussell. Knoxville: University of Tennessee Press.

Ritzer, G. 1996. *The McDonaldization of Society*. Thousand Oaks, CA: Pine Forge Press.

Rollins, J. 1985. *Between Women: Domestics and Their Employers*. Philadelphia: Temple University Press.

Smith, C. 1999. "Food and Culture in Appalachian Kentucky: An Ethnography." Unpublished Special Studies Paper. Smith College, Northampton, MA.

Sobal, J., and D. Maurer, eds. 1995. *Eating Agendas: Food and Nutrition as Social Problems*. New York: Aldine de Gruyter.

Spivey, D. 1999. *The Peppers, Cracklings, and Knots of Wool Cookbook: The Global Migration of African Cuisine*. Albany: SUNY Press.

Warde, Alan. 1997. *Consumption, Food, and Taste*. London: Sage.

West, C., and S. Fenstermaker. 1995. "Doing Difference." *Gender and Society* 9, 1.

West, C., and D. Zimmerman. 1987. "Doing Gender." *Gender and Society* 1, 2.

Whitehead, T. 1992. "In Search of Soul Food and Meaning: Culture, Food, and Health." In *African Americans in the South: Issues of Race, Class, and Gender*, ed. H. Baer and Y. Jones. Athens: University of Georgia Press.

Witt, Doris. 1999. *Black Hunger: Food and the Politics of U.S. Identity*. Oxford: Oxford University Press.

Zafar, Rafia. 1996. "Cooking Up a Past: Two Black Culinary Narratives." *GRAAT: Ethnic Voices* II, No. 14.

Indian Spices across the Black Waters

SHARMILA SEN

Crossing the Kala Pani

In a London saturated with South Asian curry houses, the Trinidadian novelist Samuel Selvon's search for Indian food as he knew it provides an illuminating anecdote about the location of contemporary Indo-Caribbean culinary culture. At a conference on Indo-Caribbean history, Selvon once said, "In all my years in England, I never came across the kind of curry we ate in Trinidad, and I searched all over London for a dhall pourri, and never saw one until one enterprising Trinidadian started up a little cookshop."[1] In order to fully appreciate the complexities involved in Selvon's search for Indo-Caribbean food on English streets lined with "Indian" restaurants run by immigrant Sylhetis from Bangladesh, it is necessary to remember those original vessels—or to use Mahadai Das's phrase, those "wooden missions of imperialist design"[2]—setting out from the Hooghly harbor near Calcutta, bound for Port of Spain or Georgetown in the nineteenth century. Between 1838 and 1917, indentured laborers from India crossed the dreaded kala pani (black waters) in thousands in order to compensate for the post-emancipation labor shortage in the British colonial sugar estates. While some Indian indentured laborers were taken to islands such as Jamaica, Barbados, Martinique, and Cuba, the majority landed in Guyana and Trinidad. Of the 551,000 indentured laborers brought from India to the Caribbean and South America, 238,909 arrived in British Guiana and 143,939 arrived in Trinidad.[3] East Indian[4] laborers transported (often as punishment for such activities against the empire as taking part in the so-called Mutiny of 1857)[5] to the British Caribbean colonies form a large part of the South Asian diaspora. These coolies[6] labored on the sugarcane fields to provide a sweetener for the tea produced by peasants in Assam and Bengal, as well as for coffee and chocolate, the two other

185

bitter colonial beverages. In England, from the late eighteenth century onwards, relatively cheap Caribbean sugar had begun to replace many Indian spices as a fruit and vegetable preservative.[7] And, ironically, at the same time when Eastern spices were being ousted by New World sugar at the English table, coolies were importing their Indian condiments and recipes across the oceans into their new home in the Caribbean colonies. While subcontinental cultures have been part of Caribbean traditions since the arrival of the first Indian cane-cutters in 1838, the Indo-Caribbean population has started to receive serious critical attention within academic circles only over the last two decades. To the already existing set of stock images which come to mind when speaking of the Caribbean—it is a place for tourists, a paradise, an area of contemporary poverty, a realm of natural disasters; it produces juicy fruits and fast bowlers on the cricket field; it is the promise of sugared profit and the site of unspeakable taboo acts such as cannibalism—we must add a new image: the East Indian coolie, working in the sugar estate under conditions scarcely better than that of slavery. The image of "fields and fields of swaying sugar-cane [planted by coolies] to give the taste of sweetness to us," Rajkumari Singh writes, can exist only in juxtaposition to the memory of "how often this sweetness became bitter gall to them [the coolies] for seeking their rights."[8]

If the East Indian population in general has been largely ignored in Caribbean discourse, the East Indian woman has been even more marginalized. Among the better-known Indo-Caribbean writers, especially those recognized by the Anglo-American readership, women's voices are sadly missing. Moreover, as Rawwida Baksh-Soodeen argues, "since the dominant discourse within Caribbean feminism is Afro-Centric, [. . .] feminist analyses of Caribbean society have tended to focus on the black and coloured population and 'creole' culture."[9] However, some contemporary fictions by Indo-Caribbean writers have begun to reconstruct the nearly forgotten coolie woman's story. In his most recent novel, *The Counting House* (1996), the Indo-Guyanese writer David Dabydeen focuses on the experiences of coolie women in nineteenth-century Guyana. This novel, pieced together from seven artifacts found at Plantation Albion, owned by the Gladstone family, creates two rival female narratives about a colonial sugar estate: Rohini's Indian tale and Miriam's Afro-Caribbean tale. *The Counting House* is (at times problematically) tenacious in its desire to trace the development of an emerging Indo-Caribbean literary identity which seeks to distinguish itself from a more dominant Afro-Caribbean discourse. To this end, curry and crab callaloo are symbolically pitted against each other in order to classify the identifying culinary traits of two so-called rival populations who were brought to the Caribbean for the specific purpose of producing the sweetest commodity of all: sugar. This essay is a reading of the cultural work performed by Indian and other food products in the making of a distinct Indo-Caribbean identity in Dabydeen's novel.

Sweet Biscuits in a Sugar Estate

David Dabydeen's *The Counting House* is a rather clear response to the voices raised in conferences across the world and to the increasingly audible complaints heard in Indo-Caribbean academic circles demanding increased focus on East Indian women's experiences.[10] The novel charts the life of Rohini and Vidia, a young couple who flee mid-nineteenth-century rural India gripped by the violence of the so-called 1857 Mutiny, and arrive as indentured laborers in a sugar estate in British Guyana. The estate, Plantation Albion, is the site of the coolies' encounter with the newly freed African slaves. While Rohini eventually strikes up a friendship with an older Black woman, Miriam, Vidia fails to find succor in the sugarcane fields and attempts to make the voyage home to India, only to drown in a shipwreck.[11]

Although Dabydeen uses Indian foods as well as practices and tools which accompany them to draw attention to a distinct Indo-Caribbean experience, it is another type of colonial cuisine, one that requires a global network and global labor, which stubbornly appears at the very moment East Indian cultural identity is about to be fixed. Therefore, before turning our attention to the uses of Indian food in representations of coolie culture, it is necessary to analyze the English biscuit tin which survives as a material witness to the indentured laborers' presence on a sugar plantation and their relationship to the colonizing nation. The prologue to *The Counting House* consists of two quotations from Fielding and Gladstone and a paragraph listing the seven artifacts out of which the author invents his novel:

> In the ruined counting house of Plantation Albion, British Guiana, three small parcels of materials survive as the only evidence of the nineteenth-century Indian presence. The first two parcels consist mostly of lists of Indian names, accounts of the wages paid to them, and scraps of letters. The contents of the third parcel are a cow-skin purse, a child's tooth, an ivory button, a drawing of the Hindu God, Rama, haloed by seven stars, a set of iron needles, some kumari seeds, and an empty tin marked "Huntley's Dominion Biscuits", its cover depicting a scene of the Battle of Waterloo.[12]

Last in an order of ascending rhetorical importance, the Huntley's biscuit tin is a surprising culinary witness to what, at least according to

Dabydeen, may be called a vanishing nineteenth-century coolie history. Huntley's dominion is vast indeed.[13] Taking our cues from anthropologists and sociologists such as Sidney Mintz[14] and Jack Goody, we can place the biscuit tin marked with British military triumph on a number of watery pathways. Goody writes that "it was this general context of colonialism, overseas trade and long-lasting foods that saw the development of the great British Biscuit industry."[15] Companies such as Huntley and Palmers, Carrs, and later Peek Freans were, by the mid-nineteenth century, rapidly growing and establishing an international clientele. Their impact on the eating habits of Britons both at home and abroad was tremendous, as was their impact on the industrial revolution.[16]

These tinned sweets circumnavigated the globe from India and the Far East to Africa and the Caribbean, arriving at last at the very estates that produced the sugar for relatively cheap, mass-marketed edibles. Rohini scarcely gets a taste of sugar biscuits in the coolie logie. In fact, her only encounter with Huntley and Palmers's product takes place when Gladstone gives her an empty tin as reward for her work in his house. The coolie woman in Dabydeen's novel, of course, is not knowledgeable about the network of political and economic systems in which the biscuit tin is embedded when she brings it home to her husband. Barred from experiencing the taste of sweet biscuits, Rohini satisfies herself with the visual pleasures the colorful tin offers. That the Huntley and Palmers tin is decorated with a scene from the battle of Waterloo the prologue had already revealed. However, through Rohini's eyes, we see the battle as an unfamiliar abstraction of blues and reds: "On the cover was painted a battle scene, a set of whitemen in red in one corner firing canons, a set of whitemen in blue in another firing back; in the middle was a field where a third set of whitemen mingled, some in blue, some in red, all on black horses, and all with raised swords" (150–151). Ignorant as the female coolie might be of European struggles for power and of the importance of the sugar economy, her highly ocular understanding of the biscuit tin as a system of symmetrically placed red and blue figures is quick to equate it with economic profit. Rohini brings the biscuit tin home to her husband so that he can hoard his meager savings of a few coins in it. Moreover, the symbolic status of the biscuit tin is reiterated again in the novel when Miriam, the ex-slave, divulges that she cannot risk her privileged status on the estate for a coolie insurrection: "I taste too much cadbury and sweet-biscuits to go back . . ." (168). As Goody and Mintz have both argued, capitalist global networks produce industrial foods *and* create a market for their consumption. Tinned products were invented for the most pragmatic of reasons—sustenance during long journeys, civil or military. On Plantation Albion, however, the tins of biscuits which Rohini and Miriam cherish are not just intended to satisfy one's physical appetite but hold the promise of satisfying psychological desires as well. They are a bit of the imperial center suspended in sugar and flour. Thus, while Gladstone may look upon biscuits from Huntley and Palmers as barely palatable physical necessities in an alien environment, the coolie woman and the ex-slave see the same tins as desirable luxuries, intimations of a bountiful world far from servitude. These two sugar estate workers, Dabydeen's ironic portrayal of Huntley and Palmers's ideal consumer, remain adamantly blind to their own labor in the cane fields that produce the necessary raw materials for the biscuit factories in Britain.

For Rohini, and for many female indentured laborers like her, the voyage from India was intended as a journey away from economic and social hardships.[17] In the coolie barracks of Guyana, a frustrated Rohini is tempted to think that not only a departure from India but also a complete abjuration of Indian customs—ways of eating, marital relationships, even religious practices—is the only effective route to emancipation. In this context, the plantation owner Gladstone's eating habits seem to fascinate her at first: "In the coolie hut she squatted before the plate, mashing the food into a colorful mess, before scooping it into her mouth in hasty movements. Gladstone ate with graceful cutlery, his hands carving the meat as absent-mindedly as they moved over the globe" (154). *The Counting House* repeatedly attributes two qualities to Indian food: colorful and messy. The vibrant hues of this particularly symbolic diet within the novel are rarely muted. Echoing those popular tourism tracts of our own times which belabor the tired banalities of brilliant colors and attendant chaos when describing India, the Caribbean, or just about any place in the so-called Third World, Rohini's plate of "colorful mess" contains an entire discourse of travel, tourism, and colonization. What stands in opposition to the "mess," in both its incarnations, as food and as chaos? Gleaming rows of silverware, the usage of which reached new and fanciful heights in the Victorian era. Just as the biscuit tin represents the efficiency of European colonizers to Rohini, the use of cutlery to manipulate the meat on the plate symbolizes the British ability to order the world to its convenience. Awed by what she perceives as Gladstone's dexterous control over both meat and the world, Rohini plans to bear the plantation owner's child, "swelling her body to the roundness of the globe which one day it would inherit" (155).

Miriam, the ex-slave, herself addicted to Cadbury's products and sweet biscuits, does not want the coolie woman to usurp her place in the white master's household. Using a potent mixture of mara-bark, she drugs Rohini and takes her to the local medicine woman in order to induce an abortion. The East Indian coolie's first attempt to insert herself into the Caribbean propelled by a heady mixture of Huntley's sugar biscuits and elaborate Victorian silverware usage is successfully checked by the Afro-Caribbean woman. Just as Rohini's ability to bear the white man's child creates a potential friction between the East Indian and the Black population, her cooking can become an arena of ethnic conflict as well.

The Coolie Woman's Kitchen

The discourse of food in Caribbean texts—of both Indian and African origins—pervades both literary and critical practices; non-Western foods, for instance, are often used to signify creolized cultures. In Dabydeen's fictions, Indian food functions to signify a non-European heritage *and* to specify a non-African/Amerindian ethnicity. But such a clean distinction is not always possible. In fact, as the following pages will suggest, Dabydeen's work is most successful at the moment of its failure to reconstruct a discrete India in the Caribbean. In the novel, the coolie woman's attempt to create a discrete Indian identity faces its greatest competition not from the patriarchal husband but from the ex-slave woman. There are intimations of writers as diverse as Eric Williams[18] and George Lamming[19] in Miriam's nineteenth-century voice when she forcefully reminds Rohini that

> Albion is *we* land, *we* man and *we* story and *I* tell it how *I* want. I start the story and I kill it so *you*, Rohini, hush and listen, for you is only a freshly-come coolie. When I give you freedom to talk, then you talk, but I can wave my chisel any time and interrupt you and take over the story and keep it or throw it away. What right you have to make story? What right you have to make baby for Gladstone? Albion is a nigger, we slave and slaughter here, Albion is we story, and you coolie who only land this morning best keep quiet till you can deserve to claim a piece. (170–171)

Miriam and Rohini's ambivalent battle—a struggle that is centered around their mutual hatred of the colonial system *and* their mutual claim on the colonizer, Gladstone—reaches a climax when Rohini discovers that she is pregnant with the plantation owner's child. Miriam, who has played mistress to Gladstone for years before Rohini's arrival in Guyana and had aborted a number of fetuses conceived with Gladstone, is aghast that a newly arrived coolie woman can dare to bear the master's child so publicly. Reproduction, for these two women, is quite clearly linked to making a narrative gesture, writing a history of Guyana. Before her arrival in Guyana, Rohini had rather assiduously avoided such narrative possibilities with liberal use of the kumari seeds her mother had secreted to her before marriage. The kumari seeds, literally translated as virgin seeds, are part of Rohini's inheritance from India. Dabydeen, we remember, opens his novel by cataloging those kumari seeds found in the ruined counting house of Plantation Albion.

In English texts, the link between food and pharmacy is an old one. For instance, in Gervase Markham's *The English hous-wife* (1653), one of the earliest published cookbooks in England, the chapter on food is nestled between pharmacy and perfumerie.[20] The arrangement of Markham's book, which is characteristic of its time, indicates that in the zone between the curative and the cosmetic lies the discussion of food. In *The Counting House*, Rohini's Indian kumari seeds also function within this liminal zone. As a contraceptive device, the seeds are Rohini's protection against an unwanted pregnancy early in her marriage to Vidia. By the time Rohini has transported those seeds to the Caribbean, the reader already knows of their deadly potential. In order to facilitate the process of emigration, Rohini uses a potent mixture of kumari seeds to kill the cow in her in-laws' house. The inauspicious death of the cow, which transpires as smoothly as the young bride has planned, is read as an ominous sign and hastens the departure of Rohini and Vidia to Guyana, a land of rich promise deftly sketched by the wily recruiters of British India. Contraception, then, can both impede and hasten the creation of new life. Kumari seeds, as the name suggests, are not only curative in that they can defer conception or induce abortion, they are also cosmetic. These seeds, with their eponymous promise of virginity, can erase the past and help maintain the illusion of innocence, of a new beginning. When Rohini finally stops re-creating virginity through these grains, her pregnancy with Gladstone's child threatens to create a new history of the Caribbean, a history that Eric Williams will summarily relegate to the sidelines a century later. The discourse of Indian food products in the Caribbean, even in their pharmacological incarnations, refuses to conform to the identity politics of late-twentieth-century scholars. While inspiring the creation of a self-consciously Indo-Caribbean text, Rohini's kumari seeds and the Huntley's Dominion biscuit tin veer toward shared and fluid histories much more than toward the imagining of a discrete India in the Caribbean.

Despite the complicated genealogies of the kumari seed and Huntley's Dominion biscuits, the novel continues its attempt to invoke images of specifically South Asian food products to re-create the Indian laborer's Guyana. For instance, the episodes of collision between the two worker communities of Plantation Albion, the freed Blacks and the coolies, are marked by consumption or preparation of Indian foods. One such collision, which is meant to cement the difference between the two communities, is the scene where Kampta, a creolized East Indian, is whipped publicly. The indentured laborers feast on rotis and potato curry and the Afro-creoles sell trinkets in the crowd which has been gathered to witness Kampta's punishment. The Afro-Caribbean and the Indo-Caribbean population commune in a grotesque lunch party where colonial violence mingles freely with West Indian rum and East Indian curry.

> The remaining Sundays [of Kampta's whipping] became occasions of festivity, the coolies squatting in the grass and unwrapping rotis and potato curry whilst their children ran about with homemade kites. A nigger fiddler, glad for a taste of free food and rum, joined the picnic, slapping the frail backs of a few coolies in a show of instant camaraderie. The food jolted free from their hands or mouths. Pieces of potato lay on the grass and the nigger fiddler smiled maliciously as ants scrambled over them. (83)

Significantly, the encounter between the African and the Indian populations occurs against a backdrop of curried potatoes. In this passage the two rival communities both adopt and reject certain foods as the definitive marker of their racialized selves. The creole[21] adopts and resists the new tastes brought by the coolies to Guyana. While the Black workers are tempted to try the potato curry cooked by women such as Rohini in *The Counting House*, they are also scornful of the new tastes imported by these usurpers. At Kampta's whipping, Miriam tries a palouri (fritter) and spits it out in disgust, crying for coconut water to combat the piquancy of pepper. A scene such as this, of course, does less to cement static, antagonistic Afro-creole and East Indian cultures and, in fact, points to the very porousness of such lines of cultural distinctions. The coconut water in which the New World Afro-creole seeks refuge originates in tropical southeast Asia. The pepper which adds piquancy to the palouri would not have found a place in Rohini's kitchen if Dutch traders had not carried the New World product to India. And the humble potato itself, the base of the curry which the fiddler gleefully watches fall on the grass and be wasted on the ants, is also a vegetable introduced to Asia by traders who had voyaged to the Americas. No doubt Rohini and Miriam do not question the origins of spices or their familiar staples. Yet, when David Dabydeen attempts to reach back to an originary point in Indo-Caribbean history through a creative rewriting, the thorny question of authenticity muddles neat categories. The very product which adds piquancy to the curry and marks it as East Indian in the novel was not native to India prior to the sixteenth century. The transformed ecology of nineteenth-century South Asia, however, had absorbed the New World product, and the once foreign chili pepper had transformed the taste of Indian curry markedly.

Dabydeen, as well as some other writers from the Caribbean, continues to invest curry and its associated spices and smells with the sign of East Indian difference. Dabydeen's project of writing a coolie history and reinscribing a forgotten South Asian culture rests on female production of particular foods. If women are to be the keepers and producers of culinary and cultural traditions, then how does the association of coolie identity with the East Indian woman's kitchen affect interracial relationships within the Caribbean?

Another form of cultural production in Caribbean, the calypso, offers some possible answers to this question. In his writing about twentieth-century calypsos, the West Indian scholar Gordon Rohlehr argues that an Indian feast, especially one at which East Indian women were present, often turned into an "arena of ethnic confrontation" between the creole and the East Indian. In calypsos, the "Talkarie" [cooked vegetables] became for the Afro-creole the thing to which the "alien Other" [East Indians] could be "comically reduced."[22] In the lyrics of such artists as Atilla, Executor, or Fighter, which Rohlehr mentions, the rejection of East Indian food by an Afro-creole man is complicated by his sexual desire for an East Indian woman. In Invader's 1939 calypso, "Marajh daughter," the protagonist is clear about his intentions regarding the East Indian woman:

> I want everybody to realize
> I want a nice Indian girl that is creolize
> I don't want no parata or dhal water
> I want my potato and cassava
> Crab, callaloo, and of course I want my manicou
> And how about my stew pork and pound plantain too
> I want my own vermouth and whiskey
> And they must agree to maintain my family . . .[23]

While the abjuration of dhal water and parata is no doubt a commentary on perceived Indian frugality, a stereotype that exists in Guyana and Trinidad even today,[24] Invader's final line betrays his protagonist's real interest: the East Indian family's wealth. The complex economic rivalry between Asian and African groups in Guyana during the twentieth century, and particularly in the post-independence decades, is reiterated in the calypso artist's shrewd lyrics and in Dabydeen's fiction. The Indian feast (or even a picnic at a public whipping in the case of *The Counting House*) is a particularly charged scene where the accusations from disgruntled Afro-Caribbeans regarding East Indian plenitude *and* frugality collide upon the figure of the Indo-Caribbean woman. *The Counting House*, rather disappointingly, resorts to the age-old tactic of charging Rohini with the responsibility of safeguarding the so-called Indian traditions while also portraying her as a vulnerable, sexually promiscuous, and ultimately unreliable custodian of that Indianness. The kumari seeds that Rohini secretly imports to Guyana may prove to be her only resistance to the thankless task of preserving an India in the Caribbean.

The Counting House, nonetheless, attempts to recreate an authentic Indian voice from the debris of forgotten artifacts through the strategic use of Hindustani words. In fact, the great majority of Hindustani words used in the text are related to food or cooking. What are the exigencies of a fiction in which the dialogue in Indo-Guyanese English is littered with Hindustani words for food such as "palouri" (fritter), "channa" (chick peas), "roti" (unleavened bread), "massala" (spices), and "jilabie" (syrupy, fried sweet)? As important, what impact does the transliterated Hindustani word have on a Caribbean anglophone text? From the moment it styles itself as a narrative derived from records left in a colonial office, *The Counting House* places great emphasis on the significance of the written word. In the novel, Miriam and Rohini understand the value of learning to read the colonizer's languages—English and Latin—as they roam in the Gladstone graveyard, scrutinizing gravestones. They are both drawn to one particular Latin engraving: "Sunt Lachrimae Rerum"—a phrase that remains untranslated throughout the novel. For the coolie and ex-slave alike, the translation of the Latin phrase into English seems to be a key to grasping the power of the family that owns the fruit of their labor. In such a context, the untranslated Hindustani stands in peculiar opposition to the untranslated Latin on the pages of the novel: The Englishman's tears (borrowed from Virgil's Roman Empire) confront the Indian coolie's comestibles via the medium of a third language, English.

When Indian spices and cooking utensils[25] are carried across the kala pani, the words used to describe them travel alongside. Rohini and Vidia's curries are accretive products, reflecting the impact of centuries of trade, travel, invasions, and colonization, but they remain distinctively alien in colonial Guyana and cannot be separated from their South Asian signifiers. The last vestige of nineteenth-century India in the Caribbean, then, seems to lurk in words for describing a taste, a vegetable, a sweet, or a recipe. And women are most often presented as the guardians of these recipes, the preparers of dishes bearing non-English names. Dabydeen's representation of the East Indian woman's kitchen as a repository of migrant culture in this novel is an echo of earlier feminist essays by Indo-Caribbean women. Here is Rajkumari Singh in her attempt to retrieve an ethnic identity from her grandmother's kitchen:

> Surely you cannot forget Per-Agie our great Coolie-grandmother squatting on her haunches, blowing through the phookni to help the chuha-fire blaze so that your parents and mine could have a hot sadha roti and alu chokha before they leave for the fields! Can't you hear her bangles tinkling as she grinds the garam massala to make her curries unforgettable? Does not your gourmet's nostril still quiver with the smell . . . the one and only unforgettable smell of hot oil, garlic, onions, pepper, geera, to chunke the daal that was and still is a must in our daily diet? . . . Daal, rice and baigan choka, or coconut choka, or alloo choka . . . All this they gave to us and more. In return for our HERITAGE what greater tribute can we pay them than to keep alive the name by which they were called. COOLIE . . .[26]

At the linguistic level, a distinctive feature of the English (or even the patwa) used to describe Indo-Caribbean experiences, as seen in Singh's rallying cry, is the frequent use of a Hindustani gastronomic vocabulary. In her exhortation to keep the coolie grandmother's memory alive, many of those words, such as "baigan" or "geera" could have easily been written as "eggplant" or "cumin" without sacrificing the meaning. But, for Singh, the "baigan" and "geera" are far more evocative than "eggplant" or "cumin" because they are fossil sounds bearing the impression of over a century-old Indo-Caribbean presence.

Despite the remnants of a selective vocabulary derived from Hindustani words, the East Indian woman risks becoming a nearly invisible figure, confined to cooking the roti and curry which serve as a symbol of far-away India. While Indian masala acts as the line dividing the Afro-creole from the East Indian, Rohini, who grinds those spices, is silenced by the textual strategies of *The Counting House*. Dabydeen's novel, while ostensibly attempting to give a voice to Rohini, finds itself unable to articulate that experience in the first person. Of the three sections of the novel—"Rohini," "Kampta," and "Miriam"—only the last one is narrated in the first person. Miriam, the ex-slave woman, confides to the reader her inner thoughts about the "freshly-come coolie" or about her secret recipe for substituting mara-bark for cinnamon to poison the white mistress of the plantation. But Rohini's Indian recipe remains largely untold, just as her newly arrived coolie language remains largely unheard on Dabydeen's page, barely leaking out in the form of a few culinary tidbits.

In a recent cultural representation of the East Indian woman originating from another island with a large Caribbean population, Britain, the bhangramuffin singer Apache Indian's[27] song "Arranged Marriage" brings together some of the discourses on sugar and femininity, and attempts to locate the nineteenth-century coolie woman's descendant within the syrupy spirals of a popular South Asian dessert, the "jilabie"— an untranslated word in Dabydeen's novel.[28] With a pronounced sense of satire, the self-styled Indo-Caribbean sings: "Me wan gal sweet like jelebee."[29] While reading *The Counting House*, we must watch for its intersections with other forms of Indo-Caribbean cultural expression in order to gauge the complex irony of being "sweet like jelebee" for the female descendants of those coolies who toiled in Caribbean sugar estates.

Notes

1. Samuel Selvon, "Three into One Can't Go—East Indian, Trinidadian, Westindian," in *India in the Caribbean*, ed. David Dabydeen and Brinsley Samaroo (Warwick: Hansib/University of Warwick, Centre for Caribbean Studies, 1987), 18.

2. Mahadai Das, "They Came in Ships," in *India in the Caribbean*.

3. David Dabydeen and Brinsley Samaroo, introduction, *Across Dark Waters: Ethnicity and Indian Identity in the Caribbean* (Warwick: Warwick University Caribbean Studies and Macmillan Caribbean, 1996), 1.

4. "East Indian" is the term most frequently used in the Caribbean context to indicate a South Asian heritage. Although the term bases itself on a genealogy of ludicrous misnomers and can lead to typically comic conjunctions such as East Indian West Indian, I have retained "East Indian" throughout this essay to refer to peoples and cultures in the Caribbean associated with places that are now called India, Pakistan, or Bangladesh. My term for the literature of the East Indian community, once again taking my cue from scholars such as Dabydeen and Frank Birbalsingh, is "Indo-Caribbean."

5. In *From Pillar to Post*, the Guyanese novelist Ismith Khan says, "[My family came to Guyana] because of the Indian 'Mutiny' when Indian soldiers were called upon to shoot on fellow Indians. Some soldiers rebelled and turned their guns on the British instead. My grandfather was one of these rebellious soldiers. Consequently, he was on the run from the British authorities. I know that my family left from Kanpur Railway Station, but I don't know how they made it to Guyana" (139). For the complete interview, see *From Pillar to Post: The Indo-Caribbean Diaspora*, ed. Frank Birbalsingh (Toronto: Tsar, 1997), 139–146.

6. There is undoubtedly a history of degradation associated with the term "coolie" and in some parts of the Caribbean it continues to carry all the viciousness of a

150-year-old invective. Nonetheless, in more recent years, scholars, writers, and activists have begun to revive the term in order to assert the East Indian presence, indentureship and all, in the Caribbean. In "I Am a Coolie," *Heritage* 2 (Georgetown, Guyana, 1973): 24–27, Rajkumari Singh writes: "Not only in the Guyana context must COOLIE be given new meaning, but in every land of the Caribbean Sea, the Indian Ocean, the seas of the East, in Africa and Europe. Proclaim the word! Identify with the word! Proudly say to the world: 'I AM A COOLIE.'" In this essay and elsewhere, I use the term "coolie" in this spirit of reappropriation and resistance.

7. Anne Wilson, *Food and Drink in Britain* (London: Constable, 1973), 267. Wilson also attributes the decrease in spice usage to the availability of fresher meat due to modifications in livestock management and improved transporation systems.

8. Singh, "I Am a Coolie."

9. Rawwida Baksh-Soodeen, "Issues of Difference in Contemporary Caribbean Feminism," *Feminist Review* 59 (Summer 1998): 79.

10. The following essays offer a range of views on this topic: Aruna Srivastava, "Images of Women in Indo-Caribbean Literature," and Verene A. Shepard, "Indian Women in Jamaica, 1845–1945," in *Indenture and Exile: The Indo-Caribbean Experience*, ed. Frank Birbalsingh (Toronto: Tsar, 1989); Ramabai Espinet, "Representation and the Indo-Caribbean Woman in Trinidad and Tobago," in *Indo-Caribbean Resistance*, ed. Frank Birbalsingh (Toronto: Tsar, 1993), and "The Invisible Woman in West Indian Fiction," *World Literature Written in English*, 29 (1989): 2, by the same author; and Jeremy Poynting, "East Indian Women in the Caribbean: Experience and Voice," in *India in the Caribbean*.

11. Vidia's fictional return to India may have ended in a fatal disaster, but the actual coolies who did try to go back after their period of indenture did not fare much better. For a historical account of those return voyages, see Marianne Soares Ramesar, "The Repatriates," in *Across the Dark Waters*. The novelist, it should be noted, quite conspicuously kills his male Indian protagonist Vidia, surely something of a reference to Vidiadhar Surajprasad Naipaul, to make room for a female Indian voice in Guyana. However, the reader can never comfortably quell the suspicion that Rohini's female East Indian voice is perhaps too constrictively locked in resistance to that of the male writers from the Caribbean.

12. David Dabydeen, *The Counting House* (London: Jonathan Cape, 1996), xi–xii. Subsequent references will be made parenthetically in the text.

13. In her discussion of the Huntley and Palmers biscuit tin, Anne McClintock writes: "In the flickering magic lantern of imperial desire, teas, biscuits, tobaccos, Bovril, tins of cocoa and, above all, soaps beach themselves on far-flung shores, tramp through jungles, quell uprisings, restore order and write the inevitable legend of commercial progress across the colonial landscape." McClintock, *Imperial Leather* (New York: Routledge, 1995), 219, where this argument is elaborated.

14. See Sidney Mintz, *Sweetness and Power: The Place of Sugar in Modern History* (New York: Viking, 1985).

15. Jack Goody, *Cooking, Cuisine, and Class* (Cambridge: Cambridge University Press, 1982), 155.

16. In chapter 5 of *Cooking, Cuisine, and Class*, Goody notes that some of the innovations in biscuit production, especially those at Huntley and Palmers, led to

the development of a secondary industry which specialized in trade machinery. He writes:

> In 1859, these firms [Huntley and Palmers, Carrs, and Peek Freans] sold 6 million lbs of their products. Changing eating habits in the shape of earlier breakfasts and later dinners led to a further increase in consumption, and by the late 1870s the figure had risen to 37 million lbs a year. Huntley and Palmers had become one of the forty most important companies in Britain, and within fifty years their biscuits were distributed not only throughout the nation but throughout the world. As with the early canning industry, much of the production of biscuits had first of all been directed to the needs of travellers, explorers and the armed forces. Such produce sustained sailors, traders and colonial officers overseas; only later did industrial production impinge upon the internal market in England or upon the local market overseas, eventually becoming part of the daily diet of the population. (157)

17. Many of the female indentured laborers were single women fleeing their ancestral villages to escape social stigmas such as pregnancy before marriage. In fact, the novelist V. S. Naipaul's grandmother was one such unmarried mother who crossed the kala pani to the Caribbean.

18. In his authoritative work *From Columbus to Castro*, Eric Williams devotes only fourteen out of five hundred and fifteen pages to Indian indentured laborers. Given the fact that Williams's own island, Trinidad, boasts an Indo-Caribbean population equal in number to the Afro-Caribbean one, this oversight is ironic indeed. See Eric Williams, *From Columbus to Castro: The History of the Caribbean, 1492–1969* (New York: Harper & Row, 1970).

19. See, for example, George Lamming, "The Indian Presence as Caribbean Reality," in *Indenture and Exile*. This paper, based on Lamming's personal recollections of his childhood in Barbados, only affirms the invisibility of East Indians, an invisibility which is further subsumed under the author's call for a pan-Caribbean identity.

20. Gervase Markham, *The English hous-wife* (London: Printed by W. Wilson for E. Brewster and George Sawbridge, 1653).

21. In a recent publication, Patricia Mohammed writes that, in East Indian communities in the Caribbean, the term "creole"—a historically slippery word—is used exclusively to refer to peoples of African descent. See Patricia Mohammed, "Towards Indigenous Feminist Theorizing in the Caribbean," *Feminist Review* 59 (Summer 1998): 29–30.

22. Gordon Rohlehr, "Images of Men and Women in the 1930s Calypsoes: The Sociology of Food Acquisition in the Context of Survivalism," in *Gender in Caribbean Development*, ed. Patricia Mohammed and Catherine Shepherd (Mona, Jamaica: UWI, Women and Development Studies Project, 1988), 235–309.

23. Invader quoted in Espinet, "Representation and the Indo-Caribbean Woman in Trinidad and Tobago," 49.

24. In Janice Shinebourne's *The Last English Plantation* (Leeds: Peepal Tree Press, 1988), the Black students resurrect the stereotype of miserliness when they deride the East Indians by calling them "Coolie water rice." Meanwhile, the East Indians retaliate by calling the Afro-Caribbeans "Pork-Eater" and "Black Pudding Lady."

25. It is really the spices and utensils (alongside cooking methods) which make the coolie's cuisine distinct. The rest of the ingredients are mostly locally procured.

26. Singh, "I Am a Coolie."

27. Bhangramuffin music combines Jamaican ragamuffin influences with Punjabi bhangra folk rhythms and samples from Bombay film music (which itself is a mongrel of sorts). A welder from a working-class neighborhood, which includes both Asians and West Indians, in Handsworth, U.K., Steve Kapur first appeared on the British music scene in the early nineties under the name Apache Indian. His stage name made references both to his Punjabi roots and to his artistic influence, the Jamaican ragamuffin singer Super Cat, who was also known as the wild Apache. See George Lipsitz, *Dangerous Crossroads: Popular Music, Postmodernism, the Poetics of Place* (London: Verso, 1994), for a musicologist's perspective on rai, reggae, ragamuffin, and bhangra music in the migrant communities of France and Britain. Chapter 6 of Lipsitz's book includes a more detailed discussion of Apache Indian. Also see John Hutnyk's argument about the misinterpretation of Apache Indian as symbol of cross-over popular music in "Hybridity Saves?" *Amerasia Journal* 25, 3 (1999/2000): 39–50.

28. See Vera M. Kutzinski's *Sugar's Secrets: Race and the Erotics of Cuban Nationalism* (Charlottesville: University Press of Virginia, 1993) for an extensive discussion of the intersecting discourses on sugar and femininity in nineteenth-century Cuban literature.

29. Apache Indian, "Arranged Marriage," rec. 1991, *No Reservations*, Island Records Ltd., 1993.

The Border as Barrier and Bridge: Food, Gender, and Ethnicity in the San Luis Valley of Colorado

Carole M. Counihan

> We are the porous rock in the stone *metate*
> squatting on the ground.
> We are the rolling pin, *el maíz y agua,*
> *la masa harina. Somos el amasijo.*
> *Somos lo molido en el metate.*
> We are the *comal* sizzling hot,
> the hot *tortilla*, the hungry mouth.
> We are the coarse rock.
> We are the grinding motion,
> the mixed potion, *somos el molcajete.*
> We are the pestle, the *comino, ajo, pimienta,*
> We are the *chile colorado,*
> the green shoot that cracks the rock.
> We will abide.[1]
>
> Gloria Anzaldúa 1987, 81–82

Gloria Anzaldúa uses strong images of foods and cooking to define Chicana identity. "We are . . ." the poem chants again and again—the stone *metate*, the rolling pin, the *comal*, the coarse rock, *el molcajete*, the pestle—common tools of many Chicanas' once daily labors. "We are . . ." the poem sings—*el maíz y agua*, *la masa harina*, *lo molido*, the hot tortilla, the *comino, ajo, pimienta*, the *chile colorado*—the enduring grains and pungent spices that sustain body and soul in Chicano communities. In Anzaldúa's poem, women labor hard, they sustain life, they hunger, and they "will abide." She links survival, women, and cooking in her poem, affirming the centrality of food in women's lives.[2]

Following Anzaldúa's poetic lead, this essay uses food as a window into Hispanic female identity and relationships in the San Luis Valley of Colorado. It examines how a *Mexicana*[3] named Bernadette[4] living in the small town of Antonito in southern Colorado sometimes crossed and sometimes crashed against gender and ethnic borders through commensality and its negation. For Bernadette, for *Mexicanos*, and for many people all over the world, commensality signifies intimacy, equality, and inclusion; and not eating together signifies distance, hierarchy, and social exclusion (Mauss 1967). Eating habits express cultural identity and mark cultural borders (Counihan 2004). Food borders are sometimes a bridge and sometimes a barrier between ethnic, class, and gender groups.

This essay takes a feminist anthropological approach to food.[5] Because food is so often the domain and language of women, focusing on it emphasizes their importance. Because women are sometimes obligated to cook for and serve others, food can be a channel of oppression. Yet because cooking, feeding, eating, and fasting can be significant means of communication, food can be a channel of creativity and power. Many women speak eloquently and avidly about food, and they reveal important memories and feelings. I have been collecting food-centered life histories in diverse field settings for twenty years (Counihan 1999, 2004). I have found that they can provide a voice for women who have not had a chance to speak publicly and provide a weapon against the silencing that has always been a central weapon in women's oppression. The challenge to feminist ethnographers is to work with diverse women and to use their voices in empowering ways.[6]

This essay is based on the food-centered life history of Bernadette gathered as part of an ongoing ethnographic project I have been conducting since 1996 in southern Colorado with my husband, anthropologist Jim Taggart (Counihan 2002, Taggart 2002, Taylor and Taggart 2003). I have tape-recorded interviews with nineteen women and four men centered on food production, preparation, consumption, and exchange. I have asked about past and present diet, methods of food preservation, important recipes, everyday and ritual meals, healing foods, breast-feeding, and food exchanges.[7] Antonito is in a poor rural region almost entirely devoid of study.[8] The stories of diverse women like Bernadette are important because they contribute to understanding the enduring *Mexicano* culture in the Southwest and show the race-ethnic, class, and gender obstacles people have run into and sometimes overcome.

Food and the Geographic Context

Bernadette was born and raised in Antonito, a town of 900 just six miles north of the New Mexico border in the southern San Luis Valley. Approximately the size of the state of Connecticut, the San Luis Valley

stretches across southern Colorado from the Sangre de Cristo mountains in the east to the San Juan Mountains in the west, and from the
New Mexico border north eighty miles to Saguache. The valley lies
between 7,500 and 8,000 feet and has a high desert climate with little
rainfall, extremely cold winters, strong westerly winds, and a short
growing season—all of which have contributed to limiting the valley
population to approximately 40,000 inhabitants.

Only one hundred and ten miles north of Santa Fe, Antonito is on
the northern edge of the centuries-old Hispanic presence in the Southwest, two miles southeast of Conejos, the tiny county seat, and three
miles from Guadalupe, the oldest Hispanic settlement in the area, settled in 1854.[9] Unlike those towns and the surrounding hamlets of San
Antonio, San Rafael, San Miguel, Ortiz, Las Mesitas, and Mogote
which were agro-pastoral settlements along rivers, Antonito was established in an arid spot as a commercial center and railroad depot in 1881
when the Denver and Rio Grande railroad came from Alamosa en route
to Española and Santa Fe and laid out a town site. Many contemporary
Mexicano residents came to Antonito—or their parents or grandparents
came—from one of the surrounding riverine hamlets and have roots in
an agro-pastoral tradition.

Bernadette's mother, for example, grew up in the hamlet of San Antonio, where her grandfather and uncles were sheepherders. She moved
to Antonito after marrying Bernadette's father, who came to Antonito
as a young man from Walsenberg, just over the Sangre de Cristo mountains east of the San Luis Valley. He worked in a grocery store and her
mother oversaw the household and the five children. They had fruit
trees and a big vegetable and flower garden—with spinach, rutabagas,
turnips, carrots, onions, potatoes, beans, peas, cabbages, tomatoes, and
corn. They raised and slaughtered pigs, chickens, and occasionally an
orphaned lamb, and they preserved the meat by drying it into jerky,
freezing it, making sausages, and curing ham.[10]

Today ranching and agriculture are marginal occupations except for
a few large landowners; unemployment is high; and Antonito's few busi-
nesses are struggling to survive. The town has a locally owned supermarket, two liquor stores, one video rental outlet, two auto repair shops,
two gas stations, four modest gift shops catering to the meager stream
of tourists, a bank, bar, pharmacy, hardware store, Laundromat, post
office, and discount store full of random goods.

Today poverty is widespread in Antonito and Conejos County, which
is the second-poorest in Colorado (Aguilar 2002). Lucky are those who
work for public entities or the nearby Perlite mine, for they draw regular salaries. Many people work for minimum wage in the service econ-

omy in the city of Alamosa, population 8,000, thirty miles north. Many others get by on odd jobs, baby-sitting, trading in used goods, public assistance jobs, and welfare. In the summer there is a modest tourist economy due to hunting, fishing, and vacationing in the nearby San Juan mountains and to the popular Cumbres & Toltec Scenic Railroad which runs trains between Antonito and Chama, New Mexico.

Antonito has three restaurants and two Mexican food stands (as well as a soda fountain in the pharmacy). Named Dos Hermanas, the Dutch Mill Cafe, Stefán's, the G-6, and Lee's Texaco, they are all owned and run by *Mexicanos* and they serve similar food—a mix of Anglo food like beef, burgers, steaks, and chicken fingers, with Colorado Mexican cuisine like fajitas, burritos, enchiladas, tacos, tamales, green chili, red chili, beans, and red rice. (Lee's Texaco also sells pizza.) These eateries serve as meeting places for residents, tourists, and travelers.

The population of Antonito in the 2000 census was officially 873 people, 90 percent of whom were Hispanic[11]—of both Spanish and Mexican descent—and the remaining 10 percent consisted of European Americans of diverse ethnicity and provenance. The cuisine of Antonito—its widely shared practices of cooking and eating—shows a strong Mexican influence, modified by the cold, dry climate. Potatoes, beans, and chili with flour tortillas or bread have long been the staples of the diet, supplemented by vegetables, game, fish, beef, pork, and mutton. In many conversations with *Mexicanas* in Antonito, food has emerged as a compelling topic and center of social relations.

Food and Female Identity

A major constituent of Bernadette's and many *Mexicanas'* identity was cooking and feeding. Bernadette said, *The responsibility of providing food was instilled in us. Because I saw it when my grandmother did it for my grandpa, I saw it when my mother did it for my daddy, and I saw that it was my duty too. That's the cultural thing that you have to do. Now I've seen it, I know I do it, and my sister Virginia does it for her husband.* For Bernadette cooking was not only an obligation but also a pleasure: *I love to cook, like for my little ones, my nephews, until they say, "Oh, Aunt Bernadette, we can't eat any more, we can't eat any more." I like to cook everything. Everything. And if I can find a new recipe, I'll try it—anything, you know. I just love cooking.*

But not all women cooked or enjoyed it. Sometimes they rejected the role and the perceived servitude that went with it. Bernadette said, *But my sister Anna, who's the baby of the family, she doesn't cook. She says, "And if he ate, he ate. And if he didn't, he didn't." And she's not going to get up. You know, she's not going to do it.* Most women in Antonito, however, shouldered domestic duties as their lot and relied on reciprocity with female relatives for help and support. Sharing food chores, recipes, and childcare provided important ways for women to forge familial and extra-familial relationships.

Bernadette expressed connections to her mother and daughter through their macaroni, which was one of her favorite comfort foods. *Oh my mom made the best. She used to boil the macaroni, and then while it was boiling she'd add milk, canned milk, and then she would put the cheese, and then she would crush up all these soda crackers, and she would put that on top, and then she would stick it in the oven, so that the cheese would melt into the crackers, and then salt and pepper.*

And there is another way to make macaroni. My daughter Gloria makes the best. She fries the macaroni and she toasts it. And then after it's getting toasty she adds water, and then she lets it get soft, and then she puts tomato sauce, and she fries hamburger, and then she puts in the hamburger. She puts the macaroni, she puts fried hamburger, tomato sauce, and she sprinkles cheese. Oh, that little girl is getting good. Bernadette took both pride and pleasure in her mother's and daughter's cooking and kept alive cultural traditions and a female-centered family identity (see Beoku-Betts 1995).

Another food that expressed family identity for Bernadette was deviled eggs. She said, *I was thinking it's really funny how whenever we get together, the Vigil clan, it seems like that's all we eat—deviled eggs! For whatever occasion—bring on the deviled eggs! Isn't that weird? I was thinking maybe it's a comfort food. It's associated with the warmness of a family. Deviled eggs themselves mean we're all getting together, as a family, as a unit, and that's one of our good foods that we're going to share. You know, it's like a comfort.*

Food also represented cultural identity for Bernadette: *To me, I'm Mexicana. I associate myself with being Mexicana. Because I speak Spanish, I speak the language. And then I eat the food. I have the customs. So, to me that falls into the category of being a Mexicana. I can't classify myself as anything else.* Although we were talking in English, Bernadette used Spanish to define her preferred ethnic identifier, *"Mexicana."* She admitted that others in Antonito did not like that word because they said, "We aren't Mexican—we're American." But many use *Mexicano* to mean not Mexican but what they are: citizens of the United States born to families of Spanish and Mexican origin. Bernadette continued, *So we're all Mexicanos. And where in the heck do we get the frijoles and the tortillas and all that if it wasn't from the Mexicanos? We all eat the same tortillas. We all eat the same way. So what's the big difference between Hispanic, Mexicano, and Spanish?*

Bernadette used food both to enact her Hispanic ethnicity and to demonstrate her multiculturalism. When Jim asked her in Spanish about her family background, she said, *Somos Mexicanos, Irish, Jewish, y todo está—we're Mexicanos, Irish, Jewish, and all that*. Bernadette was *Mexicana* on her father's side and a mix on her mother's side, with both Irish and native Navajo or Cheyenne ancestors. She wasn't sure about her Jewish heritage but thought it might have come down on both sides. Claiming diverse ethnic ancestry was not uncommon in Antonito, where many people professed a Spanish or Mexican core with strains of French, English, Irish, Scottish, Lebanese, Navajo, Apache, Pima, or other ancestors. The extent of cultural diversity needs to be explored further—its factual basis and its meaning. Is claiming multiple ethnicities a way to partake more fully in the national culture and combat the oppression of being *Mexicano*?

Bernadette revealed her openness to other cultural traditions through the array of foods she fondly described in her interview. These included Puerto Rican rice, green chili, red chili, macaroni, her grandmother's meat-ball soup with dill and onions, rice pudding, elk, rabbit, enchiladas, lasagna, sweet-potato-corn-flake-marshmallow croquettes, Chinese chicken, and potatoes—fried, mashed, and abundant.

Potatoes were the most basic food and staple crop of the San Luis Valley. Bernadette loved them: *And me—I'm a potato person. As long as I have potatoes, I'm all right. My sister Virginia said, "That must be the Irish in you." Because of that potato famine when they all came, they didn't have any potatoes. I go, "I guess so," I go, "Because I've got to have them."* Potatoes symbolized the Irish, but they were also central to the San Luis Valley-style Mexican-American cuisine that was the heart of Bernadette's culinary passion. She said, *To me the best food is fried potatoes, green chili, or red chili, and sometimes tortillas if you know how to make them.* Bernadette's comfort foods similarly revealed her *Mexicana* core. She said, *To me comfort food is fried potatoes, mashed potatoes, maybe green chili. Green chili is a comfort food for me, because I like it on anything. Red chili, that's good too. Macaroni.*

Red and green chili were at the heart of San Luis Valley and northern New Mexico cooking, and Bernadette described them in detail: *Oh my green chili, here's how I make it. First of all, I . . . cut the pork into little cubes. Then I put some oil in a frying pan, and I fry the pork with a little bit of flour. Then you put your garlic in and your onion, and then you put your green chili, the fresh ones, chopped up. . . . Then you add some water and let it boil. Yeah, and then you get that Bouquet Secret, that browning stuff, and add a little bit of that, just a dash to give it a little bit of color. And then you put your green chili in there.*

205

Green chilis will be coming in August. You can buy them by the bushel or you can buy them by the sack, I think it's twenty pounds. I buy two sacks. Two. Honey, I roast my own. It's a hot job. When you get your green chili, you soak it in water. And then you spread them evenly on the rack in the oven. And make sure your oven is at 400 degrees because it needs to be hot. And you give them about four minutes on one side and then you turn them, and keep turning them, because you don't want to burn them. If they burn, you've lost them, and they're too expensive to lose, so you've got to be real careful. Then after you get them out of the oven—as hot as they are—you get them and you stick them in a baggie and toss them right in the freezer.

Now the red chili. What I do is I buy the lean meat, lean hamburger. You fry it, put your onions and your garlic and then put your chili powder. But you've got to be careful what kind of red chili you buy. Because the one that's already prepared for you—you don't know what's really in the prepared one. So if you buy it rojo, which is just plain simple toasted in the oven, then you can put your own stuff into it. And if you want to make your own chili, you can get these ristras, they're called ristras de chile colorado. Or you can get them in the bags, and just clean them and soak them, and stick them in the oven. But you've got to watch real good too, because they'll toast wicked, and once they're burned, oh, you get the most awful taste. So you just toast them real light, and then you put them in a blender if you want to, and you add your seasoning to that, and you get the wildest, hottest red chili. You can use comino, and you can use, maybe a little bit of cilantro—maybe, but not very much. And garlic for sure, and salt, and that's about it.

Bernadette's description of red and green chili revealed the importance of preparing food correctly, at home, with care and foresight to maximize quality and minimize cost. She shared with poet Gloria Anzaldúa a culinary culture where key foods were symbols of women's identity, strength, and survival.

Food and Ethnic Relations

Eating together forged social connections; not sharing food marked social distance. In Antonito, for much of the twentieth century, Anglos and Chicanos rarely ate in each other's homes, and then usually only within similar class ranks. One reason for scarce interactions was that there were very few Anglos in the largely Hispanic town. In Bernadette's high school class, there were only two Anglos out of forty students. She described the ethnic character of her town: *Antonito is basically Hispanic—you might feel like an outsider because you're almost the only white people that are here. Besides you and Peggy Jones—and I never considered Peggy anything but Peggy. There was never an issue with me about being*

206

white or not white. We're all Hispanic, I mean everybody here. There wasn't a big issue about being white—or whites against us. But you know, even with the few white people that were here, they would try to put the Hispanic people in their place. Because they did have the better jobs. They were better educated.

Many of the few Anglos in Antonito attained upper-class status because they were white, they were relatively wealthy, and they were landowners, professionals, and politicians. Bernadette implied that they lived relatively separately from *Mexicanos*, most of whom were of modest means. Anglos and *Mexicanos* interacted in the public sphere of commerce and work, but most did not share meals in each other's homes, and those who did defined it as an exception. There was some social mixing between Anglo and *Mexicano* children around school and sports. Bernadette remembered Anglo as well as *Mexicano* school friends dropping by her house because they knew there was always a pot of beans on the stove and plenty of tortillas. This pot of beans, however, marked the ethnic border as both bridge and barrier, for the Anglo children crossed to come to her house, but she did not traverse it to eat at the Anglo children's houses.

Food sometimes successfully united Anglo and Hispanic women in public places, for example at church suppers and the like. Bernadette described the cooperative cooking of *Mexicanas* and Anglo women when their children all had a religious retreat in the local Theatine Fathers' seminary prior to their confirmation. The mothers prepared all their meals and snacks for two days and had such a great time together that the priest had to come and tell them to quiet down because they were disturbing the children. Cooperative cooking and eating forged temporary ties across ethnic boundaries between women.

But foods associated with mourning the dead marked ethnic borders that Bernadette found difficult to cross. When a Hispanic friend or relative died, Bernadette often cooked food for the bereaved family. She said that typically the mourning family held a big meal at the church hall or at home after the funeral. Some people had sandwiches of cold cuts, but if they really wanted to make a good impression, they had a big dinner of turkey, ham, mashed potatoes, gravy, ice cream and cake. I asked if people ever cooked Mexican food and she said maybe beans and green chili, but not usually home-made tortillas or enchiladas because they took too much time.

I asked Bernadette if Anglos had similar funeral customs, and she described a local prosperous Anglo family's funeral. Since she was a friend of the family, she roasted a couple of hens and made mashed potatoes, potato salad, muffins, and cupcakes, which she brought to her friend's house. But at the post-funeral meal, they just served little tea sandwiches, salad, and cake—not the big meal *Mexicanos* had. Bernadette wondered if she had committed an impropriety by bringing food. This occasion underscored the different commensal customs of Chicanos and Anglos. Funeral food linked Bernadette to her Anglo friends but also created barriers between them when she found herself unsure about the culturally appropriate behavior for their funerals.

Food and Class Relations

Mexicanos expressed sociability and social equality by sharing food, and marked class differences and borders by not eating together. People in Antonito defined class according to wealth and education. Bernadette described the higher class thus: *Some of them had a little more money. Their parents were better educated. Education played a big deal, a great deal. Their mothers were volunteers, they would do this; they would do that. They would be involved in a lot of school activities. They would help with the nuns. They were more involved in the church. Things like that.*

Mexicanos from the laboring classes rarely ate in the homes of the wealthy *Mexicano* landowners and professionals unless they were working for them, in which case the offer of a meal marked the employer's good will (Taylor and Taggart 2003, 85). Bernadette described the class barriers she encountered by telling a food story: *I was in Girl Scouts. The mothers that thought they were better would know that my mother was a good cook. So they would call and say, "Well, Bernadette is in the Girl Scouts so please bring us five cakes," or, "Please cook us four pies. But since you're not elite like us, just bring us the goodies, but don't come, don't try to associate with us." That kind of attitude.*

And my daddy saw that one time. They played that on my mom one time, Beverly Garcia, did, she was my Girl Scout leader. She called up one day on the phone and she told my mom, "Would you make us four cakes?"

And my mom goes, "Sure." You know, Mexicana, "Okay, whatever."

And my daddy asked her, "Why are you making four cakes?"

And my mom said "Because the Girl Scout leader wants Bernadette to take four cakes for the Girl Scout meeting."

And my dad told her, "Why aren't you going to take them?"

My mom replied, "Well no, she's going to take them because they don't want me. I don't go because they don't invite me to go."

And my dad said, "Well that's going to stop right here." So he waited for Mrs. Garcia. And he didn't let my mom bake the cakes. And when Mrs. Garcia came for the cakes he said, "I don't think so. If my wife isn't good enough to associate with you, then you're not good enough to eat her cakes."

And that ended that. That was one thing about daddy, boy, you didn't mess with him.

Bernadette's father refuted the class subordination expressed through making food for others but not eating with them. Class hierarchy has been perhaps more important than ethnic division in Antonito because segregation has kept the races largely apart, but class divisions have been continually reenacted. Bernadette and others lamented the lack of unity among her people and their infighting;[12] food sometimes brought them together at church suppers, weddings, and funerals, but at other times kept them separate.

Food and Gender Relations

The gender division of labor around food defined separate but complementary roles for men and women. In some homes, the cultural assumption that women serve and defer to men by feeding them became a means of reinforcing gender inequality. Food lay at the heart of Bernadette's relationships with men and sometimes enabled her to cross the borders of their differences but at other times loomed as an oppressive barrier. Bernadette's first husband, José, was Puerto Rican and originally from New York, though she met and married him in Pueblo, Colorado, two hours northeast of Antonito on the other side of the Sangre de Cristo mountains. She met him at a dance after she had gotten *"thin, real thin"* for the first time in her life after a period of misery and homesickness. She had never dated anyone before and she romanticized José as the gorgeous and suave stranger. She quickly married him, and then had a daughter Gloria. But soon the marriage became increasingly awful as José slid into alcoholism, drug dealing, and violent abusive behavior.

Bernadette's narratives about her marriage used food imagery to communicate both the attraction and the aversion she felt for her husband. His Puerto Rican food was different and appealing. Cooking and eating it were ways she participated in her husband's culture: *I tried to learn a lot—because it's just a really delicious kind of food. That's the only thing I got out of that Puerto Rican culture, you know. It's just really, really good food, and the way they add their herbs and their ingredients, that's what caught my eye. Because they use a lot of different herbs for a lot of different things, which we never did. We just used the basic. Not them.*

On the better side—we would get together on weekends, and it was just the most wonderful time, it was just fun. When he was in a good mood, it was a lot of fun. We would go to the park in Pueblo, or to a private home, and the guys would dig a hole in the ground, and then they would go and get branches of trees with a lot of leaves on them. And they would dig a hole, put the leaves inside the hole, and then they would get heavy-duty aluminum foil and put that on top, and then they would go and get a pig, a dead pig, you know. They'd clean out the pig real good, and they'd put a stick in him, and they'd rub him down with oil, and I remember with garlic, fresh garlic, and then they would use some kind of chili, like a red chili, and put that on top, and then they'd cover up the pig with more aluminum foil. But on the bottom they would put charcoal, and then the aluminum foil, and then the pig, and then more aluminum foil. They would do that the night before. And then that pig would be roasted—the meat would be just falling off. Oh, it was wonderful!

And then they'd make pastelitos, little pastry pies—and I can't find anybody to give me that recipe—but it is one of the best recipes, it is just wonderful. It's like what we call in Spanish empanaditas, to them is pastelitos. But this was not made sweet, this was made with a meat, the pork meat, and then it was made with some kind of bean, garbanzo bean, I think it was, and some other things, but I just can't find that recipe.

Bernadette appreciated and tried to learn Puerto Rican cooking but unfortunately she describes her husband teaching her with abuse and dominance. *I learned the hard way how to make rice, let's put it that way. That's about the basic thing. José used to show me, he used to tell me, this is how you make the rice, . . . but if I didn't get it right, oh, he'd beat me, until I got it right, really. That's how you learn the hard way, eeeh, he'd give me a good one. And it was a brutal kind of way, but hey, I learned how to cook rice, let me tell you. . . . And if the food wasn't done the right way, he'd throw it, it would be all over the ceiling. Then I thought that I was the only one going through that, but I wasn't. There was another little gal, and she had the same problem with her husband. She would cook and she was a good, good cook, and he'd just toss it against the wall if it wasn't just the way he wanted it. And you couldn't very well tell them, "Make it yourself," because you know we were so leery of them, that, hey, we'll learn, we'll learn.*

But that's how I learned to make rice, because he'd make me—one night, he made me make eight bowls of rice until I got it right. Now I think all the tears in between, all the tears and all the fear, but that's how I learned how to make rice. I got it right.

Food not only stood for the incompatibilities and power imbalance between Bernadette and her husband, but also for all that was wrong in his life: *I think that when things weren't going his way, and he wasn't happy with the food, that was the way that he showed that he wasn't happy. Because he . . . wasn't happy with his life to begin with. . . . I think all of that emotion was in him, and I just met him at the wrong time. He was just like a little volcano waiting to erupt. He had quite a temper. And I think that food was his way of getting out his anger when things weren't going the right way. And with the food, if it was any little bad way, he'd get mad, if it didn't come out just the way he wanted it.*

José used Bernadette's inadequate cooking as a reason for abusing her. Although she tried to please and forge ties with him by cooking Puerto Rican style, he refused her offering. Rather than allowing food to be a bridge between them, he used it to shut her out. His behavior illustrated how culturally sanctioned expectations that women defer to and serve men through feeding them could threaten gender equality and sometimes justify violence.[13] José's abuse became so great that Bernadette decided she had to leave: *I didn't want that kind of life for my daughter. I thought no. I would rather live alone. Like there's that saying, mejor sola che mal acompañada—better alone that in company with somebody that's bad and evil.* She eventually divorced José. Their incompatibility over food reflected and symbolized deeper barriers in the marriage.

Several years later, Bernadette crossed another cultural border when she made her second marriage to an undocumented Mexican migrant worker named Manuel. Again her stories described food as both a bridge and a barrier to cultural communication: *I found that when I married my husband from Mexico, it was the same way, their cooking was really good, with different spices. It was the darnedest thing, because when I went to Mexico, it was the most wonderful experience, it was wonderful. And one evening my mother-in-law wanted to drink some tea. And I thought, "Oh, let's get the tea bags out," you know.*

But she goes, "No, we have to go and look for our own."

I go, "Okay." So we took a hike up a hill, and she was just picking a—it was like a branch of a little tree, and she picked certain branches, you know, from the ground. They weren't roots because they were already out, and then she got them, and we took them down and we washed them, and we boiled them. And they made the best tea, but I'll be darned if I can remember what the name of it was. And it was just really, really good. So we just had tea, and I thought that was just great, I thought it was just so wonderful.

In this story and others, Bernadette used food to express her appreciation for Mexican culture, yet also its foreignness. Eventually, however, Manuel's foreignness became too much for her; the border became a barrier. He was kind to Bernadette and her daughter but had trouble finding work, got depressed, did not speak much English, and depended on Bernadette for too much. As she got more and more debilitated from an incurable physical disease, she found it harder and harder to deal with him and his needs. Bernadette described the end of the relationship: *Finally, I just thought, "This is it. I'm sorry, I just can't live with you any more." I told him, "I just can't put up with you."*

He was always, "Teach me this, teach me that." I was in so much pain. And I just couldn't do a lot of things—oh, it was just getting to be a hassle. And then, I felt it was my job to get up with him at six o'clock in the morning, or five, fix him his breakfast, his lunch, even though I had to drag myself. And he told me, "Don't get up." But I had to; it was just something that I felt I had to do. So I would get up and make him breakfast and stuff like that, but it was a killer.

And then finally I told him, "No, it's just not going to work." So we went and we got our divorce.

Here again, Bernadette used the language of food to describe her incompatibility with this man whom, like her first husband, she had crossed a cultural border to marry. His neediness and her nurturance were reflected in her feeding him. Repudiation of feeding him represented her decision to take care of herself rather than of a man who was not giving enough back to her. In both marriages, food became an expression of failed gender relations and the pitfalls of the traditional domestic division of labor when not accompanied by gender equality. With José, Bernadette's food work was the site of her oppression. Food was Bernadette's voice, and her husband tried to silence her by controlling her cooking, by forcing her to make it his way, and by shattering her creations against the wall. With Manuel, feeding was a different source of oppression; Bernadette was exhausted by taking care of Manuel, when she herself was becoming more in need of care. In both cases, the reciprocity essential to gender equality was missing.

Where reciprocity and food-sharing have been possible, Bernadette has crossed race ethnic, class, and gender divides. But such reciprocity was relatively rare and unlikely unless women had strong socioeconomic positions by virtue of education and earning power as Bernadette did not have. Not having attained reciprocity with a man, Bernadette lived alone. She still loved cooking and was continually recreating ties with the women of her family—her mother, daughter, sisters, and sisters-in-law—through food-sharing. Perhaps Bernadette's experience reflected Margaret Randall's words, "Now I cook as a woman, free at last of that feeling of enslavement with which a male culture has imbued the process of preparing food" (1997b, 120). Perhaps her cooking was empowering because she cooked freely and received esteem for her labors through reciprocal relationships with her female relatives.

Conclusion

Food and talking about it have been both bridge and barrier between Bernadette and others, including myself. Conversations about food where she was the expert and I the acolyte enabled us to build connections across our race-ethnic and class differences. But there remained a distance between us symbolized by the fact that although Bernadette and I shared food gifts many times, we have not yet eaten a meal together. A border still exists which has not been crossed by commensality.

Similarly, our distance is both marked and mediated by our ongoing efforts to find a satisfactory way to get her story into print. When I wrote an earlier draft of this essay (Counihan 1998), I gave her a copy and asked for her feedback. She had some problems with it that revealed her uncertainty with my rendition of her as well as the waves caused by her speaking out. Her Anglo brother-in-law told her not to let me publish the article and not to do any more tape-recorded interviews with me. Was his effort to silence her an effort to control the stories told and the reality described? Bernadette's sister and daughter also told her not to let me use her words. They disparaged her and said she sounded stupid. Although cooking and eating together were important for the women of Bernadette's family, they tried to silence her food narrative, perhaps reflecting their own low assessment of the value of women's work and words.

Bernadette's relatives' criticisms caused her to feel uncertain about my essay and triggered a discussion that led to revisions. She felt that certain passages made her sound ignorant, and she wanted me to edit them to be more grammatical, less repetitious, and more true to her vision of herself. To protect herself from her relatives' disgruntlement, she asked me to use pseudonyms, and she chose the name Bernadette after the saint who, she said, was visited by the Immaculate Conception and made seven prophecies. Bernadette said she was proud of her interviews because they were something she could leave her child and grandchildren, but she also feared that her words would come back to hurt her. Getting her words into print in a way that she found fulfilling was an ongoing process that depended on the continuing interaction between us. Our struggles over voice mirrored the larger challenges of defining gender, ethnic, and class power in the United States. They showed that conversations across class, ethnic, cultural, and regional borders are challenging but possible and important. The food-centered life histories of Bernadette and other women in her community can keep alive their *Mexicano* culture and dignify their experiences against

213

prevailing ideologies that would devalue them. Like "the green shoot that cracks the rock," they "will abide."

Notes

I presented an earlier version of this essay at the 1998 Annual Meeting of the American Anthropological Association (Counihan 1998) in the session "The Border Counts: Subjugating Signs and Transnational Agitation." I thank Miguel Díaz Barriga and Matthew Gutmann for organizing the session and Patricia Zavella, the discussant, for her thoughtful comments. I thank my husband, anthropologist Jim Taggart, for sharing fieldwork and data with me and for commenting on several earlier drafts. I thank sociologist Mary Romero for suggesting the San Luis Valley as a possible fieldwork site and for commenting on an earlier draft. I thank Arlene Avakian and Barbara Haber for suggestions for revisions. Finally I give thanks to Bernadette for allowing me to tape-record her stories and for giving me permission to write about her.

1. *metate:* grinding stone
   maíz: corn
   agua: water
   masa harina: flour dough
   somos el amasijo: we are the kneading, the dough
   somos lo molido en el metate: we are the flour in the grinding stone
   comal: flat pan for cooking tortillas
   somos el molcajete: we are the mortar
   comino, ajo, pimienta: cumin, garlic, pepper
   chile colorado: red chili

2. As I was making final revisions to this essay, I learned of Gloria Anzaldúa's death on May 15, 2004, due to complications of diabetes. May her words and her courageous spirit live on.

3. I use *Mexicanas/os* in this paper to refer to people of Spanish and Mexican descent residing in Antonito. This is a term many in Antonito use. Some use "Hispanic," "Spanish," or "Spanish American," and some, especially younger people or those involved in political activism, use Chicana/o, a term which other people hate. In northern New Mexico, some people identify themselves as *Hispanas/os* (Madrid 1998) but these terms are rarely used in southern Colorado. See Elsasser, MacKenzie, and Tixier y Vigil (1980, xv) for the terms used in northern New Mexico.

4. All informants' names in this essay are pseudonyms.

5. Some feminist studies of food are Adams 1990, Avakian 1997, Bordo 1993, Brumberg 1988, Bynum 1987, Charles and Kerr 1988, Chernin 1985, Counihan 1999, Counihan 2004, DeVault 1991, Paules 1991, Randall 1997b, Thompson 1994, and Zavella 2001. On feminist anthropology, see Behar and Gordon 1995, Moore 1988, Sacks 1974, and Wolf 1992.

6. The Latina Feminist Group (2001) has eloquently demonstrated the importance of finding a voice in coming to power. Some women who have found a powerful voice through food writing are Fisher 1954, Esquivel 1992, and Randall 1997a. Writers who have explored food as women's voice are Beoku-Betts 1995,

Bruch 1988, Brumberg 1997, Bynum 1987, Counihan 1999, 2003, 2004, Thompson 1994, and Zafar 1999.

7. I did two interviews with Bernadette in English, which produced over one hundred pages of transcriptions and Jim did two interviews with her in Spanish which produced over fifty pages of transcriptions.

8. Notable exceptions are Taylor and Taggart 2003 and Deutsch 1987. Deutsch says, "Written History of . . . Chicanas or Hispanic women in Colorado [is] virtually non-existent." On the San Luis Valley culture and ecology see Peña 1998. See Zavella 1991 on the need to document Chicana diversity.

9. Deutsch (1987, 17) says that settlers came to Guadalupe from Abiquiu in Rio Arriba County, northern New Mexico. The southern San Luis Valley was long the territory of the Ute Indians (Marsh 1991, Osburn 1998, Young 1997) and was settled in the mid-nineteenth century by Spaniards and Mexicans from Old and New Mexico (Deutsch 1987). Anglos arrived in ever greater numbers in the late nineteenth century with the U.S. military (sent to vanquish the Utes), the Church of the Latter Day Saints, homesteading claims, and the railroad. On Hispanic and Anglo landownership, use, acquisition, and loss in southern Colorado, see Gutierrez and Eckert 1991, Martinez 1987, and Weber 1991.

10. On the food traditions of the *Mexicanos* of southern Colorado and northern New Mexico, see Cabeza de Baca 1949, 1954 and Deutsch 1987. On southwestern cuisine, see Bentley 1998.

11. Population figures come from http://dola.colorado.gov/demog/history/allhist.cfm, consulted 2/1/03.

12. Joe Taylor used the metaphor of "crabs in a bucket" to describe the ways *Mexicanos* in Antonito fought with each other and kept each other down (Taylor and Taggart 2003: 91).

13. Adams (1990), Charles and Kerr (1988, 72), DeVault (1991, 143–144), and Ellis (1983) note that men often use dissatisfaction with food as an excuse to abuse women.

References

Adams, Carol J. 1990. *The Sexual Politics of Meat: A Feminist-Vegetarian Critical Theory*. New York: Continuum.

Aguilar, Louis. 2002. "Drying Up: Drought Pushes 169-year-old Family-owned Ranch in Southern Colorado to the Edge of Extinction." *Denver Post*, July 29.

Anzaldúa, Gloria. 1987. *Borderlands La Frontera: The New Mestiza*. San Francisco: Aunt Lute Books.

Avakian, Arlene Voski, ed. 1997. *Through the Kitchen Window: Women Explore the Intimate Meanings of Food and Cooking*, Boston: Beacon Press.

Bean, Luther E. 1975. *Land of the Blue Sky People*. Alamosa, CO: Ye Olde Print Shoppe.

Behar, Ruth, and Deborah A. Gordon, eds. 1995. *Women Writing Culture*. Berkeley: University of California Press.

Bentley, Amy. 1998. "From Culinary Other to Mainstream America: Meanings and Uses of Southwestern Cuisine." *Southern Folklore* 55, 3: 238–252, special issue on Culinary Tourism, ed. Lucy Long.

Beoku-Betts, Josephine. 1995. "We Got Our Way of Cooking Things: Women, Food and Preservation of Cultural Identity among the Gullah." *Gender and Society* 9: 535–555.

Bordo, Susan. 1993. *Unbearable Weight: Feminism, Western Culture, and the Body*, Berkeley: University of California Press.

Bruch, Hilde. 1988. *Conversations with Anorexics*, ed. Danita Czyzewski and Melanie A. Suhr. New York: Basic Books.

Brumberg, Joan Jacobs. 1988. *Fasting Girls: The Emergence of Anorexia Nervosa as a Modern Disease*. Cambridge: Harvard University Press.

———. 1997. *The Body Project: An Intimate History of American Girls*. New York: Random House.

Bynum, Caroline Walker. 1987. *Holy Feast and Holy Fast: The Religious Significance of Food to Medieval Women*. Berkeley: University of California Press.

Cabeza de Baca, Fabiola. 1949. *The Good Life*. Santa Fe: Museum of New Mexico Press.

———. 1954. *We Fed Them Cactus*. Albuquerque: University of New Mexico Press.

Charles, Nikki, and Marion Kerr. 1988. *Women, Food, and Families*. Manchester: Manchester University Press.

Chernin, Kim. 1985. *The Hungry Self: Women, Eating, and Identity*. New York: Times Books.

Counihan, Carole. 1998. "The Border as Bridge and Barrier: Food, Gender, and Ethnicity in the San Luis Valley of Colorado." Paper presented at the 97th Annual Meeting of the American Anthropological Association, Philadelphia, PA.

———. 1999. *The Anthropology of Food and Body: Gender, Meaning and Power*. New York: Routledge.

———. 2002. "Food as Women's Voice in the San Luis Valley of Colorado." In *Food in the USA: A Reader*, ed. Carole Counihan. New York: Routledge, 295–304.

———2003. "Food Contagion." *Slow: The Magazine of the International Slow Food Movement* 39 (May): 22–25.

———. 2004. *Around the Tuscan Table: Food, Family and Gender in Twentieth Century Florence*. New York: Routledge.

Deutsch, Sarah. 1987. *No Separate Refuge: Culture, Class, and Gender on an Anglo-Hispanic Frontier in the American Southwest, 1880–1940*. New York: Oxford.

DeVault, Marjorie L. 1991. *Feeding the Family: The Social Organization of Caring as Gendered Work*. Chicago: University of Chicago Press.

Ellis, Rhian. 1983. "The Way to a Man's Heart: Food in the Violent Home." In *The Sociology of Food and Eating*, ed. Anne Murcott. Aldershot: Gower, 164–171.

Elsasser, Nan, Kyle MacKenzie, and Yvonne Tixier y Vigil. 1980. *Las Mujeres: Conversations from a Hispanic Community*. New York: The Feminist Press.

Esquivel, Laura. 1989. *Like Water for Chocolate*. New York: Doubleday.

Fisher, M. F. K. 1954. *The Art of Eating*. New York: Morrow.

Gutierrez, Paul, and Jerry Eckert. 1991. "Contrasts and Commonalities: Hispanic and Anglo Farming in Conejos County, Colorado." *Rural Sociology*, 56, 2: 247–263.

Latina Feminist Group. 2001. *Telling to Live: Latina Feminist Testimonios*. Durham: Duke University Press.

Madrid, Arturo. 1998. "Missing People and Others: Joining Together to Expand the Circle." In *Race, Class and Gender: An Anthology*, ed. M. Anderson and P. H. Collins. Belmont, CA: Wadsworth, 21–26.

Marsh, Charles. 1991. *People of the Shining Mountains: The Utes of Colorado*. Boulder, CO: Pruett.

Martinez, Ruben. 1997. "Chicano Lands: Acquisition and Loss." *Wisconsin Sociologist* 24, 2/3: 89–98.

Mauss, Marcel. 1967. *The Gift*. New York: Norton.

Moore, Henrietta. 1988. *Feminism and Anthropology*. Minneapolis: University of Minnesota Press.

Osburn, Katherine. 1998. *Southern Ute Women: Autonomy and Assimilation on the Reservation, 1887–1934*. Albuquerque: University of New Mexico Press.

Paules, Greta Foff. 1991. *Power and Resistance among Waitresses in a New Jersey Restaurant*. Philadelphia: Temple University Press.

Peña, Devon, ed. 1998. *Chicano Culture, Ecology, Politics: Subversive Kin*. Tucson: University of Arizona Press.

Randall, Margaret. 1997a. *Hunger's Table: Women, Food and Politics*, Watsonville, CA: Papier Mache Press.

———. 1997b. "What My Tongue Knows." In *Through the Kitchen Window*, ed. A. Avakian, 117–133. Boston: Beacon.

Sacks, Karen. 1974. "Engels Revisited: Women, the Organization of Production, and Private Property." In *Women, Culture, and Society*, ed. Michelle Zimbalist Rosaldo and Louise Lamphere. Stanford: Stanford University Press.

Taggart, James M. 2002. "Food, Masculinity and Place in the Hispanic Southwest." In *Food in the USA: A Reader*, ed. Carole Counihan. New York: Routledge, 305–313.

Taylor, José Inez, and James M. Taggart. 2003. *Alex and the Hobo: A Chicano Life and Story*. Austin: University of Texas Press.

Thompson, Becky. 1994. *A Hunger So Wide and So Deep: American Women Speak Out on Eating Problems*. Minneapolis: University of Minnesota Press.

Tushar, Olibama López. 1992. *The People of El Valle: A History of the Spanish Colonials in the San Luis Valley*. Pueblo, CO: El Escritorio.

Weber, Kenneth R. 1991. "Necessary but Insufficient: Land, Water, and Economic Development in Hispanic Southern Colorado." *Journal of Ethnic Studies* 19, 2: 127–142.

Wolf, Margery. 1992. *A Thrice-Told Tale: Feminism, Postmodernism, and Ethnographic Responsibility*. Stanford: Stanford University Press.

Young, Richard K. 1997. *The Ute Indians*. Norman: University of Oklahoma Press.

Zafar, Rafia. "The Signifying Dash: Autobiography and History in Two Black Women's Cookbooks." *Feminist Studies* 25, 2: 449–470.

Zavella, Patricia. 1991. "Reflections on Diversity among Chicanas." *Frontiers* 12, 2: 73–85.

———. 2001. "Tenemos que Seguir Luchando." In Latina Feminist Group, *Telling to Live*, 348–355.

RESISTANCES

Women's studies scholarship and women's activism have not always considered women as active agents of resistance to our oppression. Early proponents of women's studies, who had worked hard to legitimize women as a valid category of scholarship, at first focused on the similarities among women's lives—women as victims of an all-encompassing patriarchy. Women of color critiqued this approach both in women's activism and in the academy, often citing the critical role of race and class in their lives as well as the centrality of women of color to resistance movements in their communities, and women of color continue to produce some of the most exciting scholarship in the field. As women's studies became more acceptable in many fields, even de rigueur in some, feminist analyses have become much more complex and nuanced, including a greater focus on women's resistance.

The essays in this section look at women in three very different sites with very different approaches, but they all view women's resistance within the contexts of gender, national, and ethnic oppression. Laura Lindenfeld's analysis of the film *Fried Green Tomatoes* questions the extent of the resistance to gender and sexual norms in a work that purports to celebrate women's social and economic independence in a story of two women's commitment to each another. She also explores how viewing this film sates her appetite for both popular culture and food, but only with a heavy overlay of guilt. Analyzing another film, the Indian work *Spices*, Beheroze F. Shroff argues that women's use of the chili pepper represents both the oppression of women under colonialism and patriarchy and women's resistance to domination by Indian men and the colonial domination of Indian people by the British. Eating and cooking, for a group of Armenian American feminists interviewed by Arlene Avakian, are ways to maintain their sometimes tenuous hold on their ethnicity and a way to assert that identity with non-Armenians. These essays complicate notions of resistance, recognizing it but never celebrating it outside of the context of the very real power of patriarchy, colonialism, and genocide.

Women Who Eat Too Much: Femininity and Food in *Fried Green Tomatoes*

LAURA LINDENFELD

I never cease to be amazed how many conflicting feelings and experiences I have in relationship to food and eating. I am able to bask in the glorious pleasures of the culinary, to relish in the delights of food, only to find myself—still after so many years of contemplating this very issue—experiencing residual feelings of guilt. Sometimes those feelings are less than residual and in fact more prominent. I always imagine that I should be able to deal with this cycle so much better, that consuming food should become simple, nonproblematic, pleasurable, guilt-free. I find myself puzzled over the difficulty of coming to simple terms with food and eating. After all—I have studied the feminist literature that addresses women, food, and bodies. I have taught classes on food culture and American identity. I have written and thought about this topic endlessly, and I should know better than to attach my value as a human being to the amount of chocolate mousse cake that I've eaten. In my efforts to better understand what seems to me to be a ridiculous method of self-torture, I have turned—of all things—to film. Watching films, I have noticed, provides me with a similar cycle of pleasure and guilt. How is it that I am able to immerse myself in the narrative world of a mainstream film and find pleasure and even at times empowerment in something that simultaneously feels troubling and wrong to me? My guilty pleasure in consuming film closely echoes the sentiments I experience around food. I enjoy it, but. . . .

As a scholar whose efforts strive toward dissecting media products in order to understand better how they shape hegemonic understandings of self and other, I find that this essay has proven particularly challenging. Watching film, like eating, is laden with various issues for me. Constantly calling myself to awareness of what lies behind the products I consume—whether it be food, film, furniture, or clothing—has become almost habitual, and I am not quite certain what happens to plea-

221

sure in this constant struggle for awareness. The film *Fried Green To-matoes* (Avnet, 1991) poses an interesting puzzle for me, as it is seemingly progressive in its treatment of race, gender, and sexuality. Yet each time I have "consumed" this film it has felt like the guilty pleasure of eating foods that are "wrong." The fact that this film looks at the relationship between gender, race, food, and power makes it an especially fruitful starting point to enter into this discussion.

In her essay "Eating the Other: Desire and Resistance," bell hooks explores the commodification of Otherness in mass culture, emphasizing how often "within commodity culture, ethnicity becomes spice, seasoning that can liven up the dull dish that is mainstream white culture."[1] She expresses her concern about the way contemporary media focus on race and Otherness and describes discussions she has had with people who regard this seemingly progressive type of representation as positive. hooks writes, "After weeks of debating with one another about the distinction between cultural appropriation and cultural appreciation, students in my introductory course on black literature were convinced that something radical was happening, that these issues were 'coming out in the open.'" She concludes strongly, "we cannot, however, accept these new images uncritically."[2]

This essay is a response to hooks's challenge to critically analyze both my pleasure and my discomfort. *Fried Green Tomatoes* offers various alternatives for women in relationship to food. At the same time, however, it takes back with one hand what it gives with the other by deemphasizing and negatively reinscribing some of the subversive tendencies it exhibits, especially in its treatment of race. While working through the subversive, utopian possibilities this film offers about women, eating, and identity, I will look at the ways in which it simultaneously supports the status quo. Through a close reading of the film, the following pages walk through my consumption of *Fried Green Tomatoes* on terms that, as hooks writes, "begin to conceptualize and identify ways that desire informs our political choices and affiliations." In this sense, this framework of analyzing my relationship to this film provides me with a method to map out and challenge the pleasure that I, as a heterosexual white woman, am able to experience in viewing it. In closely taking apart my pleasure in this film while simultaneously addressing the critical voices I hear while watching it, I wish to shed light on how this critical act might feed my understanding of the interconnectedness of consumption, pleasure, and guilt. To follow through with hooks's challenge, I analyze this cycle of pleasure and guilt in order to better understand, as hooks writes, "how desire disrupts, subverts, and makes resistance possible" by critically taking my relationship with this film to task.[3] In focusing this analysis around my own spectator position, I will map out the ways in which *Fried Green Tomatoes* undermines many of the possibilities of change that the film appears to offer.

My reading of *Fried Green Tomatoes* is a result of how I, as a viewer, have negotiated my relationship with this film to be a means of personal empowerment despite the ways in which the film undermines much of what it accomplishes. In particular, I will focus on how representations of food and eating in *Fried Green Tomatoes* subvert standardized notions of gender and sexuality as well as the ways in which it questions patriarchal political structures and the inequitable distribution of food. Thus, I would like to illustrate the very oscillation I experience in viewing this film, drawing on moments of empowerment and pleasure only to then visit the flip side of this coin.

Based on the book by Fanny Flagg, *Fried Green Tomatoes at the Whistle Stop Café*, a text that has become something of a cult classic among U.S. lesbians, the film *Fried Green Tomatoes* has received a fair amount of critical attention. A number of these essays focus on the intertextual relationship between novel and film, looking critically at the ways in which feminism, gender, race, and sexuality are treated in the transposition from written text to celluloid image. Jennifer Ross Church's essay "The Balancing Act of *Fried Green Tomatoes*" questions how a film that deals with such a controversial issue as a cannibalized husband was able to make the successful leap from novel to film. Church emphasizes the influence that *Fried Green Tomatoes* had on the Hollywood film industry, writing, "How could such a quiet, female buddy movie attract a wide audience? Not even reviewed in most major journals and advertised largely by word of mouth, the film and video grossed over $42 million in the year following its release, prompting the movie industry to try to define and cash in on its audience."[4] Her essay goes on to question precisely what "the draw" of this film was, how it was able "to balance extremes and to touch on serious issues of sexuality, race, and modern-day alienation without losing any large segments of its audience."[5] In a similar fashion, Shari Zeck looks at the role humor plays in her essay "Laughter, Loss, and Transformation in *Fried Green Tomatoes*." She draws on a comparison between novel and film to discuss the limitations of humor as a transgressive power in the film.[6]

My analysis of this film stems from Zeck's and Church's readings, both of which analyze moments of upheaval and change while also looking at hegemonic reinscriptions of race, gender, and sexuality.[7] Precisely the fact that *Fried Green Tomatoes* unexpectedly made the leap from novel to film makes it an interesting object of study. This is the point where I wish to begin my discussion. I view the popularity of the film as intrinsically linked to its ability to present material that challenges cultural norms while also adhering to what Raymond Williams refers to as "emergent culture."[8] By "emergent," Williams means, "first, that new meanings and values, new practices, new significances and experiences, are continually being created. But there is then a much earlier attempt to incorporate them, just because they are part—and yet not a defined part—of effective contemporary practice. Indeed it is significant in our own period how very early this attempt is, how alert the dominant culture now is to anything that can be seen as emergent."[9] In this sense, the film, unlike the novel, carefully navigates the waters that lie between what Williams calls "effective dominant culture" and "oppositional culture,"[10] that is, it gives its audience enough newness and difference without running the risk of alienating a hegemonic reading of itself. In this sense, *Fried Green Tomatoes* is a relatively open text that allows for a certain degree of potentially empowering polysemic readings, readings that, however, to a large extent reinscribe effective dominant culture. As I will show, the power and creativity of the individual to create meanings of one's own, to which, as some would argue, media texts open themselves, are overshadowed by ideological elements in the film that affirm mainstream, hegemonic culture.[11] This film is able, as Church argues, to treat quite subversive material in a way that does not challenge mainstream culture *too much*, but rather just enough that the film, instead of running the risk of losing a mainstream audience, actually became a quite successful box-office hit.[12]

Fried Green Tomatoes is not a subversive, fringe text as is, to a certain extent, the book upon which it is based. It is mainstream, and despite its many problems, it has managed to offer me some comfort and empowerment in relationship to food and eating. Analyzing my own spectator position in regard to this film might serve as a means to think about how change becomes incorporated and ultimately usurped by mainstream culture. With each further viewing, the film becomes more and more regressive in my eyes, undoing much of the "feminist" work that it sets up, creating problematic issues around race, gender, and sexuality, and undermining its progressive narrative of food and eating. Nonetheless, the film has somehow managed to provide me with alternatives, and I am certain that this is a reflection of my own race, sexuality, and gender.

Fried Green Tomatoes, a film that in many ways attempts to challenge traditional gender roles and heterosexism, seems to challenge the stereotypical ways in which women and food have been represented in mainstream. The mainstream media creates laughter around women who are "larger" than what hegemonic culture holds to be acceptable. Women who take up space and enjoy eating are equated with animals and positioned as the proverbial butt of jokes. Even among slender actresses, there exist few examples who are allowed to partake of culinary delights on the screen without being either demonized or sexualized. The options are lean at best. We are left to choose between unrealistically sculpted and stylized bodies or images of the marginalized, ridiculed fat woman. In her book *The Invisible Woman: Confronting Weight Prejudice in America*, W. Charisse Goodman discusses the dearth of positive large female characters in film:

> Of the approximately 70 movies I randomly surveyed—mostly mainstream commercial American films—only 17 had any large female characters at all in the script, most of whom represented the standard domineering mother figure, the comically unattractive women, the whore figure, and Bates as her *Misery* psychopath character. Only six of these 17 films presented a big woman as a positive figure, and of these six, only three—*Daddy's Dyin'*—*Who's Got the Will?* and John Waters' *Hairspray* and *Crybaby*—featured fat women as romantic figures and central characters.[13]

Certainly, the number of larger women allowed to occupy positive roles in mainstream film *and* enjoy food is incredibly small.

When women do eat in mainstream cinema, the situations that allow for this are narrowly defined. There are the lovely, thin goddesses whose eating serves to enhance their erotic attraction to men. *Flashdance* (Jennifer Beals), *Pretty Woman* (Julia Roberts), and *When Harry Met Sally* (Meg Ryan), to mention only a few, position, as Susan Bordo writes, "the heroines' unrestrained delight in eating . . . as sexual foreplay, a way of prefiguring the abandon that will shortly be expressed in bed."[14] In all of these films, the heroines' bodies conform to contemporary ideals of female body norms, leaving us to assume that it's okay to eat, but only if one doesn't get fat and if the indulgence precedes heterosexual intercourse. The other circumstances, according to Bordo, under which, "[women] are permitted to lust for food itself [are] when they are pregnant or when it is clear they have been near starvation."[15] The possibilities appear bleak.

Mainstream representations of women eating are generally quite problematic, and I do not wish to imply that those in *Fried Green Tomatoes* are not guilty, as well, of perpetuating stereotypical and judgmental images. Rather, my focus here remains on how this particular film offers narratives of empowerment in the face of a culture that

perpetually bombards viewers with unrealistic, unhealthy, and dangerous images of bodies and food while it simultaneously contradicts this
tendency.

Fried Green Tomatoes tells the story of two generations of southern
women by interweaving the narratives with each other. Evelyn Couch,
who constantly stuffs herself with candy bars to escape the dreariness of
her everyday life and her dull marriage with husband Ed, meets Ninny
Threadgoode, an eighty-two-year-old woman living in the same retire-
ment facility as Ed's aunt. Through the many visits with Ninny, Evelyn
hears stories of two women from the 1920s–1930s, Idgie and Ruth, as
the camera cuts back and forth between past and present (1980s).
Through the relationship with Ninny and the stories of Idgie and Ruth,
Evelyn comes to recognize that she must take responsibility for herself
and her life. Through narrative, visual, and acoustic parallels that link
present and past, the film relates Evelyn's development and empowerment directly back to the stories that she hears about the women's pasts.
The narrative technique of interweaving past with present provides a
framework through which the viewer can compare and contrast Evelyn's story to the Idgie/Ruth narrative. Ultimately, it is the story of these
women and their relationships to food and each other told through
Ninny that help to heal Evelyn and empower her to challenge her relationship with her husband and with herself. Through these tales, she
is also able to overcome a painful compulsive eating disorder and actually form a strong, healing connection with Ninny through food, so that
food comes to play a central role in this narrative of self-empowerment
and self-assertion.

Food is constantly present throughout the film, and much of the
narrative is embedded in images of cooking and eating. Already in the
first scene, the camera displays an image of the run-down Whistle Stop
Café, the words "peach pie, pecan pie, blueberry pie, cherry and peach
cobbler" written on the window and the "fried green tomatoes served
hot" still legible but chipped and faded on the door. The camera alternates between medium shots of the café and of Evelyn as she stares
longingly at the café and takes a bite into a candy bar. The viewer is
already set up to contrast Evelyn's world of junk and fast food to the
stories behind the aging, chipping remnants of Idgie and Ruth's café, an
establishment, as the sign tells us, for "fine food at fair prices." The past
becomes present to Evelyn and the viewer through the soundtrack.
Rustling leaves turn into the sound of trains pulling through town as
the camera tracks over the railroad line to emphasize the interconnectedness of past and present. The cinematography and editing have al-

ready established food as central link between the contemporary and the historical in this opening scene.

While mass-produced candy bars dominate Evelyn's world, Idgie and Ruth's is filled with sumptuous homemade pies, cakes, and southern home-style cooking, all perfectly beautiful and lovingly prepared. In the scene that depicts Idgie's sister's wedding, for example, the camera pans over a table of sweets that would leave even Martha Stewart filled with envy. The contrast between these two cultures plays itself out continuously throughout the film. Evelyn devours entire boxes of Krispy Kream Donuts while Idgie and Ruth connect over highly aestheticized, thoughtfully prepared picnics of homemade pies, casseroles, lemonade in mason jars, and fresh berries. The aestheticization of food in the Idgie/Ruth narrative positions eating and cooking as nurturing and healing, whereas Evelyn appears as ridiculous and even pitiful via her relationship with food. For Idgie and Ruth, food comes to signify community, connectedness, and togetherness. For Evelyn, who eventually develops a similar relationship to food, eating initially means alienation, loneliness, and pain. Representations of food mirror respectively the emotional and psychic space that the women in this film inhabit. Clearly, Idgie and Ruth's relationship is coded as "good" and "relational" while Evelyn's becomes "bad" and "destructive." Food becomes one of the means of facilitating viewer identification with Idgie and Ruth, thereby supporting the narrative that idealizes their relationship with each other as a means of overthrowing traditional power relations, a role that eating eventually plays for Evelyn and Ninny as well. The film thus comments on a culture that mass-produces meaningless food, and it causes the viewer to prioritize food, cooking, and eating that creates relationships and connectedness.

The film's challenging of stereotypical gender through representations of food and eating operates in a similar fashion. In various ways, food becomes a source of empowerment and a vehicle for positive change for all the women in this narrative. Idgie and Ruth's story takes place during the Depression, and the widespread scarcity of food for many in the United States at this time becomes an issue of basic survival. It is striking that Idgie and Ruth, rather than suffering from a lack of food, are actually able to gain economic independence through food and eating. Food, in this respect, is power, and these two women use their access to food to challenge political and economic hierarchies.

Idgie's character clearly defies traditional standards set for women. Already as a young girl, she refuses to wear feminine clothing and embodies the classic tomboy. Even as a young adult, the nonfeminine gender role she inhabits (which, although irritating to many of the towns-people and her family members, everyone seems to accept in an almost utopian fashion) serves as the central signifier for her character. Idgie appears tough, strong, boyish, and utterly rebellious.

The "honey scene" displays Idgie's toughness and creates strong links between gender, female sexuality, and food. In this scene Idgie self-assuredly marches to a tree swarming with bees and fetches a piece of honeycomb for Ruth (and the viewer, who watches from Ruth's point of view) as she looks on in amazement and fear. At the same time, the film disrupts Idgie's tough, masculinized character by showing that she has the capacity to nurture with food, a traditional female role through which she is able to express her affection for Ruth. In this sense, Idgie's character challenges dualistic understandings of gender. She is not sim-ply the tough tomboy but rather a gender conundrum, refusing some traditional female roles while taking on and playing with others. Most important, Idgie's ability to nurture while also rejecting stereotypical female defined roles questions how gender becomes defined.

The honey serves as a means for the women to express their sexual longing for each other and to subtly underline the lesbian relationship that exists between the two. Idgie, the "Bee Charmer," as Ruth calls her, hands the jar to the object of her affection, Ruth, who proceeds, framed in a medium long two-shot, to dip her fingers into the sticky, sweet, golden honey. Honey comes to signify the love and affection between these two women in this "quietly stated study of (un)requited lesbian love, of two women sharing friendship, obstacles and joys as their reli-ance on one another deepens over the years," as James Parish writes.[16] The place where this scene is situated in the film's plot underlines the connection between food and female sexuality. Although the film never explicitly represents sexual acts between the two women, Parish empha-sizes how "the lesbian subtext remains a deliberate undercurrent to the main thrust of this comedy drama."[17] Ruth's birthday party immediately follows this sexually charged scene. The non-diegetic soundtrack plays a sexy African American vocalist singing the blues as the camera cuts from the two-shot of the women and the honey jar to a group yelling "Surprise!" Immediately, once again, we see a medium long shot of feminine Ruth and tomboy Idgie, who is now dressed in suspenders and tie. Holding a bottle, Idgie puts her arm around Ruth. The sexual over-tones continue into the next scene where the two women swim in the lake, and Ruth emerges in a wet, almost transparent, honey-colored slip from the water and kisses Idgie on the cheek. At the end of the film we see yet again a jar of honey on Ruth's grave with a note from the "Bee Charmer" next to it, a sign of Idgie's undying love for her deceased

partner. Here, food represents sexuality, pleasure, and connection between women.

The film, in its humorous, light-hearted style, immediately frames
this segment of the Idgie/Ruth narrative by cutting back to Evelyn in
the present, who is unable to look at her vagina because she cannot take
her girdle off at her women's group. The "source of our strength and
our separateness" as the teacher of Evelyn's women's class refers to the
vagina in this quite funny, ironically positioned scene (Idgie and Ruth
apparently have no problems getting in touch with their genitals), is
inaccessible to Evelyn, who is literally wrapped up in the garments of
standardized femininity. Evelyn's body size, the result of her relationship to food, and her adherence to standardized gender roles stand in
the way of her experiencing her sexuality. Thus the film comments on
the relationship between women's sexuality and normative gender roles,
linking these to each other through food.

Here the film undoes much of what it potentially sets up. In creating
dichotomies of "good eating" and "destructive eating," it links "good-
ness" with thinness and fatness with lack of control and hysteria.[18] I
imagine what it would be like to see Kathy Bates cast as Ruth, and Mary
Stuart Masterson or Mary-Louise Parker as Evelyn. It is indeed essential to the plot that Ruth be an "attractive" female who meets the expectations of what counts as a beautiful body capable of manipulating men,
and Bates clearly does not meet these standards. The choice to cast
Masterson as Idgie and Parker as Ruth is anything but coincidental.
Mainstream media's politics of body size and shape are extremely conservative. In the transposition from novel to film, for instance, Ninny's
body size undergoes a substantial change. In the novel, she describes
herself as a "big women. Big bones and all."[19] Jessica Tandy, cast as
Ninny in the film, is a very slight, petite, small-boned woman who
appears almost frail. An example out of Kathy Bates's career further
exemplifies this tendency. After having played the role of Frankie on
stage in *Frankie and Johnnie*, Bates was passed over for the film role for
Michelle Pfeiffer, an actress whose appearance has helped to set contemporary standards for beauty and attractiveness. As W. Charisse
Goodman writes, "This is typical. If the heavy woman has any consistent role in commercial American films, it is as the peripheral, asexual
mother or 'buddy,' and rarely, if ever, the central, romantic character.
Message to all large women: You're not sexy. The only beautiful woman
is a thin woman."[20]

The lesbian subtext of the film undergoes a similar treatment. While
the Gay and Lesbian Alliance Against Defamation (GLAAD) honored
Fried Green Tomatoes with a Media Award explicitly for its positive rep-

resentation of a lesbian relationship, the representation itself remains quite vague.[21] As Rebecca Bell-Metereau writes, mainstream cinema takes "pains to establish the heterosexuality of the woman characters, even in the case of *Fried Green Tomatoes*, where the literary source presented the main relationship as lesbian."[22] As the film presents possibilities for difference, it also takes them away. Jennifer Ross Church emphasizes how "the film depends upon looks between the two women that can be interpreted in very different ways and upon a more mature, public proclamation of their love."[23] According to Church's analysis, the film clearly opens up different spectator possibilities: Ruth's "love" proclamation for Idgie in the courtroom can therefore be viewed as an affirmation of either a lesbian partnership or a nonsexual female friendship. It insinuates the possibility of sexual love and partnership between women, but it does so in a manner that is careful not to alienate a mainstream heterosexual viewing audience. The emphasis on both Idgie's and Ruth's physical beauty (their facial features, bodies, and anachronistic 1990s hairstyles adhere closely to the Hollywood standards of what is held to be "beautiful") further undermines the gender-disruptive tendencies the film attempts to set up. While Idgie, for example, is indeed tomboyish and tough, her outward appearance remains within the parameters of what mainstream heterosexist culture understands as beautiful.

As problematic as many of the representations of sexuality, gender, and food are, the film offers other transgressive and empowering images of gender and food. By subverting the traditional model of the woman as server and caretaker and turning the role of feeder into a means of overthrowing male dominance, *Fried Green Tomatoes* challenges traditional concepts of power. Food and servitude thus become sources of strength throughout the Idgie/Ruth narrative. In her book *Feeding the Family: The Social Organization of Caring as Gendered Work*, Marjorie DeVault argues that "feeding work has become one of the primary ways that women 'do' gender."[24] Performing the roles of cooking and feeding thus often serves as reaffirmation of gender roles, so that for many women this work "has become an apparently 'natural' part of the gendered self."[25] *Fried Green Tomatoes* displays woman as the classic feeder and server and then subverts this very role. Food—initially a means of entrapment for Evelyn, who relies on doughnuts and candy bars for emotional warmth—takes on strikingly different meanings when it is prepared, eaten, and served by Idgie and Ruth. As Evelyn is able to form a strong connection with Ninny, her relationship with food changes parallel to this development. This becomes a means of overthrowing traditionally gendered power relationships, and cooking and serving represent acts of personal, social, and political assertion.

Fried Green Tomatoes critically displays the flip side of this coin. Evelyn Couch's life revolves around the classic "female" duties of serving and pleasing her husband. Suffering from "empty nest syndrome" now that her son has left home, Evelyn, married to the proverbial "couch potato," Ed, anxiously awaits his arrival home from work every day. Dressed primly and properly, she meticulously prepares meals and decorates the table with flowers for her husband, who prefers to dine alone in front of the television. To soothe her distress and deal with the anxiety she experiences over the loss of the traditional mother/feeder role, Evelyn turns to junk food as a source of self-nurturing. By dressing her in muumuus and good-girl southern belle clothing with carefully coifed curls, the film emphasizes Evelyn's inability to take action and deal with her life. She feels "so useless, so powerless," as she explains to Ninny. Her feelings of powerlessness revolve around food, as she is unable to recognize how fully she has given herself over to traditional gender norms. "I can't stop eating," she cries. "Every day I try and try, and every day I go off. I hide candy bars all over the house." The camera pans alongside her as she stuffs herself, carefully situating the viewer in Ninny's position. We look at Evelyn with a mixture of pity and humor, glad that we are not made to be "in her shoes." The cinematography cautiously provides us with just enough distance from Evelyn that we can empathize with her without having to fear *becoming* her.

In its treatment of Evelyn, the film takes back many of the possibilities that it offers for viewers. While Evelyn eventually becomes—despite her body size—an admirable, self-assured character, the ways in which the narrative, cinematography, and editing comment on her figure undermine the transgressive possibilities the film sets up. The fact that *Fried Green Tomatoes* even takes up the issue of representing a woman with a compulsive eating disorder and attempts to place it in a sociocultural and psychological framework distinguishes it from most representations of women and eating in mainstream U.S. cinema. Nonetheless, the representation of Evelyn positions overweight women in a negative light and reaffirms biologically determined theories about women's bodies and their relationships to food. When Evelyn breaks down and confesses to Ninny that she feels helpless and out of control, Ninny tells her that the onset of menopause and thus a hormonal imbalance are to blame for her distress. In effect, the film blames Evelyn's female anatomy and her aging process for what feminist eating-disorders specialists view as an effect of socially reinforced gender patterns that make women believe they are sick if they like to eat.[26] In essentializing Evelyn's relationship to food and reducing it to biological terms, the film undermines many of the subversive moves that it makes, reinforcing hegemonic, patriarchal understandings of women's bodies as naturally flawed and therefore in need of correction.

The camera often positions Evelyn as an object of laughter. At times, this works to strengthen her character. The humorous characterization of Evelyn often facilitates empathy and understanding with her. When she begins to identify as "Towanda the Avenger," for example, who destroys the cute red convertible of two skinny young women who wrongfully steal her parking spot and make fun of her for her age and body size, I have repeatedly found myself rejoicing. But this humor, as Shari Zeck argues, is limited in its capacity to transgress. Zeck writes, "After all we have seen how in this film, moments of laughter, even when combined explicitly with gender transgression, are so readily re-cuperated by the gaze of a benign mother, a useless husband, and a feckless sheriff, suggesting how fragile humor as a weapon of rebellion can be."[27] The humorous elements are quite often judgmental and harsh. In a supermarket scene, for instance, the camera frames Evelyn next to a huge pile of dog food packages. As she exits the store, the camera shoots her in a long shot walking toward her car with the super-market logo in bright red letters in the background, indicating to us that Evelyn is one of "The Beef People." In the next shot, a young man calls her a fat cow and causes her to drop her groceries on the ground. Once again, the film gives the viewer enough distance to empathize with Evelyn, while the humor keeps us from taking her problems all too seriously. Certainly, these representations are anything but subver-sive and transgressive. Rather, they serve to elicit laughter at the "fat woman's" expense, and American audiences, culturally prepared to find this humorous, instantaneously get the joke.

In contrast to Evelyn, for Idgie and Ruth food, cooking, eating, and nurturing serve as realms of empowerment, and here the camera has us view from and thus identify through their perspectives. Ultimately, it is through her relationship with Ninny and through food itself that Eve-lyn is able to empower and heal herself, but initially she provides a stark contrast to Idgie and Ruth. When Idgie rescues Ruth from her physi-cally abusive husband, the two women move in with each other and open a restaurant, the "Whistle Stop Café." Indeed, almost everything about this space comes to represent subversion of traditional hierar-chies. Here, women and people of color run the show, and the Ku Klux Klan of this small Alabama town does not like this at all. Unlike Evelyn who stuffs herself with Cracker Jacks, a not-so-subtle yet humorous link

232

to the traditional southern "cracker" good girl role that has been shoved down her throat, Idgie refuses to acknowledge threats by the Klan and continues to serve food to whomever she wishes. When warned by Sheriff Grady that she should stop "selling to coloreds," Idgie defiantly pokes fun at him and his friends "under those sheets" for "marching around in one of those parades you boys have. . . . How come they don't have enough sense to change their shoes?" She teases him, "I'd recognize those size 14 clodhoppers you got anywhere, Grady," situating herself on the side of her African American friends whom she consistently treats with friendship, warmth, respect, and dignity.

Ruth participates in transgressive gender behavior as well. She turns the role of the passive female into parody by consciously employing passive-aggressive tactics around food in order to challenge male dominance. From the beginning, she inhabits a traditionally feminine role. Yet as she grows in her relationship with Idgie, she begins to subvert serving into a form of conscious manipulation. In support of Idgie, who directly challenges Grady's (and thus the institution of the police's) authority, she bats her eyes and plays the "sweet" female as the camera cuts to a close-up of her interrogating him with a smile feigning sweetness, "Would you like some more pie, Grady?" Serving thus becomes a means of diverting Grady's attention away from the task at hand and undermining his power.

Ruth's character passive-aggressively assaults male figures—always with a warm, feminine smile—numerous times throughout the film. When the inspector comes to investigate the murder of her husband, Ruth once again masquerades in the feminine role of the subservient as a means of asserting power by suggesting, "Could I interest you in some pie?" in order to divert his attention from the task at hand. The mask of femininity serves as a shield against the male figures that unconsciously link femaleness with passivity. I certainly do not wish to imply that women rarely gain access to power through feeding. I would, quite the contrary, argue that this realm is one in which women traditionally have often been able to assert certain forms of power. My point is that representations in film rarely show food and cooking as forms of self-empowerment, and *Fried Green Tomatoes* consistently plays with these traditional gender associations. Food, cooking, and eating are the realms where this upheaval manifests itself, always in the context of women bonding with each other. Eating and food never stand in the service of appeasing men and appealing to their sexual desire as is so often the case in Hollywood cinema.

This paradigm becomes most strikingly apparent in the context of Evelyn's personal development. As harshly as the film treats her throughout the initial parts of her story, Evelyn slowly emerges as a strong, respectable, attractive character despite her body size, and this transition manifests itself in part through her relationship to food. Indeed, it is precisely through food that she is able to find to herself. After attempting various diets, changing her clothing style to look more contemporary and upbeat, and exercising, Evelyn begins to take responsibility for her life. This is a mixed blessing. In order to find herself, Evelyn plays out roles prescribed by society that will supposedly "heal" her, and these focus on regulating her body.

As much as Evelyn's character regulates her body in an "appropriate" and "normal" manner, she does eventually break away from this regulatory discipline. Evelyn goes through various permutations of rebellion. During her "Towanda" phase, she serves her husband sushi, crudité, and crackers for dinner. He accuses her of trying to kill him with this food, to which she responds, "If I was gonna kill ya, I'd use my hands." As she develops a relationship with Ninny and with herself, her attitude toward food changes. Toward the end of the film, Evelyn seems "together" and happy. Her hairstyle and dress change so that she appears less as a caricature of a good girl gone awry and more as a well-balanced, content woman. This development culminates in her ability to eat the fried green tomatoes she has brought in to Ninny to celebrate her birthday. Problematic as the representation of Evelyn's character throughout the majority of the film is, the image of Evelyn biting into a fried green tomato, enjoying the food and the company of her female friend, and not experiencing guilt over the consumption of (heavens forbid!) fried food is quite striking. I cannot think of any other scene in contemporary mainstream U.S. cinema that represents a large woman—otherwise positioned as a "woman who eats too much"—enjoying food in the context of female friendship and bonding.

The image of Kathy Bates eating fried food and feeling comfortable in her body has had an empowering effect on me. The food fight scene in the Idgie/Ruth narrative provides an interesting example as well of how *Fried Green Tomatoes* comments on the ways in which women have been taught to identify around food and their bodies.

The food fight scene begins with cinematography and editing techniques that evoke classic food advertising, setting the viewer up for what appears to be a "beautiful" food scene. We hear the voice of Marion Williams singing "Cool Down Yonder" as the camera opens on a close-up of green tomatoes frying in a cast-iron skillet. Slowly, paced to the music, the film cuts to a stunning bowl of deep red tomatoes, followed by a shot of a luscious, dense bowl of chocolate icing being stirred by a spatula. Also in close-up, we see a bowl of eggs and then a shot of

234

glistening ripened blackberries. The food is perfect and simultaneously quite sexy in its simplicity, reminiscent of illustrations from *Gourmet* magazine. The camera then cuts from the kitchen to the restaurant space of the café, where we see policeman Grady, a classic emblem of patriarchal authority and white supremacy. As the camera cuts back to the kitchen, we see Idgie feeding one of the fried green tomatoes she has prepared to Ruth in a flirtatious manner. The scene gradually builds up the sexual tension between the two women, and it comes as no surprise that the most sexually charged and physical scene between the women in the film occurs in conjunction with food.

While this scene associates masculinity with the public restaurant space, the kitchen is clearly coded as female and private. As Ruth roles her eyes in the obviously "hot" kitchen (it is both physically hot and the sexual overtones of the scene emphasize its erotic "heat"), she comments to Idgie, "They're terrible." Idgie, to the words of the song "cool down" proceeds to splash Ruth in the face with a glass of water, "I just thought you needed a little cooling off." The loaded meaning behind this exacerbates the sexual tension. From a water fight between the two women, the scene progresses to a food fight. Idgie's hand reaches in a close-up into the blackberries that she then smears in Ruth's face. The women proceed to rub ingredients necessary for making fruit pie all over each other's bodies, holding and stroking each other with the food as they then fall to the floor. "We need to make a little paste," Ruth says as she strokes flour on Idgie.

The camerawork then forces a direct comparison between Ruth and Idgie's world of upheaval, connectedness, and female dominance by cutting to a medium close-up of Grady attempting to eat a perfect slice of cherry pie, only to be disrupted by the noise in the kitchen. The camera tilts from the plate to his face as he glares to the left of the screen toward the kitchen. His neat, orderly, masculine pie remains on its plate while their messy, chaotic, female pie becomes a tool for sexual play and intimate contact, and this is clearly upsetting to him. Here, policeman Grady is the outsider, and as the viewer, we are invited to participate in the jokes the women play on him. The film turns the tables and prioritizes the female over the male.

As Grady enters the kitchen, the women are rolling around on the floor. "What in the name of Christmas are you two doin?" he inquires, attempting to assert his dominance in a space that is clearly not under his domain. Idgie's response emphasizes the close connections that the film makes between sexuality, gender, and food: "She's trying to teach me how to cook." Cooking, clearly meant jokingly, is indeed a form of rebellion in this film, and it takes on various meanings. Cooking becomes sexual play that excludes men and thus serves as a direct challenge to male authority.

The women continue to challenge Grady's authority. When he states, "You betta stop this or I'm gonna hafta arrest you for disorderly conduct," Ruth laughs and says, "Well arrest us then." The camera then cuts back to the same exact shots we saw in the beginning of the scene. We see the hand stirring the harmless, aestheticized sweet chocolate frosting, yet in the next shot Ruth takes the metal spatula and smears the mixture down Grady's face. The simple kitchen tool becomes a symbolic assault weapon, humorously challenging male dominance and simultaneously foreshadowing the frying pan that later becomes an actual murder weapon. The play of subversion turns into actual upheaval as the "passive" domain of woman, the kitchen, becomes a real threat.

This scene challenges the association of femaleness with chaos, disorder, and uncleanliness and of masculinity with order and cleanliness in a striking manner. The film clearly prioritizes Idgie and Ruth's relationship with each other over patriarchal norms. Thus the cinematography and editing that position food as harmless and aesthetically pleasing (much in the same manner that female bodies are so often served up for male viewing gratification) subvert the narrative of food. The glistening chocolate turns into a symbolic weapon of assault, and the cinematographic narrative of "beautiful food" turns into a realm where female passion, lesbian desire, and the exclusion of men play themselves out. The visual elements of this scene support the ways in which the narrative otherwise challenges patriarchy through food.

The linkage of food with the political takes on a transgressive quality. Despite screenplay and novel author Fannie Flagg's statement that "It's not a political film at all," food becomes overtly political in *Fried Green Tomatoes*.[28] The whole town talks of "Railroad Bill," who jumps on trains and throws government food to the impoverished people living along the railroad tracks. It is indeed interesting that the townspeople assume this person to be male, when in fact, as we learn, it is Idgie herself. Early on in the film we see Idgie and Ruth out on one of their first encounters as they climb into a boxcar. As the train moves along, Idgie throws food to poor people living in a settlement camp. When Ruth points out that this is not Idgie's food to take, Idgie reverts to the biblical quote, "give unto others" as a means of justification for her theft, drawing on traditional values to support her subversive actions. A series of high and low angle eyeline matches between the desperate faces gradually becoming happy and Ruth and Idgie forms a visual connection between the women and the plight of the economically disadvantaged families. Providing food is Idgie's political act.

236

Similarly, food becomes a source through which Idgie and Ruth form bonds with wandering hobos like Smokey Nowhere who have no income, lodging, or food. We watch as the women take these vagabonds into their café, provide them with lodging, subsistence, and nurturing, thus attempting on a small, local scale to undo the politics of food distribution that the government practices. By feeding the economically underprivileged and throwing food off the train, Idgie plays a contemporary Robin Hood attempting to sustain the masses. She consistently identifies with and supports the underdog, and food is her weapon of choice for challenging social, economic, and racial inequalities.

Less overtly political yet equally significant are the bonds Idgie and Ruth form with African Americans through food and cooking. The film consistently affirms a connection particularly between Idgie and the African American characters through the narrative and the non-diegetic soundtrack. The non-diegetic soundtrack links Idgie and Ruth's experiences with African American culture. The film opens to a haunting African American female voice humming. Slowly the voice breaks into singing as we see Frank Bennett's car being lifted out of the lake. Sexy, bluesy vocals accompany the "love scene" by the lake, and the food fight scene in the café's kitchen plays itself out to the tune "Cool Down Yonder" sung by Marion Williams.

This association of the white female experience with that of the African American experience is, however, as Jennifer Ross Church argues, quite problematic. She states, "Just as the lesbian relationship remains largely undefined against a heterosexual background, black characters are placed against a white background, and the story relies heavily on stereotypes and familiar images to establish their identity. Like lesbianism, race is invoked for its emotional power yet is emptied of its content."[29] As Church points out, many of the scenes from the novel that explicitly represent African American communities in Troutville, the African American section near Whistle Stop, and Slagtown, a large neighborhood outside Birmingham, are absent from the film. These communities, have the "effect of grounding the black characters and making them seem more real, just as the consequences that black characters suffer as a result of their actions are more serious."[30] The film simply avoids these scenes.

I challenge this film on its insufficient representation of African American culture and myself on my ability to "enjoy" it despite this. The narrative as presented in the film represents African American characters almost solely in relationship to whiteness.[31] The "strategic use of black characters to define the goals and enhance the qualities of white characters," as Toni Morrison writes, is nothing new to the history of American narratives.[32] Just as the founding writers of the United States were able to "engage, imagine, and create an Africanist presence and persona" that served, among other things, as a backdrop against which whiteness could define itself, so does contemporary mainstream culture perpetuate this trope by viewing African American characters from outside their own perspective.[33] Ultimately, *Fried Green Tomatoes* focuses on how the African American characters support and rescue the white characters, a trope that by now has become so commonplace in mainstream film that one could refer to it as a "Whoopie Goldberg syndrome."[34]

What Church does emphasize in regard to race is that this film, despite the fragmented, stereotypical representations, "offers more freedom and possibilities to the white characters, who are not in danger of being redefined against a white norm."[35] This space of escape and change that develops between the female characters offers them possibilities for change. I question the need to represent freedom and possibility to one group of oppressed people, in this case women, at the expense of another, African Americans. *Fried Green Tomatoes* reinscribes what many feminist theorists have sought to challenge, namely the notion, as Elizabeth Spelman writes, of a "generic woman" which "obscures the heterogeneity of women and cuts off examination of the significance of such heterogeneity for feminist theory and political activity."[36] *Fried Green Tomatoes*, like many feminist texts written by white women that, as Audre Lorde writes, "ignore their built-in privilege of whiteness and define *woman* in terms of their own experience alone" faces what she calls "the pitfall of being seduced into joining the oppressor under the pretense of sharing power."[37] Change and opportunity for white women can and must be represented alongside images that offer change and opportunity for other oppressed groups. Both my initial inability to recognize this dynamic and the filmmakers' blindness to racial dynamics reiterate what Ruth Frankenberg consistently emphasizes in her study of whiteness, namely that "in a social context where white people have too often viewed themselves as nonracial or racially neutral, it is crucial to look at the 'racialness' of white experience."[38]

The experience of white women becomes linked (albeit highly problematically) with that of African Americans in this film through food and cooking. Particularly the parts of the narrative that deal with the murder of Frank Bennett, Ruth's violently abusive husband, serve to form connections between Idgie and Ruth and Big George, Sipsey, and Naughty Bird, the African American characters who work in the café. Out of support for Ruth and Idgie, Sipsey murders Frank Bennett by hitting him over the head with—of all things—a cast-iron skillet. The kitchen as a source of power and strength embodies itself in the image of Sipsey heaving the heavy skillet over the white, wife-abusing Bennett's head, literally overthrowing traditional hierarchies. The viewer learns of this only at the very end of the film so that one is left to assume that Idgie herself or Big George has killed Bennett, but certainly not the small, reticent Sipsey who constantly appears in the background but is hardly ever placed in center screen. The film, constructing and thus anticipating a "white" spectator, plays with viewers' expectations of which characters are important, as one is never led to assume that this small, unassuming African American woman might be responsible for Bennett's death.[39] In expecting that the viewer will get this "irony," the film speaks from a position of whiteness. We then see how Idgie, Big George, and Sipsey have bonded together over this secret in order to protect Big George (whom the white authorities automatically assume to be guilty) from an inevitable death sentence.

It is, of course, in the café's kitchen and food storage areas where this bonding process takes place. Through the bond forged between the African American characters and the women, white masculine dominance literally becomes an object of consumption. In order to get rid of evidence (i.e., Bennett's corpse), Idgie has Big George start the "hog boiling" season a little early, and the sexist pig Bennett becomes a barbecued pig, a "secret" that, as Sipsey states, gets "hidden in the sauce." Here, again, the film is anything but subtle as it cuts from Idgie performing in drag on stage with Grady dressed as a women to a medium close-up of a piece of raw meat into which a large cleaver cuts. The non-diegetic soundtrack comments humorously once again with the song "Barbeque Bess" sung by Patti La Belle. We then see that it is George who is preparing what we later find out to be Bennett's body for the grill. The diegetic soundtrack emphasizes the sizzling sound when the meat hits the hot grill. In the following set of shots, Idgie and Ruth serve plate after plate of "the best damn barbecue in the state of Alabama" to the inspector. Revenge is as sweet and tasty as the barbecue sauce, and I must admit that I have found myself rejoicing as patriarchy consumes itself.

The film consistently underlines a constructed similarity of experience between people of color and women without adequately differentiating between the forms of oppression that white women face as opposed to those of people of color. The inspector, for example, condescendingly refers to Idgie as "girlie girl" only to then call Big George by the racialized term "boy." In treating race and gender alongside each other in this fashion, the oppression of "women" comes to the forefront at the cost of failing to represent the African American side of this tale. While Shari Zeck argues that "white women and African Americans are not opposed in this film, but rather they cooperate in ridding the world of evil white men," the film's lack of distinction between oppression faced by white women and by women (and all people) of color is one of the elements of this film that I find, in conducting a closer analysis, to be most alienating and unpalatable. *Fried Green Tomatoes* repeats the paradigm of analogizing racism and sexism, which, according to Trina Grillo and Stephanie Wildman "perpetuates patterns of racial domination by minimizing the impact of racism, rendering it an insignificant phenomenon—one of a laundry list of isms or oppressions that society must suffer."[40] This film's consistent comparison of the experience of white women with people of color offers "protection for the traditional center" and thus supports the privilege that hegemonic culture assigns to whiteness.[41]

I think of the many times, however, that I have viewed *Fried Green Tomatoes* and how easy it has been for me, as a heterosexual white woman who has experienced so many privileges because of my ethnicity and sexuality, to distance myself from the issues of race, gender, and sexuality that this film glosses over. In writing this, I cannot avoid the privilege I have been handed that I can so easily overlook when viewing mainstream films. Thus, I most certainly do not wish to redeem *Fried Green Tomatoes* from its treatment of race. In underlining similarities in experience between women, people of color, and economically disadvantaged social classes, the film perpetuates myths about different forms of oppression and fails to show how excruciating and yet how unalike the experiences of race, class, gender, ageism, heterosexism, and body size prejudice can be. By doing this, *Fried Green Tomatoes* fails to adequately differentiate the multiple forms of oppression that operate in a sexist, racist, heterosexist culture, and in doing so begs the question of how this film actually serves to reinscribe these as opposed to challenging them.

I find myself compelled to understand the position from which I encounter this film as a means of understanding how its narrative is able to speak to me in this manner. Without questioning my own positionality, delving into the issue of how the film has offered me possibilities for change loses its meaning. My position as a white heterosexual woman certainly has much to do with my experience of this film as potentially empowering. This is, after all, a story about white women finding ways to empower themselves. Despite all of its flaws and its need to consistently recuperate hegemonic ideals, I have been able to find these moments. I wonder, however, what it might feel like to watch this film from a different position. What might it be like, for example, to watch *Fried Green Tomatoes* as a white male? Or as a person of color? What appears to my eyes as a form of empowerment might be experienced by another viewer as male-bashing or as terribly racist. The film was clearly produced and distributed with a viewer like myself in mind. Its marketing tactics underline the position of whiteness from which *Fried Green Tomatoes* operates. The film poster and video jacket, for example, feature pictures of the four central characters, all of whom are white women played by well-known Hollywood actresses. The narrative on the back of the video jacket states that this is "the story of a simpler time," and I have to question for whom the 1930s were a time of simplicity. Certainly the lives of African Americans living in the South at this time were anything but "simple."

Clearly, *Fried Green Tomatoes* offers forms of "newness" and change, but the emergent elements are contained within residual cultural patterns. This film, like so many of the cultural products that we create and consume, stands on the edge of creating change, yet remains anchored in residual cultural values, closely echoing what Raymond Williams states about the arts of creation and performance: "They contribute to the effective dominant culture and are a central articulation of it. They embody residual meanings and values, not all of which are incorporated, though many are. They express also and significantly some emergent practices and meanings, yet some of these may eventually be incorporated, as they reach people and begin to move them."[42] The way *Fried Green Tomatoes* treats gender stands in direct contrast to its treatment of race and how it caters to white, mainstream American audiences' desire to continually have African Americans serve as caretakers. In this sense, the film remains, to use Williams's term, residual.

Were this film to be produced now, almost fifteen years later than it was made (1991), I am certain that the lesbian relationship, for example, would be more prominently defined; representing lesbianism on television and in film has become "fashionable."[43] Perhaps, the African American figures might take on a more central role, but I believe the film—as does contemporary mainstream film—would still subordinate these characters. Like bell hooks, I wish to voice my concern over the degree to which emergent cultural forms become usurped by mainstream cinema as a new way to create objects of consumption while reaffirming hegemonic values. Seeking to understand the social, economic, and political consequences of such texts would prove a most worthy endeavor. The lucrative body of female buddy films that has been produced since *Fried Green Tomatoes*, many of which modeled themselves on this film, opens up some answers to this query.[44] The oscillation between residual and emergent elements within the same media product appears to sell very well: it offers the illusion of difference, newness, and change but simultaneously reinscribes hegemony. It is also important to question whether a text that provides someone like myself with empowerment and opportunity necessarily fosters positive social change.

I return to the cycle of pleasure and guilt. There is no simple answer to this dynamic, but through writing, I have come more and more to realize the value of discourse as a means of understanding where pleasure comes from and what its ramifications are. The challenging and yet satisfying tasks of writing and teaching have become forms of sorting through, of digesting texts and claiming elements of empowerment while transforming guilt into responsible action. It is precisely this form of engagement that has allowed me to question my position in relationship to this film and go beyond the cycle of pleasure/guilt. With more critical awareness, perhaps we can create and consume cultural texts that foster growth and change without having to excuse themselves for making waves. The more I confront this dynamic, the less I experience guilt both in consuming films and in consuming food, and I am more able to recognize where my personal responsibility lies.

Notes

1. bell hooks, "Eating the Other: Desire and Resistance," in *Eating Culture*, ed. Ron Scapp and Brian Seitz (Albany: State University of New York Press, 1998), 181.

2. Ibid, 200.

3. Ibid.

4. Jennifer Ross Church, "The Balancing Act of *Fried Green Tomatoes*," in *Vision/Re-Vision: Adapting Contemporary American Fiction by Women to Film*, ed. Barbara Tepa Lupack (Bowling Green: Bowling Green State University Popular Press, 1996), 193.

5. Ibid.

6. Shari Zeck, "Laughter, Loss, and Transformation in *Fried Green Tomatoes*," in *Performing Gender and Comedy: Theories, Texts, and Contexts*, ed. Shannon Hengen (Ontario: Gordon and Breach, 1998), 219–229. Zeck discusses the comical role that Idgie plays in the film. She writes, "The power of Idgie Threadgoode is not in the *isolated fact* that she tells tall tales or is a jokester. After all, we have seen how in this film moments of laughter, even when combined explicitly with gender transgression, are so readily recuperated by the gaze of a benign mother, a useless husband, and a feckless sheriff, suggesting how fragile humor as a weapon of rebellion can be[. . .]. To take the character as the joke itself is not to dismiss her transgressive qualities, but to understand the limits of that transgressiveness and to remind us of the important point: it is not just that Idgie is the tall tale teller, but rather that that

action's particular significance takes shape in the exaggerations of her gender identity, in turn tied to her continuous mourning" (224). James Robert Parish discusses the lesbian subtext of *Fried Green Tomatoes* in *Gays and Lesbians in Mainstream Cinema* (Jefferson, N.C.: McFarland), 1993.

7. One, in many ways, very interesting psychoanalytic reading of this film by Jane van Buren does a wonderful job of analyzing the "refreshing psychic space that bursts out of what we have come to accept as the dominant film discourse of male subjectivity," yet she never questions its many problematic issues relating to race, sexuality, and gender. Jane van Buren, "Food for Thought in the Film *Fried Green Tomatoes,*" *Psychoanalytic Inquiry* 18, 2 (1998): 291.

8. Raymond Williams, "Base and Superstructure in Marxist Cultural Theory," in his *Problems in Materialism and Culture* (London: Verso, 1980), 41.

9. Ibid.

10. Ibid., 40.

11. John Fiske, for example, defines polysemy as a "multiplicity of meanings." He writes of television that a "program provides a potential of meanings which may be realized, or made into actually experienced meanings, by socially situated viewers in the process of reading." John Fiske, *Television Culture* (London: Routledge, 1987), 15–16.

12. In toto, the film grossed $80.1 million in U.S. box offices and $37.403 million in video sales. Internet Movie Database, www.imdb.com, March 10, 2000.

13. W. Charisse Goodman, *The Invisible Woman: Confronting Weight Prejudice in America* (Carlsbad, CA: Guerze Books, 1995), 58.

14. Susan Bordo, "Hunger as Ideology," in her *Unbearable Weight: Feminism, Western Culture, and the Body* (Berkeley: University of California Press, 1993), 110. Her previous sentence reads: "When women are positively depicted as sensuously voracious about food (almost never in commercials, and only very rarely in movies and novels), their hunger for food is employed solely as a metaphor for their sexual appetite."

15. Ibid.

16. Parish, *Gays and Lesbians,*147.

17. Ibid.

18. Susan Bordo explores the cultural associations of fatness with "the taint of matter and flesh, 'wantonness,' mental stupor and mental decay" (*Unbearable Weight*, 233).

19. Fannie Flagg, *Fried Green Tomatoes at the Whistle Stop Café* (New York: McGraw-Hill, 1988), 6.

20. Goodman, *The Invisible Woman,* 56. Some non-mainstream and non-American films provide striking contrasts to the body politics of Hollywood. *Antonia's Line* (Marleen Gorris, 1995), a Dutch film, features a large, well-rounded woman as its central character. She is allowed to eat, throw dinner parties, *and* be quite sexy and appealing. The Australian film *Muriel's Wedding* (P. J. Hogan, 1994) is another wonderful example that deals directly with the protagonist's body size and her own issues of feeling unattractive. During the course of the film, Muriel is allowed to become sexual and beautiful. *Out of Rosenheim* (Percy Adlon, 1988), starring the German actress Marianne Sägebrecht, provides another striking contrast to standard American fare.

21. Parish, *Gays and Lesbians*, 87.

22. Rebecca Bell-Metereau, *Hollywood Androgyny* (New York: Columbia University Press, 1993), 251.

23. Church, "The Balancing Act of *Fried Green Tomatoes*," 194.

24. Marjorie L. DeVault, *Feeding the Family: The Social Organization of Caring as Gendered Work* (Chicago: University of Chicago Press, 1991), 118.

25. Ibid., 119.

26. Barbara Ehrenreich and Deirdre English point out in *For Her Own Good* (Garden City, NY: Anchor Press, 1978), 110–120, how theories that "guided the doctor's practice from the late nineteenth century to the early twentieth century held that woman's *normal* state was to be sick. . . . Medicine had 'discovered' that female functions were inherently pathological." In linking Evelyn's eating disorder to her female organs, the film underlines what Ehrenreich and English refer to as a "dictatorship of the ovaries."

Some of the literature that looks specifically at the relationship between the treatment of women's bodies and eating disorders includes: Patricia Fallow, Melanie Katzman, and Susan Wooley, *Feminist Perspectives on Eating Disorders* (New York: Guilford Press, 1994); Bordo, *Unbearable Weight*; Laura Fraser, *Losing It: America's Obsession with Weight and the Industry That Feeds On It* (New York: Dutton, 1997); Morag MacSween, *Anorexic Bodies. A Feminist and Sociological Perspective on Anorexia Nervosa* (New York: Routledge, 1993); and Sharlene Hesse-Biber, *Am I Thin Enough Yet? The Cult of Thinness and the Commercialization of Identity* (New York: Oxford University Press, 1996).

27. Zeck, "Laughter, Loss, and Transformation in *Fried Green Tomatoes*," 224.

28. Parish, *Gays and Lesbians*, 149.

29. Church, "The Balancing Act of *Fried Green Tomatoes*," 202.

30. Ibid.

31. Zeck argues that the film is fairly sensitive in its treatment of African American characters. About the casting of Cicely Tyson as Sipsey, for example, she says that "while Sipsey may be narratively in the background, verbally silent, it's Cicely Tyson, perhaps the most celebrated actress in this much-celebrated cast, who is present to us visually" ("Laughter, Loss, and Transformation in *Fried Green Tomatoes*," 226–227). Similarly, she argues, "the subversive African American is linked to the gender subversive Idgie," pointing out that Sipsey contributes substantially to the humor of the film by telling two central jokes. "The first, a joke about white men who won't sit in a restaurant with black men but will 'eat eggs, shot right out of a chicken's ass' and second—'the secret's in the sauce' (and so is Frank Bennett)— hide power within their folksiness" (227).

32. Toni Morrison, *Playing in the Dark* (New York: Vintage Books, 1992), 52.

33. Ibid.

34. I thank Arlene Voski Avakian for this point, made to me in personal communication.

35. Church, "The Balancing Act of *Fried Green Tomatoes*," 203.

36. Elizabeth Spelman, *Inessential Woman: Problems of Exclusion in Feminist Thought* (Boston: Beacon Press, 1988), ix.

37. Audre Lorde, "Age, Race, Class, and Sex: Women Redefining Difference," *Sister outsider: essays and speeches* (Freedom, CA: Crossing Press, 1984), 117.

38. Ruth Frankenberg, *White Women, Race Matters: The Social Construction of Whiteness* (Minneapolis: University of Minnesota Press, 1993), 1.

39. Toni Morrison writes, "the readers of virtually all of American fiction have been positioned as white" (*Playing in the Dark*, xii). *Fried Green Tomatoes* constructs its ideal viewer in a similar fashion by assuming that the reader will view from a position of whiteness and racial unawareness.

40. Trina Grillo and Stephanie M. Wildman, "Obscuring the Importance of Race: The Implications of Making Comparisons between Racism and Sexism (or Other Isms)," *Critical White Studies: Looking Behind the Mirror*, ed. Richard Delgada and Jean Stefancic (Philadelphia: Temple University Press, 1997), 621.

41. Ibid., 622.

42. Williams, "Base and Superstructure," 45.

43. One need only look at "Ellen's" coming out on network television to see an example of how the commodification of sexuality has changed and shifted. This is certainly not to say mainstream media represents homosexuality in a positive manner. Rather, the parameters around what can be represented have shifted since the early 1990s, and *Fried Green Tomatoes* would most likely reflect this tendency were it to be filmed today.

44. As Jennifer Ross Church writes, the success of *Fried Green Tomatoes* prompted "the movie industry to try to define and cash in on its audience" ("The Balancing Act of *Fried Green Tomatoes*," 193). There have been a row of successful women's films since the early '90s. One of the most popular ones is *The Joy Luck Club* (Wayne Wang, 1993), which also deals with women's identity and food. In 1995 three lucrative films about women's relationships were produced: *How to Make an American Quilt* (Jocelyn Moorhouse); *Boys on the Side* (Herbert Ross); and *Waiting to Exhale* (Forest Whitaker). All of these films would lend themselves to an analysis similar to the one of *Fried Green Tomatoes*.

Chili Peppers as Tools of Resistance:
Ketan Mehta's *Mirch Masala*

BEHEROZE F. SHROFF

Resistance . . . may be no more than a negative agency, an absence of acqui-
escence in one's oppression. The act of reading resistance can be an important political recognition.

Rajeswari Sunder Rajan, Real and Imagined Women

It is one of the paradoxes of Indian film, as of Indian life, that the woman is,
on the one hand, victimized as a wife and, on the other, venerated as a mother.
. . . Self-sacrificing, martyred, and ill-used by the husband, or by fate, she is
shown as indestructible when it comes to protecting her sons. . . . Thus the
implication is that a woman's only hope of salvation lies in becoming the
mother of sons.

Aruna Vasudev, "The Woman: Myth and Reality in Indian Cinema"

India has the reputation of churning out, on an average, two films per
day,[1] and is generally considered the leading producer of films in the
world. The Hindi language film has dominated the Indian distribution
scene, and produced from one of the major film centers, namely Bombay, this body of films is often referred to as the "Bombay film" and
more recently as Bollywood cinema. Analyzing the Bombay films in the
post-independence years, Eric Barnouw and S. Krishnaswamy in their
seminal study of Indian cinema write:

> The *formula* as dictated by exhibitor and distributor, called for one or
> two major stars, at least half a dozen songs, and a few dances. The
> story was of declining importance. . . . The subject matter with in-
> creasing concentration was romance. An overwhelming number of
> Bombay films now began with the chance acquaintance of hero and
> heroine, often in an unconventional manner and novel setting. . . .
> there was strong bias towards the *glamorous*. . . . Dance and song pro-
> vided conventionalized substitutes for love-making and emotional
> crises.[2]

The commercial Hindi film with these formula elements also has been popularly referred to as the *masala* film, and with increasing emphasis on Westernization and "glamour," these films follow formulaic plots with recognizable icons such as the heterosexual love triangle—often rags to riches romances with song-and-dance routines. Thus Bombay as a major film center has been called Bollywood.[3]

In the 1960s and '70s, a series of independently made films, called the "New Cinema" or the "Parallel cinema"[4] appeared on the Indian scene. These films mostly funded by the Indian government body, the Film Finance Corporation, thematically and stylistically attempted to break away from the mainstream, commercial cinema aesthetics and themes. Ketan Mehta, who made *Mirch Masala* (translated in English as *Spices*) in 1986 falls under the category of "New Cinema.". But Mehta's work in this film and in his 1980 film *Bhavni Bhavai* (translated in English as *A Folk Tale*) skillfully bridges the gap between the *masala* film and serious, engaged cinema, which is how much of "New Cinema" was characterized[5] since many of the "New Cinema" films dealt with the problematic issues of caste, class, and gender inequality in postcolonial India. Mehta's use of *masala* in the title *Mirch Masala*, then, playfully references the "masala" Bombay Bollywood films (since he uses some of the elements of *masala* like the chase sequences, slapstick comedy, songs, and dances) inasmuch as the word "masala" refers to the chili peppers that he employs as the central metaphor and motif of resistance among the women of an Indian village.

In this essay, I discuss Ketan Mehta's imaginative uses of chili peppers as a trope that has multiple connotations. The first is an important aspect of the livelihood of the villagers—most women of the lower caste in the village are employed in a factory where chili pepper is ground and made into spices. The chilis in the film also symbolize women's sexuality from a dual perspective. "The male gaze" is embodied in the lusty and power-hungry *Subedar* (Tax Collector) and other male characters who view women as attractive spices to be consumed—in other words, women's bodies are viewed as commodities to be enjoyed. From the women's perspective, however, the chilis offer a literal and metaphoric form of resistance. Through the events of the film, the women learn to mobilize, get empowered, and collectively use the chili pepper against the patriarchal authority in that society.

Set in the 1940s, *Spices* portrays India under British colonial rule. The Subedar, the Indian representative of the British colonial government, visits different villages with his soldiers from time to time, plundering and pillaging and operating through corruption. As part of the economic corruption, women are exploited and become sexual objects of the Subedar's pleasure. Among the women featured, Sonbai and Saraswati stand out as they challenge patriarchal oppression—Sonbai resists the dominant patriarchal power of the State, embodied in the Subedar, and Saraswati offers challenges to the patriarchal control of her wayward husband, the Village Chief, within the family.

The story revolves around the Subedar's unabashed and public demand for Sonbai from the village at any cost. Sonbai fleeing from the Subedar seeks refuge in the spice factory, where she and other village women grind chili peppers to make different *masalas* or combinations of spices. Denied his wish, the Subedar storms the spice factory, killing the old gate keeper Abu Miyan. However, the women jointly confront the Subedar and teach him a lesson.

The subplot involves Saraswati's acts of rebellion. As the wife of the Village Chief or *Mukhi*, Saraswati rebels against her subservient role. Her first act of rebellion is to lock the Mukhi out of the house when he comes home in the morning after spending the night with his mistress. As her second act of resistance, she enrolls her daughter in the village school, defying age-old taboos against educating women. Finally, Saraswati organizes a demonstration to protest the villagers' decision to hand over Sonbai to the Subedar. In this way, Mehta's film skillfully weaves the micro (family) and macro (state) levels of oppression as exerted on women, along with their resistance to this domination.

In the film, the powerful imagery of the chili pepper is interwoven with the women's struggles. Visually, the image evolves in the film from a plant growing on the vine, to a harvested cash crop laid out on the ground to dry in the sun. As the women then grind the raw chilies, the chili powder becomes the end product of women's labor.

The Subedar, almost salivating, regards woman's bodies in general and Sonbai's in particular as a spice to be consumed. When he demands that Sonbai be brought to him, the Subedar and Jeevan Seth, the spice factory owner, have the following exchange:

SUBEDAR: "Well in that factory of yours, there's a certain spice that I like very much."

SETH: "Tell me what spice Sir, I'll have whatever you want made up freshly for you."

SUBEDAR: "You don't understand. There's a certain woman inside your factory. She's hot as a spice."[6]

The fact that Sonbai is a married woman is hardly a deterrent to the Subedar. His male desire to consume her female body mirrors the occupation of the land by the colonizer.[7] Here, the Subedar, as Tax Collector, also embodies the colonizer's power. Hence, resistance against the Subedar is also a struggle against colonial exploitation and conquest. Both Sonbai and Saraswati struggle to reclaim their bodies, a struggle in which eventually all the women of the village participate.

The filmmaker evokes the importance of chili pepper to the livelihood of the people cultivating the land by opening with a creation myth. The camera pans across the green fertile land, parrots fly as the camera tracks fields of chili pepper, and an itinerant minstrel's song echoes over this verdant landscape:

> After creating matter, man and mind
> God was bored
> So he sprinkled some chilis and spices
> and made the world more colorful

This creation myth extols the cosmic status of spices in the Indian psyche and evokes India as the land of spices that drew the colonizer to its shores. Later, in an ironic twist, the God who was bored and sprinkled the land with spices turns into the Tax Collector/colonizer who while playing god becomes bored and demands a particular woman's body which is characterized as a "hot spice."

After the opening creation myth, the credit titles appear on a close-up freeze-frame shot of the red chili pepper growing. This image of the luscious chili, red on the outside, spicy and explosive on the inside, prefigures its role as the chief ingredient in this narrative and emphasizes from the outset its double meaning—the sexual power of the women and their ability to use their power to resist oppression within the family and society.

The Subedar, a native dressed in colonial authority, along with his soldiers bursts upon the idyllic opening scene, disrupting its harmony with the thundering sound of horse-hooves and horse-neighs. As the camera starts to pull back, the entire frame is filled with the vibrant red color, foregrounding the red chili peppers spread out on the ground, drying in the sun. The low camera angle emphasizes the soldiers' trampling horses in the background. The peppers lying on the ground are trampled carelessly by the Subedar and his soldiers, who treat everyone and everything as an object to be trampled.

The underlying tension of the image with the red color of the chilis dominating the frame evokes the image of blood spilling, and the usual violence that follows in the wake of the Subedar and his men. As representatives of the colonizers, their presence evokes the pillaging of the land and the exploitation of the villagers. In fact the entire system of taxation imposed by the British colluded with the existing feudal land-holding system and worsened it by encouraging corruption among the local authorities such as the Mukhi. The women were at the very bottom of this system, exploited both economically and sexually.

Resistance to the Subedar and his pillaging soldiers is also set up immediately in the character of Sonbai, whose defiant actions in their first encounter lead him to refer to her later as a fiery and delectable spice. The Subedar and his men, riding at top speed, arrive at the river bank where women are at their daily task of washing clothes and collecting water. All the women flee, fearing the Subedar and his soldiers. Sonbai alone stands up to him and challenges the senseless stampede. She speaks up against the indiscriminate use and pollution of precious water resources: "My Lord, only human beings drink water here, animals over there."

A soldier attempts to silence Sonbai, but for the Subedar, the beautiful woman's words are perceived as an invitation into a game of seduction, because he knows that the power invested in his person is totally understood and accepted under threats and duress by all the villagers. Obeying Sonbai's wishes, he commands the soldiers to take the horses to the other side, while, excited by her defiance, he coyly responds to Sonbai: "Can this animal [meaning himself] drink here?" Sonbai stands her ground and meets his gaze, attempting to be an equal. Perhaps, she recognizes that the Subedar's attraction to her sexuality gives her the upper hand as she orders him: "To drink like a man, kneel and cup your hands."

She brings the Subedar to his knees, and in obeisance, he kneels and cups his hand to drink water from Sonbai's pot. While for Sonbai this is an act of resistance by a villager to the Subedar's unchallenged powers, for the Subedar the interaction is full of sexual tension. The reversed power dynamic—the woman/subject in command—the man/ruler submissive—undoubtedly titillates his sexual fantasies. For the power-hungry Subedar, Sonbai becomes a desirable sexual object that he will demand from the villagers at any cost, as if in a continuum with his tax-collecting duties. Just as he is entitled to gather taxes, he also has the limitless power to demand Sonbai's body or that of any woman he fancies.

The visual imagery of the red chili peppers and Sonbai's struggle against the Subedar form some of the key scenes in the film. The Subedar wants Sonbai because of her defiance; her resistance is a power that excites him. But in their second encounter when Sonbai has the upper hand, her power is perceived by the Subedar as an act of transgression that violates his honor, and takes away from his role of playing God.

At his camp, the all-powerful Subedar habitually surrounds himself with village elders and village leaders, holding court like an emperor. He displays Western objects like the gramophone to show his power and his modern status to the rustic folk, impressing them with his material acquisitions. During one of his princely public shaving rituals, the Subedar interrupts the routine and accosts Sonbai, who is passing by the camp on her way to the river. The Subedar, in trying to convince Sonbai to spend a night with him, familiarly touches her face. Offended by this intimate gesture, Sonbai slaps him, but fearing reprisal she flees the scene. At this point, Mehta sets up an interesting intercutting of shots dramatizing the hunt for Sonbai, in which the red chili peppers play a key role, emphasizing their multiple meanings in connection with women and sexuality.

This is how the shots are set up: fleeing from the Subedar, and with the Subedar's soldiers on horseback in pursuit, a desperate Sonbai heads toward the village spice factory for refuge. Mehta cuts to the peaceful interior of the spice factory, where the other women of the village are at work. An older woman sprinkling water on a mound of chili peppers, smells one to evaluate its potency and comments: "They are very pungent." Another woman responds: "These will make a strong *masala*."

The very next cut shows the fleeing Sonbai falling onto the red chili peppers that have been laid out to dry in the sun. The overhead camera angle and the slow-motion speed of the shot once again evoke the image of blood spilled on the land onto which this pursued woman falls. The red color of her garments blends into the red of the chili peppers. Subsequent low-angle shots show the soldiers' horses trampling red peppers in a tight frame. The rapid intercutting here between a full frame of red chili peppers and Sonbai hiding in the mounds of the dark vermilion-colored dried peppers, or Sonbai actually running over the red chili peppers (in one shot the camera tracks her bare feet as she runs over a carpet of peppers) inscribes multiple meanings onto the chili peppers.

The filmmaker uses this intercutting together with the statement: "these will make a strong *masala*" to evoke several layers of meaning—the drama heating up, the hunt for and conquest of Sonbai intensifying, the playful reference to the chase sequences in the Bollywood "masala" films, and finally the evolving consciousness and imminent explosive empowerment that the women will experience in the concluding sequence of the film. Significantly this final scene unfolds within the confines of the spice factory, where the women grind chili peppers to make different *masalas*. Throughout the film, through parallel cutting, the filmmaker moves between the two women, Sonbai and Saraswati. The potentially explosive power inside the red chili pepper extends to Saraswati's acts of resistance, which begin quietly within her family. Saraswati knows that her husband, the Mukhi, has a mistress, that he comes home whenever he chooses and basically keeps his wife as a servant to maintain his house and cook and clean for him. As part of her defiance against the traditional role of woman and wife, Saraswati enrolls her daughter in the village school, an all-male institution. With this act, Saraswati takes her challenge to patriarchal authority into the open, into a public space, very much like Sonbai.

The filmmaker interweaves the two women's defiant acts or explosive acts of rebellion. From the moment that Sonbai slaps the Subedar, she has posed a very serious challenge to his unquestioned authority and also to his unquestioned manhood. Similarly, Saraswati challenges the Mukhi's notions of masculine authority within the family and before the village. In an interesting scene, the village barber narrates Sonbai's humiliation of the Tax Collector to the jubilant Village Chief, who enjoys the Tax Collector's emasculation. However, in the very next moment, the smirk is wiped off the Chief's face when he is told that his own daughter is sitting in a classroom full of boys at the village school. The Village Chief's emasculation is similar to the Tax Collector's because both men feel publicly humiliated by women.

The filmmaker spends a considerable amount of time on the final sequence, where the struggle unfolds inside and outside the factory and finally comes to a head. The women workers inside the factory attempt to make sense of the events that have transpired because in order to protect Sonbai, they too are held as prisoners. While they are trapped inside, and are complicit in Sonbai's act of defiance, Saraswati operates from the outside. She brings food for the imprisoned women into the factory—significantly, the meal consists of a green chili pepper and a *roti* (flat bread). A green chili is the young plant that eventually becomes red. The women inside the factory who are as yet green chilis (politically) will evolve into red chilis (a spicier chili pepper) and develop their strength to fight back. It is important to note here that Saraswati, an upper-caste woman and the wife of the Village Chief, steps out of her caste and class as she extends a helping hand to the lower-caste women in the spice factory, an act of courage that links her own struggle with that of Sonbai and the other women.

That the women are aware of their status in society is obvious from the telling comments they make in response to the food Saraswati brings them: "What a relief from the usual chores"; "Only a woman would think of bringing us *rotis*."

Inside the factory, the women also debate the issue of whether Sonbai should give herself up and not make the situation threatening to the entire village. They regard her resistance to the Subedar's demands as a self-serving and individualistic assertion, not thinking of the repercussions for the entire community. To add to the debate, an older woman in the factory relates a story from the past when the women of the village were raped and no one came to their rescue.

Unbeknownst to the women in the factory, another discussion about Sonbai is going on outside at a meeting called by the Village Chief and held on the front porch of his home. The meeting, attended by men only, has one surreptitious female audience member, namely Saraswati, who as the Chief's wife is present inside her home, a silent witness to the village men's inability to come to any decision regarding the Subedar's absolute and authoritative demand for Sonbai. Not cowed by her husband the Chief's anger and threats upon discovering his daughter at the village school, Saraswati once again decides to challenge him and the village men. She organizes a demonstration which takes the form of a popular women's street protest that involves the use of kitchen utensils, objects used by women in a private space—a stainless steel plate (*thali*) and a rolling pin (*latni*)—which become the machinery of expressing an antagonistic opinion in public. The women hold a loud demonstration, banging the rolling pins on the steel plates. Confronted by this act of defiance, the men of the village led by their Chief of course respond with the only tactic usually employed by them and displayed by the Chief himself in an earlier scene—violence. The women's action is brutally put down by the Mukhi and other men, but not before the women have made a statement about their disagreement with the men's decision to give up Sonbai to the Subedar. One can analyze Saraswati's style of protest as a strategy of covert resistance that James C. Scott delineates as "the powers of the weak."[8]

The Subedar, in a final show of power representing the authority of the State, storms into the spice factory, breaking down the old wooden doors. The drama surrounding the taking of the factory is shot from various angles by the filmmaker in order to emphasize the element of sexual assault, especially with the wide-angle shots showing the repeated attacks on the factory gates with a battering ram. In this violent encounter, the Subedar's men kill the old Muslim gate keeper, leaving the defenseless women inside to fight on their own. The death of the gate keeper becomes the catalyst of change in the consciousness of the women.

In a spontaneous act of resistance, the women use the only weapon they have against the Subedar and his men—the ground chili peppers. They blind the Subedar by throwing the peppers—the *mirch masala*—into his eyes. In her essay "Dialectic of Public and Private," Ranjani Mazumdar[9] points out usefully that "the factory which is the workplace and therefore the public space of the women is turned into the site of struggle and it is no longer Sonbai alone but also the others who decide to fight. The 'masala' (spice) that they make, the commodity that is produced for the owner of the factory, is used as a weapon in their final attack."

The women discover their power collectively—the power of their labor and the power to organize against their sexual exploitation and the oppressive colonial and patriarchal power structures in society. The sequence in the factory is a culmination of the process of the women's empowerment through the film; and as the final act of resistance, it is a very powerful and dramatic moment when the women hurl the ground chili pepper powder at the Subedar, blinding him. It is worth noting here that the action of the women in the factory has an interesting parallel in history. In their incisive essay "That Magic Time" on peasant women's participation in the uprising that was called the Telangana People's Struggle, Vasantha Kannabiran and K. Lalitha write: "Accounts tell us how two hundred peasant women stood together . . . and chased the police out of the village. Women encircled a police van, attacked the police with pestles and chili powder and secured the release of their. . . . activists."[10]

In the imagined terrain of *Spices*, in some ways, the women metaphorically blind "the male gaze" which looked upon them as a hot spice. In the final succession of shots, the Subedar is brought to his knees, reminiscent of Sonbai's first encounter with him, when full of his power as a man and a representative of the colonial power, he had flirted with Sonbai; at the level of metaphor, the women destroy the power of his lustful gaze, at least temporarily.

Using the red chili pepper as the central trope of women's resistance, *Spices* raises significant questions about that resistance. In the concluding sequence, Sonbai does not participate in hurling chili powder at the Subedar. Earlier, she had picked up a sickle as a means of self-defense, and amid slow dissolves of showers of red chili powder and the Subedar screaming in pain, Sonbai with her sickle stands still in the foreground. In the rather abrupt concluding freeze-frame shot, she is seen in a medium close-up shot with the sickle in her hand. Perhaps Ketan Mehta wants us to see Sonbai as the leader of a successful rebellion. But the last image demands of the viewer further questions about the issues of power relations that govern women's lives. The successful act of resistance of the women does not end here. The use of the chili powder has helped them recognize themselves as powerful agents who have only just begun their work. The sickle in Sonbai's hand reinscribes the past history of similar peasant struggles onto the concluding freeze frame.

Notes

Epigraphs: Rajeswari Sunder Rajan, *Real and Imagined Women: Gender, Culture, and Postcolonialism* (London: Routledge, 1993), 12. Aruna Vasudev, "The Woman: Myth and Reality in Indian Cinema," in *Cinema and Cultural Identity: Reflections on Films from Japan, India, and China*, ed. Wimal Dissanayake (Lanham, MD: University Press of America, 1988), 109.

1. "Since 1971 India has been leading the world in film production, and over the last decade or so the film factories have churned out an average of 800 films a year." Sumita Chakravarty, *National Identity in Indian Popular Cinema, 1947–1987* (Austin: University of Texas Press, 1993), 9.

2. Eric Barnouw and S. Krishnaswamy, *Indian Film*, 2nd ed. (New York and New Delhi: Oxford University Press, 1980), 155, emphasis added.

3. Kishore Valicha comments: "The parallel of the popular Hindi film with Hollywood is, besides being practically unavoidable, rather revealing. The Hindi film unquestionably borrows heavily from its Hollywood counterpart. But it is an interesting fact that it reworks what it borrows within strongly Indian conventions, transforming it to express typically Indian preoccupations." *The Moving Image: A Study of Indian Cinema* (Bombay: Orient Longman, 1988), 39. In recent times critics such as M. Madhav Prasad in *Ideology of the Hindi Film* (Oxford: Oxford University Press, 1998) and others like Jyotika Virdi have undertaken a serious analysis of many of these films.

4. In "The Two Cinemas of India," Mira Reym Binford writes, "Although New Cinema is not a single cohesive movement with a clearly articulated political or aesthetic ideology, its film makers are linked by their rejection of commercial cinema's values, themes and stylistic approaches." In *Film and Politics in the Third World*, ed. John D. H. Downing (New York: Praeger, 1987), 148. Also see Chakravarty, *National Identity in Indian Popular Cinema*, 235–248.

5. For a discussion of *Bhavni Bhavai*, see Binford, "The Two Cinemas of India," 155.

6. All quotations from the film are taken from the English subtitled version on video (VHS), *Spices*, directed by Ketan Mehta, distributed by Mystic Fire Video in the United States. Unfortunately, the English translation does not do justice to the original words. The Subedar actually describes Sonbai as a "garam masala," which is a combination of particular, flavorful hot spices.

7. Several feminist scholars have undertaken a provocative analysis of the conflation of women's bodies with the land/nation. For further reading on this issue, look at Kumari Jayawardena, *Feminism and Nationalism in the Third World*. (London: Zed Books, 1986). Also see Kumkum Sangari and Sudesh Vaid, eds., *Recasting Women: Essays in Colonial History* (New Delhi: Kali for Women, 1989).

8. James C. Scott, *Weapons of the Weak: Everyday Forms of Peasant Resistance* (New Haven: Yale University Press 1985), xvi.

9. Ranjani Mazumdar, "Dialectic of Public and Private: Representation of Women in *Bhoomika* and *Mirch Masala*," *Economic and Political Weekly*, October 26, 1991, 84.

10. Vasantha Kannabiran and K. Lalitha, "That Magic Time: Women in the Telangana People's Struggle," in *Recasting Women*, .188.

Shish Kebab Armenians?: Food and the Construction and Maintenance of Ethnic and Gender Identities among Armenian American Feminists

ARLENE VOSKI AVAKIAN

When I was growing up in Washington Heights, the New York City neighborhood that included a large Armenian American population and community, my family had few interactions with *odars* (non-Armenians). Once I entered school those boundaries were permeated, and I encountered mostly the children of other immigrants—Jews, Greeks, Roumanians, but also some real "Americans." My interaction with non-Armenians was limited at first due to my inability to speak English, but once having mastered the language I wanted to partake of what I identified as "Americanness" as fully as I could.

Some things I learned very quickly from the images around me. I knew it was best to have light skin, blond hair, and blue eyes, and while my dark hair and olive complexion fell short of that ideal I did know that I was white and Christian. My parents, though not interested in other aspects of assimilation, realized that being white was important to our success in this country and passed on to me and my brother, often in Armenian, American racism first about African American inferiority and about the Puerto Ricans whose movement into our neighborhood in the 1950s precipitated our move to the suburbs. Although on the edges of whiteness, I felt fairly secure since I was clearly neither black, Puerto Rican, nor Jewish.

Other aspects of becoming "American" were not so easily accomplished. I eventually made friends with non-Armenian children, and was able to observe them in their homes. I noted that their families mirrored the pictures in *Life* magazine and the *Saturday Evening Post*, and what I saw on TV and in the movies. The tables in those 1950s media representations were not groaning under the abundance of food I was used to, nor did they include marinated and broiled lamb, rice of any kind that was not served with an ice cream scoop, stuffed vegetables or grape leaves, and steamed brains or raw chopped lamb mixed with fine *bughlur* and Italian parsley. While I was definitely not ready to give up *pilaf*, *dolma*, *lahmajoon*, *chee kufta*, or *shish kebab*, I also desperately wanted hamburgers, Wonder Bread, Velveeta, and the newest wonder of 1950s food technology, Lipton Instant Chicken Noodle Soup. Food was the one thing about my family I thought I could change easily. I was right about food being central to cultural identification, but I was wrong about being able to convince my family to eat "American" food. I was wrong, too, about identity being as simple as learning to speak English and partaking of American cuisine. By eating hamburgers and dehydrated soups and speaking English I could *pass* as an American, but actually *being* an American was far more complicated and, I eventually learned, was neither attainable nor desirable.

This essay explores how food practices are used in the development and maintenance of ethnic and gender identities and their interaction through interviews with Armenian American feminists. A daily material practice, cooking and eating, grounds the discussion of multiple, intersecting positionalities and resistances in lived experience that is at once concrete and symbolic. I argue that cooking and eating were central to the constructions of these women's ethnic and gender identities, continue to be significant, and can be used to transgress patriarchy and ethnic invisibility. These Armenian American women have deployed food practices to forge new identities which are both deeply embedded within their experience of being Armenian American women and consistent with their feminist, anti-racist, progressive politics.

Since what we mean by gender or ethnicity can no longer be assumed, I will first engage in definitions. White feminist activism and theoretical formulations of the 1970s posited a womanhood of similarities across time, space, and social formations.[1] Critiques came quickly from women of color and some lesbians arguing that race, class, and sexuality could not be subsumed under the all-encompassing banner of sisterhood.[2] By the 1990s these ongoing critiques along with the development of femmist/womanist theories by women of color and postcolonial, and poststructural theories marginalized essentialized notions of gender. Arguing against what she calls "biological foundationalism" Linda Nicholson, along with many other feminist theorists, posits that we can no longer make generalizations about gender, but must look at women in their contexts.[3] Advocating that feminists recognize that the body itself is socially constructed and that its meaning cannot be universalized but must be contexualized, she suggests that feminists "think about the meaning of 'woman' as illustrating a map of intersecting similarities and differences. Within such a map, the body does not disappear but rather becomes an historically specific variable whose meaning and import is recognized as potentially different in different historical contexts."[4] Judith Butler argues that "what woman signify has been taken for granted for too long" and must be deconstructed in order to "release the term into a future of multiple significations."[5] For Chantel Mouffe the question is no longer how to "unearth" the category of woman. "The central issues become: how is 'woman' constructed as a category with different discourses? how is sexual difference made a pertinent distinction in social relations? and how are relations of subordination constructed through such a distinction?"[6]

If gender is complicated by intersectionality and fluidity, analyses of ethnic identity are just as complex. Feminist theory along with postcolonial and poststructural studies has opened many questions about identities that were once assumed to be in the realm of developmental psychology or sociological or historical studies on immigration. No longer concerned with assimilation patterns through the generations or debates about ethnicity as a primordial element, scholars in a wide variety of disciplines and interdisciplinary fields explore notions of hybridity, biculturality, community, nation, and diaspora.[7] Embedded now in contexts which are conceptualized as both complex and fluid, ethnic identities are tied to international, transnational, national, and regional contexts. Just as woman has been shown to be constructed within multiple and sometimes conflicting contexts, ethnic identities are also composed of multiplicities of gender, class, and race, all of which must be put within historical contexts and the specificities of local circumstances. Stuart Hall posits that while identities are currently and rightly being decentered, we must think about them as a process which, while never completed, can neither be abandoned.[8] Identities are never fixed entities, but "fragmented and fractured, never singular but multiply constituted across different, often intersecting and antagonistic discourses, practices and positions" operating within the specificities of particular histories.[9] Identities then are about what we might become, what traditions we might invent, what self we may narrate; they "are constituted within not outside representation."[10] Focusing on diasporan people, he argues that cultural origins cannot be thought of as an essentialized past that diasporan peoples can return to, but they also undergo processes of change as they are mediated by contemporary discourses. The past then is also constructed "through memory, fantasy, narrative memory and myth."[11]

Directly addressing the relationship between ethnic and diasporan identities and the possibility for resistance, R. Radhakrishnan argues for use of the term "ethnic": "Whereas the term 'diaspora' indicates a desire to historicize the moment of departure as a moment of pure rupture both from 'the natural home' and 'the place of residence,' the ethnic mandate is to live 'within the hyphen' and yet be able to speak. Whereas the pure diasporic objective is to 'blow the hyphen out of the continuum of history,' the ethnic program is to bear historical witness to the agonizing tension between two histories."[12] Located both in the past and the present, he calls for ethnic people to be engaged in the "critical task of reciprocal invention . . . it is of the utmost importance that a variety of emerging post-colonial identities . . . establish themselves 'relationally' with the twin purposes of affirming themselves and demystifying the so-called mainstream."[13] The possibility of agency comes precisely out of the complexity of these intersections. Oppressed people experience pressure from the dominant group, but they are not without their own resources or their own histories. Even through the exigencies of slavery in the Americas, enough remnants of history and culture survived for W. E. B. Du Bois to formulate his notion of the double consciousness, creating the possibility for both individual and collective resistance. Consciousness of one's history outside of oppression and the resistance it can engender may be preserved in a variety of sites on a continuum from daily life to political revolutions.

I will now turn to the ways in which a group of Armenian American feminists conceptualize the construction, deconstruction, and reformulation of their gender and ethnic identities through focusing on the daily, material social practice of cooking and eating. The women belong to an Armenian American feminist group that I have been a part of since its inception more than five years ago. Self-identified as both feminist and Armenian American, we came together to explore our Armenian American identities within the context of our progressive antiracist feminist politics. Although most of us do not participate in any of the traditional institutions of the Armenian community, we consciously claim our ethnicity and our feminism. Because this group of women has been consciously exploring their ethnic and gender identities and the connections between them more than five years, they are ideal for this exploration, and using cooking and eating grounds the discussion in a concrete daily practice that is both material and symbolic.

I held a group interview at the end of one of our regularly scheduled meetings as a kind of brainstorming session about the place of food in our lives, and then conducted individual interviews with eleven women, all but one of the group participants. The women range in age from their early thirties to early seventies. All are or have been professionals or are seeking professional careers, having just finished advanced degrees. Four were from working-class families, one participant's family moved from working class to middle class during her teenage years, and eight were raised middle class. Most of the women would describe themselves as white, and the few who identify as women of color on the basis of the genocide or Armenians' Middle Eastern heritage readily acknowledge their white privilege in contemporary United States culture. Five of the women have children. Two identify as lesbians and one as bisexual. Six are either married (not all the same as the ones who have children) or have had a commitment ceremony or are living with a partner. All but one are children of Armenian parents; the one person whose parents are not both Armenian has an Armenian mother. All but four are daughters or granddaughters of survivors of the 1915 genocide. However, all are from Turkish Armenian families and feel connected to the trauma that resulted from that cataclysm and from the invisibility of a genocide not officially recognized by the United States.[14]

The material in the interviews clarifies and complicates. What is clear is that gender and ethnicity are not separated in either these women's experiences or reflections on them. Although I asked questions relating specifically to gender and ethnicity, I could not group the responses along gender and ethnic lines because they were so intertwined. For these Armenian American women, even those who are not descendants of survivors, the genocide, its denial, and the invisibility of Armenians and Armenian culture and history in mainstream American culture are central to their gender identities and their food practices. From the obvious issue of insuring the continuation of Armenian culture to experiences of eating disorders, cooking and eating and the issues they raise are grounded in the experiences of women who are Armenian American. Women had contradictory responses to the relationship of food practices to women's oppression. While most women do agree that cooking within the Armenian community has been compulsory for women and has signified and constructed their oppression, many also assert that their mothers and grandmothers created authority and control in their kitchens, which often became a space where they bonded with other women. These are not, however, generic women's spaces but *Armenian* women's spaces that some of the women in the study evoke in their current lives through cooking elaborate Armenian dishes or gathering to cook with friends. No longer compulsory in the lives of the women I interviewed, cooking has had its meaning subverted, and they cook to serve their own needs. For many of the women cooking becomes a vehicle to reclaim, proclaim, and enact a transformed Armenian American womanhood.

I will now look at the issues raised in the interviews, focusing on the ways in which gender and ethnicity are intertwined, enacted, and re-sisted. Almost immediately the group discussion focused on body image and the pain women experience because their bodies deviate from the images that bombard them daily. Many women in this group identify their bodies ethnically, with almost half citing their ethnicity as the reason for their difference from the tall, long-legged, thin, narrow-hipped bodies projected by the media. While understanding that the ubiquitous ultra-thin models do not accurately portray any group of women, they nonetheless feel that Armenian bodies are heavier and shorter than the "American" norm. Some women even feel support from their families whose ideas about body image do not fit the Ameri-can norm. Helen reports that her family "thought it was great that I had . . . a pretty good chest . . . at a pretty early age . . . I mean, I had some-what of a curvaceous figure I guess, and . . . all my relatives thought that was so wonderful and I was going to be so beautiful. . . . I would say . . . I should be thinner. My mother and my grandmother and my great-aunt would say, 'oh no. You look beautiful.'"

For most of the women, however, their families added to their prob-lems by continuing to overfeed them while chastising them about their weight. Lucy says, "they always want you to be thinner, but they always want to shove another *dolma* down your throat. . . . Eat! Eat! Get thin-ner! Get thinner! . . . it's so contradictory and you don't know what to do with it."

Most women think their family's high priority on an overabundance of food is directly connected to the genocide. All but two of the women agree that an overabundance of food was the norm in their families of origin. Even for working-class families, food was a priority. Emma's grandparents ate lobsters and steak at the beginning of the week even if that meant they had little money at the end of the week. Melissa says, "even if there wasn't a lot of money or lots of anything else, there was lots of food." Some daughters think that for their mothers, particularly if they were survivors of the genocide, the giving of food—feeding the family—was central to their self-esteem as mothers. Further, by feeding them Armenian food, which they considered to be healthy and contrib-uting to the legendary longevity of Armenians, they would insure the survival of their husbands and children—perhaps even by extension, the Armenian people. The image of tables groaning with food is at odds with, and perhaps created deliberately to counteract both personal his-tories of hunger and images of starving Armenians. Joanne's survivor grandmother told her she had seen her parents killed and had to bury them when she was ten. She describes her survivor grandmother's rela-tionship to food as resulting from her experiences in the genocide:

> I hesitate to use the word compulsion because that makes it sound pathological, but I feel that she is compelled to make a lot of food. . . . I think it is a survivor mentality. That you will survive if there is a lot to eat. And that's why she was so vigilant about watching what we eat, and even now, though she can't really see that well . . . she watches every bit that crosses my mouth. And she never thinks I eat enough, ever. . . .

Though neither her parents nor her grandparents were survivors, Debby connects her own compulsive eating to both the impact of the genocide on her family's food practices and the representation of women's bodies in American culture.

> The compulsiveness about eating, for me, is partly connected to sort of being—coming of age in this time and all the body garbage that a lot of women have—but also somehow that it came through my family's fear. All of the sort of psychology of our genocide experiences, that there was a lot of fear. Would there be enough? It was very unstated, but would there be enough? There always had to be enough. So there was an anxiety about food I think, as there was an anxiety about health and germs and safety in my family that I think is connected with this part of Armenian history.

While a history of genocide seems "always to be there," it is often not spoken about.[15] In some families food was used as a vehicle to communicate what could not be readily spoken. Emma related that her parents encouraged her to marry an Armenian, focusing on food as the main reason, but she feels that they had another, unspoken agenda:

> An Armenian will understand you more and the food was always part of that. This was part of it. You will eat the same food. They will understand the food you eat. That somehow if you married—I don't know, someone who wasn't Armenian you would be forced to eat corned beef and cabbage your whole life and you would never be able to eat pilaf and chicken. Or you would make pilaf and chicken and your husband wouldn't eat it and then, what would happen? The marriage would fail. How can you go through life . . . if someone doesn't understand your food, how can they understand you? But they didn't say, they won't understand your history, or they won't understand the suffering that your grandparents went through, they won't understand your language, or your culture.

In their current lives many of the women continue to prioritize food and are struggling to overcome what they describe as an unhealthy relationship to food. Three of the women self-identified as either having had or still struggling with eating disorders, and two others regularly refused to eat dinner when they were children. By their own assessment, most of the women buy too much food, cook too much food, focus on food too much, and are unable to throw away leftovers.

Despite some of the difficulties associated with conflicting messages and overabundance of food, the majority of the women also strongly feel that the giving of food is an act of love, one deeply laden with Armenian cultural meanings. Counteracting the perception that women cook only to serve men, Victoria states that the giving of food is "a place of pleasing, of pleasing others, of pleasing oneself."

> It's an attentiveness to another that is actually very generous and caring . . . in this little prayer book there is something about the word "succor" that has to do with comfort and refuge and I think in a way, food sometimes, at least my understanding of it or my connection of it with Armenian identity, has been the place of refuge in a way. That it's this place of . . . knowing that something's being attended to that matters, and that you matter. And so that kind of attention, attentiveness which is why, for me, there is this spirituality part of it that, there is a kind of attentiveness and care that is not divorced from the act of cooking and food. And not everybody has that. I mean I have some friends who—it's torture for them to eat. I mean, they just don't even want to take time to do that. Whereas, I look forward to that, that it's a place of rest and refreshment and community.

Both in the group discussion and in the individual interviews many women describe experiencing a sense of joy and safety in cooking with their mothers and grandmothers. For some, eating was one of the few pleasurable activities their families did together. Even those women who experienced conflict around eating described the family table as a loving place, as a gathering place, particularly on holidays. Anne, who often refused to eat dinner as a way to exercise control over her life when she was a child, nevertheless also relates positive feelings about family gatherings around food. Her sister Anahid characterizes her relationship to her genocide survivor mother and food as a double bind—if she ate too much she was disgusting, but if she did not eat she was injuring her mother. Nevertheless, she also describes her family table when the extended family gathered as a place of joy, and that joy was connected to the stories the adults told when they were eating together:

> The food was wonderful in those gatherings, but it was really the gathering that was . . . important to me, . . . It was really the time when I felt the most joy, and the most vitality in the sense of vibrancy. . . . That was a time to share stories. And I can still hear what *Miam-*

horakour [aunt, literally father's sister] . . . And the thing that Anne [her sister] and I talk about most is her laughter, and she, you know she [the aunt] and my father survived together. My father survived because of her. . . . *Laughing* . . . I can see myself lying down on her living room floor watching TV on a Saturday night and they gathered around the table and you could hear the laughter and the drones of the voices . . . probably some of the most important times growing up. So, I think the gathering was really, really important.

For many other women, cooking was the only time they heard their elders' stories. Emma's grandmother diced onions into bits and pieces while she told about her life, in bits and pieces.

She would take a whole onion and hold it in her hand and cut it in slices one way and perpendicular another way and then finely minced . . . lots of stories were told in that arena. You know, the genocide stories were told there too . . . food was absolutely central and the conversations, the most important conversations that I have had with my family have happened in the kitchen, usually around cooking and food preparation.

Gathering around the kitchen to cook with mothers and grandmothers or around the table to eat with relatives provided not only stories, but a clarity about what it meant to be Armenian. For a number of reasons, Armenians in the United States often feel invisible. The Armenian population in this country is relatively small, and Armenians seldom see themselves reflected in the dominant culture. Moreover, the United States is complicit in Turkey's denial of the genocide, the central historical moment in modern Armenian history, by refusing to officially acknowledge it. Food as a marker of ethnic identity is often trivialized both by scholars and by community members. Armenians who are outside the community are derided by insiders as "shish kebab Armenians." Yet to the women in my study, food powerfully conveys ethnic identity. When asked to comment on the relationship of food to her ethnic identity, Victoria responds, "I don't know, I guess it's just so . . . it's kind of woven in there. I think of the cheorag that you make, the kind that you braid together and so, for me, my Armenian identity and food are braided together." Dorothy says Armenian food is "home." The confusion about who Armenians are, particularly in the context of the New England towns she grew up in, was clarified for her by eating Armenian food.

This intense relationship to Armenian food is often characterized by a protectiveness, a feeling of ownership laced with a fear that if non-Armenians cook their dishes, their cultural value would be threatened.

Dorothy was furious with a non-Armenian friend who cooked Armenian food. "I'd be bullshit when she would try to cook my food or that— it could never be as good as mine. I felt like I was being robbed of my—I don't know it was—what made us special I think." She says the food is "all we have left" and that we have to keep it to ourselves to protect our legacy. Joanne refuses to give out her own or her family's recipes, and will refer people to cookbooks because those recipes are in the public domain. For her the way the women in her family prepare food is "almost like it's this secret code that preserves family integrity and cultural integrity that I don't want to give away." In response to my question about whether her feelings were based on the fragility of the culture, her response evokes a connection both to Armenian women and to homeland. For her, cooking Armenian food

> is part of my Armenian women's lineage and it's like a sacred act being able to prepare this food that grandmother after grandmother after grandmother has prepared. . . . the fact that basically the same food is being preserved helps [me] feel connected, something that I as well as others have been distanced from and that is the homeland . . . and the same land where they lived.

Debby shares a sense of ownership of Armenian cuisine and is also enraged by what she sees as appropriation of and erasure of Armenian food by the natural foods movement.

> Do people know Molly Katzen? She wrote *The Moosewood Cookbook* which was, when I was in college that was the college students' cooking bible. Here were all my "granolier" than thou college friends of mine who were reading this book and every dish in there that could be Armenian was either Greek or Turkish. . . . I have never seen in any of her cookbooks any mention of Armenians or Armenian cooking or Armenian food. It makes me really, really pissed off. So there are my friends making these things that they claim are Greek or Turkish and it made me really angry. It made me feel really invisible.

Helen was not so clear about her ownership of Armenian cuisine when she traveled to Turkey with her non-Armenian husband whose parents currently live there. She knew intellectually that many Armenian dishes are also eaten by Turkish people, but when they were presented as unequivocally Turkish she was confronted with the complexities of cultural processes in the context of genocide. Is the dish Armenian or Turkish? Is what she knows as that Armenian dish fixated at 1915, the date of the beginning of the genocide?

We stayed with my husband's sister and she has a maid who cooks—and of course to her it was Turkish. It was really bizarre. Some of the names were the same . . . but over the seventy, eighty years since the genocide, they have taken different paths—essential elements were there. So they would say we're having *manti* . . . and then they would serve me this *manti* but it wasn't *manti*, but it was and so then I'm thinking to myself what is the real *manti*? To her this is the real *manti* because she's never heard of any other kind of *manti*. But then what is the *manti* that I know? I think what I know is probably the way it was made in 1915 and the way she's making it is the way the dish has been evolving in Turkey since that time. . . . It's not that they've appropriated it. It's that the thought of having appropriated hasn't occurred to anyone there. So I can't go there and say how can you appropriate it. There is nothing for me to say. It is just a cuisine that is held in common. And yet, I feel that it's not right that it be owned by this other woman who doesn't know anything about the Armenians. Who knows, her grandfather probably massacred my grandfather and there she is making this food that I feel is owned by . . . Actually, I can't own it.

The issue of Turkish influences in Armenian cuisine and other cultural forms may come up from time to time, but most of the women are clear about what Armenian food is. Many actually use it to overcome their ethnic invisibility, proclaiming an Armenian identity through cooking for non-Armenian friends and colleagues. Debby prepared Armenian food when it was her turn to cook when she lived with friends during college, but was frustrated in her attempt to become more ethnically visible to her house mates.

I would spend hours preparing these meals for this group of 15 people. It was like—first of all it was my way of trying to make myself visible and gift them and show *odars* [non-Armenians] what Armenian culture was and who I was . . . but I kept having this like—you didn't get it. There was no way. They didn't know enough about what it meant to me to get it. . . . I think it is about invisibility though and trying to—you finally have something that—this is Armenian. Growing up nobody knew what an Armenian was, right? And finally your food is finally getting value and you want to claim ownership to it.

Debby's Armenian identity was obscure to her peers partly because she was not raised in an Armenian community. While she likes people to know that she is Armenian, she is also sensitive to being exoticized by non-Armenians. Yet even those who grew up in ethnic communities attest to the importance of food to their identities. Raised by parents involved in the large Armenian community in eastern Massachusetts, Helen identifies food as a "pillar" of her ethnic identity.

Anahid's use of food with non-Armenians both evokes her deceased father and allows her to be more fully present with her non-Armenian friends. She made *shish kebab* for the first time in her life when she was in her fifties for her friends.

> I think I wanted to be more engaged . . . it was something about bringing my father there, you know. And that certainly was one of the best ways I knew to do that. And I had been thinking a lot about him lately—I mean at that time. I had been thinking a lot about missing him and—a lot about my relationship with him. And so I think he was very present.

For many women, food has this power to evoke spirits of both individual people who have died and "the people." Anahid's sister Anne also speaks lovingly about her parents preparing *shishkebab* together, and like Anahid she cooked it for the first time only after their parents died. For Anne, the recipe itself is precious.

> A couple of years before my mother died, I asked her how to make *shish kebab* and I had written it on a scrap paper and it's in my recipe box. . . . I am very connected to them by that little piece of scrap paper, just all the memory that brings back.

Dorothy, whose grandmother lived with her parents when she was a child and was the adult who provided both the daily cooking and the parenting for the children, feels close to her now deceased grandmother whenever she cooks. Her sister who is a caterer says she thinks of their grandmother every day while she is cooking. For Debby, "cooking Armenian food . . . is almost devotional. It honors the memory of my grandmother. When I cook her food it brings her back to me and it honors her."

Cooking and eating can also encapsulate collective memory. For Victoria, cooking Armenian food means

> you're savoring [in] some sense the generations that are not at the table, but they're there. . . . And food and cooking, even though time is important when you cook, you enter into this other kind of timeless realm because it's so connected to recipes and the people who have done it before you. . . . I don't know how to express it, Arlene, but there is something rare about it, and people either understand it or they don't. . . .

But there are dangers for women in giving these gifts. Saying that she gives Armenian food to non-Armenian friends and colleagues as an offering, Victoria is mindful to take care that they not make assumptions about her cooking for them on the basis of her gender.

> I actually like to do in larger groups of people who aren't Armenian ... it actually allows me to be there in a way. It's another form of being present and sharing something that's important to me. And I think in whatever ways people approach it, that they actually appreciate it and so, so anyway, all that kind of caring and attention is important to me. I think the thing that I find hard, that I am learning maybe to do differently, is that I don't want it taken for granted, that if I am going to offer it's always an offering. It comes out of a generosity of spirit, and not out of a sense of duty.

While these women bring their Armenian ethnicity into their non-Armenian lives through cooking, some women also experienced the transmission of Armenian culture through food within their families of origin. Emma says that teaching their grandchildren about Armenian food was vitally important to her grandparents.

> It totally mattered to my grandparents that—what they cooked and that they taught us how to cook. It mattered to them more, I think, than telling us where they lived and who their parents were. Or maybe they couldn't talk about that but they talked about the food.

Transmitting the culture to children through food, particularly for women who are not connected to other aspects of Armenian community life, was a particularly highly charged subject for the three women in the group who are married to non-Armenian men. They are conscious that cultivating their children's Armenian palates has taken on meaning far beyond the particular foods. Two of the women are married to Jewish men, and they both feel at a disadvantage because Jewish culture is much more visible than Armenian culture in mainstream America. Also, for women who have progressive politics, the conservatism of the Armenian community makes connections with it difficult, if not impossible.

> So much about having a child has made me look at my Armenian-ness, and I often feel ripped with this fear and anxiety and guilt that it's going to be lost. It is all going to be lost because his father is not Armenian and he's, you know, half. So there is this anxiety that Haig won't get it. That it will be lost. And when I think about what can I give him—I am not going to drag him to Armenian church. I hated that as a kid. And I don't connect with it now. What am I going to give him? It always comes back to food. It absolutely comes back to food. . . . I have to be careful because it seems so loaded, but it also

seems like the only thing I feel good about—that I understand, that I know, that I can give to him, that I can pass down confidently. So it matters to me that he eats the lentil soup. I wanted him to eat my *dolma*. He spit it out the first thing. *Laughing.* And I just have to say, it's okay. That's not a personal rejection, but I want him to know the food. I want him to know more than just the food, but it's a place for me to start.

Despite their current positive feelings about Armenian food, some of the women were embarrassed by what their families ate. Joanne's mother filled her lunch box with a sandwich made with pita and sometimes, for a special treat, gave her a piece of *paklava*. While she loved to eat this food at home, Joanne did not want it at school. Dorothy's joy at finding a *yalanchi* (stuffed grape leaves) in her lunch box was cut short when she offered a taste to her best friend who pretended to taste it, made a disgusted sound, and ran into the bathroom making vomiting noises. Dorothy said she learned then that the food she ate was "bizarre." Emma's parents strongly demarcated their lives into the public/non-Armenian and the private/Armenian. Having friends over for dinner broke those boundaries, and she was embarrassed because of her parents' difference, which centered on food.

> When I was in school I could blend in, but at home it was kind of obvious that we were different—that we ate different, that our house smelled different, we didn't really sit down to eat—kind of like the Woody Allen meals, like everyone is kind of talking over each other. No one is really listening. There is never really one conversation. And it felt uncivilized. It felt like we were peasants, like who are these crude . . . people who are eating this different food and everyone's talking at the same time. . . . I feel like my cover has been blown.

Melissa's family used Armenian processes to preserve meat, and she feared that neighbors would smell the meat as it was drying. One of her favorite after-school snacks was *jajik*, a cold soup made from yogurt, but she could not eat it if a friend came to her house because she was embarrassed. Clearly, the "differences" between these women and their "American" peers were not felt as a neutral, multicultural experience, but one in which they and their families were the "uncivilized" others.

Other women felt proud of their Armenian cuisine. Ruth, who lived in a large Armenian community in Massachusetts, grew up knowing that everyone loved Armenian food because even *odars* came to Armenian picnics to get the food. While she was generally proud of the food, she also did not want to admit that her family ate *chee kufta*, an Armenian version of steak tartare. Victoria's Armenian mother regularly

270

made two dinners, an Armenian one for herself and her children and a non-Armenian one for her WASP husband, who did not like Armenian food. Yet, Victoria was always proud of Armenian food and now often makes it at public events connected with her professional position. Anahid, Anne, Lucy, and Debby grew up feeling lucky to have Armenian food. Some of these women grew up in Armenian communities, and others lived in WASP areas. Some of them are in their thirties, and others are in their fifties. Some have wonderful memories of dinnertime, and for others eating with their families was painful. It is not possible to attribute pride or shame about Armenian food to any one factor.

Also contradictory and complex are the women's attitudes about the relationship between cooking and women's subservience in their families and in the Armenian community. All agree that women in their families of origin were expected to serve men, and that they were judged by their cooking skills, though they were only rarely complimented and often criticized for not achieving what was expected of them. Elizabeth, a woman in her seventies, said she resented everything about being married, including cooking. While she provided nutritious food for her family, she rarely spent the time it would take to make Armenian specialties. Perhaps reflecting her mother's open anger about being forced to cook, Elizabeth's daughter Ruth's attitude toward Armenian women's cooking duties focuses on subservience.

> Like some women never have time to eat. Like all the women in Armenian families would often eat on the fly and they didn't always even have enough time to sit with their families became they were running around serving. It wasn't done the way you'd want it to be done. And I think the preparation of the food was resented more than it was enjoyed and then the food itself was not relished. You were too exhausted to relish it.

Other women also talked about women serving men. Discussing the gender interactions in her family, Dorothy said:

> The men would just sit down at the table and the women would start filling the table up with food and the men would start eating as soon as the food hit the table. And so all the men would be there first and get served first. I think in an unconscious way it showed a form of subservience. I mean even though it was a way to show love, I think it was also the role. I can't explain it. But to this day it's like the men get taken care of first and foremost.

Yet, when pushed to say that her mother was subservient to her father, Dorothy is less clear.

I mean, I think the subservient thing was that the men got taken care of and even though my mother was very powerful and mouthy, which she was, my father dominated by his anger and also it was just the rule. You just saw that the men—whatever the men said or wanted was truth. So, yeah, I think it did seem like a *form* of subservience. [My emphasis]

Victoria related that she had not tasted the white meat of turkey until she was in her twenties because her brothers, father, and uncles were served first, and by the time the platter got to her the white meat was gone. She was upset by what she identified as the subservience of the women when she was a teenager.

When I was a teenager, it bothered me that we, as women, were running around in the kitchen and the men were out, sitting out there and, you know it was to make sure that everything was done for them. . . .

Speaking about her grandmother's cooking, Victoria's assessment is now more complex.

She knew just how to do things easily and quickly and when you walked in on her doing that she would often be singing, sometimes she'd be singing hymns or . . . when she thought she was alone. So she loved and relished that time and so for me, actually, it's also connected with prayer, which may sound kind of funny, but it's this thing that sometimes you do that's what you lose yourself in or sometimes solitary. And it's also this offering. It's for the people [for] whom you're making it. And I have mixed reactions to that, that it's both pleasure to offer that to others and the subservience piece that you mentioned.

Relating her feelings about cooking directly to feminism, Joanne comments on gender and cooking, also noting that despite her feminism and noticing that there was a clear division of labor around cooking she did not associate it with women's subservience.

In terms of gender it just became very clear who—how the division of labor went in terms of food. I don't think that I placed a value on that. That it was bad or good. When I started to become aware of liberal feminism, when I was a teenager, having to prepare food automatically became a bad thing in my mind, but in my experience, preparing food was always a positive thing. . . . I don't think I ever associated food preparation with negativity. . . . I obviously enjoyed doing it even though I had all these other issues around food and eating. [She had an eating disorder.]

Though she describes her mother as a typical Armenian *harse* [bride], implying that she was totally subservient to her husband and his family, Melissa's assessment of her mother's relationship to cooking is complex. Her mother was expected to cook regularly not only for her own husband and children, but also for her mother-in-law and brother-in-law, who lived in a full apartment with a kitchen on the second floor of their house. The then-single brother-in-law also felt free to invite friends for dinner on a regular basis.

> My uncle used to always have his friends over and so there would be like all these single men that my mother would also be cooking for. So . . . it was insane. I mean from my perspective, I had a blast, because they were playing with me, you know, but you know, from her perspective she was just working and working and working. And she still has a tendency to do that, like we go to visit my brother's, she will be working and working and working. She almost seems like tied to the kitchen and it's sort of like the most comfortable place for her to be but also the place that she tends to resent being the most, you know. It's very, it's a very odd thing.

For Joanne, her grandmother was able to exercise control in the kitchen, and she guarded that space with a vengeance.

> With my grandmother, it [the kitchen] was definitely a woman's domain . . . And I remember, very distinctly, one time—sometime about 15 years ago we were at her house in New York for Thanksgiving. My grandfather had recently died and my father went into the kitchen to start doing the dishes and she threw a tantrum. You are not to do that. This is women's work and afterwards she said, in her inimitable way, men who go in the kitchen are sissies. . . . So, I think she felt violently territorial about it because that was the only place she had freedom in the house, from my grandfather. . . . He would never have ventured to come in. I think that was where he had no control. That was her place of control. And my mother talks about her preparing meals to excess. And she would say, Ma, you don't need all this food and her mother would say, no this is . . . I think she had complete control. I am sure she was given a budget and observed that budget to a certain extent, but other than that, he had no input. And I think it was a point of pride in her to able to serve these elaborate meals to him and please him, in that sense, and please the family.

For other women, cooking together creates a woman's space. While very critical of the rigid roles that relegated women to cooking, Ruth also thinks that the preparing of food provided an opportunity for women to be together, a practice she continues in her current life.

I see it [preparing food] as a way to bring people together to socialize. That's how I think of it even now. It did that for Armenian women in my family because they often did things together before a big event, and so they would chat about whatever while they were preparing food. But there was also such a work ethic that I am not sure these particular women would have felt okay about just sitting down over a cup of tea and talking. I think they would have had to have been doing something. . . . I am not sure it was ever even conscious on their parts that this was the way they were going to get to visit, by preparing food together, because it was just part of the fabric of their lives. Maybe it was their version of how they combined activities because they had to do this, they had to do that and they were busy and so they would visit because they were preparing food.

Women gathering together to cook was a particularly joyful part of Anahid's childhood. Her mother was a survivor and depressed most of the time. She resented daily cooking but enjoyed sharing the tasks with other women.

My mother was very depressed, so doing it [cooking] alone was, I mean, I think that she came to life when . . . not necessarily just with our family, but when those women were present and they were work-ing together and they were preparing something together. I could hear her . . . I mean those are some of the times when I can really hear her laughing. . . . She would come to life too at the beach where there were those women and they would be cooking together or pre-paring food together.

For Joanne, cooking women are powerful, and that women's power is her legacy. Done alone or with a group of women, cooking is both powerful and sensuous.

I mean there was passion around food. I think that . . . from my adult mind, in relation to gender, food and the power of women are very closely connected. I mean that's where I can see all of my foremothers showing their passion—being able to be completely alive in food preparation.

Joanne is currently in a committed relationship with a man who also loves to cook, and they argue about who will do the cooking because they both love it. She carries on the tradition she identified in her foremothers.

And then I gradually learned to cook myself and took such great pleasure in it that—it just felt like my whole being was present when I was making food. It still does now. It is one of the few things that I

274

do where I don't get distracted. I am just so immersed in it. . . . the sensuousness and the art of it and the physical touches of it. I love preparing food. *Laughing*

Also feeling sensual about food, Anahid wonders if her passion is channeled into food rather than into sexuality. "I think the way sometimes I can use food, or the way I've been—the way food has been used in my family, anyway, has been more in the service of being asexual rather than being sexual."

While many of the woman value cooking and love the *idea* of cooking, many do not cook regularly, and while they felt that cooking was a creative expression for their mothers and grandmothers not many of them expressed it as an important vehicle for themselves. Because all the women are professionals or have recently completed advanced degrees, they are less limited than their grandmothers and even their mothers in their life choices. A notable exception to the pattern is Melissa, a musician. Her modes of cooking are connected to her musical expression. When she was first composing, her major focus was on experimentation, and she felt then that cooking was a highly creative act. She never used recipes, and her husband at the time complained because she never cooked anything the same way twice. Currently, cooking has another meaning for her: "now, when I cook, it's more for nourishment because there is that feeling of—ah, washing grains, I can breathe, you know. I can relax . . . Psychological nourishment." As a young woman she associated artists with decadence: "you know there was just something macho about it that had to do with being an artist. *Laughing.*" Her attitude toward artists in general and her own craft has changed, and along with it her cooking.

> Although I am still interested in experimentation, I am also very interested in getting it right. Or getting a certain effect . . . I am much more interested in . . . harmonies, tonal qualities, you know, I may discard them, but I am more interested in them than I was before. Before I was like, I didn't want anything to do with that part. I just wanted to be as creative as possible. And so, now I am more interested in like, how do you cook the rice just right.

Melissa considers cooking to be a skill and values what she learned from her mother. And when the women of previous generations came together to cook food for holidays or family outings, they also shared their skills. But these skills were not usually recognized by the men in their lives. Many women talked about the criticism the women in their families endured about their cooking. Lucy's father consistently complained about her mother's cooking, whether it was Armenian or American; the Armenian food was always compared to what they had in the old country. She learned that her mother was a good cook from how other people, mostly non-Armenians, raved about her food. Despite her mother having to cook because she was a woman, and her father's criticisms, she feels that she learned about a particular kind of power from her mother's cooking.

> I learned that there is a lot of power in technical skills. That food is like a technical skill, like other kinds of technical skills. And that there is a lot of power and respect that goes along with having mastered those skills and not everyone does. So even though my father was just his unusual self, I knew that other people regarded her as being sort of a very good cook and came to her and asked her stuff about how to prepare things and asked her to prepare things for parties that they were having. And I know for a while she toyed with the idea of opening a catering company with a friend of hers.

Ruth feels that the women in her family took pride in their skills, but that what they cooked was

> often taken for granted. I rarely saw a man appreciate what had been prepared. I rarely heard someone say, this *yalanchi* is delicious. You might, however, hear a criticism—oh, it's a little too dry this time. It's a little too oily. . . . Women complimented other women, but I think I got the sense early on that it didn't count as much as what the men said.

Dorothy had the experience of everyone criticizing women's cooking, and she also felt a competition among women around food preparation when she was a child.

> And there was a lot of criticism about food. We'd go to my aunt's in Worcester and we'd be coming home and they'd go, "that wasn't lamb, that was mutton." *Laughter.* I always thought that mutton must be a dog or something. I just thought, oh my god they served us mutton, and all they meant was that it was tough, you know. . . . We would eat all weekend, you know. We'd have chicken and *pilaf*, and leg of lamb and *geragour*, and I don't know how my aunt did it. But I think she loved it when we came over, but it was never good enough. And I notice that now.

Leisure time among the women I interviewed is in short supply. In their current lives some find joy in cooking, but not in everyday meal preparation. Making a distinction between duty cooking and recreational cooking, Debby reported:

I don't do the daily cooking. . . . Dan [her husband] cooks every day
. . . at four o'clock when I come home from work, the last thing I
want to do is put dinner on the table. I am exhausted and cranky. . . .
See, I love to cook for special occasions. I like to bake. I like to do
holiday cooking. I like to make things for people. But I don't like to
do—to put it on the table. I guess I don't want it to be a chore, you
know. And I am lucky enough to be married to someone who loves to
do it daily. . . . But the way I love to cook and this is . . . in some ways
like the way my mother cooked, is—you know on a Sunday afternoon, I'll turn on the radio and play wonderful music and I'll spend
the afternoon cooking. And maybe I'll have a friend with me but
maybe I won't. And that's very relaxing for me to do. I think . . . it's
not so much that my mother did that, but it takes me back to those
times with her and my grandmother. It makes me somehow feel like
I have that time back. I think that my mother had trouble getting
dinner on the table when she came home weary from work and it was
hard for her. . . . So maybe there's some part of me that thought I
want to save this so it will always be special and fun for me and not
have to ever do it as a chore.

Although her father did cook, for Debby he did not do the same kind
of cooking as her mother who had to "get the dinner on the table." It
was her mother who did the "duty cooking." She wants to keep the joy
in her cooking, "the spiritual sense of this as something wonderful in
life . . . what life has to offer."

Anahid also makes the distinction between daily cooking, which her
mother resented, and cooking for "gatherings." While she no longer
has much time to have those "gatherings," she wants to make time for
them in her life again because they make her feel "rooted in someplace
that felt, probably, very comforting and vital."

For Emma the cooking itself is comforting. Upon hearing of the
death of a peer, also a young woman in her early thirties, she cooked for
an entire weekend.

The kitchen is a comfortable place for me. It is a place where I feel
good at what I do. . . . So, as I was there chopping the onions and
crying from the onions, and really crying about the onions because it
was too much to cry about Louise, I was thinking about my grandmother and how maybe it really was easier for me to deal with the
sadness if I was doing something—if I was creating something. If I
was, you know, something about food. This was going to be the food
to nurture my son, you know, my family, me. So it was kind of about
life and keeping me busy and feeling competent.

Many of the women's lives are too busy for them to do the kind of cooking they want to do. Ruth does take her turn cooking in the cooperative house she has lived in for many years, but she does not do the kind of cooking she would if she had more time.

> Well, my belief system is one thing, what I put into practice is another. I think that food and the preparation of food is really important and I think it's a lost art and practice in many respects. . . . I probably would, if I had time . . . like I would probably make *yalanchi*. I do that occasionally . . . And I keep the recipes and I share it. And occasionally, if there is going to be a social gathering, if there needs to be like something for a community works benefit or something where we need to make it and I've got my mother doing it, we'll get a few people and we'll do it here at our house and get some help, because it's too much for one person to do—*yalanchi*. So, that's been one thing we've done over the years, is to prepare things together that are labor intensive, kind of make it a social event at the same time. . . . And I like preparing foods as a group. It's a lot of fun. You know, you can talk about anything. Talk politics too.

As feminists, most of the women are concerned that what they do in the kitchen is appreciated and not expected from them because they are women. Some women also struggle with their tendency to judge themselves in terms of how well they can cook.

> It is a kind of compulsion. You know my mom would get very anxious before people came over for dinner, like for holiday meals—to the point where she would actually get some chest pains. . . . She wouldn't be able to breathe because of the pressure, and anxiety. And I have really worked around that because it's important for me to have people around. I want people over, but I don't want to—she made herself sick over it. So when people came over I used to feel that I needed to have everything ready so people would walk in and I would be relaxed and that was part of the show. It was like—and I did theater—having people over for dinner is like a well-constructed theatrical performance as far as me and my family were concerned. Because you wanted to have it look easy.

Food, cooking, and eating are carriers of a patriarchal culture, yet these feminists claim these food practices as their legacy as Armenian American women. Armenian food evokes memories of individual people and "the people," particularly important for Armenians because of the genocide and its invisibility. They deploy cooking as a way to define themselves ethnically both for themselves and to others outside of an Armenian context. For those who were not raised in an Armenian community or whose parents did not participate in Armenian events, Armenian cuisine often represented their only clarity about being Armenian. Even those who were deeply immersed in Armenian activities, however, identified food as important to their sense of themselves as Armenians and a way to convey their ethnicity to non-Armenians. Some have used cooking Armenian food as a gift, an offering of caring, friendship, and love while mindful of the dangers inherent in an activity so closely connected to women's subservience.

This group of feminists view their identities as Armenian American women as constructed through the intersection of *all* of the issues we discussed. Their sense of themselves as Armenian American women is impacted by Armenian history in Turkey, Armenian ethnicity in the United States, and their analysis of Armenian culture as a patriarchy. The genocide and Armenian invisibility in this country shapes their lives as much as their inability to participate in the Armenian community because of their assessment that women must continue to be subservient to men. They do, however, insist on their right to claim their ethnicity and to enact it in their own ways, resisting both Armenian invisibility within the United States and women's limitations within the Armenian community.

Notes

1. Ann Oakley, "A Brief History of Gender," in *Who's Afraid of Feminism: Seeing through the Backlash* (New York: The New Press, 1997).

2. The literature of women of color critiquing white feminism is voluminous. A few important titles include: Toni Cade, ed., *The Black Woman* (New York: Signet, 1970); Cherríe Moraga and Gloria Anzaldúa, eds., *This Bridge Called My Back: Writing by Radical Women of Color* (Watertown, MA: Persephone Press, 1981); Angela Davis, *Women, Race, and Class* (New York: Vintage, 1981); Barbara Smith, ed., *Home Girls: A Black Feminist Anthology* (New York: Kitchen Table/Women of Color Press, 1983); Audre Lorde, *Sister Outsider: Essays and Speeches* (Trumansburg, NY: The Crossing Press, 1984); June Jordan, "Report from the Bahamas," in *On Call: Political Essays* (Boston: South End, 1985); Gloria Anzaldúa, *Borderlands/La Frontera: The New Mestiza* (San Francisco: Spinsters/Aunt Lute, 1987); Gita Sen and Caren Grown, *Development, Crises, and Alternative Visions: Third World Women's Perspectives* (New York: Monthly Review Press, 1987); Chandra Talpade Mohanty, Ann Russo, and Lourdes Torres, eds., *Third World Women and the Politics of Feminism* (Bloomington: Indiana University Press, 1991); Braidotti et al., eds., *Women, the Environment and Sustainable Development: Towards a Theoretical Synthesis* (London: Zed Books, 1994); and Amrita Basu, *The Challenge of Local Feminisms: Women's Movements in Global Perspective* (Boulder: Westview Press, 1995).

3. Linda Nicholson, "Interpreting 'Gender,'" *Signs* 20, 1 (1994).

4. Ibid.

5. Judith Butler, "Contingent Foundations: Feminism and the Question of 'Postmodernism,'" in *Feminists Theorize the Political*, ed. Judith Butler and Joan Scott (New York: Routledge, 1992), 16.

6. Chantel Mouffe, "Feminism, Citizenship, and Radical Democratic Politics," in ibid., 373.

7. The literature on ethnic, national, and diasporic identities is also vast.

8. Stuart Hall, "Introduction: Who Needs Identity?" in *Questions of Cultural Identity*, ed. Stuart Hall and Paul DuGuy (London: Sage, 1996), 2.

9. Ibid., 3.

10. Ibid., 4.

11. Stuart Hall, "Cultural Identity and Diaspora," in *Identity: Community, Culture and Difference*, ed. Jonathan Rutherford (London: Lawrence & Wishart, 1990), 226.

12. R. Radhakrishnan, *Diasporic Mediations: Between Home and Location* (Minneapolis: University of Minnesota Press, 1996), 175–176.

13. Ibid., 176.

14. The government of Turkey officially denies the genocide. The United States Congress is complicit in this denial by failing every year, to pass a resolution designating April 24 to commemorate the survivors. In 1996 Canada officially recognized the genocide, and in 1998 France followed suit, both over the strenuous objections of the Turkish government.

15. Research on holocaust survivors shows that many survivors cannot or will not talk about their experiences. For some this silence came from fear of themselves or their children being identified as survivors or Jews; others felt that no one wanted to hear about the horrors they had suffered or, if they did, could never understand, and still others wanted to put the past behind them in order to start new lives. See Aaron Hass, *In the Shadow of the Holocaust: The Second Generation* (Ithaca: Cornell University Press, 1990) and *The Aftermath: Living with the Holocaust* (New York: Cambridge University Press, 1995); and William B. Helmreich, *Against All Odds: Holocaust Survivors and the Successful Lives They Made in America* (New York: Simon and Schuster, 1992). The research on Armenian Americans shows a similar pattern. See Donald Miller and Lorna Miller, *The Armenian Genocide of 1915: An Oral History of the Experience of Survivors* (Berkeley: University of California Press, 1992). My own research on Armenian American women and the genocide also shows that many families did not talk about their experiences, yet felt they knew something terrible had happened to their parents if they were survivors or to the Armenian people if they were not. Many women spoke of always knowing about the genocide. Arlene Avakian, "Surviving the Survivors: Daughters and Granddaughters of Survivors of the Armenian Genocide," forthcoming in Proceedings of Armenian Women's International Association Second International Conference, Paris, 1997, AIWA Press.

Notes on Contributors

ARLENE VOSKI AVAKIAN is professor and director of women's studies at the University of Massachusetts Amherst. She is editor of *Through the Kitchen Window: Women Explore the Intimate Meanings of Food and Cooking* (1997), author of *Lion Woman's Legacy: An Armenian American Memoir* (1992), and co-editor of *African American Women and the Vote, 1837–1965* (1997). Avakian has also written numerous articles on a variety of topics centering on gender, race, class, and sexuality, some fiction, and a bit of poetry.

AMY BENTLEY is an associate professor in the Department of Nutrition, Food Studies, and Public Health at New York University. A cultural historian by training, Bentley is the author of *Eating for Victory: Food Rationing and the Politics of Domesticity* (1998), as well as several articles examining the cultural and historical landscapes of food. "Feeding Baby, Teaching Mother" is part of a larger history of baby food in the United States currently in progress.

CAROLE COUNIHAN is professor of anthropology at Millersville University in Pennsylvania. She is author of *Around the Tuscan Table: Food, Family, and Gender in Twentieth Century Florence* (2004) and *The Anthropology of Food and Body: Gender, Meaning, and Power* (1999). She is editor of *Food in the USA: A Reader* (2002) and co-editor with Penny Van Esterik of *Food and Culture: A Reader* (1997). Counihan is editor of the scholarly journal *Food and Foodways* and a member of the editorial board of *Slow: The Magazine of the International Slow Food Movement*. She is working on a book on women and food in the San Luis Valley of Colorado.

DARRA GOLDSTEIN is professor of Russian at Williams College and founding editor of *Gastronomica: The Journal of Food and Culture*. She is also the author of three cookbooks, *A Taste of Russia*, *The Georgian Feast* (winner of the 1994 IACP Julia Child Award for Cookbook of the Year),

281

and *The Winter Vegetarian*. Goldstein serves as general editor of the book series California Studies in Food and Culture (University of California Press) and as food editor of *Russian Life* magazine.

BARBARA HABER is the former curator of books at Radcliffe's Schlesinger Library at Harvard University, where she developed collections in both women's studies and culinary history. A food historian, she is the author of *From Hardtack to Home Fries: An Uncommon History of American Cooks and Meals*, a book that examines the relationship between women and food.

NANCY HARMON JENKINS is a writer and historian with a strong interest in both Mediterranean and North American food traditions. She is the author, most recently, of *The Essential Mediterranean* (2003).

ALICE JULIER teaches in the Sociology Department at Smith College. Her dissertation focused on potlucks, dinner parties, and other forms of domestic hospitality as enactments of inequality in everyday life, notably of race, gender, and class. She recently edited a volume of *Food and Foodways* dedicated to masculinities and food. Her new research is on evangelical Christian weight-loss programs and gender. Julier is the president of the Association for the Study of Food and Society.

LESLIE LAND writes the garden Q&A column for the *New York Times*. Her most recent book is *The New York Times 1000 Gardening Questions and Answers* (2003). In a previous life, she was a founding chef at Chez Panisse, wrote a syndicated food column, and published two cookbooks. Her writings on food, cooking, and agriculture have appeared in the *New York Times Magazine*, *Food and Wine*, *Yankee*, and *Money*, among many other publications.

LAURA LINDENFELD is an assistant professor in the Department of Communication and Journalism and a research associate at the Margaret Chase Smith Center for Public Policy at the University of Maine, where she teaches media criticism, film studies, and women's studies.

SHARMILA SEN is an assistant professor of English at Harvard University. She specializes in Anglophone literatures from Africa, the Caribbean, and South Asia.

LAURA SHAPIRO is an award-winning journalist and a food historian. She the author of *Perfection Salad: Women and Cooking at the Turn of the*

Century (1986; paper ed., 2001) and *Something from the Oven: Reinventing Dinner in 1950s America* (2004).

BEHEROZE F. SHROFF is a documentary film maker from Bombay who teaches in Asian American studies at University of California, Irvine. Shroff has made several films that range from issues of diaspora—*Sweet Jail: The Sikhs of Yuba City*—to issues of gender—*Reaching for Half the Sky*. Shroff's most recent work, *We're Indian and African: Voices of the Sidis* and *Voices of the Sidis: Ancestral Links*, focuses on the African presence in India, which goes back to the thirteenth century.

JAN WHITAKER is the author of a social history of American tea rooms, *Tea at the Blue Lantern Inn* (2002). She is presently at work on a social history of downtown department stores. Whitaker has published essays on "quick lunch" eateries of the early twentieth century, on old roadside tea rooms, and on tea-drinking customs in America and has presented conference papers on "spectacular" food and how chop houses were coded as masculine.

Index

Page numbers in italics refer to illustrations.

For Her Own Good (Ehrenreich and
English), 244n26
Fortune (magazine), 33
Fox, John, Jr., 123
Fox, Minnie C., 123
France, 181n9, 280n14
French cuisine, 95
Frankenberg, Ruth, 238
Frankfurter Küche, 44
Frederick, Christine, 45, 48, 49–50, 51,
60n13
Frederick, T. George, 48
Freidenberg, Olga, 156
Fremont Canning Company, 73, 74,
75, 76
See also Gerber Products Company
French cuisine, 95
*Fried Green Tomatoes at the Whistle Stop
Café* (Flagg), 223
Fried Green Tomatoes (Avnet), 219, 222–
41
African American culture and, 237–
40, 244n31
food as link between present and
past, 226–27
gender stereotypes, challenges to,
227–28, 232–33
humor, depictions of, 229, 232, 242–
43n6
lesbian subtext, 228–29, 229–30, 234–
35
oscillation between subversion and
regression, 222–23, 224, 231–32,
233–34, 240–41
patriarchy, challenges to, 233, 235–
36, 238–39
political statements, 236–37
popularity, 223–24, 243n12, 245n44
power, challenges to traditional concepts of, 230–33
sexual imagery, 228–29, 229–30, 234–
35
whiteness, position of, 238–40,
245n39

Friedman, Harriet, 12
From Pillar to Post (Khan), 196n5
frosted layer cake recipe, 31

Gabaccia, Donna, 170, 173, 175–76,
178, 180n2
gas stoves, 59n8
Gastronomica (journal), 1
Gay, Lettie, 123
Gay and Lesbian Alliance Against Defamation (GLAAD), 229–30
gender construction
food practices and, 8–10
West *vs.* New Guinea and Amazon,
22
gender relations
Armenian American culture, 261,
271–73
family meal and, 15
Mexican American culture, 209–12
General Electric
cross-marketing, 56
Electric Kitchen, 47
stove manufacturing, 27, 42–43, 45,
58n2
General Electric Kitchen Institute, 47
General Foods (food company), 31
General Mills (food company)
cake mixes, 35, 36
live trademark (*See* Betty Crocker)
See also Washburn Crosby
Gerber, Daniel, 73
Gerber, Mrs. Daniel, 73, 74
Gerber Baby, 75, 76, 80, 82–83
Gerber Products Company (food company), 27, 73–74
advertising, 76–80 (*See also* Gerber
Baby)
breast-feeding, role in decline of, 63
direct marketing to women, 78–79
market share struggles, 81–82
naturalization of baby foods, 76–78
reputation, challenges to, 81–83
See also Fremont Canning Company